Millennial Momentum

Millennial Momentum

How a New Generation Is Remaking America

MORLEY WINOGRAD
MICHAEL D. HAIS

RUTGERS UNIVERSITY PRESS
New Brunswick, New Jersey, and London

Library of Congress Cataloging-in-Publication Data

Winograd, Morley.
  Millennial momentum : how a new generation is remaking America / Morley
Winograd and Michael D. Hais.
    p. cm.
  Includes bibliographical references and index.
  ISBN 978–0–8135–5150–0 (hardcover : alk. paper)
  1. Political participation—United States.   2. Political culture—United States.
3. United States—Politics and government—21st century.   I. Hais, Michael D.,
1943–   II. Title.
  JK1764.W636   2011
  323′.0420973—dc22   2011001049

A British Cataloging-in-Publication record for this book is available
from the British Library.

Visit our Web site: http://rutgerspress.rutgers.edu

Manufactured in the United States of America

To Bobbie and Reena with love,
Morley and Mike

Contents

Acknowledgments *ix*

Introduction I

PART I | CHANGE CREATES FEAR, UNCERTAINTY, AND DOUBT

1   *Welcome to the Millennial Era*   9
2   *Millennials Are About to Take Over America*   26
3   *Fighting Over America's Future*   44

PART II   CHANGING AMERICA'S GOVERNMENT

4   *Judging the Fourth Turning*   65
5   *Crowdsourcing the Congress*   83
6   *The Challenge of Presidential Leadership in a Fourth Turning*   102

PART III | CHANGING THE WAY AMERICANS WORK AND LEARN

7   *Leadership for a New Economic Era*   121
8   *Confronting Corporate Life*   138
9   *Building Better Learning Communities*   156
10   *Taking Higher Education Higher*   175

PART IV   CHANGING THE WAY AMERICANS LIVE

11   *Millennial Family Lifestyles*   193

12   *Let Millennials Entertain You*   210

13   *Changing the World*   226

14   *Making Over American Politics*   245

15   *Building a New Civic Ethos*   264

Note on Data Sources and Analyses   281
References   283
Index   303

ACKNOWLEDGMENTS

ALTHOUGH WE ACCEPT FULL RESPONSIBILITY for everything we have written in these pages, we want to gratefully acknowledge the numerous contributions others have made to our efforts.

We continue to recognize and appreciate the remarkable intellectual achievement and seminal thinking of Neil Howe and the late William Strauss, the originators of generational theory. Their unique way of looking at the world provides a lens through which everyone should view our nation's history and its future. As with *Millennial Makeover: MySpace, You Tube, and the Future of American Politics*, we borrowed liberally from their theoretical insights in writing this book. We have had the wonderful opportunity since the publication of our first book to come to know Neil Howe, who has become a true friend and an ongoing source of inspiration and information to us on all things generational, for which we wish to express our special thanks.

We also must thank Simon Rosenberg, founder and president of NDN, the think tank at which both of us are fellows. Simon generously shared his deep knowledge and understanding of the details and implications of the rapid changes in America's population and political dynamics with us. He also sponsored and gave us full access to the results of three national surveys, conducted by Frank N. Magid Associates, which are cited liberally throughout this book. We are grateful for his willingness to publicize our writings and bring them to an ever wider audience.

We had the good fortune to work with two of America's preeminent research organizations—Frank N. Magid Associates and the Pew Research Center—who gave us special access to much of the survey research cited extensively throughout this book. At Magid, we specifically want to thank Jack MacKenzie, president of Magid's Millennial Strategy Program, for sharing his extensive knowledge of the behavior and preferences of the Millennial Generation, and Bob Crawford, who expertly and patiently administered and tabulated several surveys for us. At Pew, we want to express our gratitude to Scott Keeter, Pew's director of survey research, who gave us full access to Pew's ongoing attitudinal research, and to Leah Melani Christian, who provided generational cross-tabulations of numerous Pew surveys in a highly capable and timely manner.

In the course of our research we came to know many innovative leaders on the cutting edge of Millennial era change. Each of them is mentioned in the book when we share their particular insights, but we also want to acknowledge their generous cooperation and patience in answering all of our questions, which helped so much in the writing of this book. We owe a special debt to Doug Ross, a personal friend and innovative educator, for his perceptive insights about strengthening education across the United States. More important, all of America owes Doug and other educational leaders like him thanks for all they are doing to make sure that our nation's emerging civic generation is fully equipped to compete and contribute in the Millennial era. Two of those leaders—University of Michigan President Emeritus James Duderstadt, and learning technology guru Ted Kahn—were especially helpful to us in the writing of this book.

After our first book, we had the opportunity to meet many wonderful and amazing young people, all members of America's next great generation. Their unique blend of idealism and pragmatism has given us a renewed sense of optimism about America's future. At the risk of offending those we don't specifically mention, we want to give our special thanks to several who were particularly helpful to our work.

Alex Steed served as the administrator of the Millennials Changing America Web site, which provided an upfront and personal insight into the thinking and contributions of his generation. Alex Pearlman is the editor in chief of *The Next Great Generation* (*TNGG*), an online publication for and about Millennials that wittily and contemporaneously captures the thoughts off her generation. Alicia Menendez, who was our point person at NDN, has been a consummate professional to work with—upbeat, helpful, calm, and a wise team player in a wide variety of situations, many of them stressful. Meagan Carberry stayed in touch with us during her many career moves and provided us great insights on how Millennials were reacting to events as they unfolded. Chris Golden and his partner at myImpact.org, Nick Triano, reached out to us early and continue to demonstrate incredible devotion to the cause of community service. Maya Enista opened up the doors to her Mobilize.org summits and allowed us to observe and write about true Millennial consensus building on the critical issues confronting our country. Hilary Doe and Zach Kolodin also gave us an opportunity to learn the unique perspective of the generation on the nation's future as part of their leadership of the Roosevelt Institute Campus Network's Think 2040 project.

Three brilliant observers of the Millennial Generation were kind enough to share their insights and contacts with us, which greatly enriched the material for this book. Joel Kotkin, the nation's most insightful demographer, who teaches Millennials at Chapman University as part of his commitment to America's future, was particularly helpful to us in both the writing of this book and publicizing our first one. Lee Fox is the founder of the Web site KooDooZ, which provides tween-age Millennials a place to organize their instincts for service, share their ideas with their peers and adults, and make the world a better place in the process. Amy Hirsh Robinson works with companies to help them understand the Millennial Generation, enabling her clients to take advantage of the amazing skills and talent of this generation. We thank them all.

Ron Goldfarb is not only our agent but also our friend. He has never ceased to be the most loyal and tireless supporter of our efforts and of the story that we are trying to tell. His perceptive comments about our work and his extensive knowledge of publishing and marketing have been of enormous benefit to us. Ron's work on our behalf is as much of a labor of love as it is a commercial endeavor, and we continue to thank him for that.

Perhaps the greatest of Ron's many gifts to us was introducing us to Marlie Wasserman, the director of Rutgers University Press. Marlie took a chance in 2007 and agreed to publish our first book. We are honored that she was willing to come back and work with us again. Marlie is the perfect editor: willing to let us express ourselves without limitation, while consistently providing, in her typically warm and positive manner, thoughtful and smart suggestions to make our work clearer and more meaningful to our readers. Perhaps the greatest validation of the wisdom of Marlie's recommendations is our usual reaction to them: "That makes sense. Why didn't we think of that?"

As always, we appreciate the major contributions our spouses have made to our writing. Bobbie Winograd, once again, provided her time and remarkable skills as an editor, proofreader, and researcher. Her efforts saved us numerous hours and even more numerous mistakes in grammar, sentence structure, and proper citations of the wide range of sources we have used in this book. On a personal note, I, Morley Winograd, want to thank my wife for the grace and good humor with which she took the news that I was going to be lost to her once again for days and weeks on end in order to write another book. Perhaps after forty-eight years of marriage she considered it a blessing in disguise, but I am grateful enough for her support to have dedicated my contributions to this book to her.

In addition, I, Mike Hais, want to personally thank my wife, Reena. Her love and encouragement and her pride in *Millennial Makeover* made writing *Millennial Momentum* much easier and more enjoyable. Her willingness to put aside things she might rather be doing to give me time to think and write is very much appreciated, as is her cheerfully engaging in endless hours of discussion on the arcane points of generational theory and American politics. Finally, I am both amazed and grateful for her understanding and humor in dealing with the uncertainties that come along with writing a book. Perhaps more than four decades of being married to a fan of the Boston Red Sox has given her ample training for responding to that sort of angst.

And to all of our readers, we wish to thank you for your interest in our work and hope that the ideas we have expressed in this book make you even more confident that the future of our great country is in very good hands so long as we trust the Millennial Generation to guide us.

Millennial Momentum

Introduction

TO HAVE A CLEAR SENSE of where America is headed in the future requires a thorough understanding of the behaviors and attitudes of the Millennial Generation, young Americans born between 1982 and 2003. Millennials were decisive in determining the outcome of the 2008 elections and the political and societal impact of the generation is only going to grow over the coming decades, as increasing numbers of Millennials enter the electorate, go to work, get married, start families, and dominate the country's media and entertainment audiences. Of the approximately 95 million Millennials now living, only 41 percent were of voting age in 2008, and they composed less than one-fifth of the electorate that year. When Barack Obama seeks reelection in 2012, about six in ten Millennials will be eligible to vote, and about one in four American voters will come from the Millennial Generation. By 2020, when virtually all members of the generation will be of voting age, Millennials will represent more than one out every three adults (36%).

Any group of that size will be able not only to sway elections and determine public policy in such areas as health care, education, energy, and the environment but also to change the way America lives and works. Finding jobs for everyone in the generation and motivating them to provide the innovation and creativity necessary to grow the economy again will be a central challenge for leaders in America's private and public sectors. Furthermore, the technologies Millennials utilize so often and so well, from social networks to mobile smart phones, will provide communication capabilities that will undermine hierarchical organizational structures in government and business, modifying, if not entirely eliminating, the top-down, command-and-control structures built by members of the GI Generation during and after World War II. The interest of Millennials in staying in touch with anyone anywhere in the world will also have a profound impact on America's foreign policy and on the nation's attitudes toward both enemies and allies around the globe. All of these issues will ultimately be resolved, but the struggle to find the right answers will consume our nation's debate about its future for much of the next decade. Which path the United States ultimately takes will be determined by the Millennial Generation's willingness to engage in a vast civic endeavor to remake America and its institutions and the willingness of the rest of the country to follow its lead.

In spite of the Millennials' crucial impact on the 2008 election and their growing presence in the electorate, observers on both sides of the political spectrum were slow to realize their impact on that year's election, let alone the future of the country.

In September 2008, conservative commentator Jonah Goldberg said that Barack Obama was taking a big risk in counting on Millennial support "because history shows that young voters are the least reliable voters. They get distracted by shiny things—TV, iPod glare, whatever—and fail to make it to the polls . . . every four years I'm told that this is the year young people will be decisive—and every four years I say, 'no it's not.' So far I've always been right and they've always been wrong. Maybe that will change this year, but I bet it won't" (Goldberg 2008).

From the other side of the political spectrum, longtime Clinton loyalist James Carville made the same point. "There is a word in politics to describe candidates who rely on the youth vote—and that word is 'loser'" (Connery 2008).

Both Goldberg and Carville had become "prisoners of their preconceptions," a term coined by Philip Tetlock, a psychologist at the University of California at Berkeley. His landmark 1980s study of predictions about economic and political trends found that the most famous pundits were usually the least accurate, because their own fame often caused them to be guilty of the "sin of certainty" (Lehrer 2009).

Of course, every tomorrow always looks a lot like yesterday—except when it doesn't, and the world suddenly changes. Barack Obama and his campaign strategists ignored the conventional wisdom and made Millennials an important part of the voter coalition that put him in the White House. They began the campaign "with a firm but risky belief that we could radically expand the electorate," as Obama campaign manager David Plouffe revealed in his post-campaign book, *The Audacity to Win.* "We refused to accept the electorate as it was. We thought we could make it younger and more diverse and that's exactly what we did" (Plouffe 2009, 380).

But the Obama campaign did more than simply trust its instincts. It also employed the type of thinking Tetlock found was used by those political pundits whose predictions tended to be the most accurate. In this approach, any prediction, or in this case, strategy, is stated in a testable format and then continually tested against objective performance data to see if the data continue to support the prediction (Lehrer 2009). "We measured our progress exclusively with our own yardstick. We had clear internal benchmarks that the campaign leadership used to measure our progress or lack thereof. . . . We tried to shoot high but remained grounded in a hard analysis of what would truly be possible" (Plouffe 2009, 379).

Ultimately, Plouffe and the Obama campaign were proven right and Goldberg and Carville wrong. As a result, on January 20, 2009, a record number of nearly two million people personally witnessed the inauguration of Barack Obama as the forty-fourth president of the United States. There is no way to determine precisely the age distribution of those on the scene that day in Washington, but there is little doubt that individuals in their teens and twenties dominated the crowd. While the heartiness of youth may have contributed to the willingness of so many young people to withstand hours of subfreezing temperatures to celebrate Barack Obama's ascension to the presidency, there was far more involved than simply physical endurance.

Millennials had come to Washington to celebrate the election of Barack Obama—a victory their participation had clearly made possible. Voting-age Millennials supported Obama over his Republican opponent, John McCain, by greater than a 2:1 margin (66% to 32%); older generations split their vote almost evenly (50% for Obama to 48% for McCain), creating the largest disparity between younger and older voters ever recorded in four decades of modern polling. The turnout gap between younger and older voters in 2008 was also the smallest it had been since 1972, when the voting age was lowered from twenty-one to eighteen (Pew 2010b). As a result, Millennials provided Obama with nearly 7 million, or 80 percent, of his 8.5 million popular vote popular vote margin. The overwhelming support of Millennials put Indiana and North Carolina and possibly Virginia and Florida into the Obama column, adding at least 26 and perhaps as many as 66 electoral votes to his total. While Barack Obama might have been elected president without the overwhelming support of Millennials, his appeal to that generation turned what would have been a very narrow victory into a mandate for change.

Obama's victory further reinforced the generation's inherent confidence in its ability to save the world from its most destructive tendencies. As one Millennial, Derek Anderson, wrote in a blog on the Web site aptly entitled *The Next Great Generation*, "we are the rising heroes of the planet, whether we want to be or not. . . . We need to put on the big-kid-pants, suit up, and deal with the problems handed down to us, I don't think there is a more prepared generation for the job. . . . We are an over-qualified super weapon that is being presented with unreal opportunities for both good and bad." But as Anderson also pointed out, quoting Uncle Ben's reminder to Spiderman, "with great power, comes great responsibility." By electing America's first African American president, Millennials created a watershed event in American history that placed enormous responsibility on the generation's shoulders to ensure the changes that they favored kept "the world spinning in the right direction" (Anderson 2010).

The causes their candidate had supported, the rhetoric Obama used to advance his candidacy, and the campaign's adroit adoption of social network technologies to create a legion of grassroots supporters suggested that Millennials were ready to support the new president's efforts to send the country in a completely new direction, not just redress historical wrongs. Obama's victory signaled that new forces in the American electorate had realigned the political and ideological dynamics of the last forty years, ushering in a new era of increased civic engagement and societal change (Winograd and Hais 2008). But whether those changes would turn out the way Millennials hoped would depend on the leadership skills of their hero and the generation's willingness to stay involved in the process of change they had initiated.

Just as the Obama campaign did, our book, *Millennial Makeover: MySpace, You Tube, and the Future of American Politics*, written in 2007, took a view opposite to those of Goldberg and Carville about the power of this generation to impact America's future. Even though we never communicated with anyone in the campaign, we were able to foresee, more than a year before Barack Obama was elected to presidency, the affinity of Millennials for the candidate they ultimately supported so overwhelmingly and enthusiastically:

> In 2007, survey research data, as well as the approach and tone of the announced 2008 presidential candidates, provided some clues as to who might be best positioned among the candidates to capture the hearts and minds of a new generation. Senator Obama, the youngest major party candidate, a late Baby Boomer born on the cusp of Generation X, distanced himself from the rest of the candidates in a crucial way that demonstrated his awareness of generational differences and his sensitivity to the concerns and political style of the Millennial Generation. (Winograd and Hais 2008, 3)

Our ability to forecast the importance of the Millennial Generation and Barack Obama's ability to appeal to it did not rely on any psychic abilities on our part. We based our predictions on the theory of generational cycles developed by William Strauss and Neil Howe, and we tested our hypotheses against hard survey research data to see if they aligned with that theory. The strength of the data's correlation with events as they unfolded made us increasingly certain we were right. We use the same approach in this book because we still believe it is the best way to understand the arc of history. Survey data continue to validate the importance of generational differences generally, and of the Millennial Generation specifically, in defining America's future. We remain convinced of the ability of America's youngest generation to be the country's next great generation.

Looking at today's debates from a generational perspective also continues to provide insights about where the nation is headed. This is not the first time that a powerful civic generation, similar to the Millennials in its beliefs and attitudes, has provided new momentum to the nation's constant quest to find the best way to organize and govern a democratic society. To understand this moment in history and where it might lead, it is essential to begin with an understanding of generational cycles in American history.

PART ONE

*Change Creates
Fear, Uncertainty,
and Doubt*

CHAPTER 1

Welcome to the Millennial Era

In May 1964, President Lyndon B. Johnson journeyed to Ann Arbor to address the graduating class of the University of Michigan at the "Big House," the university's 100,000-seat football stadium. Forty-six years later, another president, Barack Obama, drew almost 80,000 people to hear him address the university's 2010 graduating class. The two speeches had more in common than venue and large crowds, however. Both presidents implored their listeners to join in an effort to revitalize and rebuild the United States and to rekindle a sense of community in the nation. Those dual goals reflected the values and attitudes of America's two most recent civic generations, Johnson's own GI Generation and the Millennial Generation that had done so much to elect Obama president. Both generations earned the sobriquet "civic" because of their interest in fixing societal problems and building new institutions.

To a large extent, President Johnson's address was a valedictory plea to the GI Generation, which, in its youth, had overcome the ravages of the Great Depression and the threat of fascism. In 1964, his generation was at the height of its political power and the nation enjoyed a full measure of prosperity and tranquillity. In that positive context, the president, using the military language so familiar to his generation, urged those in attendance, to join him in making one final effort to perfect the Great Society in America:

> Will you join in the battle to give every citizen the full equality which God enjoins and the law requires whatever his belief, or race, or the color of his skin?
>
> Will you join in the battle to give every citizen an escape from the crushing weight of poverty?

Will you join in the battle to make it possible for all nations to live in enduring peace—as neighbors and not as mortal enemies?

Will you join in the battle to build the Great Society, to prove that our material progress is only the foundation on which we will build a richer life of mind and spirit? (Johnson 1964)

As a member of a civic generation, he was certain his call would be answered and that Americans would unite once again to achieve great things. But history now remembers the speech as the end, not the beginning, of an era dominated and shaped by a civic generation. The first members of the Baby Boom Generation arrived on campuses the next semester and openly rebelled against the president's war in Vietnam, specifically, and the beliefs of the GI Generation, generally. It was the beginning of a bitter political debate both over the efficacy of government and over social issues such as abortion, societal disorder, and crime that divided the generations and the country for forty years.

Barack Obama, by contrast, spoke at the beginning of a new era, at a time of great economic difficulty and frenzied political debate. An emerging civic generation, Millennials, born between 1982 and 2003, in numbers even larger than Boomers, had elected him president, and his rhetoric and behavior reflected that younger generation's beliefs and attitudes. He offered a different formula for ensuring that American democracy would thrive in the years ahead—a formula that captured the fundamental beliefs of the Millennials seated before him.

He began by extolling the value of a government capable of helping the nation respond to change. He described "two strands in America's DNA." One favored limited government and individual freedom; the other recognized "the need for a government that, while limited, can still help us adapt to a changing world" (Obama 2010).

"There are some things," Obama said, "we can only do together, as one nation—and our government must keep pace with the times." Quoting Abraham Lincoln, "the role of government is to do for the people what they cannot do better for themselves," and citing Theodore Roosevelt, "the object of government is the welfare of the people," he sought to rise above partisan debate about the size of government and to focus instead on what type of government would be needed in the twenty-first century. He called for a government that "shouldn't try to dictate your lives, but should give you the tools you need to succeed," a government that doesn't guarantee results, "but guarantees a shot at opportunity for every American who is willing to work hard."

The second requirement Obama listed for a thriving democracy was a civil public discourse that didn't question the patriotism or motivation of those on either side of the debate. "We can't expect to solve our problems if all we do is tear each other down. You can disagree with a certain policy without demonizing the person who espouses it. . . . That is what makes us Americans—our ability at the end of the day to look past all of our differences and all of our disagreements and still forge a common future." To loud cheers from his Millennial listeners, who had been raised to always be nice to one another, he emphasized the importance of following the Golden Rule and listening to all sides of the debate in order to find common ground.

His third, and final, requirement for a thriving democracy spoke even more directly to the beliefs and behaviors of Millennials. Reminding his audience that John F. Kennedy had called for the creation of a Peace Corps on the steps of the Michigan Union fifty years earlier, he urged the graduating class of 2010 to remain engaged in public life. Just as Kennedy, the first GI Generation president, had underlined the importance of citizen participation in ensuring the future of a free society, Obama told members of the newest civic generation that they held the keys to America's greatness in their hands. "If you are willing, as past generations were willing, to contribute part of your life to the life of this country, then I, like President Kennedy, believe we can [thrive]." But if, as citizens, this generation doesn't participate, then "that's when democracy breaks down."

President Obama accurately summarized the debate over what America's civic ethos should be, which has engulfed previous presidents who came into office at a time of great political turmoil and rancor, as he did. Contrary to the president's hope, however, the balance between the "two strands of America's [political] DNA" has never been struck in quiet discussions and civil conversations. Instead, throughout history this debate has generated heated and sometimes violent arguments over the fundamental principles of American democracy. This time would be no exception. Still, the president was right in pointing out one of the most distinctive characteristics of the Millennial Generation—its desire to serve—and offer it as a guide to the way in which the current conflict over the nation's future ultimately would be resolved.

Before the president spoke, Alex Marston, a graduating senior chosen to deliver remarks on behalf of his fellow Millennials, had used the setting to invoke a metaphor for his generation's willingness to respond to the challenge of change. Referencing the failure of the Wolverine football team to thrive under its new coach, as it had done in the years prior to the arrival of his class, Marston said change was "a funny thing. We desire change, yet we fear it. We grow uneasy as the world around us changes." He urged his classmates to "embrace change and the opportunities that come with it" (Marston 2010).

The question confronting the nation on that summer day in Ann Arbor and every day since was exactly the one that Marston had posed: was the country ready to embrace the changes the president advocated or would it continue to adhere to the beliefs and practices of its past? The pattern of American history provides important clues as to which direction the country will choose and the role that the Millennial Generation will play in determining the nation's destiny in the twenty-first century.

WHERE WE ARE GOING DEPENDS ON WHERE WE HAVE BEEN

In their seminal books, *Generations: The History of America's Future 1584 to 2069* (1991) and *The Fourth Turning* (1997), William Strauss and Neil Howe described a recurring pattern of four generational archetypes that has cycled throughout Anglo-American history. The span of each generation, especially those that have been born and come of age since the United States became an independent nation in the last quarter of the eighteenth century, is about twenty years. Thus, the resulting generational cycles last about eight decades from beginning to end. Strauss and Howe maintain that the United States is now in its fifth historical generational cycle, the Millennial cycle, which began around 1968 and will end in the middle of the twenty-first century.

According to these authors, with the exception of the Civil War period, each cycle has consisted of four types of generations that reappear in the same order within that cycle. Each generational type has distinctive attitudinal and behavioral characteristics, regardless of when it appears in American history.

- "Idealist." Idealists are reared in an indulgent manner by their parents, permitting them to develop the strongly held values, or ideology, that guide their behavior throughout their lives. As adults, the members of Idealist generations are driven by those uncompromising values, even though half of the generation tends to hold to one set of values and the other half believes exactly the opposite. For example, both Bill Clinton and George W. Bush are members of this generational archetype, even though they believe strongly in very different philosophies. Idealists have very little confidence in the ability and willingness of societal institutions to implement their deeply held beliefs and, as a result, frequently attempt to weaken or even destroy those institutions. Baby Boomers (born 1946–1964) are the Idealist generation of the current generational cycle. The positions of power and leadership they hold today will be challenged and tested over time by the rising Millennial Generation.

- "Reactive." The children of this generational type are reared in an unprotected manner by their parents and are frequently criticized and condemned by adults. As grownups they tend to be individualistic, alienated, risk-taking, entrepreneurial, and pragmatic. Generation X (born 1965–1982) is the Reactive generation in the current cycle. Former Alaska governor and 2008 Republican vice-presidential nominee Sarah Palin (born 1964), and House Republican Whip Eric Cantor (born 1963), are late-wave Boomers born on the cusp of generational change, both of whom possess the in-your-face, chip-on-the-shoulder demeanor typical of reactive generations. GOP Representatives Kevin McCarthy (born 1965) and Paul Ryan (born 1970), the co-authors, along with Cantor, of the conservative manifesto *Young Guns*, are the first members of Generation X to achieve national political prominence through their leadership positions in the House of Representatives.

- "Civic." Members of civic generations are reared in a protected manner that emphasizes adherence to group and social norms. As adults they focus on resolving societal challenges and building institutions. Despite coming of age during periods of intense stress and turmoil, civic generations invariably exhibit a uniquely high degree of optimism about where they and the nation are ultimately headed. Tom Brokaw's book *The Greatest Generation* celebrates the GI Generation (born 1901–1924), the highly revered civic generation of the previous cycle. The Millennial Generation is the civic generation of the current cycle. It will become the primary force shaping America until at least the middle of this century. This transformation will occur in stages as Millennials emerge to prominence first as voters and consumers and, in two or three decades, as governmental and private sector leaders in their own right.

- "Adaptive." This generational archetype is reared in an over-protected, smothering manner, in large part in reaction to major societal crises that occur during its childhood, producing adults who tend toward conformity, risk aversion, and compromise. Senator John McCain and Vice President Joe Biden are members of the Silent Generation (born 1925–1945), the Adaptive generation of the last cycle. The Adaptive generation in the current cycle (born beginning in 2004) has not yet been given a name by generational theorists.

Although all of the generational archetypes occur at predictable intervals, they do not have an identical impact on America. Our book, *Millennial Makeover*, demonstrated that the emergence of the two dominant or dynamic generational archetypes—idealist and civic—along with the deployment of a new communication technology, produces the electoral and political realignments, or shifts in party dominance, that occur about every four decades in U.S. politics. Increased birth and immigration rates in the twenty years before the coming of age of idealist and civic generations give these two archetypes the numbers to change and truly dominate U.S. elections and most other aspects of American society, as well. But, it is more than demography that makes idealist and civic generations decisive. The differing attitudes, values, and behaviors of these two dominant generational archetypes have led each of them to make over the country and its institutions in distinctive ways throughout its history (Winograd and Hais 2008).

Each eight-decade-long generational cycle is divided into two eras of about forty years each that are driven by the two dynamic generational archetypes—idealist and civic. Eras that begin with the coming of age of a divided, anti-establishment idealist generation have been characterized by less identification with the existing political parties, resulting in more split-ticket voting, lower electoral turnout, more negative attitudes toward government and politics, policy gridlock in Congress, a contraction of government, and increased economic inequality. These were all characteristics of America's most recent idealist era, 1968–2008. By contrast, the emergence of an optimistic, unified civic generation has historically produced a higher degree of partisan loyalties within the electorate, causing greater straight-ticket voting, increased voter participation, more interest in fixing governmental and political institutions, policy breakthroughs—particularly at the federal level—activist government, and greater economic equality. These are quite likely to be the characteristics of the country's Millennial-dominated civic era that began with the 2008 presidential election.

THE FOURTH FOURTH TURNING IN AMERICAN HISTORY

This is not the first time in American history that a young civic generation intent on fixing the institutions its elders had built is about to send the nation on a dramatically new course. About every eighty years a generation with attitudes and beliefs similar to today's Millennials has forced the nation to deal with its most fundamental challenges. Each time, the tension between those intent on defending the status quo and those committed to creating a different future has generated a crisis that threatened the very existence of the country. Strauss and Howe term this particular alignment of generational change and challenge to the old order a "fourth turning" of the generational cycle.

There have been three previous fourth turnings since the United States became an independent nation:

American Revolution fourth turning (1773–1789)

Civil War fourth turning (1860–1877)

New Deal fourth turning (1929–1941)

Each one has followed a specific sequence of events. Each phase builds upon the previous series of events as the country's historical turning heads toward a climax and ultimate denouement, or resolution. From a perspective of decades or even centuries, the progression from one phase to another may seem precise. For those living through it, however, the sequence of events unfolds gradually with the appearance of one step backward for every two steps forward generating as much confusion as clarity about just what direction the country wants to go. In order of occurrence, the specific events in each fourth turning are:

- "Catalyst." A startling event, or sequence of events, that produces a sudden shift in mood. The collapse of America's financial systems in September 2008, and the Great Recession that followed, are generally considered to be the catalyst for the fourth turning, or transition, that America is now experiencing. It arrived almost exactly eighty years after the 1929 stock market crash that triggered the nation's previous civic era. The election of Abraham Lincoln to the presidency followed by the firing on Fort Sumter and the formation of the Confederacy was the catalyst for the Civil War fourth turning. The Boston Tea Party (1773) and the harsh British reaction to it were the catalysts for the American Revolution fourth turning. The fact that the catalytic events in all of America's fourth turnings "were foreseeable but poorly foreseen gives rise to a new sense of urgency about institutional dysfunction and civic vulnerability" that eventually triggers "a fierce new dynamic of public synergy" (Strauss and Howe 1997, 257).

- "Regeneracy." In all previous fourth turnings, a reenergizing of civic life has begun about three years after catalytic events trigger a new era as "collective action is now seen as vital to solving the society's most fundamental problems" (Strauss and Howe 1997, 257). Regeneracy begins when the country is presented with a new vision of the nation's future and a set of values for the community to live by, which then become the subject of intense political debate. Generational theory suggests that President Obama's first term in office was destined to be a time in which a new civic ethos was proposed and became the center of sharp political debate. The period of regeneracy in the American Revolution fourth turning was the Revolutionary

War itself, as the thirteen colonies embarked on a new course of independent nationhood. In the Civil War fourth turning, according to Strauss and Howe, the regeneracy occurred after the Northern defeat in the first Battle of Bull Run, when "Americans realized that the struggle would be neither glamorous nor painless" (Strauss and Howe 1997, 257), leading to an unprecedented growth of government authority on both the Union and Confederate sides. In the New Deal fourth turning, the period of regeneracy was the first one hundred days of Franklin Roosevelt's administration that set America in a new economic direction, with the government playing a much more central and critical role. The bailout, or TARP, legislation passed in the last several months of George W. Bush's administration; the massive stimulus bill adopted early in Obama's first year in office; and the enactment of health care reform legislation about a year after Obama's inauguration suggested the regeneracy in the current fourth turning might also involve an expanded federal government economic role. But all of these actions have become sufficiently contentious that it is not yet clear if they represent the future civic ethos of the country or simply another in a series of events that will lead to a new consensus with a completely different role for government. Almost certainly, the 2012, and probably the 2016, elections will play a crucial role in determining the nature of the nation's next civic ethos. Government will not be able to act with full force upon whatever consensus emerges until after at least the first, and perhaps the second, of those two elections.

- "Climax." About midway through fourth turnings, crucial events occur that confirm the death of the old social, economic, and political order, and the birth of a new one. The climactic events of the nation's previous fourth turnings were the Battle of Yorktown (American Revolution); the 1864 reelection of Abraham Lincoln followed within a few months by the surrender of the Confederacy at Appomattox (Civil War); and Franklin Roosevelt's overwhelming reelection in 1936 (New Deal). The climactic events for the current fourth turning are still in America's future. Whatever the climactic event in the current fourth turning is and whenever it occurs, it will have dramatic consequences for the entire country. "The climax shakes a society to its roots, transforms its institutions, redirects its purposes and marks its people (and its generations) for life. . . . Whatever the event and whatever the outcome, a society passes through a great gate of history, fundamentally altering the course of history" (Strauss and Howe 1997, 258).

- "Resolution." A triumphant or tragic conclusion separating winners from losers finally resolves big public questions and clearly establishes a new order. Specifically, the resolution of the American Revolution fourth turning occurred with the passage and ratification of the U.S. Constitution that formally established the new nation and the institutions by which it has been governed for more than two centuries. For good or ill, the final resolution of the Civil War fourth turning was the disputed 1876 presidential election and the 1877 compromise that resolved that election and, more important, ended Reconstruction in a very different way from what Abraham Lincoln would have wanted. The resolution of the New Deal fourth turning was symbolized by the Japanese attack on Pearl Harbor and the coming of World War II. These events led to a complete, centrally controlled mobilization of American life and confirmed, at least until the presidency of Ronald Reagan, that an industrial and internationalist United States needed a strong federal government.

FOURTH TURNINGS ALWAYS START WITH FEAR, UNCERTAINTY, AND DOUBT

A generational alignment, such as the one the country is now experiencing, in which a dominant idealist generation is confronted by and then eventually gives way to an emerging civic generation leads to great political tension and conflict right at the beginning of every fourth turning. These conflicts are initiated by the catalytic event that precipitates the fourth turning and are intensified by disputes about the nation's new direction. The political rhetoric during these periods has invariably been among the most rancorous and contentious of any in American history, and has sometimes led to violence, because the stakes for all sides in the debate over what direction the country should take are enormous.

Considering the public's worried and dour mood during this time early in every fourth turning, we call the period "years of FUD," the business world's acronym for Fear, Uncertainty, and Doubt. Tension grips the nation and political debate rises to new levels of rage and frustration. Pouring fuel on the FUD fire with dramatic and hyperbolic claims of the dire consequences that will flow from any further change is a very well worn and often successful strategy in corporate life. Recent events have demonstrated that these tactics have great power in the political world as well. The shrill tone and angry tenor of FUD is likely to characterize most, if not all, of the remainder of Barack Obama's first presidential term and possibly his second, should there be one.

Periods of FUD filled with harsh dissent and rancor have occurred early in every fourth turning. More than two centuries ago, the population of the thirteen colonies was sharply divided during the Revolutionary War turning. John Adams claimed that about one-third of the colonists supported the Revolution, one-third were Tories or British Loyalists, and another third were neutral. Although more recent historians dispute Adams's numbers, it is clear that those loyal to the British Crown made up a significant portion of the population. Some put the number of British Loyalists at 30 percent of the white population, and American historian Robert Middlekauff, believes that 20 percent overall, and upward of half the population in the large Middle Atlantic colonies New York and Pennsylvania, were Tories. Middlekauff also points to a division along age lines: a disproportionately large number of Loyalists were older (or in generational terms, members of the idealist Awakening Generation) (Middlekauff 1982). Estimates are that after the war, between 60,000 and 100,000 Loyalists fled the newly born United States, primarily for Canada, the British Caribbean, or the English mother country. This represents between 3 and 5 percent of the prewar population of the colonies, a larger percentage than left France in the aftermath of its revolution two decades later.

Societal and political divisions did not disappear following the victory of the colonial rebels and the departure of the British. Conflict over exactly what type of government the new nation should have was sharp. Attempting to quantify public opinion during an era before the advent of survey research is difficult, if not impossible. No one knows precisely, therefore, how divided Americans were over the ratification of the U.S. Constitution. Today, some regard the document as divinely inspired, but estimates are that in 1787 at least half, if not more, of the population opposed its ratification. The framers of the Constitution clearly recognized these divisions; in order to win over opponents, a series of amendments to the original document had to be promised by its Federalist proponents as one of the first orders of business in the new Congress. Even so, votes on ratification in several key large states (Massachusetts, New York, and Virginia) were almost evenly split, and two states (Rhode Island and North Carolina) rejected the original document outright.

In no fourth turning, of course, was conflict more intense or violent than in the Civil War turning. The 1860 election that put Abraham Lincoln in the White House was sharply contested. Lincoln did receive about six in ten electoral votes, but only 40 percent of the national popular vote. He received virtually no votes in the eleven states that, after his election, became the Confederacy. North of the Mason-Dixon Line, he narrowly lost New Jersey and won bare majorities in other large northern states, including New York, Ohio, Indiana, and his home state, Illinois, which was also the home of his chief Democratic opponent, Stephen A. Douglas.

Once Lincoln assumed the presidency and the Civil War began, he faced opposition from all sides. Almost every white person in the Confederate States reviled him. The words of his assassin, John Wilkes Booth, after fatally wounding the president, "Sic semper tyrannis" (Thus always to tyrants) succinctly expressed the thoughts of most Southerners about Lincoln. In the North, much of the criticism was intensely personal: Lincoln was called an "ape," a "baboon," or worse. Many opposed what they perceived to be a war sacrificing the blood of white men to free blacks. Riots protesting the military draft broke out in Northern cities. In New York, blacks were lynched, and the city's Negro orphanage burned. Another indication of the divisions over the war in the North was the outcome of the 1862 midterm elections, in which Lincoln's Republicans lost 22 House seats and the opposition Democrats gained 28. Even within his own party, a faction called him timid for failing to emancipate the slaves sooner than he did or pursuing a more vindictive policy against the secessionist states. Given all this, it is little wonder that Lincoln himself thought he might not be reelected in 1864 (Charnwood 1996).

The fourth turning that began in the early 1930s was precipitated by the greatest economic crisis in American history. By the time Franklin Roosevelt assumed the presidency, one in four Americans was unemployed, and the country's financial system was on the verge of collapse. He received large popular and electoral vote majorities, and his Democratic Party dominated both houses of Congress, allowing Roosevelt to embark on an unprecedented, massively ambitious, and experimental program of federal intervention in the economy.

But FDR was hardly without opposition, some of it violent. A month before his inauguration, Roosevelt was nearly the victim of an assassin. Giuseppe Zangara, an unemployed bricklayer with anarchist leanings, fired at FDR. Although Zangara missed the president-elect, he hit and killed Anton Cermak, the mayor of Chicago.

Once in office, Roosevelt was personally criticized from the right for being a "traitor to his class." In shrill language that was to be repeated in the first years of the Obama administration, FDR's policies and programs were labeled "foreign," "socialist," "communist," and "fascist." Social Security, now an accepted and valued program, was derided as a severe invasion of privacy. At the same time, from the other side of the political spectrum, Roosevelt was criticized for not doing enough to dismantle the capitalist system and, in the words of Huey Long, "share the wealth." Long was seen as a potentially formidable opponent of FDR in the 1936 election, which he may well have been had he not been assassinated in 1935.

Roosevelt was reelected in 1936, winning 61 percent of the popular vote and the electoral votes of all but two states, the then rock-ribbed Republican strongholds of Maine and Vermont. However, a late October straw poll sponsored by the *Literary Digest* magazine predicted that FDR's Republican opponent, Alf Landon, would win the election with 57 percent of the popular vote and 370 of 531 electoral votes. Once the real election results came in, the *Literary Digest* became the laughing stock of the nation and ceased publication within two years. The problem with the magazine's poll was that it surveyed only those with telephones and auto licenses, hardly representative of the American electorate in the midst of the Great Depression. Still, in the week between the publication of the poll and the election many did believe that FDR could be defeated. On the eve of his largest electoral victory, opposition to Franklin Roosevelt was perceived to be large enough that a prediction of his defeat did not seem especially far-fetched.

From the perspective of decades, or even centuries, the successes and accomplishments of Washington, Lincoln, and Franklin Roosevelt—and of America itself—seem almost to have been preordained and easy to achieve. Nothing could be further from the truth. None of these outcomes was certain to those who lived through each of the fourth turnings, or came without furious and often debilitating debate during a period of great fear, uncertainty, and doubt.

Change Can Be Terrifying to Those Destined to Live Through It

The reaction of the country to the sudden shift from confidence in the future based upon a clearly understood set of values and beliefs to a period of fear, uncertainty, and doubt makes for powerful and dramatic storytelling. In her best-selling novel, . . . And Ladies of the Club, Helen Hooven Santmyer described all the changes America experienced from Ulysses S. Grant's election as president in 1868, when America's voters ratified the victorious Republican Party's political program during the Civil War fourth turning, until Franklin Roosevelt's first presidential victory in 1932, and the coming of the New Deal at the beginning of America's next fourth turning. Santmyer's patiently created portrayal of the wrenching end of an idealist era and the beginning of a civic one is one of the most accurate historical depictions of this period of FUD in American life ever written.

Set in the fictional town of Waynesboro, Ohio, the story begins with a description of remarks to the graduating class of the town's female college by the local Republican congressman and town hero, a Union general in the recent Civil War, speaking in support of Grant's candidacy. Extolling the virtues of the GOP as the party of Abraham Lincoln and the Union, and condemning the opposition Democrats as the party that supported slavery and rebellion, the remarks solidified the lifelong identification of Santmyer's protagonist, Anne Gordon, with the dominant civic-era party of its day. In real life, that party loyalty, forged in the Civil War and its aftermath, enabled the Republicans to win fourteen of eighteen presidential elections between 1860 and 1928, and the state of Ohio in all but two of those elections.

But the world was completely different by the book's end in 1932. The election of Franklin D. Roosevelt represented an important and, to Anne Gordon's way of thinking, disastrous, turn for the nation—an event of clear generational significance that undermined the very fabric of American life: "The young people seemed not to react as she did. . . . The [Democratic] convention of 1932 was to her wholly dismaying: that bland, patronizing demagogue Roosevelt!" (Santmyer 1982, 1169).

During the campaign, Anne's civic GI Generation grandchildren tried to reassure her that the country would survive the election of Roosevelt. Their arguments did not convince her:

> this man [Roosevelt] . . . promised everything to the poor and benighted: his schemes for sweeping reforms to bring about recovery—unemployment relief and made [*sic*] work, new laws for the stock market to save the country from another panic, . . . help for the one-third of the population "ill-housed, ill-clad, ill-fed" all summed up in the phrase "a New Deal for the forgotten man." . . . The country would outlive Roosevelt but it would not be the America in which she had grown up and lived her life. . . . She was too old, she supposed, to adjust to what young people could take in stride. (Santmyer 1982, 1170)

In 2010, early in another fourth turning and in the midst of a new period of FUD, Stephen Bannon's documentary *Generation Zero* combined the same sense of historical foreboding with visually striking images of impending doom. The movie, which was a huge hit at the Conservative PAC (CPAC) convention and Tea Party gatherings across the nation, even built its story around Strauss and Howe's generational theory. The film's executive producer and president of Citizens United Productions, Dave Bossie, explained to conservative talk show host Sean Hannity that capitalism didn't cause the catalytic events of the current fourth turning. Instead, it was "the hubris and greed . . . [and] cultural and social break down from the '60s." Blaming only the liberal half of the Boomer generation for overturning the traditional society that the GI Generation had built in America, Bossie went on to say, "the greatest generation . . . it would never dawn on them to take the type of risk that these people did. . . . The people at Woodstock in the '60s who became the yuppies of the '80s really the barons of the 2000s and really are the leaders around the country that helped cause this" (Hannity 2010).

The documentary included the thoughts of dozens of the most prominent conservative thinkers on the choices facing the country, including Republican former House Speaker Newt Gingrich, who accurately described what is at stake in each of the country's fourth turnings:

> Revolutionary War period up through creating our Constitution, the Civil War period and the Great Depression and World War II. In those three periods of choosing, people had to decide what kind of country we were going to be, where we were going to go as a nation. I think we are entering a similar period. The choices over the next few years are among the most profound we will have seen in all of American history." (Bannon 2010)

Using unidentified speakers, the documentary *Generation Zero* predicted:

> A time of testing, of adversity . . . when the best qualities of every generation comes to the surface and becomes very important in steering history in a good direction. But more importantly, fourth turnings are necessary for the evolution of civilization. There has to be a period when we get rid of what's old. Particularly what's old institutionally. We make the ground fresh again for the young. The question of what that new order will be is up to us and to the younger generations, and it always will be. (Bannon 2010)

Then in the time-tested manner of all prophets of doom, director Bannon pointed to the coming apocalypse, when the pressure of Baby Boomers' retirement on Social Security and U.S. financial obligations to the Chinese would bring the country to its knees. He argued that the only way to restore America's future was to stop government spending and eliminate the debt by breaking the unholy "alliance between the Democratic Party and big business." Otherwise, "when we add another $9 trillion under the $12 trillion we've already borrowed, we're going to have revolution" (Hannity 2010).

Although both Santmeyer's and Bannon's attempts to describe the crises the country confronted in two different eras might be considered by some to be fanciful flights of fear divorced from reality, they both focused on the question of the nation's ability to thrive, or even survive, in the future. That is the underlying question bothering the nation during every period of FUD at the start of every fourth turning.

CONCLUSION

Today, as in the 1770s, 1860s, and 1930s, America is experiencing a fourth turning. As in the past, an ideologically driven, highly divided idealist generation that has dominated U.S. politics for four decades, in this instance the Baby Boomers, is facing a civic generation that is just coming onto the stage. Led by Barack Obama, a president to whom it has special affinity, the emerging Millennial Generation, like previous civic generations, is focused on revitalizing the nation's institutions and dealing with long-standing issues deferred during the idealist era that is passing from the scene. Other Americans are arguing just as strongly that only a return to what they perceive to be the nation's original governmental and economic conception can provide a path to stability and prosperity in the future.

Previous fourth turnings provide insights into what lies ahead. At the beginning of civic eras, as Strauss and Howe point out, "society starts propelling itself on a trajectory that nobody had foreseen before the catalyzing event" (Strauss and Howe 1997, 257). It is the underpinnings of that trajectory which this book is designed to illuminate, to help the country understand the choices before it and the course of action it should pursue.

This particular generational alignment provides opportunities for great achievement and problem resolution, but also, invariably, major tension and conflict. The outcome will inevitably produce major changes in the nation's politics and public policy, as well as its public and private-sector institutions. Ultimately, every aspect of American society from its schools to its workplaces, from its sources of entertainment to its family life, even its role in the world, will be radically different from what it was in the twentieth century as the nation moves from an idealist era to a civic one. Because the Millennial Generation will play such a powerful role in shaping these changes, any attempt to understand the trajectory the country is on now must begin with a clear understanding of the distinctive attitudes and behaviors of these 95 million young Americans.

CHAPTER 2

Millennials Are About
to Take Over America

DURING AMERICA'S GREAT DEPRESSION an exciting
new technology, movies coupled with sound, provided a temporary
escape from the feelings of fear, uncertainty, and doubt that had
descended on the nation. Busby Berkley's art deco–inspired choreogra-
phy was melded with tales of individual success to offer, as the original
poster for *42nd Street* blared, "A New Deal in Entertainment." The
movie's plot and cast of characters presented a perfect allegory for
American attitudes and popular culture in February 1933, just before
Franklin D. Roosevelt's first inaugural. The villain is a conniving,
underhanded Wall Street tycoon, the financial backer of a Broadway
musical whose interference nearly destroys the show. The lead character
is, in today's vernacular, a cynical, self-centered diva whose future is rescued by an FDR-like, father-figure director who shows her a different
way to approach life. Once she learns to trust her supporting cast, a band
of GI Generation actors and dancers, the show is saved from ruin and
prosperity beckons. The GI Generation took the message of *42nd Street*
and other popular movies, such as *A Star Is Born* and *Stage Door*, to heart
and endorsed the idea that too much focus on individual pursuits led to
trouble, but success could flow from a new "sense of community and
interdependency" (Dickstein 2009).

This same collective spirit animates the Millennial Generation, born
eighty years after the GI Generation. Popular television shows like *High
School Musical* and *Glee!* capture the same spirit of camaraderie as 1930s
musicals did. At the heart of today's new technology, social networks,
which Millennials use so well, is the ability to stay connected with a
wide variety of friends, creating communities far larger and more diverse
than those of any previous generation. A record number of Millennials

are acting on their belief in collective action by signing up for community service to help those in need. The share of college graduates who believe their community is more important than their job has doubled since 1982, the single largest shift in basic values between members of Generation X who graduated that year, and those who finished college in 2008 (N. Howe 2010b). Even though the 95 million members of the Millennial Generation, born between 1982 and 2003, are the children of Baby Boomers and Gen-Xers, in many key respects they are more like their GI Generation (born 1901–1924) great-grandparents than their own parents.

Millennials are the largest and most racially diverse generation in American history. About 40 percent of Millennials are African American, Latino, Asian, or of mixed racial background. This compares with about 25 percent of the two next older generations—Gen-Xers and Baby Boomers. The oldest living American generation of any significant size, Silents, are 90 percent white. While this was also true of the GI Generation, many in that cohort were either immigrants themselves or the children of Catholic and Jewish immigrants from eastern and southern Europe who composed the last large European immigration wave in the late nineteenth and early twentieth centuries.

Both the Millennial and GI Generations were large in comparison to the generations that immediately preceded their own. There are now about 27 million more Millennials alive than members of Generation X and 17 million more Millennials than Baby Boomers, gaps that will only grow as the older generations age and die. In 1930, just two years before the GI Generation was instrumental in propelling Franklin Roosevelt to the White House, there were nearly as many members of that generation living at that time as there were members of the two previous American generations combined. Then, just as now, the sheer numbers of that generation allowed its beliefs, attitudes, and behaviors to dominate American life and politics for the next four decades.

CIVIC GENERATION CHILDHOODS ARE A LOT ALIKE

The economy made modest recoveries from mild recessions about ten years before the oldest members of the two civic generations reached voting age. These rebounds were characterized by rising stock markets and economic productivity, along with increased economic inequality and questionable practices in the financial sector, which contributed to major economic declines just as large numbers of both young Millennials and members of the GI Generation were first beginning to enter the job market.

Partially in response to economic hard times, in both of the idealist eras during which Millennials and members of the GI Generation were children, there were vociferous demands for limiting immigration to protect American jobs. Even as young civic generation immigrants and children of immigrants from each generation were beginning to change the country's values and culture forever, calls for preserving the traditional American way of life from foreign influences gained significant political traction.

Older members of idealist generations also demanded large government efforts to eliminate addictive substances—Prohibition during the GI Generation's youth and the War on Drugs when Millennials were children—as another way to protect the young from the sins their elders had committed.

The childhoods of both the Millennial and GI generations were at first marked by a lessening U.S. involvement in international affairs. For the GI Generation, it was the end of World War I in 1918 and the rejection of the League of Nations and foreign alliances in the 1920s and 1930s. For Millennials, the end of the Cold War provided an opportunity for the country to turn its attention inward, and the nation's memories of the Vietnam War reinforced that tendency. In both time periods, however, events—the rise of fascism in the 1930s and the 9/11 attacks and a growing threat of terrorism in this century—eventually forced Americans to pay greater attention to events elsewhere in the world than they might otherwise have wished. It was members of the two civic generations who bore most of the military burden in dealing with these concerns—the GI Generation in World War II and Millennials in the Iraq and Afghanistan wars.

In addition to being shaped by similar events, both generations were molded more directly by the distinctive child-rearing practices and attitudes toward family of their parents. In both cases, parents of civic generations raised their own children in ways dramatically different than the way in which they themselves had been raised. Many Boomers were permitted, even encouraged, by their parents to form the strongly held personal values that have guided members of that generation for a lifetime, and that were so humorously portrayed in the arguments between Meathead and his father-in-law, Archie Bunker, on television's *All in the Family*. Many Gen-Xers were often raised at a distance or left alone by their parents, being forced to cope with adversity and to figure out their own ways of getting along in an often hostile world, as poignantly portrayed in the movie *The Breakfast Club*.

By contrast, Millennial children were almost invariably highly valued by their parents and perceived as the most important requirement for a full and happy life. In many ways their childhood upbringing reflected the lessons imparted by Cliff and Clair Huxtable, the parents on the *Bill Cosby Show*, one of the most popular family situation comedies ever. Just like the Huxtable children, young Millennials were revered, praised, sheltered, befriended, and carefully guided by their parents to lead well-structured lives based on adherence to clear and mutually agreed-upon rules. This has produced a generation of young people that is, by most measures, accomplished, self-confident, group-oriented, and optimistic.

Some critics have also argued that this child-rearing approach produced a generation of self-important, entitled and, ultimately, indecisive young people (Twenge 2006). In one particularly notable rant, conservative commentator Glenn Beck decried what he perceived to be the entitlement attitudes of Millennials, blaming it all on their "dope-smoking hippie" parents, and a liberal government determined to protect them from the rough and tumble of life in a free and unregulated society:

> Here's the problem with the Millennial generation. . . . They don't give a flying crap about anybody but themselves, because they're special, look at all the trophies they won. . . . Soon the government will be able to protect everyone so you'll not be able to fire anyone. You can live more like they live in France where . . . countries [*sic*] have whole sections of floors dedicated to people who just sit in an office and do nothing because the state won't let them fire them. . . . That's where we're headed. (Beck 2008)

This is not the first time that such a charge had been leveled at a civic generation and the way it was raised. At the outset of World War II, army psychiatrists complained that their GI recruits had been "over-mothered" in the years before the war (Strauss and Howe 1991, 264). History will tell us if the Millennial Generation will ultimately be as successful in the decades ahead at overcoming its supposedly soft upbringing as was the Greatest Generation. To date, however, the results are positive. Juvenile crime, teen pregnancy, abortion, and substance abuse rates are lower and standardized academic test scores and community participation rates are higher among Millennials than they were among both Baby Boomers and Gen-Xers.

The parenting they received and the societal and economic environment in which Millennials were reared and came of age created a distinctive mindset labeled "pragmatic idealism" by David Burstein, who writes about his "Change Generation" for *Fast Company* magazine. Three-quarters of all Millennials believe that "as Americans we can always find a way to solve our problems and get what we want." Burstein sees a clear generational difference in how each cohort has approached problems when they were young. Earlier generations "have tended to be either excessively pragmatic (1950s [Silent Generation]) or excessively idealistic (1960s [Boomers])—or excessively cynical (Generation X), but the combination and balance of pragmatism and idealism in my generation is providing some exciting results" (Burstein 2010).

Once again, the parallels to America's last civic generation—the GI Generation—are striking. Facing even worse economic adversity in the 1930s than what Millennials are experiencing today, young GI's deferred careers and marriage and adopted a philosophy of "apple-pie radicalism, more economic than cultural or moral. . . . Even the most committed ideologues agreed . . . that the main argument was over what system worked best" (Strauss and Howe, 1991, 271). "Throughout their lives [the] GI's have been America's confident and rational problem solvers" (ibid., 261).

Just as that can-do attitude served the country so well when the GI Generation became adults, the Millennial Generation's new brand of pragmatic idealism is arriving just in time to undo the political gridlock created by its Gen-X and especially its Boomer parents. Burstein believes that his generation's mindset is not a passing youthful fad. "Perhaps the most exciting thing about this is its sustainability . . . this generation will be working on major challenges for a lifetime, not just in their youth" (Burstein 2010). The Millennial Generation's distinctive mindset will be the dominant force shaping the behavior of the country's body politic and guiding the course of American life for the coming four decades.

TO MILLENNIALS, WE ARE ALL BROTHERS AND SISTERS UNDER THE SKIN

The ethnic diversity and group orientation of the Millennial Generation is clearly reflected in its attitudes. Millennials, more than other generations, support racial and ethnic equality and inclusion, and look for win-win solutions that advance the welfare of everyone, whether it's their friends or all of society. They have taken to heart the lessons imparted to them as toddlers when their parents sat them in front of the TV to watch a show about a purple dinosaur named Barney. The program made it clear that even though on the outside Barney was "as different as he could be, on the inside he was just like you and me."

In 1987, a Pew Research Center survey indicated that fewer than half of all Americans (48%) believed that "It is all right for blacks and whites to date each other." Two decades later, acceptance of interracial dating is broadly acceptable, especially among Millennials (92% as against 81% for older generations). Millennial support for racial equality and inclusion is not confined to individual relationships, but extends to matters of societal and governmental policy, as well. Millennials are far more likely than others (46% to 28%) to agree that "we should make every possible effort to improve the position of blacks and other minorities, even if it means giving them preferential treatment" (Pew 2007).

Black-white relations are not the nation's only ethnic concern. The hot-button issue of immigration became fuel for the FUD fire now gripping the nation's political debate. In April 2010, Arizona enacted SB 1070, which required local police to ascertain the immigration status of those "reasonably" suspected of being in the United States illegally. Proponents and opponents of the new law demonstrated throughout the country and talk show participants argued about it incessantly. Boomers were more likely than Millennials to believe that the Arizona law was "about right" (as opposed to "going too far" or "not far enough"). Older generations were also more likely to say that no newcomers should be allowed to enter the country, while younger generations favored a welcome-all approach (Cave 2010).

For most Millennials, the impact of immigrants on American life and immigration policy is no longer a matter of much debate. In May 2009, only one-third of Millennials agreed with the proposition that "immigrants threaten American values and customs" (Pew 2009b). However, 55 percent of older Americans, a full 20 percentage points more than Millennial respondents, agreed with the statement. One year later, 41 percent of Boomers believed immigration levels should be decreased, but only 24 percent of Gen-Xers and Millennials agreed (Cave 2010).

Although the diverse ethnicity of the Millennial Generation undoubtedly contributes to these egalitarian and inclusive views, it is not the only reason for them. Among the 60 percent of Millennials who are white, virtually all disagree with the contention that they "don't have much in common with people of other races," with a clear majority (57%) completely disagreeing. By contrast, in the late 1980s, when members of Generation X were the same age that Millennials are now, only one-quarter completely disagreed (Pew 2009b) For Millennials of all backgrounds, racial and ethnic equality and inclusivity is a message they have been hearing all their lives and one in which they firmly believe.

LIVE AND LET LIVE IS THE MILLENNIAL MOTTO

For much of the Boomer-dominated idealist era of the past four decades, social issues, such as the role of women, gay rights, and abortion triggered the most heated political debates and sharply defined a candidate's political philosophy. While those issues produce shrill disputes among older generations, most Millennials wonder what all the shouting is about.

Americans have increasingly accepted expanded social and economic opportunities for women. According to Pew, currently three-quarters reject the contention, "women should return to their traditional roles in society," with a majority (54%) disagreeing completely. But, generational differences still remain. Members of the Silent Generation grew up, and lived much of their adult lives, in an environment in which gender roles were clearly defined. As the author of *Generational Dynamics*, John J. Xenakis, nostalgically recalled in the conservative documentary

Ground Zero, "People really misunderstand the 1950s. They think in terms of, like, June Cleaver and Donna Reed. As if everybody was discriminating against women, forcing them to stay at home" (Bannon 2010). Only 40 percent of those over sixty-five completely reject the idea of women returning to their traditional roles, a position shared by approximately half of Baby Boomers and Gen-Xers. By contrast, 84 percent of Millennials disagree at least to a certain extent and two-thirds (67%) completely disagree with the idea (Pew 2009b).

Civic eras have always produced greater educational opportunities for women. Female members of the GI Generation attended public high schools in the same proportion as men, and Millennials are the first generation in U.S. history in which an equal or even greater number of women than men attend college and professional schools. Among urban Millennials who are single and childless, women earn 8 percent more than men (Luscombe 2010). Based on these experiences, Millennials are far less likely than older generations to perceive sex discrimination as a concern. Only half of Millennials, as compared with 55 percent of Boomers, and two-thirds of members of the Silent Generation, agree that "women get fewer opportunities for good jobs than men" (Pew 2009b).

Americans are also increasingly tolerant of homosexuality, and, once again, Millennials are leading this change in beliefs. Over the past twenty years, the number of Americans who believe that "school boards ought to have the right to fire teachers who are known homosexuals" has dropped by almost half (from 51% to 28%). Only one in five Millennials express any degree of support for this opinion, as compared with 30 percent of all older generations and nearly half (43%) of members of the Silent Generation. Millennials are also significantly more positive about gay marriage than are older generations (43% to 32%) (Pew 2009b).

The only social issue on which the Millennial Generation is not more liberal or nontraditional than some older generations is abortion. The Millennial Generation is split on the issue. Forty-eight percent believe that abortion should be legal in all or most cases, while the same number say it should be illegal all or most of the time. By contrast, a slight majority of Generation X (50% to 41%) and a plurality of Boomers (47% to 43%) believe that abortion should always or usually be legal rather than illegal (Pew 2009b). Unlike Boomer feminist women for whom "the personal was political," abortion does not appear to be a major personal concern for most Millennials. Many in the younger generation see abortion as less a matter of women's rights than a conflict between individual rights and societal values. As with civic generations before them, Millennials more often than not place a greater premium on the latter than the former.

Overall, however, while many older Americans remain focused on social issues, Millennials have turned the page on matters of individual morality and overwhelmingly demonstrate tolerance and openness in their dealings with others. In the last fourth turning, the civic GI Generation could not understand why its elders had expended so much energy fighting over Prohibition and arguing about evolutionary theory. The Great Depression and the threat of fascism were much more pressing concerns. So, too, have Millennials moved on to the concerns of a new era—unemployment, economic inequality, financial regulation, access to health care, the ability of the United States to compete economically with other nations, and the role of government in dealing with those issues. Although not all politicians immediately recognized this shift in the nation's agenda, those that did found an attentive audience within a civic generation interested in new solutions to these enduring challenges.

MILLENNIALS PREFER AN ACTIVIST GOVERNMENT

Just as their great-grandparents did, Millennials emerged into young adulthood—and the job market—as the economic structure and assumptions of previous decades ground to a halt and went into reverse. For Millennials the greatest economic downturn since the 1930s became their own personal Great Depression.

In October 2009, unemployment among 16- to 19-year-olds reached nearly 28 percent. Among those 20 to 24, it was almost 16 percent, and in the 25 to 34 age cohort (a group that contained the very oldest Millennials and the very youngest Gen-Xers), more than one in ten did not have jobs. A Pew survey conducted that month reported that nearly two-thirds of Millennials (61%) came from households in which someone was unemployed at some time during the previous year (Pew 2009d).

Millennials looked to the government for help with their economic difficulties, just as other civic generations had done before them. More than older generations, Millennials favor a wide scope of governmental activity, especially on the federal level. An October 2009 Pew survey indicated that a solid majority of Millennials (57% to 35%) preferred a bigger government that provides more services to a smaller government that provides fewer services (Pew 2009d). Similarly, a June 2010 survey found that 58 percent of Millennials, as compared with 52 percent of older generations, favored a federal government that actively attempts to solve societal and economic problems (Winograd and Hais 2010b). More specifically, Hispanic Millennials preferred that government play a major role in creating jobs and improving the economy over the free market by a similar two-to-one margin (Bendixen and Amandi Associates 2010). Older generations had nearly the opposite response, preferring a smaller government to a bigger one by a 55 percent to 35 percent margin.

This generic endorsement of activist government is reflected in the specific preferences of the Millennial Generation toward the Obama administration's initiatives designed to deal with the economic downturn. Like other civic generations, Millennials disproportionately favor economic regulation of business and the financial industry. About eight months after the collapse of the financial industry, nearly 69 percent of Millennials, compared with 61 percent of older generations, agreed with the contention that "a free market economy needs government regulation in order to best serve the public interest." Millennials were a bit less likely than older generations (50% to 56%) to believe that "government regulation of business usually does more harm than good" (Pew 2009b).

Millennials also offered disproportionate support for increased government spending to alleviate unemployment. In June 2009, two-thirds of Millennials (65%, compared with 53% of older generations) favored the $800 billion Economic Recovery Act or stimulus enacted the previous February (Pew 2009c). By October 2009, in the face of continued economic sluggishness, Millennial support for the stimulus had fallen to 57 percent, but that was still well above the 41 percent favorable opinion among older generations (Pew 2009d).

Although all generations solidly supported federal infrastructure spending on roads, bridges, and other public works, Millennials also favored the otherwise unpopular government bailouts of financial institutions and auto companies. About half of Millennials, in contrast to one-third of older generations, supported government loans to banks, brokerages, General Motors, and Chrysler (2009d). Millennials' team orientation and pragmatic idealism provide the underpinnings for this sustained belief in the efficacy of collective, government action.

Civic Generations Are All for One and One for All Economically

The GI Generation's support for the federal government taking the lead in ensuring economic prosperity came from the deep and persistent poverty it experienced growing up in the 1930s. Here is how one member of that generation described his teenage years:

> I was born May 22nd, 1922, the oldest of six children. My dad was working 6 days a week for $17.00. . . . We lived close to the railroad tracks in the poor section of town. . . . When I came home from school my mother would make me change my clothes right through to the skin and put on old clothes. . . . After which I would take pails and walk the railroad tracks, picking up coal that fell off all the coal cars heading North. . . . When I came home with the coal, I would find my younger brothers whining, "Mama, I am hungry." I would ask my mother, "Ma, what's for supper?" She would snap back, "Wind pudding and air sauce." I would then find her crying. I felt so bad. (Brokaw 1999, 138–39)

Fortunately, while they have suffered disproportionately in the recent Great Recession, most members of the Millennial Generation have not experienced the same level of economic deprivation as did their generational forebears. But they still resemble the GI Generation in their endorsement of a greater level of economic equality and a wider range of economic opportunity. For instance, a May 2009 Pew survey found that a large majority of Millennials (69%) agreed that the government should guarantee every citizen enough to eat and a place to sleep. This contrasts with 59 percent among older generations. Millennials are also significantly less likely than their elders (65% to 74%) to believe that poor people have become too dependent on government assistance (Pew 2009b). Fifty-three percent of Millennials, as compared with 47 percent of older generations, believe that the federal government should ensure that all Americans have a basic standard of living and income even if this increases spending (Winograd and Hais 2010b).

The Millennial Generation's endorsement of greater economic equality and broader economic opportunity is also reflected in a level of support for labor unions that may be unmatched since the GI Generation was in the forefront of the organizing battles of the 1930s. More than three-quarters (78%) of Millennials, as opposed to 58 percent of older generations, agree that labor unions are needed to protect the rights and economic well-being of workers. Millennials are also substantially less likely than other age cohorts (53% to 62%) to believe that unions have too much power (Pew 2009b).

In previous hard economic times, the hostility of civic generations to economic inequality led to progressive taxation and increased spending on transfer payments or entitlements. As this civic era began, the very same debate broke out among older generations seeking to preserve their economic status, while Millennials urged a more inclusive and egalitarian approach to economic policy making.

Will Millennials Still Love Government and the Democratic Party When They're Old and Gray?

In the 1950s and early 1960s, when the civic GI Generation dominated U.S. politics, Americans trusted government leaders to a degree that appears impossibly naïve today. Large majorities believed that public officials cared about what most people think, that government was run for the benefit of the many and not the few, and that it could effectively deal with the major issues confronting the nation. During the subsequent four decades of the idealist era that followed, perceptions of government soured. Most of the country came to see the very institutions held in such reverence a few decades earlier in a new and negative light.

But, as with civic generations before them, Millennials have more positive perceptions of government than other generations. Fewer than half of Millennials (42%), compared with nearly two-thirds of older citizens (61%), agree with the statement "when something is run by government, it is usually wasteful and inefficient." By almost the same margin, Millennials, in contrast to their elders, reject the contention that "government controls too much of our daily lives." And by a significant 60 percent to 46 percent margin, Millennials are more likely than other generations to believe that "government is run for the benefit of all" (Pew 2009b). Millennials also exhibit a disproportionately high level of what political scientists label political efficacy, a sense that they can utilize and influence government and the political process. They are more likely than older generations to disagree that "it's not worth it to deal with the federal government" (55% to 48%) and that "people like me don't have any say in what government does" (52% to 46%). They are more inclined than older cohorts to agree that "voting gives people some say in what government does" (74% to 67%) and that "most elected officials really care what people like me think" (46% to 36%) (2009b).

Conservatives, however, take comfort from one of the brightest pearls of conventional political wisdom, which suggests that although people may be liberal and supportive of government action when they are young they become increasingly conservative and antigovernment as they age. An aphorism variously attributed to Winston Churchill, George Bernard Shaw, and World War I–era French Prime Minister Aristide Briand holds that "the man who is not a socialist at twenty has no heart, but if he is still a socialist at forty, he has no head."

As so often happens when conventional wisdom is tested with real-world data, the truth turns out to be quite different. First, as Republican pollster Kristen Soltis points out, young people are not always liberals or Democrats. After all, she comments, "in the presidential elections from 1980–1992, the 18–34 age group was the most Republican age group." Young people in those elections were older members of Generation X, for whom Ronald Reagan was as much of an icon as Franklin D. Roosevelt was to the GI Generation. To this day, older Gen-Xers remain among the most stalwart Republicans within the electorate. It is this stability of political attitudes and identifications, once they are firmly formed, that leads Soltis to advise her fellow Republicans on the need to forthrightly address the concerns of Millennials, rather than to assume that time alone will inevitably transform them into conservative Republicans (Soltis 2009).

And, as conservative activist Grover Norquist sadly realized, people do not always move to the political right as they age. Seven decades after Franklin D. Roosevelt won his first presidential election, Norquist gave a decidedly unorthodox description of the generation perceived by many to have been America's greatest. Norquist was interviewed in English by the Spanish newspaper *El Mundo* in 2004. The process of retranslating his comments back into English made it unclear if he described the beliefs and voting behavior of the civic GI Generation as "anti-American" or simply "un-American," but the implication was clearly the same:

> This generation has been an exception in American history, because it has defended anti-American policies. They voted for the creation of the welfare state and obligatory military service. They are the base of the Democratic Party. . . . Their idea of the legitimate role of the state is radically different than anything previous generations knew, or subsequent generations. . . . The government moves people around like pawns on a chessboard. One-size-fits-all labor law, one-size-fits-all Social Security. Very un-American. (Continetti 2004)

Recognizing that once a generation's political attitudes and behavior are set, they rarely change, Norquist offers death as the only solution to the political problem created by the GI Generation's statist beliefs:

> The age cohort that is most Democratic and most pro-statist are those people who turned 21 years of age between 1932 and 1952. . . . That age cohort is now [in 2004] between the ages of 70 and 90 years old, and every year 2 million of them die. So 8 million people from that age cohort have passed away since the last election [2000]; that means, net, maybe 1 million Democrats have disappeared. (Continetti 2004)

Although his sensitivity may have been overwhelmed by his conservative ideology, Norquist's description of the GI Generation was correct. It was, indeed, a cohort of Democrats and statists, one that favored governmental activism and international intervention throughout its adult life. Its votes underpinned the Democratic Party domination of American national politics that continued until the late 1960s and supported the public policies that Norquist decried.

Norquist correctly perceived the partisan proclivities and policy preferences of the GI Generation and its importance in shaping U.S. politics during much of the twentieth century, but he mistakenly viewed American history as linear rather than cyclical. This misperception led him to believe that the Greatest Generation was a one-of-a-kind phenomenon that only surfaced in the unique circumstances of the Great Depression and World War II, but whose ilk would never be seen again.

He was wrong. Much to Norquist's dismay and that of the conservative leadership group he convenes every Wednesday morning in Washington, D.C., Millennials are now making their presence felt in the electorate, just as the very last members of the GI Generation are passing from the scene. At least so far, a solid majority of the Millennial Generation shares the Democratic identification and activist policy preferences of its GI Generation great-grandparents. In fact, in the 2004 presidential election, there were only two generational cohorts that gave defeated Democratic candidate John Kerry majority support—the first small sliver of Millennials eligible to vote and the last measurable segment of the GI Generation, many of whom were participating in their final presidential election.

Most Millennials started out as Democrats and show no signs of changing their mind about which party reflects their beliefs. In 2007, the Democrats held nearly a 1.75:1 party identification advantage (52% to 30%) over the GOP (Pew 2007). A series of Magid surveys since then indicated that the Democratic lead among Millennials has not changed significantly, regardless of the political setting at the time the surveys were conducted. In October 2008, just before Millennials were instrumental in putting Barack Obama in the White House, 53 percent of Millennials called themselves Democrats as compared with 29 percent who said they were Republicans. In January 2009, as Obama was about to be inaugurated, the Democratic lead over the GOP among Millennials was 50 percent to 32 percent. And, in June 2010, after a year and a half of political rancor, the Democratic advantage over the Republicans within the Millennial Generation was 51 percent to 26 percent (Winograd and Hais 2010b). Decades of political science research suggests that the Democratic preferences of most Millennials, like those of the GI Generation, are likely to last a lifetime.

The concept of party identification was first described in the 1950s by four social scientists affiliated with the University of Michigan's Institute for Social Research in their landmark book *The American Voter*. Based on national surveys, the authors reported that upward of nine in ten American adults identified with or leaned to one of the major political parties. For the large majority, this psychological attachment to a party was formed when they were young adults and remained constant throughout the remainder of their life (Campbell et al. 1960). Nearly six decades later, in a replication of the original work, *The American Voter Revisited*, researchers used a panel of survey respondents interviewed at four different points in time over a seventeen-year period (1965–1982) to once again clearly demonstrate the long-term stability of party identification. A large majority of Americans (more than eight in ten) identified with or leaned to one of the parties, and upward of eight in ten identified with the same party at the end of the period that they did at the beginning. More recently, in the presidential election years 2000 and 2004, a similar panel showed an equivalent level of willingness to identify with a party and stability in that identification over time (Lewis-Beck et al. 2008). What is especially remarkable about the recent persistence in party identification is that it occurred in an idealist era, when commitment to political institutions, including political parties, is normally at low ebb.

The tendency of people to retain their political viewpoints and preferences throughout their lives suggests that once they are set, Millennial attitudes toward government's proper role in the economy will persist for decades. Economists Paola Giuliano and Antonio Spilimbergo's analysis of survey data collected annually since 1972 concluded that experiencing an economic recession during one's "formative years" (18–25 years old) led Americans to favor "leftist" governmental policies that would "help poor people" and lessen "income inequality." These attitudes were not influenced by experiencing a recession either before or after the formative years and remained in place even when controlled for demographic variables, such as sex, race, and social class (Giuliano and Spilimbergo 2009).

However, the same data suggested that the deeper and more sustained the recession, the lower the confidence levels were in governmental institutions, such as Congress and the presidency. Conservative *New York Times* columnist Ross Douthat used this finding to express the hope that all was not lost for the Republicans in eventually winning the support of Millennials. Recessions, Douthat argued, only benefit liberals—and Democrats—when an activist government is perceived to have the answers to a crisis. When liberal interventions seem to be effective, a downturn can help midwife an enduring Democratic majority. But if they don't seem to be working—or worse, if they seem to be working for insiders and favored constituencies, rather than the common man—then suspicion of state power can trump disillusionment with free markets (Douthat 2009).

In other words, the success of governmental action in dealing with the Great Depression of the 1930s and World War II in the 1940s put the GI Generation on the path of lifelong support for governmental activism and the Democratic Party. After the nation's victory in the Second World War and the economic boom that followed, positive perceptions of government and political efficacy among Americans were as universal as support for the Union—and Republican causes—were among Anne Gordon's generation of Midwesterners after the Civil War. Douthat acknowledges the Millennial Generation's current support for activist, egalitarian government policies, but suggests that the extent to which these attitudes persist in coming decades will depend on how well the country deals with the problems confronting it during the first years of the Obama presidency. Millennials continued to be one of the most stalwart constituencies in favor of the president's performance through the 2010 election, leaving Douthat's hypothesis as yet unproven.

CONCLUSION

Millennials entered the electorate in significant numbers in 2008, helping to elect President Obama and sending America in search of a new civic ethos. Because of their size and unanimity, the attitudes and beliefs of America's newest and largest civic generation provide the best clue as to what direction the country is likely to take as that debate unfolds. Just as their archetypical great-grandparents brought a new sense of collective action and group orientation to the country during the New Deal, Millennials are likely to place similar values at the center of the country's civic life in the future. Their increasing presence should lead to a more tolerant, inclusive society that sees government as a force for good and economic inequality as a problem to be solved. With their unique combination of pragmatism and idealism, Millennials will force the country to address the long-simmering challenges it has steadfastly avoided dealing with over the last several decades.

Democrats placed universal access to health care at the top of that list of problems during the 2008 campaign. Acting upon that conviction, President Obama spent most of his political capital in the first year of his administration trying to solve the problem once and for all. The subsequent political battle demonstrated how difficult it can be to convince those who grew up in earlier eras that the beliefs of an emerging generation should guide the country going forward. The debate over health care reform became both the template for, and the symbol of, political conflict in a time of FUD and generational change.

CHAPTER 3

Fighting Over America's Future

THROUGHOUT AMERICAN HISTORY, transitions to new eras have never gone smoothly, particularly when the shift is from an idealist or ideological era to a more pragmatic, civic one. Whether it was the fear of mob rule in a democracy that gave pause to the delegates to the Constitutional Convention in 1787; or concern with what even the Great Emancipator, Abraham Lincoln, in his debates with Stephen A. Douglas, termed "social equality," if slaves were freed; or the end of capitalism and economic freedom that so many felt Franklin D. Roosevelt's New Deal would bring to the country in the 1930s, the political tactics of FUD (fear, uncertainty, and doubt) have always been present when Americans have been asked to choose a new way forward. Warning of the dangers of the unknown and unproven is an easier political argument to make than praising the benefits that might flow from a future that has yet to be experienced.

As a result, even though potentially realigning presidential elections, such as the one that occurred in 2008, create an opportunity for the newly elected president to set a new direction for the country, the winning candidate immediately confronts the challenge of how to gain support in Congress for the vision that energized his campaign. As Yale University political scientist and presidential historian Stephen Skowronek points out:

> The leader who is propelled into office by a political upheaval in governmental control ultimately must confront the imperatives of establishing a new order in government and politics. Naturally enough, this challenge is resented by the favored interests and residual institutional support of the old order and once it has been posed, the unencumbered leadership environment that was created by the initial break with the past quickly fades. (Skowronek 2008, 34)

This historical truth returned with a vengeance in the first year of the country's newest civic era, as Barack Obama sought to enact the linchpin of his domestic policy agenda—health care reform. Although he was ultimately successful in enacting the most sweeping social legislation since the passage of Medicare in 1965, the cost to his popularity and the potential risks the battle posed to his presidency in the future demonstrated how difficult it can be to generate change people will believe in during the initial years of a civic era.

The debate illuminated the country's philosophical divisions that would need to be reconciled before this particular period of FUD would end. Boomers, who make up the majority of those now serving in Congress, bring their deeply held set of values to every political debate, reflecting the great importance of ideology to the generation. Millennials, on the other hand, are not interested in letting ideological posturing stand in the way of "getting stuff done," as Obama liked to say. Their generation's idealism is always accompanied by a pragmatic impulse focused on finding solutions, not on confrontation. As with civic generations before them, Millennials want to reinvigorate the nation's civic institutions, giving government a much greater role in determining basic citizen responsibilities in areas as diverse as health care, education, and environmental protection.

Unlike the last civic generation, the GI Generation, however, Millennials do not want to place responsibility for achieving their desired results in a remote, opaque bureaucracy. They see government's role as being more like that of their parents, who set the rules but left room for negotiation on what the consequences and rewards would be for abiding by those rules. In this Millennialist approach, government provides information and resources to help individuals connect and learn from each other but allows each person to decide how best to discharge their civic obligations. Ultimately, the health care reform legislation that was forged out of the partisan debates in Congress came surprisingly close to this model, even as it set off a bitter debate across the fault lines of American politics.

AMERICANS HAVE A SPLIT POLITICAL PERSONALITY

Lloyd A. Free and Hadley Cantril wrote *The Political Beliefs of Americans* in 1968, just as the New Deal civic era was about to end.

Their creative and seminal work was the first to describe and analyze the paradox of public opinion that underpins U.S. politics. Americans consistently express a deep conflict between their "ideological" and "operational" beliefs about government. In idealist eras, much of the political debate centers on ideology and values, whereas in civic eras, the country argues about the best operational solutions to pressing problems.

Free and Cantril defined ideological beliefs as overriding attitudes toward "the proper role and sphere of government in general and the Federal Government in particular" (Free and Cantrill 1968, 24). By contrast, operational beliefs refer to attitudes toward specific governmental functions and programs. According to Free and Cantril, at least since the New Deal, most Americans have been both ideological conservatives and operational liberals.

The very first Gallup polls, conducted in the mid-1930s, found clear evidence of this divide in public opinion. In 1935, Gallup asked Americans, who were still burdened by the worst effects of the Great Depression, "Do you think expenditures by the government for relief and recovery are too little, too great, or just about right?" Only 9 percent said they were too little, 31 percent said "about right," and the rest (60%), said they were "too great." But just three months later, Gallup asked "Are you in favor of government old-age pensions for the needy?" The concept that led to our Social Security system was endorsed by 89 percent of the public (Caplow, Hicks, and Wattenberg 2001, 40). Gallup polls in 1936 and 1937 showed large majorities in favor of the government providing free medical care to the poor (76%), extending long-term, low-interest loans to farmers (73%), and implementing the newly created Social Security program (64%). By contrast, only a minority wanted the government to take over railroads (29%) and banks (42%), or limit private fortunes (42%). And two-thirds of the public at the time of the 1936 presidential election, in which Franklin D. Roosevelt won reelection overwhelmingly, wanted the government to balance its budget (Pew 2010h). This pattern of ideological conservatism and operational liberalism—a generalized rejection of a large federal role in the economy, with a simultaneous endorsement of specific governmental programs—continues to the present day.

Free and Cantril illuminated this pattern of political beliefs, using several national surveys, which they had commissioned the Gallup organization to conduct during the 1964 election campaign. Those extensive surveys contained five specific questions from which the authors constructed an "ideological spectrum," and five questions from which they calculated an "operational spectrum." The results showed that most Americans preferred limited government and individual responsibility at the theoretical or ideological level, as opposed to the more liberal notions of ensuring equality and strengthening societal or community institutions. At the same time, when they focused on the operations of government, most favored a wide array of specific government programs, including those that created a social safety net, the goal of many liberals since at least the 1930s. Overall, about two-thirds of Americans were operationally or programmatically liberal but half were, at the same time, ideologically conservative.

In the 1960s, for most Americans, operational preferences trumped ideological attitudes. Virtually all ideological liberals (90%) and a large majority of those in the middle of the road (78%) on the ideological scale were operational liberals, but so too, were a clear plurality of ideological conservatives (46%). In the four decades that followed, however, ideological conservatives such as Ronald Reagan and George W. Bush came to dominate the Republican Party and win the presidency. Most of the governmental programs that a majority of Americans favored in those 1964 Gallup polls were eliminated, curtailed, or, at the very least, not expanded in the years afterward. In effect, Americans' operational liberalism was overtaken by their ideological conservatism during this idealist era, which lasted from 1968 to 2008.

In response, rather than adopting a clearly liberal philosophy and label, many Democrats rejected that political brand, preferring to call themselves moderates, progressives, or even conservatives. Bill Clinton, one of the two Democrats elected to the White House in this era, famously declared, in his 1996 State of the Union address, "The era of big government is over." But in 2004, Howard Dean's presidential primary campaign gained momentum when he challenged this "New Democratic" approach to public policy by declaring that his candidacy represented "the Democratic wing of the Democratic Party." Ideological liberalism was once again on the rise.

AMERICANS ARE STILL OF TWO
POLITICAL MINDS, AT ONCE

Data drawn from the Political Values and Core Attitudes Survey conducted periodically by the Pew Survey Research Center underlines the durability of this duality of American public opinion since Free and Cantril published their work. Based on questions asked in 1987, 1994, 2002, and 2009 that offer a reasonable facsimile to those in the 1964 Gallup surveys, it is possible to recalculate the operational and ideological spectrums since 1987. As tables 3.1 and 3.2 demonstrate, the dichotomy between the ideological and operational beliefs of Americans persists until the present time. Across the four Pew surveys, ideological conservatives outnumber ideological liberals by 39 percent to 11 percent, or a ratio of 3.5:1. By contrast, operational liberals outnumber

TABLE 3.1

The Distribution of Attitudes on the Ideological Spectrum 1987–2009

Ideological scale	1987 (%)	1994 (%)	2002 (%)	2009 (%)	Cross-survey total (%)
Liberal	9	7	13	13	11
Middle of the road	50	46	54	50	51
Conservative	41	47	32	38	39

SOURCE: Data drawn from 1987, 1994, 2002, and 2009 Political Values and Core Attitudes Surveys, courtesy of Pew Research Center. See Note on Data Sources and Analyses.

TABLE 3.2

The Distribution of Attitudes on the Operational Spectrum: 1987–2009

Operational scale	1987 (%)	1994 (%)	2002 (%)	2009 (%)	Cross-survey total (%)
Liberal	45	31	39	40	41
Middle of the road	38	44	41	42	40
Conservative	16	25	19	19	19

SOURCE: Data drawn from 1987, 1994, 2002, and 2009 Political Values and Core Attitudes Surveys, courtesy of Pew Research Center. See Note on Data Sources and Analyses.

operational conservatives across the four studies by 41 percent to 19 percent, or 2.2:1.

This pattern occurred in each of the selected four points in time. There were always more ideological conservatives than ideological liberals, and there were consistently a greater number of operational liberals than operational conservatives. Regardless of the year, a greater number of Americans endorsed limited government (particularly at the federal level), individual responsibility, and unfettered business, as concepts. At the same time, a greater number wanted specific governmental programs to ensure their own economic well-being and security, as well as that of their fellow citizens.

What has varied over time is the direction and balance between ideological and operational attitudes. As expected, conservative beliefs, particularly on the ideological scale, were at their peak in the two points in time that coincided with Republican Party ascendency. In 1987, toward the end of the Reagan administration, there were 4.6 ideological conservatives for every ideological liberal; in 1994, in the year of the Gingrich revolution that gave the Republicans control of both houses of Congress for the first time in four decades, the ratio of ideological conservatives to ideological liberals rose to 6.7:1. Also in 1994, the spread between operational liberals and operational conservatives was at its narrowest across the four surveys (1.2 operational liberals for each operational conservative).

Since then, coincident with crises that signaled the end of the most recent idealist era, such as the 9/11 terrorist attacks and the Great Recession of 2008, the balance between conservatives and liberals on the ideological scale has narrowed, and on the operational scale it has widened. In 2002, the ratio of ideological conservatives to liberals fell to 2.5:1. It remained at about that level in 2009 (2.9:1), causing many Republicans to insist that the country's politics was still "center right," despite Obama's electoral triumph. But what those Republicans failed to acknowledge was that there were also substantially more operational liberals than operational conservatives in both 2002 and 2009 (2.1:1) than there were in 1994 (1.2:1). The outcome of the 2010 midterm elections notwithstanding, the country is no more ideologically conservative than it was in the previous idealist era, primarily because of the influence of newly enfranchised Millennial voters, and remains at least as operationally liberal as it was after the catalytic events of 2008 (CNN 2010).

IT'S TIME FOR A CHANGE

Generational cycles offer the best explanation of the movement of operational and ideological attitudes over time. As new generations emerge, holding different and distinctive beliefs from those of the older generations they replace, there is a constant pushing and pulling between ideological conservatism and operational liberalism. Each strain of American political philosophy first wins new converts to its side, and then loses the advantage when events and a new generation change the country's fundamental assumptions about how the world works. In eras dominated by idealist generations, Americans place greater emphasis on their ideological beliefs. In civic eras, operational concerns are more important. The paradox of American public opinion that Free and Cantril identified is an eternal verity in U.S. politics, but because of generational cycles, the relative importance of operational and ideological attitudes varies with time, rather than being stuck in one place forever.

The swing of this constant pendulum in American politics is captured in the history of three generations of the Bush family political dynasty. The GI Generation president George H. W. Bush, despite his conservative ideology, spent a lifetime in government service. Faced with the need to deal with the problem of a growing deficit, he rejected the ideological straitjacket of his Republican Party and endorsed a compromise with Democrats to raise taxes as well as cut federal spending. Boomer politicians, such as Newt Gingrich, pilloried the first President Bush for breaking his pledge of no new taxes, and Bush's son George W. took that lesson to heart. Like his fellow Boomers, George W. Bush stuck to his belief in lower taxes and private enterprise, even when confronted by evidence, such as ballooning government deficits, that might have argued for trying alternative approaches. Only when the country's financial system was approaching collapse was he willing to abandon his ideological beliefs and support a program that saw the government take an equity interest in those financial institutions whose failure would most threaten the economy. But George W. Bush's Millennial children have returned to a political approach closer to that of their grandparents. His Millennial daughter Barbara Bush is president of Global Health Corps, an organization that champions global health equity. She told Fox News that she was glad that health care reform legislation passed. Sounding just like other members of her civic generation, she posed a rhetorical question to her interviewer: "Why do, basically, people with money have good health care and why do people who live on lower salaries not have good health care? Health should be a right for everyone" (Yahoo! News 2010).

Pew Research data underlines the importance of generational change in driving this shift in the balance between America's two major political belief systems. In 1994, for example, the ratio of ideological conservatives to ideological liberals was larger within the idealist Baby Boomer Generation, despite its reputation as a liberal generation, than in any other. In 2002 and 2009, by contrast, the civic-oriented Millennial Generation contained more ideological and operational liberals than did any other generational archetype.

In civic eras, such as the period between 1932 and 1968, operational attitudes that support governmental activism are uppermost in voter's minds. In idealist eras, such as the one from which the United States is now emerging, ideological attitudes that endorse the limitation, or even scaling back, of activist government dominate political thought. At the beginning of this civic era, most notably during the health care debate, some Democrats, joined by almost all Republicans, refused to recognize that this shift was taking place and continued to advocate policies more aligned with the public's attitudes in the previous idealist era. Older generations responded enthusiastically to Republican warnings about the danger of an overreaching government in line with their ideological beliefs, even as younger voters continued to express their preferences for programmatic solutions to the problems confronting the nation.

THE BATTLE IS JOINED

The congressional debate over health care brought a new level of activism to those with the deepest conservative ideological and operational beliefs. Libertarians, Tea Partiers, and their Republican allies were able to generate large and boisterous crowds that confronted members of Congress at local town hall meetings in August 2009 with loud, if not entirely accurate, assertions of how wrong "ObamaCare" would be for America's health. They demanded that their senator or representative vote no on establishing "death panels" that would "kill Grandma" or impose "socialized medicine" on an unwilling public.

The tactics the opponents of change used were reminiscent of the way conservative Baby Boomers, as members of Young Americans for Freedom, shouted down liberal Republican New York Governor Nelson Rockefeller when he warned during his speech to the 1964 GOP Convention of the dangers of nominating Senator Barry Goldwater for president. Although it may not yet have been clear in 1964, it was these conservative ideologues that would soon transform the Republican Party and move America into a new, more ideological, idealist era. Now, the same ideological fervor energized those intent on stopping a new wave of civic institution building. As one protester's sign at a town hall meeting proclaimed, "I'll keep my freedom, my guns, and my money. You keep the change." But unlike the angry shouting matches brought into living rooms in the 1960s via network television, the action this time was captured on flip cameras and cell phones for distribution on YouTube, to be picked up and picked over by cable news commentators.

In 1993, near the middle of the last idealist era, when antipathy to ideological liberalism was at its peak and acceptance of operational liberalism at a low ebb, Hillary Clinton encountered similarly passionate crowds that opposed everything Bill Clinton's administration stood for, including health care reform, in starkly ideological terms: "When loud jeers and catcalls came, some of the nurses tried to talk to the protestors. They were answered with furious expressions of rage—and not about health care alone. Exhibiting a deeper level of resentment, those protestors shouted that Bill and Hillary Clinton were going to destroy their way of life. They were going to ban guns, extend abortion rights, protect gays, socialize medicine" (Johnson and Broder 1997, 462).

The outcome of that idealist era debate was disastrous for the Clintons and the Democratic Party. In spite of having majorities in Congress similar in size to those the Democrats enjoyed after the 2008 elections, the Democratic effort to remake America's health care system foundered and died. A year later, the Republican Party, led by Newt Gingrich, won both the Senate and House, giving it a majority status it did not relinquish until 2006.

Many observers thought these same ideological passions would bring down another new president's plans to transform America's health care system, and with it, his attempt to build new American institutions in the Millennial era. One of the most dedicated opponents of the plan, South Carolina GOP Senator Jim DeMint, openly expressed his hope that the battle would prove to be "Obama's Waterloo." But the America of 2009 was no longer in an idealist era, driven by the antigovernment beliefs of Generation X and the conservative half of the Baby Boom Generation. It had entered a civic era, propelled by the emerging Millennial Generation. While the legislative battle over health care would generate a large number of casualties among congressional Democrats in the 2010 midterm elections, President Obama was successful in passing his proposal, and the Democrats were able to solidify the loyalty of a new group of operationally liberal, pragmatic voters.

Even as the increasingly hot rhetoric brought encouragement to the Republican Party's ideologically conservative base, it threatened to further alienate civic-generation Millennials from the GOP cause. As Maegan Carberry wrote on *Huffington Post*, "The new politics is: community organizing, vested interest from multiple and non-traditional political alliances, equality of opportunity, personal responsibility and efficient government. . . . This is the philosophy of the Millennial generation, and it will ultimately permeate political discourse as we assume more influential leadership roles." Exhibiting her generation's fundamental optimism, she predicted, in the middle of all of this generational Sturm und Drang, "If Americans could remain poised, rely on facts, and be bold instead of submitting to fears about this confusing time, we might find ourselves face-to-face with the antidote to our long-held complaints about government. We'll be more collaborative, individually empowered, and capable of perfecting the American dream" (Carberry 2009).

CALLING THE QUESTION ON THE NATION'S CHARACTER

Conservative attacks on government intervention in the medical decisions of individual Americans found a sweet spot of support within America's tradition of ideological conservatism. An August 2009 Pew Research poll found that only 34 percent favored the "health care reforms being discussed in Congress," while 47 percent were opposed. At the same time, operational liberalism in support of specific health care reforms was also alive and well. The most popular provision, supported by almost 80 percent of the public, required insurance companies to sell policies to people with preexisting conditions. Two-thirds supported mandating that everyone buy health insurance, the idea at the heart of the reforms, so long as there were financial subsidies available for those who couldn't afford insurance (Pew 2009d).

Among Millennials, these programmatically liberal ideas were even more strongly supported, with 70 percent also endorsing employer mandates and 64 percent favoring taxes on the wealthy to pay for the reforms, ideas that ultimately were not part of the reforms that Congress adopted. Eighty percent of Millennials supported the ideologically liberal goal of "changing the health care system in this country so that all Americans have health insurance that covers all medically necessary care." Only about one-third of Millennials (36%), as opposed to nearly half of older generations (47%), told Pew interviewers in May 2009 that they were concerned with the government becoming too involved with health care. By October 2009, after a summer of acrimonious town hall meetings and congressional debate, a plurality of Millennials (42%), compared with 31 percent of other age cohorts, still favored the Obama administration's reform package. Notably, whatever fall-off in support the reforms suffered among Millennials tended to be driven by a desire to see Congress do more, not less, to reform the system.

The death, in late August 2009, of Massachusetts Senator Ted Kennedy, the liberal lion of the Senate who personally symbolized the battle over health care reform, gave President Obama a new opportunity to try and reconcile the ideological and operational dimensions of his proposal by subsuming the arguments over cost and coverage within the larger issue of the nation's civic creed. Speaking to a joint session of Congress immediately after Labor Day 2009, Obama used Kennedy's words to remind everyone what the debate was really about. In a letter written before his death, the senator had emphasized the moral imperative behind the push for health care reform. It "concerns more than material things; what we face is above all a moral issue; at stake are not just the details of policy, but fundamental principles of social justice and the character of our country" (B. Obama 2009c).

Then the president presented his own view of America's civic ethos and emphasized how well within the mainstream of American political philosophy his health care reform proposal fell. "The unique and wonderful thing about America's character," he said, is its "self reliance, rugged individualism, fierce defense of freedom, and a healthy skepticism of government." But that was only one strand of America's civic DNA. The other encapsulated the country's "large heartedness, concern for others, the ability to stand in other's shoes, a recognition that we are all in this together and a willingness to lend a helping hand." Articulating American democracy's unique duality that has been part of our national character since the time of the Pilgrims (Winograd and Hais 2008, 248), Obama linked the two elements into one belief, which he asserted all Americans shared. We all believe that "hard work and responsibility should be rewarded by some measure of security and fair play" (B. Obama 2009c). By articulating this linkage between freedom and social equity, Obama attempted to embrace both ideological conservatism and operational liberalism in order to find common ground on which to build support for his reforms.

REENERGIZING AMERICA'S CIVIC ETHOS

The president's speech provided the momentum needed for Democrats in the House to pass a health care reform bill that was in line with Obama's principles. Exhibiting the steely determination of her Silent Generation to compromise, when necessary, to get what it wants, House Speaker Nancy Pelosi allowed Michigan Democratic Representative Bart Stupak, to introduce an amendment she personally opposed, which prohibited any of the new federal subsidies for health insurance to indirectly pay for abortions. It was the final concession she needed to make in order to win enough Democratic votes for final passage. The bargain was a classic tradeoff between ideological purity and programmatic necessity.

But the Republicans were still not ready to go along. The attempt to build a bipartisan coalition remained in deep trouble, with Republican senators united in opposition to "ObamaCare." The legislative wrangling over health care reform created a convenient vehicle that both sides could use to underline what was at stake in the contest between the Republican's vision of the role of government and the alternative vision put forth by the president. This intense debate over how to reenergize the country's civic creed has occurred every time a catalytic event has initiated a fourth turning. During a critical December discussion on ending debate, Senate Republican Leader Mitch McConnell complained that Democrats were intent on "reshaping America." Senate Majority Leader Harry Reid enthusiastically embraced the accusation in his response. Reshaping America, he said, "was the whole point." A period of regeneracy, with all of the sharp debate that always accompanies such times, had once again arrived in American politics.

Without Republican support, the Democrats were forced to find a way to reconcile the tensions between ideological conservatism and operational liberalism within their own caucus. Reid suggested they fall back on the Depression-era solution of restraining private sector behavior through government regulation. In the 1930s, the power of utilities to charge what they pleased, and deliver service as they saw fit, was curtailed by creating state utility commissions empowered to set "reasonable rates of return" and monitor customer service practices. This time, the Democratic solution was to use the government's regulatory powers to reduce health insurance costs by putting a limit on the percentage of revenue an insurance company could spend on administrative expenses. The concept was far from the more liberal idea of having the government take over the payments of all health insurance claims, or even the more center-left notion of putting the government in competition with other insurance companies (the so-called public option), but it still represented an extension of the government's role in the economy, something ideological conservatives could not abide.

Ideologues from the other side of the political spectrum also rebelled over the compromise. Howard Dean, 2004 Democratic presidential candidate and former Democratic National Committee chairman, declared that Democrats should vote to "Kill the Bill" rather than pass something as ideologically tainted as the Senate's version. Liberal blogger Jane Hamsher stuck to her Boomer ideologically driven opposition, even when her more Millennial-minded readers began to defect. One suggested her blog, Firedoglake, had "seriously damaged their credibility with this [stance]—they are an ideologue in this debate and after 8 years of an ideologue [George W. Bush], our country needs some pragmatism" (Burns 2009). Even Hamsher's hero, Vermont's Independent Senator Bernie Sanders, who called himself a "Democratic Socialist," indicated he would vote for legislation containing all the pragmatic compromises the liberal blogosphere couldn't swallow. The ideological intransigence of Hamsher and her ilk caused some, like the *New Republic* columnist Jonathan Chait, to express amazement at the spectacle of liberals rejecting a piece of legislation he labeled as "the greatest social achievement of our time" (Chait 2009).

Admonished by Democrats who had experienced the price of failure in 1993 and 1994, the Senate decided not to let the ideologically perfect be the enemy of the operationally good, and passed its version of health care reform on Christmas Eve.

A New Civic Ethos Emerges

This new Democratic consensus on how to reconcile the differing opinions of their members on ideological and programmatic approaches had been accomplished with the usual backroom deals and concessions to local interests that legislators consider part of the normal way of doing business in Congress, but which the public finds contrary to its belief in the need for each representative to do what is right for the entire country. This dichotomy was captured perfectly in the 1939 movie *Mr. Smith Goes to Washington*, in which Jimmy Stewart portrays a naive, principled politician who fights political corruption and guards American values as a moral hero. The role, which made Stewart a star, provided the template for the campaign of Republican State Senator Scott Brown to fill the vacancy created by Senator Kennedy's death. Shaking hands outside fabled Fenway Park before an outdoor Boston Bruins hockey game in the freezing January cold, he decried the unwillingness of those in power to listen to the economic needs of ordinary citizens; Brown rode his pickup truck and the rising wave of voter frustration with how Congress does business to become the forty-first vote Republicans needed to successfully filibuster any changes in the Senate bill that a conference committee might adopt. Al Hunt, Washington executive editor for *Bloomberg News*, called Brown's election to Kennedy's seat, "a tragedy of Greek proportions," for the cause of health care specifically and for liberalism generally.

Senator Brown's election made it clear that finding the right programmatic and ideological solution to the problem of health care would not be enough to ensure victory. Unless the president and his Democratic allies could also convince the public that the discredited legislative process had nevertheless led to legislation that was consistent with the nation's values, health care reform, and with it the civic-era impetus of the Obama administration, would be dead. Inadvertently, House Republicans gave him an opportunity to do just that by deciding to provide national television coverage of his meeting with their caucus. Obama's spontaneous defense of the need to pass the reforms, using the same combination of detailed knowledge of the bill's provisions and appeals to the nation's character that he had used in his September address to Congress, was considered a game changer by the White House.

Despite congressional Democrats' misgivings, Obama pressed the advantage by inviting a bipartisan group of congressional leaders to meet with him at Blair House, in an unprecedented daylong meeting under the glare of C-SPAN's television lights, in order to see if there was any way to thrash out their differences. Once again, Millennial preferences for transparency and civility in political discussions about how to fix the nation's broken civic institutions struck a responsive chord among those watching.

Although the Republicans thought the entire day was a waste of time, the discussion was of enormous help to the Democrats, who found they could unite all but the most conservative ideologues in their caucus around achieving the operationally liberal goal of universal coverage. Ironically, the consensus that had previously eluded the Democratic team had been revealed in the aftermath of their party's loss in the Massachusetts's special election. This new-found Democratic consensus was crystallized in the actions of Democratic Congressman Bart Stupak from Michigan's Upper Peninsula as the House took up the Senate's bill. Faced with a slightly weaker abortion provision than he had previously authored, Stupak was persuaded by his mentor, fellow Michigander John Dingell, to vote for the bill anyway, in exchange for clarification of the language pertaining to abortion in an executive order that Stupak himself had helped write for the president. Dingell was the oldest member of the Silent Generation in the House. Since first being elected to Congress in 1955, at the age of twenty-nine, he had introduced the national health insurance bill his father, a member of the Lost Generation born in 1894, had first sponsored when the older Representative Dingell was a member of the House, in the 1930s, early in America's last civic era. The

Dean of the House convinced his Boomer protégé to take the deal and sacrifice a bit of his conservative ideology for the sake of enacting a liberal program in the tradition of the New Deal (Cohn 2010).

The House's debate brought the country's disagreements over ideological and operational issues to a fever pitch. Unable to stop legislation, which only months before had been declared dead, the purveyors of FUD let loose with one final volley of epithets and warnings of political retribution. Echoing Ronald Reagan's warnings, uttered when Medicare was passed in 1965, that "one day you and I are going to spend our sunset years telling our children and our children's children what it was like in America when men were free," true believers in conservative ideology screamed that socialism was about to descend on America (Davidson 2009).

After presiding over the final House vote, liberal Democratic Congressman David Obey of Wisconsin returned the sentiment by playing a Boomer protest song, "Blowin' in the Wind" on his harmonica (Neuman 2010). Within months both Stupak and Obey announced their retirements, exhausted from the debilitating debate over health care reform and the future of the country. Both their districts elected Republicans sympathetic to the Tea Party movement in the 2010 midterm election, underlining how divided the country's politics had become.

THE PRESIDENT FINDS HIS TIME

Confrontation was not Obama's style, however, just as it was not the style of his Millennial supporters. His intellectual tendency was to look for consensus instead. This trait may stem from his unique multiracial, multicultural upbringing, which taught him how to live, in his words, "as an outsider" (B. Obama 2007, 111). The president's birth in Hawaii in 1961 also placed him on the cusp of a major generational change—the end of Baby Boomer births and the emergence of the first Gen-Xers— giving his style a bit of both generations' approach to political disputes. Liberal Boomers appreciate his idealism and commitment to economic equality. On the other hand, as with many members of Generation X, Obama tends to distance himself from the divisive, ideological debates of the recent, Boomer-dominated past. At the same time, the president's political style did not square with the more strident, sometimes sarcastic

approach of Gen-Xers. The result was a style that integrated high
ideals with a deep streak of pragmatism, the very traits that his loyal
Millennial Generation supporters most admire. This unique combination was clearly on display as the health care reform debate evolved into
a fundamental reexamination of the nature of America's civic ethos.

Even as Obama moved from a more consensual to a more confrontational leadership style during that debate, as Ron Brownstein,
Atlantic Media's political director, observed, the president never lost
sight of his goal to change "the trajectory of American politics":

> Obama's aim was to establish a long-term political direction—one
> centered on a more activist government that shapes and polices the
> market to strengthen the foundation for sustainable, broadly shared
> growth. . . . Obama's core health care goals have been to establish
> the principle that Americans are entitled to insurance and to build a
> framework for controlling costs by incentivizing providers to work
> more efficiently. He has been unwavering about that destination but
> flexible and eclectic in his route. (Brownstein 2010a)

The adoption of Obama's health care reform proposal signaled that the
debate over the best way to reform and reconstitute America's institutions, so characteristic of a civic era, had begun in earnest. By rejecting a
single payer system at the outset and eventually abandoning the compromise notion of a public option, the president made it clear that he was
not willing to sacrifice pragmatic operational solutions to the nation's
problems on the altar of ideology. By building a framework for universal coverage on the scaffolding of the existing private insurance system,
he found a way to achieve his ideological goals by using liberal schemes
of regulation and national mandates to create a new operational role for
government. The destination the president finally arrived at had set the
nation's public policy on a new course, setting off an even more furious
debate over the wisdom of the policies he was advocating.

The shape of the reform reflected a new approach to reconciling the
tensions between ideological conservatism and operational liberalism in
this civic era. Just as Millennials believe social rules are important but want
to maximize their ability to choose how to behave within those rules, the
Obama presidency would pursue other ways to set national standards that
encouraged, or, as in the case of health care, required individuals to make

their own choices about how to comply. The trajectory of public policy in the Millennial era had been established. But the foundation required to build political support for this new approach, the second key task identified by Skowronek of every "reconstructive president," was not yet in place.

CONCLUSION

The conflict between the ideological and operational beliefs of Americans is an enduring element of the nation's politics and is often sharpest at the beginning of civic eras. The president's signature on the health care reform legislation hardly ended this most recent debate. Republicans vowed a campaign to "repeal the bill" as strenuous as Alf Landon's 1936 presidential campaign to repeal Social Security. Officials in more than twenty states initiated judicial challenges built on constitutional arguments heard during the Civil War and New Deal fourth turnings. Whatever the outcome of those battles, the country, pushed by the Millennial Generation, will eventually find a new consensus on how to reconcile these seemingly opposing ideas and enter a period of institutional reform and growth, which has occurred in all of America's civic eras.

To find that consensus and to accomplish all of the societal transformations the new civic era will demand, all three branches of government will need to change how they do business. The executive branch will need to find new ways to involve and inspire the public beyond an occasional televised debate between the president and members of Congress. The failures and anachronisms of the legislative branch in a new age of transparency and accountability, all of which were exposed during the health care debate, will need to be completely overhauled if it is to have any legitimacy in the minds of voters—or the courts. Indeed, the first salvos of the judicial battle over health care to come made it clear that the Supreme Court will also get enmeshed in the debate over the new role for government that President Obama and the Congress envisioned. Until those institutional changes take place, the nation will be burdened by the fear, uncertainty, and doubt that have been present each time America takes its first tentative steps down a new path to a very different future.

PART TWO

Changing America's Government

CHAPTER 4

Judging the Fourth Turning

AT THE BEGINNING OF FOURTH TURNINGS, when the influence of a new civic generation is just beginning to be felt, the Supreme Court has been heavily populated by justices who are members of an earlier, idealist generation, the archetype least willing to compromise and most insistent on imposing its moral values and ideological beliefs on the rest of the country. But whereas idealist generations, like today's Boomers, are usually about evenly divided on both sides of the political fence within the electorate, those appointed to the Court have tended to reflect most strongly the political philosophy of the party that dominated America's politics during the previous four decades. Invariably, as the debate about which direction the country should be taking unfolds in an atmosphere of fear, uncertainty, and doubt, a majority of the Court has felt compelled to step in to maintain the prevailing political order and to resist forces demanding new approaches to the issues and concerns confronting the nation.

The political nature of the Court stems directly from the way justices are appointed. Eighty-five percent have been members of the political party of the president who nominated them, and on the rare occasions when they were not, those nominees almost invariably supported the president on the important issues of the day. As Alexis de Tocqueville remarked in the early nineteenth century, "There is hardly a political question in the United States which does not sooner or later become a judicial one." Furthermore, the Supreme Court has felt compelled to enter the "political thicket," to borrow Justice Felix Frankfurter's phrase, most dramatically and decisively during fourth turnings, when political passions run highest, and the country seems most in need of what Justice Antonin Scalia called "democratic stability" (Garrett 2003, 145).

In each instance, however, the Court's attempt to settle the nation's inherently political disputes has backfired and deepened divisions in the electorate. Only when the two other, democratically elected branches of government finally settle on a new direction for the country have the wounds healed and a new consensus emerged. Not until the events of the fourth turning have reached a climax has the Supreme Court been willing to at least acquiesce in the new direction in which America is headed. The most famous example of this phenomenon was the decision by at least one justice to change his views on the constitutionality of New Deal legislation after Franklin D. Roosevelt, flush with his landslide victory in 1936, attempted to pack the Supreme Court (Hoffer, Hoffer, and Hull 2007). As no less an expert than Peter Finley Dunne's always savvy Irish American bartender, Mr. Dooley, remarked at the turn of the twentieth century, eventually "the Supreme Court follows the election returns," and responds to the developing political consensus after doing its best to prevent it from emerging.

A DREADFUL DECISION

Article III of the Constitution simply says that there shall be a Supreme Court whose judges hold their offices for an unlimited term "during good behavior." In Federalist 78, Alexander Hamilton maintained, "The judiciary is beyond comparison the weakest of the three departments of power." Largely based on its humble beginning and this spare constitutional underpinning, the Supreme Court was so quiet, and of such little significance during most of the first two decades after the ratification of the Constitution in 1787, that there was little reason for his eighteenth-century contemporaries and subsequent historians to quarrel with Hamilton's appraisal. In fact, the Court did not deal with or decide a single case during its first three terms.

All that changed in 1803 with the decision of Chief Justice John Marshall in *Marbury v. Madison*, which asserted the Supreme Court's authority to interpret the Constitution and to decide what actions by governments, organizations, and individuals legally fit within its purview. On the surface, this exercise of judicial review might appear to have been an apolitical act, attempting to sort out, in the nation's formative years, the roles each branch of the government should play. But the decision actually stemmed from a very intense political controversy between the outgoing Federalist administration of President John Adams and the incoming Democratic-Republican administration of President Thomas Jefferson. Both the concept of judicial review and the Court's willingness to insert itself into political disputes have been a part of American democracy ever since.

On occasion, the Court has actually been invited to insert itself in such disputes by the other two branches of government, especially when the politics of fear, uncertainty, and doubt have created gridlock over issues that dealt directly with the nation's values or civic ethos. In the sixty years following the implementation of the Constitution in 1789, efforts to compromise regional disputes over slavery was the issue that raised this question most pointedly and generated the most controversy.

The Kansas-Nebraska bill of 1854, sponsored by Abraham Lincoln's future debating nemesis, Senator Stephen Douglas, embodied the concept of "popular sovereignty," which left it up to the citizens of each new state to determine the issue of slavery. But because there were conflicting opinions on whether or not Congress had the ability to give such latitude to the states, this legislation left it up to the Supreme Court to decide if there were any constitutional limits on a state's actions with regard to slavery (Jaffa 1982). That legislation did not end the debate over slavery, however, as many had hoped. As he prepared to take office in 1857, President-elect James Buchanan wrote to Justice Robert Grier in an attempt to make sure the Supreme Court understood how important a return to stability was for the new president. "The great object of my administration will be, if possible, to destroy the dangerous slavery agitation and thus restore peace to our distracted country." In his inaugural address, he opined that the Supreme Court was about to issue a ruling that would do just that. As in so many other things, Buchanan was wrong, but not because of a lack of effort by the justices.

The primary legislation governing the legal status of slavery in new western states was the Missouri Compromise of 1820, which prohibited slavery in U.S. territory north of latitude 36′30° and allowed it south of that line. As a matter of practicality, states were admitted to the Union in pairs—one slave and one free state at a time. By the 1850s, however, willingness to abide by this formula diminished, and the Compromise was repealed as part of the Kansas-Nebraska legislation. This change reflected the movement of the country to an era increasingly dominated by members of an idealist generation, who were less able to compromise their deeply held, but divided, beliefs on the subject.

Congress's inability to settle the issue of slavery in "Bleeding Kansas," along with the emerging strength of the Republican Party at the presidential level in the 1856 election, contributed directly to the Supreme Court's attempt to finally put an end to almost eighty years of debate over slavery (Jaffa1982). In the Court's infamous opinion in the 1857 *Dred Scott v. Sandford* case, Chief Justice Roger Brooke Taney held that slavery must be recognized as legal by any state to which a slave owner transported his human property, effectively spreading the hateful practice beyond its regional boundaries and making it truly national in scope.

The case involved a Missouri slave, Dred Scott, who was taken by his master first to the free state of Illinois, later to the free territory of Wisconsin, and then back to Missouri. Scott argued that because he had entered, and resided, in jurisdictions in which slavery was not permitted, he should be given his freedom. After asserting that Negroes, even those who were free, could not be citizens of the United States, and therefore had no right to sue in a federal court, the Supreme Court, in a 7–2 decision, went ahead and issued its infamous dictum declaring the original Missouri Compromise of 1820 unconstitutional. The decision denied the validity of a law that had governed the United States for thirty-four years. Just for good measure, the Court also asserted that the first Congress of the United States, in which sixteen of the thirty-nine signers of the Constitution had served, had also violated the Constitution by prohibiting the establishment of slavery in the states to be formed from the Northwest Territory. The Court stated that the right of property in a slave was expressly affirmed in the Constitution of the United States, under the Fifth Amendment's requirement of due process for any government taking of personal property; under Section 9 of Article I, which deals with migration between states; and under Section 2 of Article IV, which requires states to uphold the status of laborers from other states (Jaffa 1982). In effect, the decision barred the national government from prohibiting the owning of slaves in any part of the country, even in presumably free states, if the human property had originally been acquired legally under the laws of any other state.

Looking back through a civil war, a century and a half of civil rights legislation, subsequent Supreme Court decisions, and the lens of contemporary morality, the Dred Scott ruling seems hard to fathom. But, looked at from the mid-nineteenth-century generational and partisan alignments of a nation about to enter a fourth turning, the fact that the Taney Court could have made such a ruling is more understandable. In fact, the generational and political composition of the Supreme Court is one of the best predictors of just how and when this branch of the federal government is likely to intervene in an attempt to set the future direction of the country, even if it means overturning decisions made by the other two branches.

THE COURT IS THE LAST TO TURN

Of the nine justices who ruled on Dred Scott, all but two were born in the eighteenth century. Four were members of the Transcendental Generation (born 1792–1821), the idealist generation that shaped the tone of American society and politics in most of the first half of the nineteenth century. A fifth justice was born in 1790, on the cusp of generational change. The Transcendental Generation was, at the time, the largest in U.S. history—more than twice the size of the previously largest generation. Like other idealist generations, Transcendentals were sharply divided along regional and ideological lines based on the politics of the day.

From the election of Andrew Jackson, in 1828, to that of James Buchanan, in 1856, Democrats won six out of eight presidential elections and occupied the White House in twenty-four of thirty-two years. The Democratic Party was also the majority party in the U.S. Senate in eleven of fourteen congressional sessions between 1829 and 1857. Not surprisingly, therefore, seven of the justices who issued the Dred Scott decision were Democrats, or had been appointed to the Court by Democratic presidents. As a result, Lincoln charged, the *Dred Scott* opinion was issued both as a response to the results of the 1856 election, which showed the Democrats, at the presidential popular-vote level, to have lost their majority status, and to serve as a warning to "the Republican party to disband" (Jaffa 1982, 286).

Of the seven justices who decided against Dred Scott's bid for freedom, four were from Southern states that later attempted to secede from the Union. Chief Justice Taney, who wrote the majority decision, hailed from Maryland, also a slave state. With one exception,

John Catron of Tennessee, all of the justices who resided in Southern or slave-holding states were appointed to the Court by Democratic presidents.

With the ascension of Abraham Lincoln to the presidency in 1861, however, the regional and political complexion of the Supreme Court changed quickly and decisively, and with it, the Court's position on issues relating to slavery and the Civil War. During his one complete term in office, Lincoln appointed a majority of the Court. In contrast to the justices who decided *Dred Scott v. Sandford*, all five of the Lincoln nominees were born in the nineteenth century. Although they were also Transcendentals, they came from the opposite side of that idealist generation's philosophical divide. Every Lincoln nominee came from a Union state, and four of five were Republicans. The fifth, Stephen Field of California, was a strong pro-Union Democrat. The reconstituted Court came down solidly on the side of President Lincoln's conduct of the Civil War.

In the Prize Cases of 1863, owners of ships seized in Charleston harbor and sold after South Carolina took Fort Sumter claimed that the president and the military could not legally do so without a formal declaration of war by Congress. The Supreme Court ruled against the ship owners and in favor of President Lincoln, holding that "the President could deal with the situation presented after Sumter as a war and employ what belligerent measures he deemed necessary without waiting for Congress to declare war" (Schwartz 1993, 131). In a second key case, *White v. Texas* (1871), issued after the climax of the Civil War fourth turning, the Supreme Court legally confirmed what the force of arms had determined: states do not have the constitutional right to secede from the Union.

It is possible, of course, that had the Supreme Court retained its distinctive generational and Democratic, Southern political complexion, during and just after the Civil War, it, too, would have changed, as did the nation and its politics. However, the fact that three Democrats, who were appointed to the Court as far back as the Van Buren and Polk administrations, cast the only dissenting votes in the Prize Cases suggests that this was unlikely. In any case, the composition of the Court did change during this fourth turning to reflect new partisan and generational alignments. That change was accompanied by recognition that

America had entered a new era, with a new understanding of the role, responsibilities, and powers of government.

Trying to Turn Back the New Deal Clock

If slavery and race were the nation's focus in the decades leading to the mid-nineteenth-century fourth turning, it was the extent and type of governmental intervention in an industrial economy that was at the center of America's politics in the next fourth turning, eight decades later. As with all others in U.S. history, this fourth turning occurred at a time of intense national crisis, but this time the cause was the greatest economic calamity in U.S. history—the stock market crash of 1929 that led to the Great Depression. Once again, the crisis was accompanied by a period of intense FUD, or fear, uncertainty, and doubt and, once again, the Supreme Court entered the political thicket in an attempt to determine the country's direction on the issues that sharply divided America's political parties.

The pattern of Supreme Court actions during the Great Depression fourth turning was identical to that of the previous one. First, members of an idealist generation (Missionary) and the political party (Republican) that dominated the nation in the forty years prior to the fourth turning heavily populated the Court. As a result, the Court's initial decisions attempted to reinforce the old political order and to continue the public policies that characterized the earlier era. Then, underpinned by the emergence of America's next civic generation that had shaped a new partisan alignment, the Court, made up of younger justices, came to accept the civic era policies favored by most voters from that GI Generation.

From the election of William McKinley in 1896 until FDR's victory in 1932, the prevailing economic approach was to minimize government involvement, particularly that of the federal government, in the economy. According to one present-day historian of the Court, "upper-middle class Democrats and Republicans, including politicians and judges, all agreed that the sole valid goal of legislation was to be of general applicability and to promote the general welfare by being neutral among classes" (Powe 2009, 150). The Supreme Court supported this laissez-faire approach in decision after decision throughout this idealist era. In no case did it do so more clearly and dramatically than in 1905 in *Lochner v. New York*, which "aside from *Dred Scott* itself, . . . is now considered the most discredited decision in Supreme Court history" (Schwartz 1993, 190).

Joseph Lochner violated a New York statute, enacted in order to protect workers in a potentially unhealthy occupation, by requiring a worker in his bakery to work beyond the limit of sixty hours per week. The Supreme Court ruled against the state's attempt to enforce its statute by an 8–1 margin. Writing for the majority, Justice Rufus Peckham argued that the New York law is "not, within any fair meaning of the term, a health law, but is an illegal interference with the rights of individuals, both employers and employees, to make contracts regarding labor upon such terms as they may think best." To decide otherwise was to have government assume "the position of a supervisor, or *pater familias*, over every act of the individual." This was the Supreme Court standard on virtually every economic case that came before it for the next three decades (Schwartz 1993, 195). However, it is the opinion of the one dissenting justice, Oliver Wendell Holmes Jr., that has been most often cited since the *Lochner* decision was issued. "When [present-day] commentators discuss the case at all, they use it as a vehicle to illustrate the drastic change in jurisprudence during the twentieth century, which has seen the Holmes dissent in *Lochner* elevated to established doctrine" (ibid., 190).

Holmes, born twenty years after the final birth year of the idealist Transcendental Generation and twenty years before the next idealist generation, Missionaries, first emerged, took an entirely different view of the role of government than the laissez-faire approach of his colleagues. He argued that the liberty of contract was not absolute, especially when the parties to a contract are as potentially unequal in power as an employer and an employee. The right of an individual to absolute freedom, he wrote, "is interfered with by school laws, by the Post Office, by every state and municipal institution which takes his money . . . whether he likes it or not." Instead, Holmes wrote government has broad police powers through which "laws may regulate life in many ways . . . which equally with this interfere with the liberty to contract" (Schwartz 1993, 196). However, it took three decades, the greatest economic catastrophe in U.S. history, and a fourth turning, before first the American electorate and later the Supreme Court came to accept Holmes's point of view.

After three years of complete economic devastation, in 1932, the Democrats took control of both houses of Congress and Franklin D. Roosevelt overwhelmingly captured the presidency, winning 57 percent of the popular vote and carrying forty-four of forty-eight states. For the entirety of his first term in the White House, FDR and his Democratic congressional allies responded to the Great Depression with a massive legislative outpouring. New Deal laws were enacted that created governmental programs to provide old-age pensions, brought electricity to rural areas, created public employment jobs by building America's infrastructure, and regulated virtually every aspect of the U.S. economy—agricultural production, manufacturing, banking, and the financial markets.

In 1934, for the first and only time in American history, the party of the incumbent president gained congressional seats in a midterm election during his first term, signaling the public's approval of the New Deal. The early 1930s were also a period of FUD , however, and FDR's policies met with vociferous opposition from the left and, most especially, from the right. With the elective branches of the federal government firmly under Democratic control, it was the Supreme Court that attempted to unravel the New Deal by reasserting *Lochner*'s laissez-faire doctrine from the previous idealist era.

At least one justice sensed the changes that were coming several years before Roosevelt was elected, and saw it as his duty to resist. Two weeks after the stock market crash, chief justice and former president William Howard Taft wrote to his brother of his fear that President Herbert Hoover, at the time viewed as a progressive Republican, might make appointments to the Court: "I must stay on the court in order to prevent the Bolsheviki from getting control" (Powe 2009, 200). If Taft felt that way about Hoover, one can only imagine how he would have reacted to the New Deal.

Taft died in 1930, but other justices, especially Willis Van Devanter, James McReynolds, George Sutherland, and Pierce Butler, referred to as the "Four Horsemen of Reaction," stood ready to resist FDR and his New Deal at almost every opportunity. All four were born during the Civil War fourth turning and brought a strong, ideological bent to the Court's deliberations. Arrayed against them were liberal justices Louis Brandeis, Benjamin Cardozo, and Harlan Fiske Stone, also known as the

"Three Musketeers." The two groups' opposing ideologies reflected the divisions of that era's idealist Missionary generation as much as Boomer liberals and conservatives do today. At the center of the Court were two other, slightly less ideologically driven, members of the Missionary Generation, Chief Justice Charles Evans Hughes, who more often than not joined the progressives, and Owen Roberts, who normally voted with the conservatives to give that philosophy the majority on most cases.

In 1935 and 1936, the Supreme Court invalidated the National Industrial Recovery Act (in *Schechter Poultry Corp. v. U.S.*), the Agricultural Adjustment Act (in *Butler v. U.S.*), and the Guffey Coal Act (in *Carter v. Carter Coal*), all of which attempted to regulate and set prices and working conditions in key segments of the economy. In each case, the Court said the clause giving the Congress the power "to regulate commerce . . . among the several States" referred only to transportation, not to the production of goods or the extraction of minerals. Having ruled that the laws were an illegal federal infringement in state matters, the Court decided to go one step further in resisting the New Deal by declaring that state minimum wage laws were also unconstitutional. By using the *Lochner* precedent in *Morehead v. Tipaldo*, the Supreme Court, according to President Roosevelt, put the nation in a "constitutional no-man's land," unable to react to the Great Depression at either the federal or state level.

Partisanship also played a role in these decisions, going beyond the missionary zeal the Four Horsemen of Reaction brought to their deliberations. Seven of the nine justices were Republicans, or had been appointed by Republican presidents, including three of the Four Horsemen. The fourth, James McReynolds, nominated by Woodrow Wilson, was a conservative Tennessee Democrat and anti-Semite, who refused to talk to, or acknowledge, the Court's two Jewish justices, Louis Brandeis and Benjamin Cardozo.

A SWITCH IN TIME SAVED NINE

As in the Civil War fourth turning, the Supreme Court emerged from its own regeneracy debate and eventually came to accept much of the New Deal. In short order, during its 1937 session, the Court accepted the constitutionality of Social Security (*Helvering v. Davis*); the right of labor to organize as protected in the Wagner Act (*Jones & Laughlin Steel*

Corp. v. NLRB); and the legality of state legislation establishing working conditions and minimum wages (*West Coast Hotel Co. v. Parrish*). Within the next five years, the Supreme Court ruled in favor of legislation codifying national labor standards (*United States v. Darby*, 1941) and agricultural production (*Wickard v. Filburn*, 1942). The Court moved in Roosevelt's direction as the justices who occupied the middle ground between the Four Horsemen and the Three Musketeers, Hughes and Roberts, began to side with the latter consistently.

Years later, in 1951, Justice Owen Roberts wrote, "Looking back, it is difficult to see how the court could have resisted the popular urge for uniform standards throughout the country" (Schwartz 1993, 235). Or as Justices Sandra Day O'Conner, David Souter, and Anthony Kennedy wrote in explaining their votes in a 1992 decision on a far different matter (an abortion clinic), "the Depression had come and with it the interpretation of contractual freedom protected in *Adkins* [a 1923 case confirming *Lochner*] rested on a fundamentally false factual assumption about the capacity of a relatively unregulated market to satisfy minimum levels of human welfare" (*Planned Parenthood of Southeastern PA v. Casey*).

Once again, politics and generational change led to a change of heart by the Supreme Court, this time in what some have called the "Revolution of 1937" (Powe 2009, 213). In 1936, Franklin Roosevelt was reelected in a landslide, receiving 61 percent of the popular vote and beating Republican Alf Landon, who had campaigned on the repeal of Social Security, in the Electoral College 523–8. The Republicans were left with about 20 percent of the seats in both houses of Congress.

In the wake of that victory, FDR announced a plan to expand the Court's membership to fifteen. This was being done, the president said, to ease the burden of work on the "nine old men." At that point in time, the youngest justice, Roberts, was sixty-two, and the oldest, Brandeis, was eighty-one. Opposition to his plan to pack the Court arose almost immediately. Gallup polling conducted between March and May 1937 indicated that only 39 percent of the American public supported Roosevelt's attempt to expand the Court while 46 percent were opposed, a number that grew larger the longer the plan was discussed. FDR's plan died in July 1937, when the bill in which it was proposed was returned to the Senate Judiciary Committee with instructions to strip the Court-packing provisions from it.

No one can really know if it was just the pressure from Roosevelt's Court expansion proposal that moved the Supreme Court toward greater acceptance of New Deal legislation. On the one hand, "It is too facile to state that the 1937 change was merely a protective response to the Court-packing plan . . . [but] there *was* real conversion in a majority of the Supreme Court and its effects do justify the 'constitutional revolution' characterization." FDR himself claimed that although he lost the Court-packing battle he won the policy war. "It would be a little naïve to refuse to recognize some connection between these decisions and the Supreme Court fight" (Schwartz 1993, 234).

It is clear, however, that a nearly total generational shift on the Supreme Court reinforced the movement away from enforcement of the laissez-faire doctrine of an earlier era and toward an embrace of governmental activism. Starting with the retirement of Van Devanter, in 1937, five of the "Nine Old Men" left the Court during Roosevelt's second term, and three more did so early in his third. This enabled FDR to appoint eight of the nine justices before he died in 1945. Of the justices nominated by Roosevelt, six were members of a new and younger generation, the Lost Generation (born 1883–1900), and another, Felix Frankfurter, was born in the last birth year of the older Missionary Generation. As Supreme Court historian Lucas Powe observed, although "the Court-packing plan had failed . . . Roosevelt was nevertheless able to fill the Court with committed New Dealers" (Powe 2009, 213), Once again during a fourth turning, a Supreme Court shaped by the partisan and generational alignments of an earlier idealist era had given way to the differing configurations of an emerging civic era.

THE SUPREME COURT GETS ANOTHER TURN

In 2008, as in 1860 and 1932, the United States elected a new president as it moved toward another generational fourth turning. Like his predecessors, Abraham Lincoln and Franklin Roosevelt, Barack Obama proposed an agenda for major societal change to deal with the stresses and turmoil that confronted the nation. During the first two years of his administration, the president and his Democratic congressional allies successfully enacted much of that ambitious agenda. While many liberals applauded the president's legislative successes, opposition to the president was just as sharp and consistent across the partisan and ideological aisle as it had been in previous fourth turnings. And once again, the president's opponents looked to the judicial system to resist and to turn back the changes they were unable to halt in the elected branches of government.

Immediately after Congress passed, and President Obama signed, the Affordable Care Act, conservative attorneys general from more than twenty states, all but one a Republican, sued in Federal District Court to halt its implementation. Specifically, they alleged that the health care reform legislation was an unconstitutional overreach of congressional powers to regulate interstate commerce and provide for the general welfare of the United States under Article I of the Constitution because it attempted to regulate "inactivity," that is, not buying health insurance, and instituted a penalty for failing to do so. In effect, the suit raised the very same constitutional questions regarding the limits of the interstate commerce clause and the power of Congress to interfere with state actions or private contracts that had been the subject of intense debate during the Civil War and Great Depression fourth turnings.

The Obama administration's attempts to quickly settle the issue were met with defeat. Although district court judges in Michigan and the western district of Virginia, who had been appointed by Democratic President Bill Clinton, rejected challenges to the new law, another Virginia district court judge, Judge Henry E. Hudson, appointed by President George W. Bush, ruled against the federal government's assertion that the law fell well within the precedent of prior Supreme Court rulings that had established a broad definition of interstate commerce. Instead, he agreed with the assertion of Virginia's attorney general, in a suit separate from those of other state attorneys general, that the federal government had no right to require his state's citizens to buy health insurance and impose a penalty for not doing so. Although Hudson's ruling allowed the rest of the statute to stand, a later ruling by Florida District Judge Roger Vinson, appointed by Ronald Reagan, went even further and used this same line of reasoning to declare the entire health care reform law unconstitutional. The district court's ruling in the Virginia suit that "neither the Supreme Court nor any other circuit court of appeals has squarely addressed this issue" was in sharp contrast to those who believed previous Supreme Court rulings from the New Deal era were dispositive of the issue (Levey 2010). Since the New Deal, the

Supreme Court has interpreted the congressional authority to regulate interstate commerce as covering local activities with national implications, which most supporters of the new law felt clearly applied to health care. Moreover, just as established precedent backs the authority of Congress to require employees to purchase health insurance for their old age by imposing a payroll tax to fund Medicare, Americans, in their view, could be required to obtain health insurance before they were sixty-five (Marcus 2009).

Opinions written by some of the Court's more conservative members in earlier cases seemed to bolster this point of view. For instance, in a 2005 case (*Gonzalez v. Raich*), Antonin Scalia and Arthur Kennedy supported a very broad interpretation of the interstate commerce clause. In that opinion, the Court ruled that Congress could go so far as to regulate marijuana that was neither bought nor sold on the market, but was legally grown at home for ill patients. Writing for the majority, Justice Scalia asserted that "even noneconomic local activity" can come under federal regulation if it is "a necessary part of a more general regulation of interstate commerce" (Savage 2010). This broad precedent would presumably constrain at least some of the Court's conservative justices from overturning the health care reform law, unless they were prepared to overturn their own interpretation of the scope of the interstate commerce clause.

Others were less certain that precedent will bind a Supreme Court whose majority reflects the partisanship and generational attitudes of a previous era if, and when, it deals with health care reform. Conservative columnist George Will argued that "unless the commerce clause is infinitely elastic—in which case Congress can do *anything*—it does *not* authorize Congress to forbid the *inactivity* of not making a commercial transaction, of not purchasing a product (health insurance) from a private provider" (Will 2010). Liberal E. J. Dionne also expressed strong concerns that the Supreme Court would dispense with more recent precedent and practice judicial activism in nullifying progressive legislation: "Their [conservatives'] goal is to overturn the past 70 years of judicial understanding and bring us back to a time when courts voided minimum-wage laws and all manner of other economic regulations. . . . Let's ignore the claims of conservatives that they are opposed to 'legislating from the bench,' since it's their judges who are now doing the legislating" (Dionne 2010a).

A Vanderbilt University study describing the increased ideological polarization of law clerks chosen by the justices suggests George Will has reason to hope and E. J. Dionne is not just being paranoid about the Supreme Court's intentions. The study found that since 2005, when John Roberts became chief justice, the members of the Court almost invariably chose clerks that support their own ideological predispositions. This is a far cry from the situation from the 1940s to the 1980s when, according to Vanderbilt, the "Supreme Court clerkship appeared to be a nonpartisan institution." Justice Clarence Thomas explains his desire to hire only conservative Republicans and avoid liberal Democrats in a pithy, if disparaging, manner: "It's like trying to train a pig. It wastes your time, and it aggravates the pig." Cambridge University's David J. Garrow sums up the matter of a more politicized clerk staff—and Supreme Court—this way: "We are getting a composition of the clerk work force that is getting to be like the House of Representatives. Each side is putting forward only ideological purists." "The rise of 'politically oriented practice groups,'" the Vanderbilt study said, reinforces the impression that the court is "a superlegislature responding to ideological arguments rather than a legal institution responding to concerns grounded in the rule of law" (Liptak 2010).

The increased partisanship and ideological purity of the current Court is a reflection, indeed a product, of its generational composition. As in previous fourth turnings, a majority of the current justices are drawn from an idealist generation, in this instance Baby Boomers (born 1946–1964). Three members of the Court's conservative majority (Chief Justice John Roberts, Clarence Thomas, and Samuel Alito) and two of its liberal minority (Sonia Sotomayor and Elena Kagan) are Boomers. The generational archetype's resistance to compromise makes it unlikely that any review of the health care reform legislation that they might undertake will result in a reasoned, bipartisan majority opinion.

In addition, reflecting the political alignment of the previous era, a majority of the justices and of the Court's conservatives are Republicans. If the pattern of history is any guide, that conservative majority may once again see itself as a protector of the economic and societal arrangements of the past, and a bulwark against the changes typically embodied in the movement of the nation to a new civic era. In that event, regardless of existing precedents, the Supreme Court could overturn the actions of Congress, as it did when it declared the Missouri Compromise unconstitutional and nullified much of the early New Deal legislation. As with those earlier rulings, any such decision would provoke a furious debate throughout the country on whether the appointed Court's opinion or the actions of the two elected branches of government best reflected the evolving civic ethos of the country.

CONCLUSION

Whether or not the Supreme Court decides to throw more fuel on the FUD fire and bring the nation's divisions into even sharper conflict is something the nine justices will have to decide among themselves. A major factor in their decision will be the generational and philosophical beliefs they bring to the discussion. Generational theory suggests that in this fourth turning, as in the 1860s and the 1930s, the Supreme Court will resist change and attempt to protect the existing order of things. But history also suggests the political context of their decision cannot be ignored.

The best way for President Obama to avoid a showdown with the Supreme Court would be for him to be reelected in 2012 by a wide margin. Or as a professor of social medicine, Jonathan Oberlander, writing after the 2010 midterm elections, put it: "The future of healthcare reform . . . may very well depend on the next presidential election" (Oberlander 2010). The vote by the new Republican majority in the House early in 2011 to repeal the law in its entirety, although mostly symbolic in terms of its ultimate legislative impact, certainly could be interpreted by the Supreme Court as an invitation for it to settle an issue the Congress seems unable to agree upon. But if President Obama is reelected in 2012 and Congressional Democrats stage a comeback, then the Roberts Court might be more hesitant "to launch a sustained challenge to the core of the Democratic agenda" (Friedman and Rosen 2010). Furthermore, once the emerging civic generation of Millennials determines America's new direction, history suggests that the Supreme Court will get the message and decide to get along by going along.

But in the interim, the 2010 electoral success of the Republican Party and of libertarians, such as the Paul family duo and others associated with the Tea Party, may cause the Court to feel that the best way to follow the election returns would be to try and rehabilitate the legal doctrines first espoused in the *Lochner* decision of 1905, beginning with a decision on the health care law, but perhaps extending to many other aspects of economic and social policy as well. Judge Richard Posner, who is strongly influenced by the economic theories of Milton Friedman and the Chicago school of economics, is the most prominent advocate of just such a course of action. "That school has never reconciled itself to the fact that . . . the 'invisible hand' of Adam Smith has increasingly been replaced by the 'public interest' as defined in regulatory legislation and administration" (Schwartz 1993, 200).

In addition, the Court, as an institution, currently enjoys much more popular support than the Congress does and could use that standing as part of a campaign to limit or overturn the output of a divided Congress. Forty-two percent of Millennials, for instance, had a favorable opinion of the Supreme Court in a June 2010 Magid survey, well above the 34 percent who expressed an unfavorable opinion. By contrast, Millennials rated Congress unfavorably by an almost 2:1 margin (54% unfavorable versus 27% favorable). The differences were even starker among older generations, who were split evenly on their opinion of the Supreme Court but rated the Congress negatively by more than a 4:1 margin (74% versus 17%) (Winograd and Hais 2010b). Such an environment creates an opportunity for the Court to act upon its historically "strong distaste for the congressional process" (Garrett 2003, 160).

The Court previously did that in December 2000. With the presidential election of that year at an impasse over which candidate had carried Florida, the Supreme Court decided to resolve the issue and, thereby, the election. The court's 5–4 decision in *Bush v. Gore* was remarkable in many ways, not the least of which was its willingness to issue a closely divided opinion on a matter of such heavy political consequence. Indeed, one of the dissenters, Justice John Paul Stevens, wrote, "The identity of the loser [in the long run] is perfectly clear. It is the Nation's confidence in the judge as an impartial guardian of the law." Justice Stephen Breyer, also in dissent, suggested that the court's decision to issue a judgment in the case was a "self-inflicted wound" similar to the one incurred by the Supreme Court when it issued its fateful *Dred Scott* decision of 1857 (Garrett 2003, 142).

The Court could just as easily have declined to issue any ruling and deferred to the framework for resolving such disputes the Congress had enacted in 1886, more than a century before the 2000 election. The Electoral Count Act was passed following the public outcry over how Congress resolved the disputed presidential election of 1876, at the end of the Civil War fourth turning. After that campaign, with twenty-two electoral votes from three Southern states (Florida, Louisiana, and South Carolina) and Oregon in dispute, Republicans in Congress promised to withdraw federal troops from the South. In return, Democrats agreed to let Republican Rutherford B. Hayes become president, even though their candidate, Samuel J. Tilden, had decisively won the popular vote. The deal effectively ended Reconstruction in the South and ultimately led to decades of Jim Crow segregationist laws. The bargain was defended ten years later, using the same rationale as the Court used in its 2000 decision—by pointing to the need to end a dispute that, according to at least one senator at the time had brought the country "to the verge and brink of revolution" (Garrett 2003, 239). With the country's political rhetoric now once again at a fever pitch, and with some lower courts ruling the new law constitutional and others saying it is not, the Supreme Court may well decide it is the only institution with the credibility to settle the debate and bring some calm to the body politic. If it does so, it will once again have a say in the age-old conflict between America's ideological and operational beliefs.

In fact, the history of previous fourth turnings suggests it is more than likely that the Court will issue another round of momentous decisions in the years ahead as it tries to resolve the crucial issues that invariably divide America during periods of great generational change. Whether those decisions uphold or overturn the workings of the Congress will be determined by the results of future elections, as well as the generational and political makeup of the Court and the degree to which the public believes the legislative process still retains at least a dollop of legitimacy. Millennials are the most likely generation to express such support for the political process, but their future loyalty can only be earned if Congress summons the will to transform the way it makes decisions and who it listens to when it does. Nothing in the institution's behavior at the beginning of the Millennial era suggested it was up to the challenge.

CHAPTER 5

Crowdsourcing the Congress

ALTHOUGH GENERATIONAL CHANGE does not come to the Congress as slowly as it does to the Supreme Court, the power of incumbency and the age requirements for holding office do present obstacles to younger generations trying to get elected to that body, even when those generations become an increasingly larger share of the electorate. For instance, even though Millennials turned out in record numbers to vote for Barack Obama in 2008, no Millennials were elected to Congress that year. And, although many new representatives were elected to Congress in 2010, the average age of House members did not change appreciably from what it had been in the previous Congress (Sasso 2010); once again, none of those elected that year were Millennials. History suggests the nation's newest civic generation won't have a real toehold in the nation's legislature until the end of this decade and a majority in a decade or two after that. But their electoral power still provides an opportunity for Millennials and their technology to influence how Congress does business.

Even though Millennials continue to register strong allegiance to the Democratic Party, they hardly favor maintaining the congressional status quo. Three-fourths of the American public disapproved of the job Congress was doing in a February 2010 New York Times/CBS poll, the highest level of disapproval since 1977, when the question was first asked. Even Millennials disapproved, albeit by a slightly smaller margin of 2:1, despite the relatively positive attitudes toward societal institutions that characterizes civic generations like theirs (Winograd and Hais 2010b). Dissatisfaction with Congress's institutional anachronisms helped fuel the anger voters expressed in the 2010 midterm elections, and put both parties on notice that the public wanted to see major changes in how the legislative branch operated. Without fundamental reforms, however, the transformation of that institution in a way that meets the demands of the public and is commensurate with the serious challenges facing the country will remain elusive. In the long run, as Millennials come to dominate American politics, the only way for Congress to restore its reputation will be for it to respond to the beliefs of this generation through comprehensive changes in its practices and procedures.

For that to happen, Congress will have to give up its comfort with closed-door decision-making and adopt a more transparent process that shares more information and power with the American people. Unless Congress is willing to strike such a bargain, it risks losing what remains of its legislative credibility as America's newest civic era unfolds.

CREATING A CONGRESS FOR THE MILLENNIAL ERA

As Democrats struggled to find a way to pass health care reform in the face of united Republican opposition, only one of ten voters thought members of Congress deserved reelection. Four of five Americans thought Congress was more interested in helping special interests than in serving voters. About two-thirds of those interviewed believed the two parties should compromise more. Similar percentages felt President Obama was trying to do just that and that Republicans were not willing to work with him (Nagourney and Thee-Brennan 2010).

The numbers did not improve much after the passage of health care reform. Sixty-five percent of the public disapproved of Congress in an April 2010 Pew survey, with only 25 percent willing to give the institution a favorable rating. Pew's final poll before the midterm elections revealed levels of anti-incumbent sentiment as high as in any midterm election cycle dating back to 1994 (Pew 2010f).

A sampling of comments on the Web site *Millennials Changing America* captured the generation's disenchantment with the behavior of congressional incumbents and illustrated the desire of Millennials to see a different decision-making approach in Washington:

> Neither the far left or far right seems interested in any sort of compromise. Any congressional member displaying moderation or centrism is regarded as a party traitor and immediately attacked as such. Stifling debate is dangerous. (Viger 2009)

Congress is getting worse every day. I do not feel that they represent my interests or even care about much else than staying in power. I wouldn't trust most politicians to run a large company, much less a gas station convenience store. . . . Bring back the centrists. (Lustig 2009)

Congress, for me, is a bunch of well-off suits shuffling papers just wanting to go home at the end of the day with no concern for (yet another abstraction) "the people." (Matthew 2009)

I do NOT feel that Congress, as a whole, represents my wishes and views; I think they do an OK job representing the views of middle-of-the road, leaning conservative, hetero, late-middle-age white men. Because, obviously, that's who makes up both parts of our bicameral Congress. The views and needs of women, people of color, immigrants, the queer community (the list goes on), are simply sidelined. That is because we [Millennials] are not represented. (Katie Mae 2009)

The Senate is even less representative of the general population than it used to be. As America has become an urbanized (e.g., urban and suburban dominated) nation, Senators from rural states have become disproportionately powerful. . . . This anti-urban bias disadvantages younger voters, who are highly concentrated in America's metropolitan areas. (Kolodin 2009)

Boomers, in line with that generation's tendencies, were most likely to make the criticism personal. Fifty-seven percent blamed members of Congress, rather than the political system, for the institution's difficulties, with only 49 percent of Millennials willing to put the onus on individual behavior. On a more partisan level, Millennials were the only generation to give the Democratic leaders in Congress a positive job approval rating (53% to 35%), while the strongest levels of disapproval of the behavior of Republican congressional leadership (60%), all of whom were from the Boomer and Silent Generations, came from members of those two generations (Pew 2010c).

The ability of the political right to stir up anger at the direction in which the Democratic Congress was taking the country caused many to see the dispute as strictly ideological or partisan. But the underlying dynamic was the public's frustration with Congress itself, its way of doing business, regardless of which party was in power and whose agenda it was trying to enact. More than the settling of partisan scores or the selling of legislative accomplishments would be required to change these perceptions. Only a fundamental transformation of the way Congress did business could rescue the reputation of the legislative branch of government in the Millennial era.

SHOW ME THE MONEY

In addition to the arcane parliamentary rules that govern the daily routine of Congress, the institution's reputation for opaqueness stems mostly from the public's perception that the votes of elected officials are driven more by considerations of campaign contributions than the merits of the legislation they are considering. The enormous amount of small-money donations that the Obama campaign was able to raise, coupled with its promise to change the way business was done in Washington, created a plausible promise in the minds of many voters that the link between special-interest money and congressional decision making might finally be broken as a result of the 2008 election.

The idea that Obama would be the architect of a fundamental shift in the ability of moneyed interests to secretly influence decisions in Washington took hold, even as he rejected public funds and their accompanying restrictions on campaign expenditures, for his own presidential campaign. The Obama campaign continued to tout the quantity and generosity of its small-donor, Internet-driven contributions, arguing that a system enabling individuals to contribute in this way was actually superior to a federal government grant of funds aggregated from the voluntary contributions of taxpayers who weren't personally connected to the candidate. This focus on small-donor contributions was linked by the Obama campaign to a ban on the acceptance of Political Action Committee (PAC) funds, or from any contributions from registered federal government lobbyists.

Taken together, these actions allowed Obama to argue that his election would permit his administration to escape from the clutches of influence peddlers hiding in the power corridors of Washington. In an April 2008 campaign speech, he made reducing the power of lobbyists the key to the entire campaign's promise to create change people could believe in. "Unless we're willing to challenge the broken system in

Washington, and stop letting lobbyists use their clout to get their way, nothing else is going to change."

Obama did little after his election to tackle the problem of special-interest influence in the legislative process, however, preferring to limit his good government initiatives to a set of executive orders banning lobbyists from executive branch appointments and restricting the ability of members of his own administration to become lobbyists in the years immediately following their service. Other than denying a few people lucrative post-administration employment, these rules did little to redeem the promise of the campaign to wrest power from K Street lobbyists and give it to community activists. Indeed, some of the president's more liberal supporters, who felt corporate America had corrupted Congress at the expense of the public good, expressed dismay at the number of deals the White House cut with lobbying groups to pass what these supporters considered an unnecessarily incremental reform of the nation's health care system (Brownstein 2009).

Many participants in the Tea Party movement shared the hostility of liberals to the influence of big money in the legislative process, demanding the end of special deals on behalf of Wall Street, such as in the bank bailouts of 2008. Jane Hamsher, the editor of the liberal blog Firedoglake, was able to leverage this common hostility to corporate power to create an alliance with libertarians, including the John Birch Society, which successfully pressured the Senate to require audits of the Federal Reserve's decisions as part of that body's version of Financial Services Reform legislation (Hamsher 2010). Although the attempt to undermine the principle of political independence of the United States' central bank, established in 1913 as part of the first wave of Progressive economic reforms, was watered down in conference with the House, the fact that it gained any support at all in Congress was a reflection of the degree to which the country had come to believe that big business had too much behind-the-scenes influence on congressional deliberations.

The Supreme Court felt this problem could be remedied simply by increasing the quantity and quality of what the public knew about contributions to campaigns. Its decision in *Citizens United*, which struck down a century's worth of jurisprudence restricting corporate money in politics, cited the capability of the Internet to provide instantaneous disclosure of campaign contributions as one reason for taking this unprecedented step. Evidencing the type of judicial activism that borders on telling Congress how to legislate, something that is typical of the Court's behavior at the beginning of civic eras, Justice Antonin Scalia, writing for the majority, argued:

> With the advent of the Internet, prompt disclosure of expenditures can provide shareholders and citizens with the information needed to hold corporations and elected officials accountable for their positions and supporters. Shareholders can determine whether their corporation's political speech advances the corporation's interest in making profits, and citizens can see whether elected officials are "in the pocket" of so-called moneyed interests.

But Justice John Paul Stevens's dissent eloquently expressed the limitations of this approach. "Modern technology may help make it easier to track corporate activity, including electoral advocacy, but it is utopian to believe that it solves the problem" (Sifry 2010a). The flood of undisclosed corporate money that was spent on behalf of Republican candidates in the 2010 elections demonstrated that utopia remained out of reach, as Congress was unable or unwilling to enact any of the disclosure requirements Scalia envisioned for this new source of campaign financing.

No reformer in history has found a way to effectively and completely decouple money from politics. The campaign finance laws passed in the wake of the Watergate scandal did, however, introduce a greater degree of disclosure into the process, even though the paper formats and congressional repositories it required were hardly designed for transparency. Responding to the Court's suggestion in *Citizens United* by making all campaign contributions instantly and electronically available in an age of smart phone apps and Twitter would be the logical next step for Congress to take to enhance the public's knowledge of the way money flows into the legislative process.

Ultimately, however, the best way to reduce the power of lobbyists to make backroom deals is to restructure the relationship between elected officials and ordinary citizens in the legislative process itself. Fortunately, the social networking tools that Millennials are so adept at using could enable just such a change to occur. As the reputation of Congress continued to plummet, both political parties began to experiment with ways to bring their entire crowd of supporters into the process.

CAN TWITTER SAVE CONGRESS?

The first inklings of congressional interest in changing its relationship with the citizenry were visible in 2008, when the possibilities for using the new tools of social-networking technologies to achieve the fundamental goal of every elected official—getting reelected—became evident to at least some members. Texas Republican and avid social networker John Culberson began using Twitter to issue short text messages of no more than 140 characters, called tweets, from the House floor in late June of 2008. Democratic Congressman Michael Capuano objected that this communication, not having been cleared by the Franking Commission that he chaired, did not conform to the rules of the House and should be banned.

That commission had been established in the very first years of Congress's existence, to prevent abuse of the valuable eighteenth-century privilege allowing federal elected officials to send mail to their constituents without cost. The rules assumed that all such communications could wait until Congress's Franking Commission had a chance to review the content before it was sent to make sure it wasn't for an overtly political purpose such as asking for contributions or votes. The fact that Capuano had earlier called the Internet a "necessary evil" didn't exactly bode well for a Millennial solution to the problem (Weisman 2008).

Once Democrats in both houses of Congress realized the public relations nightmare they had created by appearing as if they wanted to stifle communication with constituents, they quickly reached a bipartisan compromise. Ignoring the more fundamental point that a mechanism designed to regulate the use of costly mailings had no business being used to regulate a free service, such as Twitter, the Franking Commission approved the use of unofficial Twitter accounts by members of Congress that would not be subject to the franking rules.

The idea caught on quickly, especially among Republicans. By June 2010, 204 of the 535 members of Congress were using Twitter, with Republicans leading Democrats in their use of this new tool by 52 percent to 28 percent (Zuckerman 2010). Senator John McCain had over 1.7 million followers on Twitter, and some of the more conservative members of the House were able to build their follower numbers to around 20,000, but the tweets of most representatives or senators were of interest to fewer than 10,000 of their constituents (Carr 2010).

The appeal of Twitter is the ability of its users to create a personal news service that continuously sends them only the information they care about. By subscribing, users become instantaneously aware of what friends are thinking or doing. That notion of freshness is critical to the service's appeal. But Twitter's appeal also depends on users not being inundated by tweets from people or sources they don't want to hear from. So those who choose to "follow" someone they find particularly interesting are not automatically connected to others who might be following the sender of the tweet. Aggregating a series of tweets can be done easily enough by including a hashtag (#), indicating the subject matter, at the beginning of the message; and those who receive messages they find of particular value can choose to "retweet," or resend, the message to their followers. This only spreads the message to the user's own circle of followers, however, since each decision to follow someone on Twitter is independent from every other one. As a result, it is not a particularly good tool for creating a new level of group participation capable of influencing legislative decisions.

Most members of Congress saw Twitter as just another way to reach out to their constituents, as they would with a direct mail piece, to promote their ideas rather than to generate a discussion of the issues they were debating. One study of a representative sample of 5,000 tweets sent by members of Congress in February 2009 found that over half were essentially announcements of the member's viewpoint, the kind of informational communication found in only about 7 percent of tweets by average users. By contrast, only 7 percent of congressional tweets captured in the study attempted to engage constituents in a discussion, and only about 3 percent requested action in response to the elected official's tweet. Amazingly, just 5 of the almost 5,000 tweets examined were retweets, and fewer than 1 percent contained a hashtag to help organize the discussion. When such conventions were used, the links were rarely ones containing new information, but rather led to the elected official's own and longer press release or Web site on the subject or to favorable press stories about the topic (Ventsias 2009).

In other words, while those members of Congress who used the technology had no hesitation in answering Twitter's fundamental question, "What are you doing or thinking?" they weren't too interested in hearing the answer to the more important question, "What should I be doing and thinking?"

ORGANIZING FOR OBAMA—AND AMERICA

Barack Obama's remarkable showing among Millennials was a direct byproduct of his campaign's ability to couple the promise of change with the tools of social media. Using e-mail, texting, and a rudimentary version of Facebook, the campaign built a small army of people who were willing to turn their online enthusiasm for the campaign into offline grassroots action, especially voter registration and turnout efforts. Its Facebook-like Web site, MyBarackObama.com, ultimately drew over four million volunteers to the site, which provided an organizing resource center with tutorials on everything from canvassing to fighting e-mail smears. The campaign's carefully nurtured e-mail list had thirteen million addresses by the time Obama was elected president. A little over three million people on that list contributed more than $600 million to the campaign (Wasow 2008). After the election, like proud parents unsure of how to handle their child's success, the candidate and incoming administration wrestled with how to maintain their offspring's enthusiasm and ensure that it channeled its energies into the most productive activities.

A similar debate erupted after the 1992 election within the victorious presidential campaign of Bill Clinton, when it attempted to build a small-donor and grassroots network on behalf of the newly elected president from inside the Democratic National Committee (DNC). The focus of this effort, called Presidential Partners, was to sell the president's agenda to the public, as opposed to the Congress. Its technology toolkit was limited to the direct mail and toll free 800 numbers of its day, but the idea was the same as the Obama campaign's sixteen years later. Simon Rosenberg, who had been in charge of coordinating the fifty states' campaign efforts for Clinton, was named policy director at the DNC and told to make it happen. But DNC chairman David Wilhelm, and his liaison at the White House, political director Rahm Emanuel, became concerned that a grassroots network, once created, might take on a life of its own and undermine the traditional power centers at the DNC, especially big-money donors. Within a year, both Rosenberg and Emanuel were removed from their assignments, and the concept of Presidential Partners died shortly thereafter. Without it, Clinton found it difficult, if not impossible, to rally public support for his agenda (Rosenberg interview 2009).

With Rahm Emanuel back in the Obama White House in 2009 as chief of staff, the president's team, once again, decided, for legal reasons, to house its grassroots organization at the DNC. This time, they made it clear that it would be operated as a semi-autonomous unit, with the responsibility to act as the president's own congressional lobbying force. Now renamed "Organizing for America," OFA was charged with using the same social networking technologies and online campaign techniques that put Barack Obama in the White House to ensure passage of the president's agenda by the Congress. But an initial dry run supporting the president's budget demonstrated the difficulty of keeping alive the passion of a campaign in the more prosaic process of governing. The budget passed, mostly because of the skill of the president's legislative team, not because a large crowd of citizens was noisily cheering for its victory.

Undeterred by this experience, Obama's team redoubled its efforts to use OFA to help enact health care reform. However, President Obama's conservative opponents proved just as adept, if not more so, in the use of social media tools to organize their own supporters against the president's proposals. The Tea Party rebellion against the Obama agenda had a simple, but emotionally compelling offer: join our movement and, in return, we will preserve your liberties. Conservatives seemed much more energized by the ideological goal of stopping the nation's drift toward what they considered to be socialism than were the president's supporters, who were charged with simply lobbying Congress to pass whatever version of health care reform was up for a vote at the time. Although OFA did have a positive impact on Democrats in the Congress during the health care debate, it proved to be far less of a force in overcoming institutional prerogatives than its creators had hoped.

The effort's limitations reflected the absence of a more transparent and nonhierarchical organizational structure. Although the Obama campaign had been able to keep strategic decision making inside a small circle of advisors at the top, even as it built an army of grassroots organizers, the same organizational approach failed to ignite this effort to create a citizen-driven lobbying force on behalf of the president's legislative agenda. As the head of OFA, Mitch Stewart, explained, "Our number one mission is to support the president's agenda. . . . We have to listen to them [volunteers] on tactical stuff, we have to listen to them on messaging. . . . We hear from staff and volunteers every single day who have a very different perspective from what the conventional wisdom is here and that's extremely helpful" (Stewart and Bird 2009). Obama's former chief campaign blogger, Sam Graham-Felsen, disagreed sharply with this approach. OFA volunteers "could have been asked to take action that requires sacrifice and struggle—like pressuring the Democratic Senators who stood, for so long, in the way of passing health care reform. Instead, they've been told to voice soft, inoffensive support for Obama's initiatives, to essentially keep quiet while the President's inner circle negotiates with Congress behind closed doors" (Sifry 2010b).

The administration's decision to keep tight control of OFA caused it to miss a major opportunity to change the way Washington works. As one disappointed supporter said:

> A substantial, lasting transformation of American politics . . . would have . . . required a different approach to online political communications in 2009: truly grassroots-driven, spontaneous, organic, and innovative. . . . The American people should have been consulted the day after the election about their needs, wants, and hoped-for agenda. They should have been in the White House and before the Congress continuously, virtually and in person. We had the means and they had the fire in their bellies. It just required a will and some working out. That didn't happen. (Jacobson 2009)

As a result of these shortcomings, at the beginning of 2010 David Plouffe was brought back to run OFA and focus its efforts on organizing for the midterm election instead of lobbying Congress. The latest experiment in using the power of ordinary citizens to overcome the influence of money in politics had ended in retreat.

Everyone Wants to Get into the Act

Clay Shirky's book *Here Comes Everybody* popularized the term "crowdsourcing," first used by Jeff Howe in a 2006 *Wired* magazine article, to describe the process of involving large numbers of people to solve a particular problem or accomplish a specific goal without paying for, or outsourcing, the work (J. Howe 2006). Built off of the three principles of the open-source software movement—transparency, flatter hierarchies, and open participation—the concept fit perfectly with Millennials' desire to maximize the opportunity for the largest number of people to participate in solving problems (Duval 2010). Shirky identifies three key elements that need to be in place for such a strategy to work, not all of which were well designed in the Democratic and Republican efforts to crowdsource the Congress:

- A promise, which explains why someone should join the group
- A tool (usually involving social media), which helps deal with the difficulties of coordinating the group's activities
- A bargain, which defines what participants can expect if they join the group, and what is expected of them in return (Shirky 2008)

Neither the Republican Party's embrace of Twitter nor the Democratic National Committee's underwriting of OFA was successful in organizing large numbers of people to change how Congress did business and to whom its members listened. The attempts fell short of the goal of completely transforming the relationship between citizens and government because the promises made to those who were invited to join the process were often not fulfilled once people actually participated in the group.

In addition, even though both efforts used the tools of social media to involve thousands of people, the bargain was too one-sided to sustain the group's participation over the long haul. OFA asked little of its supporters beyond routine grassroots activities and delivered nothing more exciting in return than news about the outcome of the vote on a specific piece of legislation, or an occasional, limited exchange with President Obama. Receiving tweets from Republican, or for that matter Democratic, representatives or senators without the ability to engage them in a substantive discussion neither gives much opportunity for input nor asks much in return from any of their followers on Twitter. By contrast, the larger and more emotionally appealing bargain offered by those organizing the Tea Party movement enabled that group to sustain itself long after the health care battle was over.

A New Bargain for a
Millennial Era Congress

The way members of Congress now use social network technologies, the unwillingness of Congress to introduce new levels of transparency, and its members' continued dependence on large campaign contributions from those with the most at stake in congressional decision making suggest that the institution is far from adopting the participatory and collaborative elements of open government that Millennials favor. This resistance threatens the very legitimacy of the legislative process in the emerging Millennial era, in which inclusion and group-consensus will be highly valued. Yet it is not hard to envision what a transformation of today's legislative process to something more attuned to Millennials' values would look like.

In the twentieth century, Americans embraced the fundamental idea of the Progressive movement, that government should be "one of the most authoritative purveyors of expert knowledge" (Keen 2008). But the idea that experts hold the key to knowledge, and therefore should be given a special role in decision making, strikes Millennials as absurd. Just as they believe that the consensus of their friends' opinions represent the best answer to a problem, Millennials expect their own ideas, and those of concerned citizens, to be part of any deliberative decision-making process, including that of Congress.

Their preference for group participation in a transparent process will lead Millennials to demand greater use of "voter generated content" in congressional deliberations and in final outcomes. David Moore, the young executive director of the Participatory Politics Foundation that created OpenCongress.org, captured this desire perfectly in an interview right before the 2008 election:

> The great advantage of open-source, socially-minded websites is that they can be both rich resources and powerful tools. We're aiming to both inform and engage. It's definitely not enough to simply make Congress more transparent. There's a fairly long way to go before everyone has a voice in the Congressional process alongside

those of lobbyists and Beltway insiders, but we're building the foundation for open access now. (Scola 2008)

Or, as Chris Kelly, chief privacy officer for Facebook, explained, "The promise of social networks is that they create a new way to directly connect voters with elected officials and eliminate the influence of middlemen in the process" (interview 2009). Social network sites far more powerful than Twitter, with the capability of linking each member of Congress with their constituents whether they are supporters, followers, or just plain friends, are the tools that will turn this promise into a reality.

One example of what could be done with congressional support is the e-Democracia Project, launched by the Brazilian House of Representatives in June 2009, with the specific purpose of engaging citizens in the lawmaking process. Lawmakers in that country were anxious to find ways to enhance their visibility in the media and saw the pilot project as a way to improve their image with the public. The project's co-developer, Cristiano Ferri Faria, called the program "a kind of crowdsourcing for legislative purposes." The backbone of the initiative is its Web site, which provides online forums, chats, and notices of offline events so citizens can share information about a problem as well as identify and discuss possible legislative solutions to the problem, and a unique application that allows participants to participate in drafting the legislation (Faria 2010a).

Its most successful effort, to date, resulted in a bill to better connect the Brazilian government with the nation's youth. That focus reflects the project's origins, which began with a brainstorming session among "young multi-tasking legislative officials" who wanted to use technology to "open doors to society." Using Twitter and Orkut (Brazil's most popular social network) for outreach, these organizational activists hosted 30 forums on 145 different topics, which generated 716 contributions from 4,371 participants. At this stage, the pilot required the intervention of a legislative expert who could translate citizen input into the language of legislative sausage making or bill writing. His work was presented to the twenty-eight-year-old sponsor of the youth involvement legislation, who made the decision about which of the suggestions would be incorporated into the bill that would be submitted to the legislature. As the process moved forward, elected officials had to explain the changes they made to the citizens' input, giving those engaged in the project an even greater appreciation of the complexity of the legislative process. Although the leaders of the effort concede that their process was quite chaotic at first, and constrained by the limited penetration of the Internet in Brazil, the result, so far has met the goal of increased legislative transparency and citizen engagement (Faria interview 2010b).

The next version of e-Democracia will move to a much more open platform, enabling Brazilians not only to engage in the conversation but also to develop their own applications on how to use the data that are generated. It will offer a very simple and user-friendly tutorial mechanism to help participants understand both the legislative process and how to participate in the portal. There will also be a "virtual discussion guide" so that citizens will be able to find out where in the legislative process matters in which they are interested currently stand. Brazilians will be able to collaborate to provide Congress with information about the problems of service delivery or other executive branch performance issues. The developers hope to use the platform to create a closed-loop feedback system, providing the legislature information on whether a law is working as intended and if not, ideas on how to correct it. Faria hopes that in ten years the technology and the interactivity it promotes will have transformed completely the relationship between the legislature and the voters of Brazil (e-mail 2010c).

Using Internet technologies to make the public a full and equal participant in the legislative process is popular in this country, as well. The Congressional Management Foundation's study of twenty-one online town hall meetings found that such exercises in virtual democracy increased constituents' approval of the elected official and his position on the issue. The events were extremely popular with a diverse array of constituents and also increased their engagement in politics and the probability that they would vote in future elections (Lazer et al. 2009).

Millennial technologies are a critical element in a new system of governance that Congress will need to adopt to create a new bargain with the American people. With these new tools in place, each member of Congress will be in a position to develop an interactive relationship with his or her constituents that will provide a real return on each citizen's involvement in the process. Instead of measuring the value of an idea on the basis of the size of the campaign contributions supporting it, the new bargain would let all constituents share ideas with one another and let the ensuing debate determine which ones are most persuasive. This approach not only fits with the political style and preferences of the Millennial Generation it is also perfectly aligned with the vision expressed by America's founders, members of another civic generation, almost two and one-half centuries ago.

MAKING THE BARGAIN STICK

The challenge of how to strike the right balance between the wishes of a legislator's constituents and the judgment of the office holder was a hot topic during the American Revolution. The comments in 1774 of Edmund Burke, a supporter of the colonial cause in that war, are considered to be the most authoritative summation of how to resolve the dilemma:

> Certainly, Gentlemen, it ought to be the happiness and glory of a Representative, to live in the strictest union, the closest correspondence, and the most unreserved communication with his constituents. Their wishes ought to have great weight with him; their opinion high respect; their business unremitted attention. It is his duty . . . to prefer their interest to his own. But, his unbiased opinion, his mature judgment, his enlightened conscience, he ought not to sacrifice to you; to any man, or to any set of men living. . . . Your Representative owes you, not his industry only, but his judgment; and he betrays, instead of serving you, if he sacrifices it to your opinion. (Burke 1774)

An example of how this process should work in the Millennial era played out in the heat of the 2008 general election campaign. Shortly after winning the nomination, Barack Obama was the subject of a revolt from subscribers on his MyBarackObama.com Web site over his position on legislation granting legal immunity to telecommunications companies that had cooperated with the Bush administration's program of wiretapping without warrants. The immunity was one of the most controversial provisions of a larger bill updating the Foreign Intelligence Surveillance Act, or FISA.

Mike Stark, a veteran Gen-X liberal agitator, who had previously antagonized conservative talk radio hosts, decided to use social networking to let candidate Obama "know that he can't keep elbowing his progressive base—the people who got him the nomination—away from the policy table." In less than two weeks, the group, "Senator Obama Please Vote NO on Telecom Immunity—Get FISA Right," had 18,000 members, making it the largest public group on the campaign's own Web site (N. Cohen 2008).

Although Senator Obama had voted earlier in favor of revoking any such immunity, he was now prepared to let the legislation take effect without such a provision, in order to attain the other benefits of the revised proposal—a classic example of the kind of tradeoffs that legislators are frequently asked to make. But, given the size of the group opposing such a vote among his own supporters, he felt obligated to explain and defend his position. In early July, he posted a nine-paragraph blog on MyBarackObama.com, explaining his reasoning and asking for his supporter's understanding and feedback. Part of the blog sounds as if he were channeling Burke:

> I cannot promise to agree with you on every issue. But I do promise to listen to your concerns, take them seriously, and seek to earn your ongoing support to change the country. . . . Democracy cannot exist without strong differences. And going forward, some of you may decide that my FISA position is a deal breaker. That's ok. But I think it is worth pointing out that our agreement on the vast majority of issues that matter outweighs the differences we may have. (Rospars 2008)

The same day the blog was posted, three of his key national security policy advisors conducted an online one-and-one-half-hour-long dialogue with the "vote NO" group. Of course, none of that ended the debate. The anti-FISA group even created a wiki to keep track of all the submissions from Obama supporters, detailing why the candidate was wrong. But the openness of the dialogue and the candor of the conversation cemented the bargain of Obama's campaign with those on both sides of the debate, including some who joined the anti-FISA group to attack the group's attacks on the candidate (Vargas 2008).

This episode demonstrates the bargain that all legislators will need to make with their constituents to restore the nation's faith in the legislative process. For the process to work over time, this dialogue will need to be so open and inclusive, in the manner of the e-Democracia project in Brazil, that it can displace the prevailing public attitudes about elected officials and their ties to moneyed or well-entrenched special interests.

CONCLUSION

Since the Republic was conceived, communication technologies have evolved rapidly to reduce the time and distance that separate Congress from the public, but many of Congress's procedures and practices have remained trapped in a time warp of its own traditions. Each new generation has registered serious dissatisfaction with the institution and the laws it passes, as a result of being able to see and hear more of how Congress actually works. In February 2010, only 22 percent of the public chose "honest" as a word to describe Congress. Yet 81 percent of those responding to the same CNN/Opinion Research Corp. survey expressed the Millennial-like optimistic belief that "Our system of government is broken but can be fixed." Creating a new connection between citizens and their representatives by using the Millennial's favorite technologies to build a more transparent, open, and participatory legislative process is the essential first step in reversing this decline in the credibility of Congress. For that to happen, congressional leaders will have to throw off their generational blinders and find a way to concede power gracefully to a new generation with new ideas.

Congress needs to make a brand new promise to Millennials, using new tools to fully involve them in the decision-making process. The resulting bargain should be built on an increased level of citizen participation in the process of governing, rather than upon the current trade of access and constituency service in return for campaign contributions. Clearly, these changes did not come soon enough to save all incumbents from the wrath of an increasingly angry electorate. Depending on the willingness of the current set of congressional leaders to embrace the values and beliefs of America's youngest generation, a complete transformation of the legislative branch may have to wait until the Millennial Generation takes its place in positions of leadership in the Congress decades from now. The sooner the transformation takes place, however, the sooner Congress will be able to make its rightful contribution to America's success in the Millennial era.

The need for the executive branch to change its ways, as well, was equally clear to all those who voted for Barack Obama in 2008. The pent-up demand for change Millennials could believe in placed enormous pressure on the president's leadership style and his ability to manage one of the most complex bureaucracies in the world. The record of his administration's first two years suggested the ability to juggle all of these challenges at once was not an easy skill to learn, even for someone with the intelligence and determination of President Obama.

CHAPTER 6

The Challenge of Presidential Leadership in a Fourth Turning

EVERY MARKETING STUDENT LEARNS that the four "Ps" of the discipline—product, price, place (distribution), and promotion—are the key to a successful sales campaign. Presidential leadership also requires the mastery of four Ps in order to successfully sell the nation on the administration's vision. But the president's four Ps are different, reflecting the multiple agendas that must simultaneously be pursued in a never-ending battle to win the support of the American people for the vision and programs the president advocates. Because of the inherently political nature of the office, the president's four priorities place politics first, public relations (communications) second, policy third, and the performance of government fourth.

In the actual conduct of the office, of course, all four priorities are interrelated and no president can afford to ignore any of them. Perhaps, in part because of his conservative antigovernment ideology and also because he was guided by Karl Rove, who strongly emphasized such concerns, George W. Bush appeared to focus most of his attention on the first two P's—politics and public relations. As a result, the poor performance of the federal government in dealing with events like Hurricane Katrina eventually undermined Bush and Rove's political and PR efforts.

President Obama tended to work these four elements in almost exactly the reverse order from the way President Bush did. Obama appeared to look with disdain upon the practice of politics, except during campaigns, and publicly expressed his dismay with the coarsening of public debate that the strident partisanship of cable news and Internet blogging brought to public relations. Faced with the prospect of major Democratic losses in the 2010 midterm elections, Obama seemed to recognize that he had failed to get the balance between the four Ps of presidential leadership right. "We probably spent much more time trying to get the policy right than trying to get the politics right. . . . I think anybody who's occupied this office has to remember that success is determined by an intersection in policy and politics and that you can't be neglecting of marketing and P.R. and public opinion" (Baker 2010). Liberal columnist E. J. Dionne pointed out that presidential leadership requires an "ongoing effort to convince free citizens of the merits of a set of ideas, policies, and decisions. Voters feel better about politicians who put what they are doing in a compelling context" (Dionne 2010b). This is especially true during a fourth turning, when Americans are being asked to accept a new civic ethos with which they have had little previous experience upon which to base their decision.

CHANNELING THE ANGER OF FOURTH TURNINGS ISN'T EASY

The presidential leadership challenge in all fourth turnings, including the present one, places the occupant of the White House squarely in the cross-hairs of history. The president must lead the country through a crisis when the future is unclear and there is no consensus on a new way forward. Wrenching as they were, previous fourth turnings and the tensions facing the country in a time of FUD provided opportunities for leadership that the three men rated America's greatest presidents by historians and the public alike—George Washington, Abraham Lincoln, and Franklin Delano Roosevelt—were able to leverage successfully. Eventually, pushed by the leadership of these presidents, the country emerged from the debate over its future and flourished in a civic era built upon the new consensus.

While the American Revolution fourth turning severed the nation's ties with Great Britain, it also led to the creation of a new nation and, eventually, the constitutional order by which the United States has been governed ever since. The inauguration of George Washington as the nation's first president at the end of the period ushered in a period of relative tranquillity and expansion that lasted nearly fifty years.

The Civil War fourth turning produced a conflict that was the most costly war in terms of total deaths of any in American history and resulted in the near dissolution of the United States itself. But Lincoln's abolition of slavery was permanently enshrined in the Constitution through the Thirteenth, Fourteenth, and Fifteenth amendments, and in the decades after the Civil War the country expanded rapidly to its continent-spanning borders, accompanied by an explosion of economic growth produced by the full blossoming of the Industrial Revolution.

The New Deal fourth turning confronted America with the worst economic crisis in its history and ended with the greatest foreign threat to its democracy. But in the 1930s, Franklin Roosevelt's New Deal came to define American government and politics for at least three decades after its enactment, and many of its programs, such as Social Security, remain sacrosanct parts of American life. Once the challenges of depression and world war were met, the United States enjoyed decades of unprecedented economic prosperity amid what most observers consider the high point of its global influence.

Ultimately, these decisive turns in public opinion resulted from the triumph of a new civic generation's attitudes and beliefs over the aging and discredited ideas of an earlier idealist generation. However, the importance of presidential leadership skills in guiding the country toward a successful resolution of the debate over a new civic ethos is equally apparent in the nation's history.

George Washington's careful stewardship during his eight years as president set the country on a solid, prosperous, and expansive course. He foreswore politics or factionalism while carefully cultivating a public image of modesty and straight talk. His policies were designed to cement the fragile nature of the new country's government and prove that it could perform to the nation's expectations.

Lincoln's struggles to find generals willing and able to achieve his military policies are the stuff of historical legend. But his assassination aborted Lincoln's plans to bind up the wounds of war. In the absence of his leadership, the country suffered through a decade of bitter political partisanship, resulting in an unsuccessful attempt to impose a new civic ethos in the South at the point of a gun. Without Lincoln's soaring rhetoric to guide it, the country lost its way and turned its back on the principles of an inclusive democracy and equal justice under the law that had originally propelled him to the presidency.

FDR's fireside chats remain a model for public relations campaigns to this day. He was also a political junkie, happy to delve into the smallest matter of patronage to build Democratic Party support for his New Deal policies. The performance of his wartime government created the nation's "arsenal of democracy," which proved to be the decisive advantage in the Allies' ultimate victory.

As one historian noted, "a fourth turning generally involves an explosion of anger, and the challenge leadership faces is, on the one hand, to moderate it to the maximum extent possible (as Lincoln so wisely did), and on the other, to channel it productively, which was FDR's greatest gift" (Kaiser 2010). Telling a story that explains where he wants to take the country and how each action and initiative represents progress toward that goal is the best way for a president to deal with the FUD inherent in any fourth turning. Presidents who have woven together each of the four presidential priorities in a single, coherent narrative have successfully managed the challenge of leadership in a fourth turning and earned their place in the nation's history.

ENROLLING THE PUBLIC
IN THE CAUSE OF CHANGE

Leadership requires not just articulating a vision of an alternative future that would not otherwise occur but also the ability to enroll people in the cause of making that vision come true (Winograd and Hais 2008, 223). In times of major generational shifts and the accompanying intergenerational tensions, the importance of these skills becomes critical to the ability of the country to find a new civic ethos in which it can believe. Barack Obama's presidential campaign clearly provided a compelling narrative, offering the country an opportunity to make history with the election of its first African American president, whose ideas and values would reinvigorate the performance of the federal government. But as the honeymoon period that all new presidents enjoy began to wane, his administration seemed to have difficulty importing the brilliance of Obama's presidential campaign into the process of governing.

During his first two years in office, he was able to enact a policy agenda—the third of the four P's—as far-reaching as that of any modern American president. By *Newsweek* correspondent Eleanor Clift's calculation, Obama won 96.7 percent of the time on "votes where he staked out a clear position, beating previous record-holder [Lyndon] Johnson's

93 percent in 1965." This made Obama the most successful "president in the last five decades in working his will on Capitol Hill" (Clift 2010).

Early in his presidency, Obama also brought renewed attention to improving the performance of the federal government—the fourth presidential priority. On his first day in office, he issued an executive order directing his appointees to create a new "system of transparency, public participation, and collaboration" that reflected the Millennial Generation's values of openness and involvement. He also brought some of his most technologically sophisticated campaign talent into the government so they could utilize Millennials' favorite technologies to improve the responsiveness and effectiveness of the government's performance.

What Obama didn't seem as interested in doing was to link the less important presidential priorities of policy and performance to the politics and public relations part of the president's job in a way that would tell one unified story, rather than presenting a laundry list of isolated, albeit impressive, accomplishments. He admitted making this mistake during the 2010 election campaign in which, by the president's own accounting, the Democrats took a "shellacking." "I think that one of the challenges we had two years ago was we had to move so fast, we were in such emergency mode, that it was very difficult for us to spend a lot of time doing victory laps and advertising exactly what we were doing, because we had to move on to the next thing" (CNN Wire Staff 2010). As Americans continued to feel the pressures of the Great Recession, improving the way the government operated and getting Congress to enact an impressive set of policy initiatives were not connected by the administration's public relations and political advisors to the most important performance priority of all—getting everyone back to work.

Explosive Exposure

The lack of a narrative to explain how all of the president's efforts were building toward the same outcome became a public relations nightmare when an explosion on the Deepwater Horizon oil rig threatened to drown Barack Obama's presidency, as well as the Gulf Coast, in a sea of oil. Looking surprisingly unsure of his executive authority, the president initially sought to respond to the greatest environmental disaster in the nation's history by relying upon the existing laws and agencies

designed to deal with such a problem. Not until the president mounted a personal public relations counteroffensive with multiple trips to the Gulf, followed by a White House showdown with British Petroleum (BP) executives that extracted a commitment to provide $20 billion to clean up the mess the company had made, did the twenty-four-hour news cycle move on to other topics. The incident provided some important lessons to Obama on why a comprehensive narrative of his presidency was needed. It also suggested a possible theme for that narrative: the need for the country to pull together in new ways to meet the challenges of the Millennial era.

The inability of BP and the government to quickly contain the effects of the spill provided a daily demonstration of the dangers of relying on a governing structure designed for an earlier era. In the first half of the twentieth century, a series of presidents from Theodore Roosevelt to Franklin Roosevelt sought to remake government to more effectively address the problems of the Industrial Age. The federal government those presidents built was based on the ideas of Progressive political theorists who wanted to use the wisdom of experts to control and regulate what appeared to be a terrifying and uncontrollable external environment. The Progressives' goal was to limit the potential for corruption in a newly powerful central government that was charged with ameliorating the effects of that dangerous environment by putting decision making in the hands of apolitical professionals, or, as one leading proponent, Max Weber described them, "the personally detached and strictly objective expert" (Noveck 2009).

In this civic era, however, President Obama was actually criticized for meeting with the very experts Progressive theory suggested should be given responsibility to solve any problem. Millennials believe better answers can be found by tapping the ideas of everyone in the group and having a completely transparent debate about the best possible solutions. Unbeknownst to most Americans, one branch of the U.S. armed forces, the Coast Guard, already has been organized using this Millennial concept. This has allowed it to deliver remarkably consistent and outstanding results.

Most of those serving in the Guard below the rank of admiral are Millennials. James Loy, the Coast Guard's former commandant, described the leadership approach this branch of the armed forces takes

to bring out the best of that generation's abilities this way: "We work in small teams where there is more rapport, more communications and less bureaucracy. . . . The level of day-to-day oversight from a centralized headquarters unit is minimal" (Phillips and Loy 2003). Unlike most military or, for that matter, other large organizations, the Coast Guard requires its front-line personnel to speak up if something is not going the way they think it should. The focus is on teamwork and information sharing, not on top-down commands to be followed blindly by each individual (Duval 2010).

The person in charge of responding to the Gulf oil spill, U.S. Coast Guard Admiral Thad Allen, is a firm believer in just that approach. After he replaced the infamous Federal Emergency Management Agency (FEMA) director, Michael Brown, as the incident commander for Hurricane Katrina relief efforts five years earlier, Allen announced his intention to "open the process up, shine the light of media scrutiny on the entire recovery project, and let the American people judge their efforts" because "transparency breeds self-correcting behavior" (Kitfield 2005).

The combination of openness and group consensus proved to be perfectly suited to solving the type of complex, interdependent problems the BP oil spill created, just as it was in dealing with the aftermath of Hurricane Katrina. The Coast Guard forces Allen commanded after the earlier disaster rescued over 33,500 victims without a single accident or casualty (Duval 2010). Under his leadership in 2010, the wellhead was capped without incident weeks before the planned deadline, and the environmental damage seemed to be better contained than anyone had originally dared hope. The Coast Guard's collaborative, cooperative structure was built to reflect and take advantage of the beliefs and atti-tudes of its mostly Millennial personnel. The commitment of the orga-nization's leadership to listening and responding to its most junior members in as open a way as possible provides a template that all organ-izations would do well to follow.

The Gulf oil disaster did not turn out to be Barack Obama's Katrina, as some of his critics had predicted, but the Coast Guard's success in cleaning up both disasters did provide important insights into what type of story the president should be telling to link all four presi-dential priorities in the Millennial era. In this narrative, improving the

performance of government by displacing the existing bureaucratic culture with a bottom-up, participatory culture similar to that of the Coast Guard, as his Open Government Initiative was designed to do, could be linked to policies that also sought to encourage individual initiative in order to achieve overarching national goals. The administration's early success in expanding programs to provide additional college tuition aid to those who enrolled in the country's official public service organizations moved the country toward achieving the administration's goal of once again having the highest proportion of college graduates of any nation in the world, without any top-down, bureaucratic commands to do so. The widely praised Race to the Top initiative, which provided increased funding for school districts that introduced reforms shown to improve student learning inspired reforms in many states that earlier, more regulatory, approaches had failed to generate. Even the controversial health care reform's mandate requiring every citizen to buy health insurance left the decision of what policy to buy to individual initiative.

Connecting the dots between these and other policy initiatives would have given the president an opportunity to argue for a new civic ethos linking national priorities to personal responsibility, the theme of his inaugural address. By integrating his policies into a single, consistent PR message, the president could have taken a major step toward building political support for this new approach, a key task for any president elected at the beginning of a fourth turning. This idea is particularly attractive to the Millennial Generation, one of the president's most loyal groups of supporters. The approach resembles the way their parents established rules for their family to follow, but left the choice of how to abide by them up to each child's sense of personal responsibility. Some conservative critics see this type of governing approach as an attempt to create a "nanny state," but it had the potential to bring a new culture built on the values of the Millennial Generation into the core of the nation's civic life.

The need to cooperate in order to achieve common goals, which has been drilled into members of the Guard by their commanders and into Millennials by their parents, could also have provided a context for the politics of bipartisanship and pragmatic idealism that Obama favored, even when it was not reciprocated by his opponents. Furthermore, it could have been used as the overarching metaphor to explain the economic restructuring proposals required to restore the country's economic growth on which the political fortunes of the Obama administration depended. However, none of these linkages was made by the president during his first two years in office.

Only after Obama and his party took, to use his term, a political "shellacking" in the 2010 midterm elections, did he finally enunciate a storyline that connected all four Ps of presidential priorities into this single, coherent message. Standing before the 112th Congress with a new Republican speaker seated behind him, Obama began his State of the Union by referring to the tragic shooting of Congresswoman Gabrielle Giffords earlier that month to remind his audience of the unique American idea that links individual initiative and freedom with national unity and achievement.

> We are part of the American family. We believe that in a country where every race and faith and point of view can be found, we are still bound together as one people; that we share common hopes and a common creed. . . . That is what sets us apart as a nation. Now, by itself, this simple recognition won't usher in a new era of cooperation. What comes of this moment is up to us. What comes of this moment will be determined not by whether we can sit together tonight, but whether we can work together tomorrow. We will move forward together, or not at all. (B. Obama 2011)

With this speech, Obama finally began an effort to win public support for his vision of what the country's new civic ethos should be. His success in achieving that would be the key test of his presidential leadership for the rest of his first term in office—and perhaps beyond.

CHANGING THE CULTURE REQUIRES CHANGING THE CONVERSATION

President Obama did realize, at least initially, that it was important to "walk the talk" of transparency and openness that was part of the values he had advocated in the campaign. Early in his administration he engaged over 93,000 people in an online town hall conversation, called Open for Questions. Over 100,000 questions were submitted and participants cast 3.6 million votes to rank their importance (Scola 2009a).

The first event drew 64,000 viewers online as well as a packed house of bloggers who were given the opportunity to attend in person. The highest ranked question was on the issue of legalizing marijuana, hardly the type of question raised by the press at traditional press conferences (Scola 2009b). But the initiative failed to gain traction, and another opportunity to tie the themes of openness and transparency to the narrative of a creating a new civic ethos was lost.

Some aspects of the administration's Open Government Initiative had more staying power, but encountered enough resistance from the existing governmental culture that they were less than effective in redeeming candidate Obama's pledge to change the way Washington operated. Responsibility for implementing the president's Memorandum on Transparency and Open Government was given to a talented team of technologists and academics, many of whom had worked on the campaign. The group's responsibility was to demonstrate "how technology can make government better, democracy stronger, and citizens more powerful," to quote from the subtitle of the book, *Wiki Government*, written by one member of the team, Beth Noveck.

The team drove agencies to create over 270,000 databases, ranging from the safety ratings of children's car seats to a project-by-project breakdown of all expenditures under the stimulus bill; the data could then be as widely shared as any Millennial would do with information that could be helpful to the larger community. In direct contrast to the vision of Progressives in the previous civic era, this initiative sought to use information technology to shift power away from the experts and engage the public in the process of using data to solve problems.

The benefit of such an approach was demonstrated by the Metropolitan Bay Transportation Authority that operates Boston's bus system. Before lunch at a Web designers' conference, the MBTA announced a plan to provide, on an open-source basis, the GPS data sent from each bus as it navigated its route. By the time the conferees were done eating, someone had incorporated the data into a Google maps application. Within two days, the information was on a Web site, and within one week it was posted as an Apple widget. Within five weeks, any Bostonian could find out when the next bus would arrive at any station by pressing a button on his or her smart phone. The entire development process was completed without any government effort or expenditure beyond the initial decision to make the underlying data available to the public in machine readable form (Dempsey 2010).

This focus on thinking of government more as the provider of data, and reserving to the public the roles of interpreter and presenter of the data, was the most transformative idea about open government to be embraced by the White House. The concept was the same one used to populate Apple's popular iPhone application store, where the underlying information, such as geo-coded locations, becomes the foundation for user-friendly applications. The idea was dubbed "we government" by its advocates. In contrast to earlier e-government efforts that simply sought to automate existing transactions, we-government proponents want to use "technology, open data, and public participation to solve shared problems" (Sifry 2010b). Its emphasis on sharing information widely was perfectly aligned with the culture of Millennials. Unfortunately, that wasn't the way Washington was used to operating.

The challenge President Obama faced in introducing this new approach was an existing governmental culture that was understandably more interested in preserving the perquisites and prerogatives provided to it by a nearly century-old status quo. Only two-thirds of the 452 federal managers interviewed by *Government Executive* magazine in 2009 thought making data ready for analysis by nongovernmental groups should be part of open government. Others wanted agencies to impose order to the data, to make it easier for the public to draw conclusions from it, or at least those conclusions the bureaucrats thought were correct. Even more reflective of the culture of "we know best" that Progressive ideas about expertise had instilled in the government were the 90 percent who believed that the Obama administration should simply show the results of programs and initiatives, but not provide the supporting data, documents, or internal discussions that led to a particular outcome (Noyes 2009).

Soon, advocates for a more transparent and open government became disillusioned with the progress the effort was making. Ellen Miller, the executive director of the Sunlight Foundation, told the Gov. 2.0 conference in September 2010 that "Data.gov started with enormous promise but it's still pretty mediocre as a data repository" (Scola 2010a). Social network sociologist Dana Boyd told attendees at an earlier conference in Washington, D.C., "Transparency alone is not the great equalizer" (Judd 2010). Clearly the ability of bureaucrats to slow down or divert efforts that were not to their liking had not diminished simply because the president had issued an executive order telling them to change their ways.

The administration did make a concerted effort to use the initiative as part of a public relations campaign designed to deal with the country's ideological skepticism of government. It realized that although the idea of sharing information widely was popular with Millennials, it mattered much less to older generations. When asked about a series of strategies to improve the government's performance, most Americans thought the highest priority should be to hold government accountable for how it spends its money, rather than working on projects to open up the internal workings of government (Hart Research Associates 2010).

As a result, when Peter Orszag, then head of the Office of Management and Budget, decided to highlight the progress his management team was making on the Open Government Initiative in June 2010, he deliberately focused on the Web site recovery.gov, which tracked each of the expenditures under the massive stimulus bill. Of the nearly 200,000 prime and subcontracts that the Recovery Act awarded, just 293, or two-tenths of 1 percent, led to "consequential investigations" of fraud. Earl Devaney, the inspector general supervising the effort, said "you'd be crazy to steal from the Recovery Act; it's far too transparent, with every dollar traceable at www.recovery.gov, and there are far too many eyes on it" (Cohn 2010). The Recovery Accountability and Transparency Board developed a software system to blend tips from the public, government contracting data, news accounts, mapping, and networking principles to tease out nonobvious relationships that might suggest fraud in how the $800 billion was being spent (Scola 2010a). As a result, even Steve Ellis, vice president of the watchdog group Taxpayers for Common Sense, agreed that "the fraud and waste element has been smaller than I think anything anybody anticipated" (L. Montgomery 2010).

Republicans were unimpressed and were delighted, instead, to highlight projects that, at least based on their description, seemed to be frivolous in concept, if not in implementation. By September 2010, after months of documenting how the stimulus bill had "saved or created over three million jobs" and how wisely the money had been spent, the public was evenly split on whether or not the expenditures had made things better or worse for the nation and its economy (Seib 2010). As important as it was to change how the government performed, it was even more important politically to convince the public that doing so would improve their economic situation.

Bev Godwin, deputy director of Al Gore's reinventing government taskforce and the former director of USA.gov, cut to the heart of the problem on the basis of her government experience, which included a stint in the White House's Office of New Media. "How, as a culture of government, do we listen to people and give them opportunities to help us? . . . How do we connect to people with people?" (Sternstein 2009).

It is still too early to know whether or not President Obama will be successful in changing the government's culture and persuading the American public to support his efforts to create a civic ethos of collective action and individual responsibility in alignment with the beliefs and behaviors of the Millennial Generation that will inherit the country and shape its future. He worked hard at attempting to moderate anger toward government by improving its performance and making the workings of the executive branch more open and transparent. He also focused on the third priority of presidential leadership, generating an historic number of policy initiatives that produced an impressive set of legislative accomplishments. But without a concerted campaign to link such efforts, especially those designed to restore confidence in the country's economic future, to the larger narrative of Obama's presidency, the country remained unsure of where he was headed and if it wanted to follow him.

It's Still the Economy, Stupid

The president's handling of the economy weighed most heavily on his political future and on the minds of most Americans. By September 2010, 57 percent of Americans still did not think President Obama had a clear plan for solving the nation's problems, while only 39 percent thought he did. A majority of the public disapproved of the president's handling of the economy, only 41 percent approved, and 60 percent believed the country was on the wrong track (New York Times/CBS News Poll 2010b). Millennials were more optimistic than other generations that their personal economic circumstances would improve within a year, but, even among this loyal group of Obama supporters, just 32 percent believed the overall economy was improving (Winograd and Hais 2010b). In primaries and polls during the run-up to the midterm elections, voters increasingly voiced their frustration that in the one area about which they believed the federal government should be most concerned—the economy—the president had failed to deliver the results they had expected.

At the same time, when given a choice between a government that stays out of "society and the economy," or a government that "actively tries to solve problems," 54 percent of all Americans and 58 percent of Millennials chose the more interventionist approach (Winograd and Hais 2010b). The public continued to count on the federal government to ensure full employment and a robust economy, a performance priority first established in the New Deal fourth turning. While about two-fifths of working-class whites, along with college-educated white men, endorsed President Reagan's narrative that "government is the problem, not the solution," only one-third of Latinos and college-educated women agreed. Reflecting the beliefs typical of a civic generation, fewer than one-fourth of Millennials were ready to agree to a return to that idealist era notion of government's role. Instead, a majority of both Millennials and minorities, the most loyal components of Barack Obama's 2008 winning coalition, felt the country was moving in the right direction, even if his policies had not as yet produced the results they had anticipated (Brownstein 2010d). As Courtney Jones, a young Millennial in Virginia said about her generation's feelings, "You can't go back to blaming Obama. You have to give him a chance" (Oliphant and Hennessey 2010). All that was needed to cement their continued loyalty was a persuasive story that would explain why it was taking so long to rebuild the economy and why the ultimate outcome would be worth waiting for.

A few of the administration's public relations efforts were successful in convincing the public of the wisdom of individual policies. As the 2010 midterm campaign kicked into post–Labor Day high gear, not only were Obama's financial regulatory reforms supported by a 2:1 margin, but even the government's loans to GM and Chrysler received positive marks, despite initially negative reviews. By holding high-profile public events to highlight each company's turnaround, as evidenced by an uptick in hiring, Obama had managed to turn that part of the bailout program into a net plus.

But one element of federal economic intervention remained very unpopular. Only 18 percent of the public believed that bank bailouts made things better, while 45 percent said they had made things worse (Seib 2010). The fact that this economic intervention was initiated and signed into law by George W. Bush at the height of the 2008 financial crisis only served to underline the public relations failures of the Obama administration. The country wanted government to reform the financial system but, for clear reasons, still did not trust the "bangsters" on Wall Street. The financial service industry's tone-deaf desire to pay six- and seven-figure bonuses to its executives while most Americans saw the value of their homes plummet helped to make Wall Street the most disliked institution in America among all generations (Winograd and Hais 2010a). By almost two-to-one margins the country favored reining in "Wall Street excesses" and protecting consumers from this universally disliked industry (Winograd and Hais 2010b).

The public's disdain of Wall Street, melded with the hostility of many Americans toward government, produced a singular media moment in February 2009, when CNBC commentator Rick Santelli railed against the Obama administration's plan to help homeowners who could no longer pay their mortgages. "This is America!" Santelli exclaimed. "How many of you people want to pay for your neighbors' mortgage that has an extra bathroom and can't pay their bills?" He called for a "Chicago Tea Party" to protest the administration's economic plan, and his call was soon answered by Tea Party activists throughout the country (Judis 2010). Republicans sensed that their road to recovery could be built by hitching a ride on the Tea Party train, sowing even more fear, uncertainty, and doubt in the 2010 midterm elections about the course Obama and the Democrats were following.

The Tea Party activists' complaint about deficit spending found an especially sympathetic ear among older generations. Almost two-thirds of the Silent Generation (63%) and 56 percent of Boomers thought federal government spending was a critical issue, in contrast with only 38 percent of Millennials. This generational conflict, reflecting deeply held ideological differences on the role of government, was visible in other policy areas, as well. For instance, a plurality of Millennials (48%)

believed the health care reform law should be given a chance to work, while most (44%) within the senior citizen Silent Generation thought it should be repealed (Winograd and Hais 2010b).

All of these generational differences were reflected in the outcome of the 2010 midterm elections. The overwhelming turnout of older voters and the more tepid response from younger voters was the direct result of the president's inability to unite the country behind what appeared to be a disparate set of unconnected policies. The president paid a heavy political price for having failed to master the art of integrating the four Ps of presidential leadership.

CONCLUSION

Two years after his historic electoral victory, President Obama had been unable to guide the country toward a consensus on a new civic ethos for the Millennial era. The president needed to more clearly articulate a new vision for America's future and the civic culture that vision would require. Millennial behaviors of sharing, openness, cooperation, group-oriented decision making, and individual responsibility within the broader context of collective action would have to become part not just of how the government operated and the programmatic changes the president wanted to make, but the common thread that linked all of his priorities into one compelling narrative. In short, if Barack Obama's presidency was going to win the approval of a majority of the public, his administration would need to design a public relations and political campaign as effective as the one that got him elected. Presidential historian Stephen Skowronek succinctly summed up the challenge still confronting Obama: "Presidents change things, and they need to justify the changes they instigate" (Skowronek 2008, 83).

The president clearly recognized the challenge still before him. Appearing on *60 Minutes* after the 2010 midterm election, he said, "Leadership isn't just legislation. It's a matter of persuading people and giving them confidence and bringing them together" (Kroft 2010). Obama took on the challenge directly with his call in the 2011 State of the Union speech for America to unite in order to "win the future." The speech's focus on improving the economy by out-innovating, out-educating, and out-building the rest of the world was an even more explicit recognition that his reelection, to say nothing of the future of the nation, depended on his finding the right economic solutions—policy and performance—and explaining them to the American public—politics and PR. Finding ways to instill a civic ethos of collective action and individual responsibility that would reflect the Millennial Generation's beliefs and behaviors in the nation's economic life was not only needed to grow the economy; it was also the key to convincing the country that the president was the right person to lead the country's efforts to restore the promise of the American Dream.

PART THREE

🌀   *Changing the Way Americans Work and Learn*

_____

CHAPTER 7

Leadership for a New Economic Era

LIKE THEIR GI GENERATION great-grandparents before them, members of the Millennial Generation began to enter the work-force in significant numbers just when the American economy was shedding jobs at a record pace. Older observers questioned whether the young generation's optimism and sense of personal confidence would fade under these economic pressures, or at least cause its members to lose their taste for liberal, interventionist economic policies.

Survey results suggested the answer to both questions was a resound-ing "no." Despite enduring higher levels of unemployment than any other generation, a Pew survey conducted in May 2009 at the height of the Great Recession found that 56 percent of Millennials were pretty well satisfied with the way things were going for them financially, a sig-nificantly greater degree of optimism than aging Boomers expressed in the same survey (46%). Seventy-two percent were optimistic that Barack Obama's policies would improve the economy, and 65 percent believed those policies would reduce the federal deficit in the long run, more than any other age cohort. One year later, 44 percent of Millennials still felt that President Obama's economic policies had helped to avoid an even worse economic crisis and were laying the foundation for an eventual economic recovery. Only 36 percent agreed with the Republican mes-sage that the president's policies had run up a record federal deficit while "failing to end the recession or slow the record pace of job losses." Just 26 percent of all Millennials accepted the proposition that "government is not the solution to our economic problems; it is the problem" (Allstate/National Journal 2010). While only a third of older generations expected to be better off economically in 2011, 58 percent of Millennials expressed confidence their economic situation would improve in the coming year (Winograd and Hais 2010a).

Instead of sinking into despair, Millennials adopted a number of coping strategies to help them weather the economic maelstrom. Parents' homes and attending school became increasingly popular safe harbors. In fall 2009, 70 percent of high school graduates were headed to campus, an all-time high (Rubin 2010). Community college applications soared by 17 percent (Brownstein 2010c), and nearly one in five undergraduates decided to prolong their education until the job market improved.

To pay for their extended education, many juggled multiple jobs and moved back in with their equally cash-strapped parents, while running up additional debt. According to the census, 56 percent of men and 48 percent of women between eighteen and twenty-four years old were either still under the same roof as their parents or had moved back home (Roberts 2009). Thirteen percent of parents with grown children told Pew researchers in May 2009 that one of their adult children had returned home in the last twelve months.

Other Millennials used the lack of jobs in the private sector as an opportunity to fulfill their generation's distinctive desire to serve its community. In 2009, AmeriCorps, the national service program created by President Bill Clinton, received two and one-half times more applications than it did in 2008, and applications continued to rise by 60 percent in 2010. Peace Corps applications jumped almost 20 percent, to the highest level in the program's nearly fifty-year history. Applications doubled, to over 35,000, from young college graduates who wanted to "Teach for America" in high-need public schools. Meanwhile, the share of army recruits with high school diplomas jumped to 95 percent from its normal level of around 80 percent (Brownstein 2010c). Scotty Fay, a recent graduate of the University of Massachusetts, typified this desire to serve in the face of adversity. "If we excel and we're able to keep ourselves working, we'll be OK, we hope, because we haven't experienced anything different than that," said Fay, who worked two jobs on top of her full-time course load before heading to her Peace Corps assignment in Guinea (Moore 2009).

But the economic decline did cause some Millennials to question what they had been taught about how to get ahead. As Josh Donahue, a twenty-three-year-old Oregon State economics graduate forced to live on food stamps, said, with more insight than he may have realized, "A degree in economics doesn't really prepare you to understand the economy very well" (CBS News 2009).

No More Faith in the Free
Market or Its Leaders

The collapse of the country's financial systems that began on September 14, 2008, triggered the beginning of America's fourth civic era and called into question not just Millennials,' but also the entire country's, basic assumptions about how the economy worked. In a series of high-stake poker moves, the government decided to let Lehman Brothers fail, forced Merrill Lynch into a shotgun marriage with the Bank of America, and then, only two days later, bailed out AIG to avoid a complete collapse of the nation's banking system, which had come to rely on that company's esoteric reinsurance policies. As Congressman Barney Frank, chairman of the House Financial Services Committee at the time, said, "The national commitment to the free market lasted one day" (Wessel 2008).

Almost overnight, conservative economic principles were jettisoned by a Republican president, George W. Bush, as his secretary of the treasury and Federal Reserve Board chairman tried to halt the economic freefall. The most massive government intervention in the economy since the New Deal made General Motors and Chrysler temporary wards of the federal government. Congress was pressured into providing $750 billion to the Treasury Department to do whatever it felt was needed to provide additional money to banks and companies deemed "too big to fail." As *Wall Street Journal* columnist David Wessel wrote, "Gone is the faith . . . that the best road to prosperity is to unleash financial markets to allocate capital, take risks, enjoy profits, absorb losses. Erased is the hope that markets correct themselves when they overshoot" (2008).

The demonstrable failure of the country's economic system left the country without a coherent consensus on economic policy and ushered in years of fear, uncertainty, and doubt about the nation's future. Keynesian acolyte Robert Skidelsky laid the blame for the collapse on the "intellectual failure of the economic profession. . . . The dominant economics of the last thirty years encouraged and promoted a system in which financial blizzards like this could occur. . . . It did so from a mistaken belief that all risk can be correctly priced and that therefore financial markets are optimally self-regulating. . . . But the only perfectly informed person is God and He does not play the stock market" (2010, 28, 50, 46). A systematic breakdown of this size, however, is never the fault of theory alone. It requires an absence of imagination and courage on the part of leadership as well.

More than five decades ago, during the previous civic era, Peter Drucker, the most influential management guru of the industrial age, had convincingly argued that the job of business leaders was to balance the legitimate claims of shareholders, customers, employees, communities, suppliers, and even society as a whole, all of which he considered to have a stake in the enterprise's success. But the leading neoclassical economist of the subsequent idealist era, Milton Friedman, maintained, beginning in 1970, that the only social responsibility of a business was to "engage in activities designed to increase its profits so long as it stays within the rules of the game" (Friedman 1970). By 1997, at the height of the economic exuberance of the Boomer-driven idealist era, the Business Roundtable, made up of the CEOs of America's major corporations, had reversed its earlier embrace of Drucker's theory. The CEOs changed the group's Statement of Corporate Governance to boldly proclaim, "the notion that the board [of directors] must somehow balance the interests of shareholders against the interests of other stakeholders fundamentally misconstrues the role of directors" (Minitzberg, Simons, and Basu 2002). By 2010, however, after two years of economic difficulties caused by the mismanagement and malfeasance of the financial sector, even a well-informed segment of the public—those who read business news several times a week—expressed profound disagreement with that point of view. Fifty-two percent said "all stakeholders are equally important," and only 14 percent said CEOs should make their decisions solely on behalf of shareholders, a percentage not much higher than the 11 percent who said CEOs should think only about "society at large" (Edelman 2010).

The Roundtable leadership's abdication of the responsibility of corporate executives to create alternative futures that would benefit all of society helped pull the nation's confidence in its business leaders down to its lowest levels in the history of scientific survey research. In 2009, only 5 percent of Americans trusted what business leaders had to say, while

73 percent had not much or no trust at all in their pronouncements, a level barely above their regard for the news media and considerably below the level of trust Americans expressed toward the executive branch of government (Rosenthal et al. 2009). By 2010, after a year of continuing economic difficulty, Millennials placed banks, other financial institutions, and large corporations at the top of their list of institutions that were having a negative impact on the country's direction. Older generations took more of a "pox on both your houses" approach, with about two-thirds attributing as much negative impact to Congress and the federal government on the country's future as on banks and big business, still hardly a ringing endorsement of corporate leadership (Pew 2010c).

Charles Prince, former CEO of Citigroup, typified the Friedman approach to corporate leadership. When asked about the worrying trends in the economy and the investments his firm was making as early as 2007, he replied, "As long as the music is playing, you've got to get up and dance." This lack of vision and accountability was too much even for President Reagan's former speechwriter Peggy Noonan. "This from a banker, a leader, a citizen, a man responsible for a community" (Noonan 2010). Except perhaps for the first, those were not roles that a man named Prince thought he was required to fill. Nor, in fact, did most of America's CEOs during the heady "greed is good" days of an idealist era when the Dow was rising and regulations were disappearing. The need for a different type of leadership, more in concert with Millennials' belief in taking responsibility for the welfare of the group, was apparent to everyone except those clinging to the paradigms and perquisites of an economic era that had passed.

Mourning Bulls, Raging Bears

Once the realization that the workings of Wall Street don't necessarily trickle down to Main Street became clear to America, nothing could save the reputation of the country's corporate leaders. Even Barack Obama's treasury secretary Timothy Geithner, who had spent his career dealing with financial institutions, told a gathering of Wall Street CEOs that if they wanted him to consider any of their ideas for resolving the crisis they should submit them on a plain white sheet of paper whose source could never be traced. "If the idea is associated with any of you, it's dead on arrival in this town."

The poster child for the type of leadership that destroyed the nation's confidence in the financial industry was the former CEO of Merrill Lynch, Stan O'Neal. He took over the reins of the company in 2003 and was the principal architect of the firm's disastrous foray into the world of subprime mortgages and collateralized debt obligations that were supposed to protect it from the downside risk of those investments. On November 1, 2007, as those investments began to go sour, Merrill Lynch fired him. It was almost a year later before the decisions he made led to the demise of Merrill Lynch as an independent firm, ninety-four years after its founding. His track record of failed performance was enough to put him on CNBC's list of "Worst American CEOs of All Time" (Portfolio.com 2009).

O'Neal did more than simply make some disastrous decisions that caused the firm to lose its financial footing. He also deliberately attempted to destroy the culture that had made Merrill Lynch great in the first place. In 1940, the leaders and founders of the firm, all members of the reactive Lost Generation, gathered their company's partners and managers for a meeting designed to capture the fundamental principles of the business they had built. The first of their nine precepts was: "The interests of our customers MUST come first," a radical concept in the *caveat emptor* culture of Wall Street—then and now. Sixty years later, when Stan O'Neal took over, he explicitly rejected the culture, referred to as "Mother Merrill" inside the firm, which the company's founders had nurtured.

"To the extent that it is paternalistic and materialistic, I don't think that is healthy," he said in a 2003 interview with the *New York Times*. "I guess there is something instinctive in me that rebels against that" (Weiner 2007). Then the Boomer grandson of a slave drove the point home more directly: "I think clubs have their place, but not in modern commerce." Instead, he focused on the numbers and cutting costs, except when it came to things like using a corporate helicopter to fly him to golf games. He put in place a management team of his own choosing, focused on achieving the same high-flying growth rate as Merrill's archrival, Goldman Sachs. Dissent was discouraged with few, if any, freewheeling strategy discussions, especially among the company's Board of Directors, most of whom owed their positions to O'Neal. Unfortunately, shareholders, and not O'Neal (who left with a generous severance package) ended up paying the price for his destruction of the culture that had served "the thundering herd" so well.

At the shareholder meeting during which the merger with Bank of America was approved, the son of one of Merrill Lynch's founders, Winthrop Smith Jr., captured the emotions of all those who had seen their life's work destroyed by O'Neal's poor leadership. Addressing what he still considered to be the "Merrill family," he began by reciting the nine precepts of the company's culture and how they had been passed down from CEO to CEO for sixty years until O'Neal took over. He made it clear that "today did not have to come. . . . Today is not the result of the sub-prime mess or synthetic CEOs. They are the symptoms. This is the story of failed leadership and the failure of the Board of Directors to take action soon enough." Then he called out the directors for their dereliction of duty in representing the interests of the owners of Merrill Lynch:

> Shame on them for allowing [O'Neal] to consciously and openly disparage Mother Merrill, throw our principles down a flight of stairs and tear out the soul of the firm. . . . Shame for allowing [O'Neal] to surround himself with many people who did not share the same values that made us great and appreciate our winning culture. . . . Shame, shame, shame for allowing one man to consciously unwind a culture and rip out the soul of this great firm.

The same story of failed leadership could be told about other titans of Wall Street, but the failure wasn't limited to the nation's financial institutions. A similar lack of vision and values also brought down one of America's leading industrial age manufacturing powerhouses, General Motors.

THE BRAND IS POLITICAL

In the previous civic era, in a city at the heart of the American continent, General Motors produced cars, such as Pontiac's "Little GTO," which were celebrated in song and captured the thrill of driving Detroit's latest creations. But in the early 1970s, GM's leaders had become so enamored of the company's success that they started to make decisions as if they controlled the world, rather than the other way around, failing to anticipate, let alone invent or invest in, alternative futures.

In 1973, OPEC's embargo tripled the price of oil, but GM's insular culture failed to respond quickly enough to consumers' sudden demand for fuel-efficient cars. While the market for such cars has waxed and waned in the intervening years, GM and its Big Three brethrens' slowness in going green gave Japanese automobile manufacturers their first foothold in the U.S. market and contributed to a growing lack of brand loyalty toward American auto companies, especially among Millennials. By 2009, Ford, the one Detroit car company to avoid the stigma of bankruptcy, found that only 7 percent of Millennials considered its products when shopping for a small car (Dolan and Terlap 2009). In contrast to young Baby Boomers singing the praises of Motor City cars, Millennials seemed ready to drive their "Chevy to the levee" and to tell the company "the levee is dry." A better set of leaders could have prevented this from happening.

Attempts to nudge Detroit into producing more fuel-efficient vehicles began during the 1973–1974 Arab Oil embargo, which led Congress to establish Corporate Average Fuel Efficiency (CAFE) standards for cars and light trucks. In the face of heated resistance from the leadership of both the Big Three and the UAW, when Bill Clinton became president he agreed to delay the adoption of higher CAFE standards until it could be proven that such goals were attainable. This formulation opened the door for what came to be known as the Partnership for a New Generation of Vehicles (PNGV). Reluctantly supported by the Big Three, PNGV provided approximately one-quarter of a billion dollars in government research funds to demonstrate the feasibility of producing a midsize sedan that could get 80 miles per gallon. Vice President Al Gore, who had been in charge of the PNGV program since its inception, met personally with the Big Three CEOs regularly from 1998 to 2000 to ensure they did not forget their past commitments to build an environmentally friendly family sedan; but the answer from many in Detroit was emphatic—profits were coming from SUVs and heavy-duty trucks, not cars. And when George W. Bush became president and installed GM's former lobbyist, Andrew Card, as his chief of staff, the entire PNGV approach was abandoned in favor of a much more one-sided research effort by the federal government that critics rightly concluded was the worst type of corporate welfare, with the government giving away research dollars and asking nothing in return.

Freed from government pressure to spend money on more environmentally friendly cars, Rick Wagoner, who became GM's CEO in June 2000, embarked upon an SUV-centered strategy that briefly won the company big profits before rising gasoline prices cut its market share in half. Losses totaled $70 billion from 2005 until the government forced GM into bankruptcy in 2009. A few years before he was forced to resign as CEO as part of the federal bailout plan, when asked what decision he most regretted, Wagoner told *Motor Trend* magazine, "Ending the EV1 electric car program and not putting the right resources into PNGV. It didn't affect *profitability* but it did affect *image*" (emphasis added) (Motor Trend 2006).

The importance of a company's public image or brand value has never been greater than in this new era, where the lines between democratic decision making and private sector planning have become increasingly blurred. The organizing cry of Boomer feminists was "the personal is political," but when the government becomes a major stockholder in private enterprises, the brand becomes political. Had the auto industry taken Vice President Gore's lead a decade ago and built a positive image among environmentally conscious Millennials, GM might have built a brand loyalty to help it regain its financial footing. Now the long-term credibility of Detroit's automobile manufacturers rests on their ability to win over a growing generation, suspicious of large corporations and searching for brands that convey a sense of purpose and meaning in their products, not just in their public pronouncements.

The environmental focus and civic-minded attitudes of Millennials will challenge executives in many industries to find a way to align their private sector goals with public policy in ways the country has not witnessed since the New Deal. This generation's preferences for transparency and equal treatment will also challenge every executive, none more so than the president of the United States, to find new ways to instill trust and confidence in their leadership in order to free up the creativity and innovation of those who work for or with them.

BROTHER, CAN YOU SPARE A PARADIGM?

The Great Depression that followed the stock market crash of October 1929 forced government leaders and economic policy makers to reexamine what they knew about how national economies really worked. In the 1930s, John Maynard Keynes's macroeconomic theories provided a theoretical basis for government intervention in the economy to "prime the pump" and restore imbalances between supply and aggregate demand. Although Keynes's theories were vehemently debated at the time, by 1971 President Richard Nixon famously declared, "We are all Keynesians now," and the role of the federal government as the ultimate protector of America's economy had become firmly established in the public's mind (P. Lewis 1976). Even Milton Friedman's later neoclassical counter-revolution against Keynesian activism failed to dissuade American voters that one of the key responsibilities of the president and the government he leads is to provide an economy with full employment and stable prices.

The cycle came full circle when the collapse of America's financial system in September 2008 caused political leaders to look for a new paradigm that could explain how the Great Recession came about and provide a new source of ideas on how to prevent another one from happening. While economists on both sides of the ideological spectrum sought to find new ways to justify their conflicting theories in the face of these events, a few more imaginative theorists put forward a new policy prescription as bold and as all encompassing as Keynes's theories were in his day.

The economic policy makers who wrote a widely circulated memo during the transition to the Obama administration for the Democracy Alliance (a key group of major contributors with the ability to influence Democratic policies) described how a modern economy is much more similar to the complex, adaptive systems found in nature than to the static model described in classical economics. The memo began with the startling statement that the "traditional unfettered 'free market' equilibrium model didn't create a healthier middle class" or an economy with enough growth to both balance the budget and lift people out of poverty, "but it did make possible, perhaps even inevitable, today's terrible economic meltdown." It then offered a "new paradigm for the economy, based on complexity science" that "predicts periodic chaos and hugely disparate results unless the market is built on strong institutional foundations and is wisely regulated. . . . This new paradigm of complexity economics is neither left nor right—it is post-partisan. But it does provide an alternative to free market orthodoxy that describes a path to progressive goals" (Beinhocker, Hanauer, and Liu 2008).

In economies as in ecosystems, the authors argued, innovation is the key to success as the system "moves through constant cycles of innovation, concentration, and then reconfiguration that Joseph Schumpeter called waves of 'creative destruction'" in his classic treatise explaining the vicissitudes of industrial age economies, *Capitalism, Socialism, and Democracy.* In complexity economics, the economy is made up of not only all the economic actors "but also the expectations and interpretations" they have about what "all the other agents want and expect. And that invisible web of human expectations becomes, in a relentless spiral, both cause and effect of external circumstances." Because of that insight, complexity economic models provided new evidence in support of Keynes's original theory that "when left to itself the economy has the potential to get far out of balance, and even get stuck in dead-end traps" that only government intervention can remedy.

The memo then recommended that President Obama and his economic team follow a path that would be the Millennial era equivalent of the New Deal. It began with a definition of the true origin of wealth—information—drawn from the book *The Origin of Wealth: Evolution, Complexity, and the Radical Remaking of Economics,* written by one of the memo's authors, Eric Beinhocker. Unlike classical economics, which equates wealth with money, this new paradigm states that wealth is maximized when the largest number of people are generating ideas in a competitive, evolutionary environment. As the memo emphasized, "Equality of opportunity, then, isn't just a moral imperative. It's an economic imperative. . . . The more potentially 'fit' players you can field, the more likely your team is to succeed." In such a system, government's role is to make "sure everyone has a fair shot—education, health care, social capital, and access to financial capital—to create new information and deploy that information productively in the economy."

The framing of the economy as an ecosystem has radical implications for how government should treat markets. Rejecting the belief of traditional economists in the market as "a state of nature," complexity economics treats markets as "social constructions" that are "effective, if well-steered" rather than sacrosanct. Rejecting the notion prized by conservatives that income inequality simply reflects unequal effort or ability or both, this theory asserts, "inequality is what markets naturally create and compound and requires correction." Although the memo did not recommend attempts to eliminate inequality of outcomes, it did suggest that it was desirable and "possible to prevent inequality in outcomes from translating into inequality of opportunity, particularly across generations."

In February 2010, President Obama echoed the memo's concepts in summing up his economic message: "Our goal is to build a new foundation for long-term, sustainable economic growth, and that requires innovation. It requires a smart energy policy. It requires a health care system that is not a drag on business. And it requires an education system that is producing the most productive workers in the world" (Bloomberg Business Week 2010).

The president's program and the theory behind it were aligned with the Millennial Generation's belief in the need to use government to increase economic equality and provide broader economic opportunity in order for the entire group to be successful. Perhaps the most Millennial of all the insights generated by this new paradigm was the importance it placed on establishing a new sense of trust in how individuals deal with each other. The theory suggested that the classical economic paradigm, enunciated during the Enlightenment by Adam Smith's *The Wealth of Nations*, was wrong in suggesting that "wealth is created by the pursuit of narrow self-interest." Instead, the memo maintained that "Norms of unchecked selfishness kill the one thing that determines whether a society can generate (let alone fairly allocate) wealth and opportunity: trust. High-trust networks thrive; low-trust ones fail. And when greed and self-interest are glorified above all, high-trust networks become low-trust" (Beinhocker, Hanauer, and Liu 2008).

Here was the critical distinction that could guide the Obama administration's entire economic policy making and provide an answer to the question all Americans were asking: "Whom do you trust?" The answer, as every Millennial knows, had to be "each other." It also implicitly defined a new set of behaviors that leaders in this new economic era would have to adopt if they hoped to encourage innovation within their own organizations.

THE GREAT DEPRESSION AND THE GREAT RECESSION SHARE MORE THAN A WORD

The parallels between the prolonged economic pain the country experienced in the 1930s and what it is experiencing now provide some insights into what a president must do to gain support for an economic strategy, whether it's called a New Deal or a New Foundation, that is radically different from what has gone before. FDR's experience suggests clarity of vision, summed up by his promise to provide "a new deal for the common man," as well as careful attention to the differences between ideological and programmatic or operational appeals, and a focus on the beliefs of a young civic generation, are the keys to building majority support for a new way to manage the nation's economic well-being.

Both the civic-oriented GI and Millennial generations came of age during periods of great economic duress. The unity of belief and size of both generations underpinned first President Franklin Roosevelt's and then President Obama's political support for long-term, structural changes in the economy. In both cases, the dire circumstances in which ordinary Americans found themselves provided the impetus for the creation of major new social programs—Social Security in Roosevelt's first term and health care reform early in Obama's administration. Both presidents needed to use their support within the generational cohort most committed to change to resist the forces of reaction among older generations that sought to undo their initiatives.

Just as Republicans and some moderate Democrats today seek to impose a new round of austerity on the nation's economy by attempting to stop the funding for such basic programs as extended unemployment insurance, FDR, during his first term, dodged and ducked an onslaught of advice to scale back the New Deal from both the opposition and from many within his own party. The debate continued right through the 1936 election, when Roosevelt's Republican opponent, Alf Landon, campaigned on a platform of repealing Social Security, arguing, as those seeking to repeal health care reform do today, that it represented an unwarranted "socialist" intrusion into individual paychecks by an out-of-control federal government.

But during the entire debate, Roosevelt stuck to his guns and insisted on the need fundamentally to overturn the laissez-faire economic policies of the Roaring Twenties. As Pulitzer Prize–winning historian David M. Kennedy wrote in his book *Freedom from Fear*, "The New Deal's premier objective, at least until 1938, and in Roosevelt's mind probably for a long time thereafter, was not economic recovery but structural reform for the long run. In the last analysis, reform was the New Deal's lasting legacy" (Kennedy 1999, 372).

Just as President Obama's health care and financial regulatory reform efforts are not the second coming of socialism that opponents try to make them out to be, Roosevelt's structural solutions avoided the heavy-handed notion of government control that so many in his party favored and so many Republicans said it was. Rather than creating a government bank, the Federal Deposit Insurance Corporation (FDIC) was designed to simply give depositors a sense of security. The Securities and Exchange Commission gave stockholders new information upon which to base their investment decisions, but did not restrict their investment opportunities. The Federal Housing Administration provided more safety to lenders and new mortgage terms for home buyers, but did not attempt to have government build the houses people needed. As Kennedy correctly observes:

> To be sure, Roosevelt sought to enlarge the national state as the instrument of the security and stability that he hoped to impart to American life. But legend to the contrary, much of the security that the New Deal threaded into the fabric of American society was often stitched with a remarkably delicate hand, not simply imposed by the fist of the imperious state. (1999, 365)

None of Roosevelt's structural reforms, however, restored the country to full employment immediately. When FDR uttered his famous line "I see one-third of a nation ill-housed, ill-clad, ill-nourished" in his 1937 inaugural speech, he was speaking about the progress the country had made in his first term and warning his audience not to become complacent with what had been accomplished to that point.

IN SEARCH OF A NEW
ECONOMIC CONSENSUS

The legislative agenda of the Obama administration reflected the policy implications of complexity economics. Four of the five pillars upon which the president said he wanted to build a stronger and new foundation for the economy related directly to the memo's recommendations. Health care and education reform made the top of the list as keys to improving economic opportunity. Misallocation of resources in the market for energy, to be corrected through a system of cap and trade, was an early initiative as well, but it died in the Senate. The relatively unfettered financial system marketplace was restrained by a new set of regulations and regulators under the financial regulatory reforms that Obama signed into law in the summer of 2010. Still, the Boomers and Gen-Xers who made up most of America's private and public sector leadership showed little inclination to escape from the prison of the ideological paradigms of their generations and embrace this new path for the nation's economy. Complexity economics provided the theoretical underpinnings for the legislative agenda the president decided to pursue, but it said nothing about how to gain the support of the American public for his economic plan.

President Obama made his first attempt to do just that in his first State of the Union speech. At the beginning of his recitation of the jobs programs he was asking Congress to enact, he summarized all of complexity economics in just two sentences. "The true engine of job creation in this country will always be America's businesses. But government can create the conditions necessary for businesses to expand and hire more workers." The statement identified a new role for the federal government in guiding the nation's economy that fit squarely within the ideological and operational consensus of American politics in a civic era. Like a farmer making sure the soil, seeds, and fertilizer maximized his crop yields, Obama suggested that the government's role was to create conditions for America's economic ecosystem to grow.

About a year and a half later, the administration announced a Jobs and Innovation Partnership that attempted to use the insights of complexity economics to help local businesses grow in every region in the country. It placed the private sector at the center of cost-saving efforts to leverage and pool federal resources by creating new "acceleration centers" for jobs and innovation, chartered to promote innovative, public-private job creation clusters, technical assistance and implementation strategies. The goal of these centers was to connect entrepreneurs with those who have the resources to create companies, and connect startups more effectively to the opportunities presented by federal government initiatives to promote exports, community development, and a cleaner economy. Each federally chartered Partnership was designed to connect entrepreneurial companies to universities, community colleges, finance experts, and talented pools of workers who could engage these businesses in collaborative efforts to define regional and local business objectives and then work to achieve them (Carol 2010b). Assistant Secretary of Commerce John Fernandez announced the administration's intention to make innovation cluster development the "key driver of future jobs and economic growth." It would do this by helping to "build ecosystems where the private sector can flourish and create the 'connective tissue' that will bind together vibrant regional economic ecosystems" (Fernandez 2010). The concept was perfectly aligned with Millennials' belief in trusting one another and sharing ideas in order to come up with the best results for the entire community.

President Obama returned to these themes in his 2011 State of the Union address, calling "encouraging innovation" the "first step in winning the future." In this speech, as in Ann Arbor the previous year, he underlined the key role government can play in establishing the conditions under which America's creativity could thrive and Americans could prosper.

> Our free enterprise system is what drives innovation. But because it's not always profitable for companies to invest in basic research, throughout history our government has provided cutting-edge scientists and inventors with the support that they need. . . . And to spur on more success stories . . . we're telling America's scientists and engineers that if they assemble teams of the best minds in their fields, and focus on the hardest problems . . . we'll fund the Apollo Projects of our time. (B. Obama 2011)

The contrast with the Republican alternative—minimizing government intrusion in the economy by cutting taxes, leaving more money in the hands of consumers and entrepreneurs to begin with, and reducing and restricting the number of regulations imposed upon corporate behavior—could not have been starker. These ideas were detailed in a book, *Young Guns*, written by three of the top young House Republicans, who took the title from a movie popular when their political hero, Ronald Reagan, was in the White House. Their policy prescriptions, which included converting Medicare to a voucher system and privatizing Social Security, reflected Generation X's philosophy of individual autonomy and hostility to the type of community or collective action that President Obama was advocating.

Which approach wins the public's support will depend on the economic results the Obama administration is able to deliver, and whether he or his Republican critics are better able to convince an increasingly skeptical public that either vision is something in which they can believe.

CONCLUSION

Reenergizing the American economy is not simply a matter of determining which economic theory is correct and applying its lessons to get America out of the Great Recession. America's economy must be restructured before it can grow again, and that will be painful. This means that the country's tolerance for change will be as sorely tested in coming years as much as it was during the Great Depression. It will inevitably put President Obama's leadership skills of enrollment and persuasion to the same stern test that FDR had to pass, but it is too soon to know if this president will be as successful as Roosevelt was. So far, the Millennials' continuing support for the president's initiatives and the generation's willingness to find new ways to cope with the dire economic circumstances they face should give the president some comfort that his efforts will ultimately be successful.

However, the task of restoring the country's economic vitality is just as much, if not more, the responsibility of leaders in the private sector as it is the president's. Their leadership paradigm will have to change just as radically as conventionally accepted notions of what drives economic growth. A new type of organizational leadership that matches the values and beliefs of Millennials will be required in order to engage those fortunate enough to have a job in the process of innovation and creativity that complexity economics places at the center of wealth creation. To accomplish that task will require the older generations, which still hold most organizational positions of leadership and power, to find new ways to motivate and incentivize their newest workers, Millennials, and to persuade those young employees to join in common purpose with their workplace superiors. In many ways, meeting that challenge will be just as difficult, and just as important, as providing effective economic leadership in the Millennial era.

CHAPTER 8

Confronting Corporate Life

ONE OF THE MORE POPULAR SITCOMS of the past decade is *The Office*, a running satire on the pain and surreal nature of working in the world of corporate cubicles and hierarchy. Mining the same rich vein of the humor-of-the-absurd portrayed in the cartoon strip *Dilbert*, the show constantly reminds its viewers how unpleasant it is to have what you do and how you do it determined by either fools who outrank you or peers who dislike you. One character in the show, Jim Halpert, captured the desperation of today's workplace this way: "This is just a job. . . . If this were my career, I'd have to throw myself in front of a train" (Murray 2010).

There are, however, distinctions among generations in their reactions to the show's portrayal of office life. Many Boomers laugh at scenes from a work environment they know all too well, without recognizing their own images in the generational stereotype of self-important blather from the clueless boss who supplies the comedic dynamic for the show. Generation Xers use the show as an emotional cathartic to help them deal with the frustrations of their daily existence. Millennials laugh at the quaint beings working in cubicles, certain that they will never be forced into such a life and if, unfortunately, they are, confident that they somehow can change its culture in ways that will benefit everyone.

But the fundamental truth for all generations is that an office is not a place where most people want to work. Fewer than half of employees surveyed in 2009 were happy in their jobs, the lowest level in twenty-two years. Millennials were the least happy, with only 36 percent expressing satisfaction with their jobs. This was the lowest level of job satisfaction among workers under twenty-five years old since 1987 (Hsu 2010). When an institution reaches that level of disrepute, its days are numbered.

CREATIVE DESTRUCTION
IN THE WORKPLACE

Julian Simon's controversial idea that more people, and therefore growth, were an asset, not a liability, to a country's economy made him one of the most famous American libertarian economists. He began his career as a cost accountant for the Prudential Insurance Company shortly after getting his degree in experimental psychology from Harvard in 1953. In his autobiography, *A Life against the Grain*, he describes the working conditions he encountered in his first day on the job. Work in the office began promptly with the ringing of a bell at 8:30 AM. Each clerk was given pen and paper and assigned to check individual expenditures in a ledger, which was audited and inspected by a boss sitting in the front of a football-field-sized room filled with rows of identical desks. At precisely 10:17 AM the bell rang for mid-morning coffee break, which ended with the ringing of another bell at 10:32 AM. At noon, the bell announced a forty-five-minute lunch break. After another fifteen-minute break for afternoon coffee, the day ended with a final bell at 5 PM, and everyone went home. The environment was so bizarre, Simon quit before the week was over (Simon 2003). But Prudential was very typical of corporations in the 1950s, almost all of which were run by former military commanders who had no model of how to organize large-scale work other than a drill-sergeant-inspired, top-down approach.

Part of the Baby Boomer rebellion against GI Generation institutions was directed at this stultifying corporate environment. Those protests led to modern office designs that provided more personalized, semi-enclosed spaces for workers and offices with walls and windows for bosses. But the overall command-and-control approach to organizing work, introduced by America's last civic generation, remains all too familiar today. Millennials are determined to change the world of work once and for all. They want to create economic entities whose products or services reflect their generation's values and whose work environments generate energy and excitement among employees who, in turn, feel a sense of ownership and commitment to achieving an organization's goals.

Successfully creating a new and better way to work is the key to America's economic success in the Millennial era. As Rob Shapiro, economic advisor to businesses, governments, and nonprofits, wrote in his book *Futurecast*, "The most prosperous advanced countries over the next decade will be those that focus most successfully on what advanced countries do best—creating, adopting, and adapting to powerful new technologies and production processes; to new ways to finance, market, and distribute things; and to new approaches for organizing and managing businesses" (Shapiro 2008, 315).

But creating an environment where innovation flourishes requires leaders who don't simply dictate, "Let a thousand flowers bloom." Instead, it requires a set of actions, not commands, that instill trust among a company's employees as well as its customers. As complexity economist Eric Beinhocker writes, "There is an important correlation between trust and economic success. High trust leads to economic cooperation, which leads to prosperity, which further enhances trust in a virtual circle" (Beinhocker 2006, 433). Creating the level of trust needed to generate enough economic growth to employ all Americans, and to generate international as well as domestic demand for the country's products and services, will require the transformation of the world of work from cubicles to creativity, and from hierarchy to democracy.

REORGANIZING WORK

In his seminal book, *The Future of Work*, MIT Sloan School of Management professor Tom Malone predicted that the same technological enabler of change, the constantly falling cost of communication, and the unchanging desire for individual freedom that transformed the nation-state, would combine to transform the world of work in this century (Malone 2004). He suggested that command-and-control hierarchies would give way, first to "loose hierarchies," and ultimately to even more successful corporate democracies and markets. His ideas have been echoed since then by the authors of *Wikinomics* (Tapscott and Williams 2006), who predict that "mass collaboration" will become the new form of economic organization. Malone's ideas have also been elaborated by strategy consultant Gary Hamel, who is experimenting with an online laboratory managed along democratic lines to find innovative ideas that might help define what the new management model should look like (Murray 2010).

The fondness of Millennials for social network communication technologies, which were largely unknown when Malone's book was published, has accelerated the trends he identified. When individuals share their ideas with whoever holds similar interests and beliefs—unrestricted by cost, distance, or rules of rank—bonds of trust are built between them. Social networks exponentially increase the capacity for such activity at greatly reduced costs. Those networks not only provide the opportunity for those at the farthest edges of the organization to decide for themselves what ought to be done but they automatically generate feedback on the effectiveness and efficiency of each person's efforts. This data creates a new way to monitor organizational behavior and, potentially, to direct it without incurring much, if any, of the costs and delays associated with previous communication tools. Because conversations on social networks are built on a foundation of shared values and interests, the technology can also be used to extend the boundaries of an organization beyond its employees to its customers, who can become engaged in further refining the effectiveness of the organization's efforts.

Still, few businesses or institutions paid much attention to social networking technology as a tool to manage their daily activities until the 2008 Obama campaign demonstrated the potential of using it to create an organizational model unlike any other. Instead, social networks like Facebook and MySpace were considered to be toys for teenagers to express their inchoate generational angst, time wasters forbidden to youthful employees on the company clock, or, at best, a way for individuals to connect with their friends. Now not only political campaigns but also companies are rushing to replicate the success of the Obama team in generating equally impressive gains in creativity, innovation, and customer loyalty from their own organizations.

MANUFACTURING HOPE

One remarkable view from the inside of this new organizational model was provided by Max Harper, a Millennial videographer of extraordinary talent devoted to using the power of "moving pictures" to propel social movements. When Harper arrived at the Obama general election campaign headquarters in Chicago in late summer 2008, he was immediately struck by both its physical and organizational openness. He was welcomed into the new media team, all of whom were Millennials, without any of the ego or sense of rank that usually characterizes those who have won a hard-fought presidential nomination. That cultural value was reinforced by the layout of the office. "The entire floor was in the shape of a large 'O' with almost everyone's desk in the open. There were some low cubicle walls, but even the senior staff offices and conference rooms had glass walls" (Harper 2009). Transparency was literally built into the physical structure of the campaign offices.

Harper's job was to take the thousands of hours of video that would be recorded as the campaign proceeded and use it to tell the story of the campaign in the most effective way possible, to both the widest and narrowest audiences the campaign wanted to reach. What Harper termed the "Hope Factory" produced requests in e-mail and text message formats asking people to join the campaign, donate to it, or even become part of the "MyBarackObama.com" social network (Sifry 2009).

When those requests were successful, they generated revenue that would be spent on communicating to a wider audience of volunteers whose time and talent could be recycled into more requests and more communication. Videos were used to grease the engine of this enterprise by capturing the campaign's story and telling it to as many audiences as possible, in any way that produced a return on the costs of distributing the images.

When the particular message was critical enough, it was shared through campaign ads and blogs, as well as in-house and external social networks. Barack Obama's crucial March 2008 speech on race, and the campaign ads attacking Senator John McCain for not knowing how many houses he owned, or being a part of the Keating Five scandal, for instance, were viewed over one million times each. But at other times, the distribution channel was carefully targeted to a specific audience. For example, Obama's sister Maya recorded messages in twelve different languages ranging from Hmong to Filipino, for Asian Americans and Pacific Islanders whose video viewership totaled no more than 12,000.

But in every case, the strategy was the same—share the particular video's story online in order to facilitate offline action on behalf of the candidate. The videos not only generated unprecedented levels of customer loyalty and repeat business, but also proved to be a key element in keeping the organization on course.

Sending communications up and down the chain of command would not have provided timely and effective directions for those inside the campaign. Instead, the loose hierarchy of the Obama campaign used video as an alternative method for creating what Harper called "organizational proprioception," a term he borrowed from the world of dance, to describe the ability of the brain to know what the foot is doing and vice versa. "Video gives everyone a sense of the whole. When you read a story about 10,000 or 1,000 people at a rally it's just a matter of a few zeros on the page one way or the other. But when you see a video of tens of thousands of people at a rally it allows the entire sphere of the campaign to understand itself and what it is doing" (Harper 2009).

Video communication became the essential tool for linking the activities of the individual foot soldiers of the organization with the brain trust at the center of the campaign. Each video was reviewed before release to make sure it captured the campaign's values. The use of hand-held cameras to capture behind-the-scene moments helped to convey a sense of authenticity and transparency, while the sense of humor and cleverness the videos often conveyed helped to build trust in the candidate. As a result, the videos produced both volunteers and VIPs who knew the organization's vision and values and what they could do to advance its cause.

Managing Visually

The Millennial Generation's penchant for taking pictures of just about everything is transforming workplaces of all types, not just campaigns. Organizations as diverse as the Veterans Administration and Hewlett Packard registered 30 percent improvements in customer satisfaction and 25 percent gains in overall productivity using the simplest of two-dimensional, static visual management techniques (Liff and Posey 2004). Mike Vance, the creator of Disney University and project manager for Disney World, has lectured and written extensively on how to incorporate visual management techniques that operate "at the speed of light, not the speed of sound" into any project requiring innovation and creativity (Vance and Deacon 1996).

But to achieve true organizational proprioception, managers will need to incorporate video in their management practices as enthusiastically as Millennials embraced YouTube. One company that has already taken this step is Cisco, the technologically sophisticated purveyor of switches and computers that make the Internet work. As part of its initiative to create a more decentralized decision-making structure that uses "clusters of experts" rather than the typical organizational hierarchy to establish priorities, Cisco introduced social networking technologies to create "virtual water coolers" into this more collaborative work environment. In order to enhance communication between expert clusters, it then deployed a new tool that Cisco had developed to make laptop video recordings easier to produce and share. Cisco estimates that more than 30,000 employees watched over 100,000 videos in the first year of the tool's deployment, with the volume of video messages rising by 600 percent the following year (Jordan interview 2008).

The exponential increase in the use of video to ensure effective communications has spread to every function within Cisco. Its department of human resources is using video to improve training, marketing is employing it to explain its products, and senior executives from CEO John Chambers on down are now communicating key messages in video format. Combined with the use of its virtual conference room technology, Telepresence, Cisco has saved over $200 million per year, cut its carbon footprint by reducing travel, and leveraged its Millennial employees' penchant for sharing video to produce a more creative, and therefore more productive, work environment (Warrior interview 2010).

In line with Malone's dictum, these innovations will not only breed even greater technological wonders but continue the transformation of organizations from loose hierarchies, such as the Obama campaign, to true democracies, where decisions are made by the group, not the leader. Those organizations that embrace a consensual decision-making, participative, collaborative culture, in line with Millennials' beliefs and attitudes, will be rewarded with greater customer loyalty and a more productive workforce. In order to effectuate a change of this magnitude, leaders will need to learn how to "coordinate and cultivate" their organizations, according to Malone, rather than command and control it.

COORDINATING INNOVATION

To coordinate innovation requires a deep understanding of the role each person plays in generating value for the organization. Verna Allee, bestselling author and advisor to major corporations and nonprofits, developed a business modeling method, Value Network Analysis (VNA), which generates visual maps of the interactions between co-workers as they go about doing their jobs. By focusing on the role each person plays in producing an outcome, these network diagrams capture opportunities to enhance the exchange of both tangible and intangible value between individuals, unlocking workers' creativity and turbo-charging innovation.

Boeing made the use of VNA a top strategic initiative after seeing it deliver gains in quality that exceeded alternative approaches, such as Six Sigma, a quality program promoted by Jack Welch when he was CEO of General Electric. Unlike Six Sigma, which uses process modeling to drive out human error, VNA takes the counterintuitive approach of encouraging variation in order to explore the organizational intersections where, as in nature's ecosystems, innovation occurs. The process focuses on human contact and the gains that occur when trust builds through continuous interaction.

Corporations and nonprofits alike have used this type of analysis to coordinate innovative efforts that have produced spectacular results. Symantec, which sells computer security products and services, used the technique to redesign their Web-based customer support services and respond to their customers much more effectively. Procter and Gamble addressed needless redundancy in its internal learning systems and communities by examining its workflows from this exchange of value perspective. The nonprofit iScale used VNA to develop new understandings between banks and those advocating sustainable economies for developing countries of the global systems they were each trying to influence. Similarly, VINNOVA, a Swedish-based support network for regional innovation, used VNA to visualize and define roles for participants that would maximize each person's contribution to the organization's regional development goals.

Whether or not VNA is used to generate this level of innovation and creativity, Allee says the trend is irreversible: "Collaborative ways of working that stress the individual's role in producing better outcomes is the future" (interview 2010). Coordinating collaboration is one of the two key skills managers will need to learn to lead workplaces in the future. The ability to cultivate creativity is the other.

Cultivating a Creative Culture

Barack Obama demonstrated how a leader can cultivate creativity when he addressed his campaign staff after his hard-fought victory over

Hillary Clinton for the Democratic presidential nomination. The YouTube video of the event shows Obama walking into the room with no fanfare and no contingent of aides to point the way. He began by reminding the group that the last time they had such a gathering was in August 2007, when they were 31 points down in the polls, and the campaign had been written off by most pundits and politicians. Back then Obama had expressed his faith in his campaign's ability to win this way: "I wasn't sure I would be the best of candidates, but I was positive we could create the best organization. . . . When people submerge their egos and focus on bringing their gifts, passion, energy and vision to a common task, then great things can be accomplished" (Sternberg 2008). Using humility, rather than hubris, to generate enrollment in his vision, Obama's remarks give the campaign staff all the credit for his victory. "You lifted me up and pulled me across the finish line. . . . You created the best political organization in America and the best one in at least the last thirty to forty years. You inspired me and restored my faith in what's possible. It's not something I did. Rather, it's a great gift you gave to me" (ibid., 2008).

The speech captures the essence of what Jim Collins, leadership guru and bestselling author, calls Level 5 leadership. These are individuals who blend "extreme personal humility with intense professional will," and who lead great, rather than just good, organizations. Collins cites Lincoln as one of the few examples of Level 5 leadership among U.S. presidents, because he "never let his ego get in the way of his primary ambition for the larger cause of an enduring nation. Yet those who mistook Mr. Lincoln's personal modesty, shy nature, and awkward manner as signs of weakness found themselves terribly mistaken" (Collins 2001, 22).

Level 5 leaders "look out the window" to give credit to factors outside themselves when things go well, and, Collins points out, "look in the mirror" to assign responsibility when things go poorly. Although the job of being president would give Obama many opportunities to look in the mirror, his pride in winning the primary campaign was that of a Millennial parent, watching his children build something great, not that of a general taking credit for the tactical execution by his troops of a plan he alone had devised.

Level 5 leadership tends to produce great organizations because it creates a culture of trust that encourages creativity and innovation, the keys to success in a complex world. Obama saw his leadership role as creating and nurturing the campaign's culture of "clarity, calmness, conviction, and collegiality throughout the ranks" (Plouffe 2009, 379). Successfully fulfilling that role in organizations with multiple generations, each having its own set of ideas and beliefs, however, is easier said than done.

Bridging the Generational Divide at Work

The Bureau of Labor Statistics estimates that there are almost equal numbers of Boomers and Millennials in America's workplace today, with Generation X filling only about half the number of positions that the two larger generations occupy. Over the next decade, the presence of Millennials will grow to a near majority. Boomer retirements will reduce that generation's presence to the same proportion as Generation X, or about 20 percent each (Meister and Willyerd 2010). This tidal wave of Millennials in the workplace will change not only the leadership style executives will have to exercise in order to be successful, but also their norms of how to get work done.

Members of Generation X, who are most likely to be the supervisors of Millennials, are having the most difficulty adjusting to the youngest generation's behavior at work. One named "Copperred" on the blog Durban Bud wrote, "I work with several Millennials and they are difficult. They lack the basic communication skills necessary for face-to-face interaction and often cannot write a complete sentence. They have a hard time accepting that they might be wrong about anything and have very little regard for the experience or expertise of others. The narcissism of this group is unbelievable!" (Copperred 2007) Even Chris DeWolfe, the former CEO and founder of MySpace, who made millions by attracting Millennials to his social network, exhibited a typical Gen-X attitude toward his Millennial employees: "We put them to work on our technology. But none of them can sell. They are afraid to close. We hire Gen X to be our sales force instead" (interview 2009).

Michelle Beaudry has experienced the generational divide challenge up close and personal as director of Human Resources at Business.com, a business-to-business search engine. Her insightful approach to the challenge has been to focus on managing Millennials' expectations and teaching them the basics of corporate life, while being careful not to tread on their generational beliefs. After hearing Millennials say, "I've been here six months, so I'm ready to be in charge," she changed the expectations communicated in the company's recruitment message to emphasize that new employees are expected to be in their first job one to two years, after which they might be considered for the next higher-level position, but not CEO (interview 2010).

"There is often no filter on what comes out of a Millennial's mouth," Beaudry reports, "so we conducted workshops on professionalism using clips from *The Office* to make it clear what was acceptable behavior." Still, the company gives their employees latitude in the use of social networks and smart phones, which ring constantly at their desks. The goal is to create a culture that reflects their employees' values while making clear to this very goal-oriented generation the importance of attaining the company's objectives.

The desire of Millennials to find solutions that work both for them and the company often make Boomers, who grew up in an us-versus-them environment, uncomfortable. NASA's Jet Propulsion Laboratory (JPL), which has mostly Boomers in its management ranks, found a way to bridge this particular generational divide by utilizing mentoring relationships focused on a common desire to advance the cause of space exploration.

JPL's director, Charles Elachi, authorized the establishment of the Phaeton program to respond to the organization's Millennial Generation employees' desire for a training opportunity to provide them a "valuable end-to-end experience," something that would normally take years to acquire. Neither the request nor the response was surprising. Ninety-five percent of Millennials rate the opportunity to collaborate with peers and have an impact on the organization at the top of their job characteristics wish list; less than half rate salaries and compensation highly (Institute of Politics 2010). Elachi's response was typical of his Boomer Generation, which often finds Millennials inspire them "to provide the visionary leadership organizations need" (N. Howe 2010b, 153).

Phaeton's program design assigned senior managers, mostly Boomers, to mentor those working on a specific project to make sure each one acquired the skills and knowledge needed to make the project a success at each stage of its progress. In addition, a senior program manager was assigned to supervise the overall program and charged with anticipating the challenges each group would face, and finding ways to mitigate the risk of a project failure through training and development. Again, the program design matched generational preferences perfectly. In line with their close relationships with their parents, 58 percent of Millennials look to Boomers, rather than Xers, for professional counsel. Despite the wide differences in rank and technological expertise, Boomers are happy to return the favor, with two-thirds reporting that Millennials look to them for advice (Hewlett, Sherbin, and Sumberg 2009). A senior engineer who mentored Phaeton participants called it "an amazing experience. . . . One particularly gratifying moment came when I was presented with a thank-you card containing a handwritten note from each member of the early career hire team" (Kwok 2010).

New hires talented enough to be selected to participate in the program are expected to spend 75 percent of their time on it, while still taking care of their regular assignments, a challenge they enthusiastically embraced. The camaraderie of Phaeton produced none of the stereotypical behaviors that Gen-Xers often ascribe to the generation (B. Riley interview 2010). The program's success in engaging and motivating JPL's Millennial workforce demonstrates the potential advantages that the generation can bring to any enterprise, including large government organizations with mission-critical work assignments, when the work environment is properly structured and managed.

NASA continues to explore the future of work, making it a critical component of its capacity to explore the universe. They created a proprietary intranet, Spacebook, for the use of NASA employees, which mimics the functionality of Facebook, and they use Sharepoint and other Web 2.0 technology to provide the tools for the collaboration NASA desires. Linda Cureton of NASA underlined the reason for these investments. "Their greatest value to NASA, is the ability to help us create a culture of engagement and collaboration that makes each individual employee much more effective" (Phillips 2010).

ACHIEVING ORGANIZATIONAL PROPRIOCEPTION

Millennial attitudes are pushing other public and private sector employers to utilize more trusting management styles and cultures that can unleash the creativity and innovation so crucial to creating a more sustainable pattern of economic growth. Most organizations, however, continue to struggle with the question of how much control they are willing to give up to gain a competitive edge and what type of changes in the nature of their work, and their relationship with their customers, they are willing to make to accommodate Millennial sensibilities.

For all of its cutting-edge use of social network technology, the Obama campaign explicitly refused to incorporate more democratic governing principles in its organizational design. Plouffe quotes Obama as saying, in the very beginning, "I like the Bush [campaign] model of a few people in a room making decisions who don't talk to the press about it" (Jamieson 2009, 51). The campaign explicitly rejected the notion, first put forward by Joe Trippi during Howard Dean's 2004 presidential campaign, to move strategic decision making to the volunteer edges of the campaign. "We wanted to control the campaign. We didn't want to outsource our efforts. We had the strategy, the goals, and the metrics" (ibid., 37). Or as Joe Rospars, the innovative new media director for the campaign, said succinctly, "The bottom up stuff needs to be enforced from the top down" (Scola 2009d).

But when the scope of the work expands, as it did for Barack Obama when he became president, no single person, no matter how gifted, can have more wisdom than the group, with its inherently greater understanding of specific conditions on the ground. As James Burke, author of *Connections*, made clear, "You can't separate location, situation, previous innovation, one's peers, and community from the process of invention. Such ideas . . . are usually created within the context of a community" (Kraft 2010).

Finding the right mix between providing strategic direction and encouraging learning and growth within an organization, while still providing workers the freedom they need to produce great outcomes, remains the biggest leadership challenge facing anyone seeking to harness the energy and enthusiasm of Millennials. The answer for all leaders is to use vision and values to provide a clear sense of direction for everyone in the organization while providing each person freedom to pursue their own aspirations within that context.

Tom Malone was correct in pointing to the importance of declines in the cost of communicating as a driver of more decentralized organizational structures; but his more important insight was how critical it is for any organization to respond to every individual's desire for freedom and flexibility in order to generate creativity and innovation. Although strategic direction must come from the top, work processes and behaviors need to embrace the bottom-up values of Millennials to inspire that generation's commitment to the organization's mission. Introducing more transparent, shared, and even visual technology will not by itself build trust. Instead, leaders in the Millennial era will need to learn how to create a culture that makes interacting with their organization, for both employees and customers, more of a cause than an economic necessity.

MAKING WORK MEANINGFUL

Millennials have a strong desire to find meaning in all their transactions, whether it is in buying an eco-friendly product or in agreeing to go to work for a particular company. Eighty-eight percent of Millennials rated the "opportunity to have an impact on the world" as an important consideration in choosing an employer (Institute of Politics 2010). That's why the State Department, the FBI, the Peace Corps, NASA, and Teach for America made up half of Millennial's top ten list of ideal employers in 2009 (N. Howe 2010b). This is a generational trait that goes well beyond the naiveté of youth. Bruce Tulgan, author of *Not Everyone Gets a Trophy*, points out that Millennials "are more idealistic than any other new youth cohort since the first wave of Boomers came of age in the 1960s." The same percentage (85%) of both Millennials and Boomers say it is important that their work makes a positive impact on the world; among Gen-Xers, agreement with this belief is ten points lower. Millennials are also "more concerned about the well-being of the planet, humankind, and their communities than older cohorts were in their twenties. They often look to values issues when they are considering a new job: Do they believe in the company's mission? Do they approve of how [it] does business?" (Tulgan 2009, 112).

As Asher Platts, a twenty-something Millennial, blogged on MCAmerica.org, "The ideal career path for me would be something that either is in the field of making the world a better place, where I can make ends meet simply by pursing my ethical interests—or a job with high enough pay, and flexible enough hours that allows me to make ends meet and do all the things that change the world for the better, but sadly pay nothing" (Platts 2010).

Bryan Guffey, writing on the same Web site, captured the important link between what an employer does and how it goes about doing it this way: "A job that allows me to have flexible work hours so I can continue to engage in my community, that supports my educational endeavors by investing in me, and one that creates a positive working environment by focusing on the quality of the work produced, not the number of hours it takes to produce it" (Guffey 2010).

Such attitudes will shift employment choices and purchasing decisions dramatically over the next decade. A 2010 Cone Cause Evolution Study found that 87 percent of eighteen-to-twenty-four-year-old Millennials considered the causes a company supported in deciding where to work, compared to less than 70 percent of the overall population. Similarly high percentages of the generation linked a company's commitment to a cause to their purchasing decisions and their willingness to recommend a company's brand to others. Almost every Millennial (85%) is likely or very likely to switch from one brand to another (price and quality being equal) if the second brand is associated with a good cause (Cone 2010).

The consulting firm Deloitte found that two-thirds of Millennials would prefer working for employers that allowed them to contribute their talent to nonprofits (N. Howe 2010b). The private sector struggles with this notion of time off for doing community service or of enfolding a purpose or cause into its corporate values statement and leadership vision. The origin of most nonprofits, however, enables them to offer Millennials an opportunity to bring meaning to their employment and consumer decisions without having to strain to make the connection. As Alex Steed, a Millennial teacher and activist, wrote in his blog, Millennials Changing America:

I know a lot of hard-working Millennials in the for-good and not-yet-fully-imagined sectors. From members of Gen Y who are helping to reinvent the nonprofit organization, as we know it, to those who are trying to reform the civic sectors, there are plenty of folks my age working hard to re-imagine and implement what America can look like. After all, having been weaned on that which we were, and living through the history that we just came through, I find it unsurprising that—on the whole—we're not particularly excited about working hard to maintain the same apparatus that gave us five-figure student debt, Enron, and September 11th. My mind—my friends—is on creating a marketplace and apparatus that does not yet exist. (Steed 2010)

This desire of Millennials to put societal goals at the center of an organization's mission has even changed curricula in graduate programs in the nation's leading business schools. For example, the University of Southern California's Marshall School of Business created a Society and Business Lab in response to the demands of its student body, more than 15 percent of whom applied to be a fellow in the program during its first year of operation. The lab's director, Adlai Wertman, says the goal is to teach students how to "optimize both the bottom line and the social mission" for any type of organization, whether it's a for-profit or non-profit enterprise or a hybrid of the two. "In the final analysis, businesses aren't just businesses; they're also people eager to connect with community" (Wertman 2008).

Pepsi's decision to forgo all advertising for the 2010 Super Bowl and use the money it saved to support nonprofit initiatives is a dramatic example of how the Millennial demand for meaning can generate a new hybrid organization. Each month, Pepsi accepted up to 1,000 applications for grants from individuals, nonprofits, or "pro-social businesses" ranging from $5,000 to $250,000 that could impact communities in the United States, making Pepsi a charitable foundation as well as a purveyor of soft drinks. Facebook users were allowed to vote each day for two weeks for up to ten of the submissions that qualified for consideration, and the money was awarded based on these accumulated online votes.

To win, nonprofits, such as myImpact.org, organized on campuses in behalf of their causes, using techniques first learned in the Obama campaign. These included giving out candy for signups and pushing out e-mails with just the right frequency and urgency to encourage supporters to vote for their causes. The Center for Progressive Leadership organized a group of sixteen progressive organizations that worked together in the September round of the Pepsi Refresh Everything contest, winning fourteen grants totaling $550,000 for the nonprofits involved. "Our strategy was entirely driven by online outreach and social media . . . and we ended up recruiting just over 40,000 people who joined the campaign" (Silverman e-mail 2010). The contest has delivered over $15 million to the winners, including $25,000 to myImpact.org, and significantly differentiated its sponsor in Millennials' minds as a company that was worth buying from and working for (Golden interview 2010).

Hybrids are often a way station along the path to an even more distinct future. Horseless carriages became automobiles and wireless phones morphed into mobile computing devices. Companies that incorporate cause marketing into their organization's culture may be just way stations on a journey to a truly different way of organizing economic activity. One glimpse of what a business model that fully integrates social entrepreneurship into a company's daily activities as others might in the future can be seen by visiting one of Millennials' favorite companies, TOMS Shoes.

In 2006, Blake Mycoskie was inspired by the impoverished, barefoot children he befriended while vacationing in Argentina to found a company that would give a new pair of shoes to a needy child for every pair it sold to a customer. He created a unique style of shoe modeled after the common slip-on style worn by workers and the poor throughout South America. Since then, his distinctive line of shoes has become so popular with Millennials that the company has been able to give away over one million pairs of shoes to children around the world.

The company's altruism is at the core of its very profitable performance. It does very little traditional advertising. Instead, it uses social networks to spread the word among Millennials about both its product and cause. The savings from this marketing approach are invested in the cost of the shoes it donates. In keeping with its focus on helping others, all costs are carefully controlled to maximize the money available to meet its "One for One" corporate commitment. TOMS Shoes' headquarters is a converted sound stage with plywood walled cubicles in Santa Monica, California. TOMS Shoes are manufactured in Argentina, Ethiopia, and China; its conference room is a painted picnic bench in the center of a small room surrounded by walls covered with visual inspiration for its next line of shoes. After their first full year of employment, each member of the company's mostly Millennial staff attends a Shoe Drop where they personally place shoes on children's feet. The company's culture permeates its product, its people, and its reputation among its devoted customers.

TOMS Shoes' business model is a template for how every business will need to operate in the future. Millennial entrepreneurs and employees will demand all commercial endeavors, regardless of their tax status, contribute to the improvement of society, not just the bottom line. If they are to move from today's hybrid initiatives to a complete transformation of corporate behavior, CEOs will need to learn the fundamentals of Millennial management and incorporate them into every aspect of a company's culture.

CONCLUSION

Just as Blake Mycoskie began his company with a vision and a set of values that reflected his passion, more and more leaders will find it critical to start their institution's transformation by communicating the vision and values of the organization to its customers and its employees. These two key strategic elements express what type of future the leader wishes to create and how those enrolled in achieving that vision are expected to behave on the journey to that alternative future. The message establishes a foundation of trust that is the key to innovation inside the organization and makes it possible to generate the level of customer loyalty needed for long-term success in the marketplace. When communicated visually, especially in video format, vision and values provide the organizational proprioception that enables every person working in a far-flung, very decentralized, loose hierarchy, if not a democracy, to stay on course in achieving an organization's vision. Well-communicated vision and values will also enable each customer or employee to respond enthusiastically to the experience of interacting with the organization. When corporations transform into institutions capable of igniting the enthusiasm of Millennials, all generations will benefit.

Nowhere is this transformation more needed than in America's educational institutions. Ready to lead the charge to make this happen is the same powerful force that shaped this country's newest civic generation—the parents of Millennials.

CHAPTER 9

Building Better Learning Communities

AMERICA'S EDUCATIONAL INSTITUTIONS are critical to the country's future, and are in dire need of transformation. How Millennials are educated, what they learn, and how much it costs to teach them will go a long way in determining the generation's and the country's success. Yet in almost every setting, from primary schools to college classrooms, the teaching strategies and technologies being employed hearken back to concepts from the beginning of the Industrial Age. The result is significant dissatisfaction with the cost and quality of education among Millennials and their parents, and a determination on the part of both to fix the problem for this generation and those that follow. In February 2010, Millennials cited education as the second most critical issue facing the nation, ranked only behind jobs and the economy. Forty-one percent considered the educational system in the United States to be good or excellent, while half considered it fair or poor. Unlike members of older generations, three-fourths of whom expressed satisfaction with the education they had personally received, only two-thirds of Millennials were willing to give their personal educational experience a passing grade. Fully 70 percent of the generation felt the biggest problems facing public education were a lack of money and the management and organization of the schools they attended (Winograd and Hais 2010a).

Fortunately, there is a unified theory of learning that can be applied to any student, at any level, which has demonstrated its ability to produce the type of educational outcomes Americans desire. The parents of Millennials and their allies are leading the way in creating the political will necessary to implement these changes and transform how we learn, before the United States falls hopelessly behind in the global competition for talent and skills.

President Obama's secretary of education Arne Duncan has said, "Education is the civil rights issue for our generation" (Duncan 2010); and President Obama told Congress, "if we want to win the future . . . then we also have to win the race to educate our kids" (B. Obama 2011). As in previous civic eras, improving America's knowledge and skills will be both a moral and an economic imperative in the Millennial era.

CIVIC ERAS ARE GOOD FOR EDUCATION AND VICE VERSA

Early in the nation's first civic era, Thomas Jefferson drafted the Land Ordinance of 1785, which set aside public lands to provide educational opportunities for all citizens. Jefferson and his congressional colleagues believed so deeply in the importance of this public policy to the young democracy's success that similar provisions were incorporated into the Northwest Ordinance of 1787. One section of land in every six-square-mile township in the five Midwestern states that had been carved out of the Northwest Territories was allocated for the purpose of financing "common schools." One-room schoolhouses soon sprouted across the new nation. The idea was so popular that two sections of land were reserved in California, in 1850, and four in some of the later Southwestern states. Jefferson's support for public education was grounded in his belief that "whenever the people are well-informed, they can be trusted with their own government" (Jefferson 1789). Some of the founders joined Jefferson in underlining the importance of an educated electorate to the proper functioning of democracy, while others, such as Dr. Benjamin Rush, argued that spending public funds on education was necessary for the functioning of the country's agricultural and manufacturing economy. The debate over whether education is an inherent good—a necessity for a well-functioning democracy—or a tool to advance the nation's economy continues to this day. But whatever the rationale, the expansion of educational opportunities has been a hallmark of civic-era public policy since the nation's founding (Goldin and Katz 2008).

Expanding educational opportunities remained a popular public policy even during the most divisive period of FUD the country has ever experienced. In the decade immediately preceding the Civil War, many New England states embraced the notion of free elementary education, along with policies that made attendance at those schools compulsory.

But it was not until 1871, as America's second fourth turning moved toward its final resolution, that every Northern and Western state eliminated the practice of requiring parents to contribute tuition, or "rate bills," to help pay for their children's common schooling. Compulsory attendance laws soon followed. During Reconstruction, this system of free and required elementary education was imposed upon the states of the Confederacy, as well (Goldin and Katz 2008, 142).

The transformation required an extraordinary intergenerational bargain. Older property owners, many of whose children were grown or had attended private schools, had to agree to pay for the education of the children of younger members of the local community. Prominent leaders, such as Horace Mann, argued for a system of free, compulsory education based on its potential economic benefit. But as the country emerged from the chaos of civil war with renewed enthusiasm for strengthening American democracy, the many state referenda that spurred the adoption of that policy also attest to the strength of the civic ethos that supported mass education. As a result of these initiatives, "by the middle of the nineteenth century, America had the most educated youth in the world" (Goldin and Katz 2008, 163). Other industrialized nations did not achieve the rates of elementary school enrollment that the United States enjoyed in 1860 until almost the turn of the nineteenth century.

Economics, more than civic engagement, drove the expansion and popularity of high school education in the early twentieth century. In 1870, only 10 percent of the labor force was employed in a job requiring more than an elementary school education; by 1920, more than a quarter of the jobs in the United States required a high school, if not college, diploma. While only 9 percent of eighteen-year-old Americans had graduated from high school in 1910, by 1940 half of the GI Generation, born between 1901 and 1924, had a high school diploma; and almost three-fourths of its members had at least enrolled in high school (Goldin and Katz 2008, 167). Males went from high school to the factory floor. Women graduated from high school in numbers equal to men and used their education as a ticket to an office job that provided higher wages, and more independence, than did working as a domestic. Just as the parents of Millennials are the driving force behind the transformation of today's schools, the rapid spread of publicly funded high schools across the nation, which began around 1890, was driven by parents of the civic G.I. Generation, who also wanted a better economic future for the children they adored.

STEALTH FIGHTER PARENTS

Unfortunately, the educational institutions that were so critical to America's success as an industrial power have failed to keep pace with the economic and technological changes that have swept the country since the first Millennials were born. High school dropout rates are far too high and those who do graduate, even with good grades, often find they are academically unprepared for the demands of higher educational institutions. These shortcomings have once again become the cause of the parents of an emerging civic generation.

One of the distinguishing characteristics of Millennials is the intense interest their parents take in every aspect of their children's lives, even after they leave home. College professors and employers have learned that the parent of a Millennial is just as likely to visit and complain about a grade or a performance evaluation given to a Millennial as is the recipient of the assessment. This desire to constantly hover over their children has earned the parents of Millennials the sobriquet "helicopter parents." The younger half of the Millennial Generation, primarily parented by members of Generation X, now constitutes the greatest portion of elementary and secondary school students. These Gen-X parents have replaced the tendency to hover and talk with a desire to take action and change bottom-line results. Boomer helicopter-parents have been transformed into Generation X "stealth fighter parents," whose fierce determination to ensure the success of their kids has put parents at the top of the list of teachers' professional problems every year since the turn of the twenty-first century (N. Howe 2010b). Nowhere is the new phenomenon more visible than in the budding parent revolution that is determined to transform the schools Millennials attend.

The co-founder of generational theory, Neil Howe, predicted that

"when Gen-X "security moms" and "committed dads" are fully roused, they will be even more attached, protective, and interventionist than Boomer [parents] ever were. . . . They will juggle schedules to monitor their kids' activities in person . . . [and] will quickly switch their kids into—or take them out of—any situation according to their assessment of their youngsters' interests. Gen Xers believe their children's education should be a fair and open transaction, with complete and accurate information and unconstrained consumer choice. (N. Howe 2010a)

In states as distinct and disparate as Connecticut and California, Howe's prediction is coming true.

This particular revolution began in Los Angeles, whose sprawling unified school district (LAUSD) has been a poster child for bureaucratic stubbornness and urban educational woes. Borrowing Clay Shirky's framework for online success, Ben Austin, a long-time advocate for kids, and his allies, started a Web site, parentrevolution.org, that proposed a bargain for parents willing to participate in a grassroots effort to improve individual schools. Without any understanding of how they would deliver at their end, the organizers promised that if half of the parents in a school-attendance district joined their cause, they would "give you a great school for your child to attend." When parents whose Millennial children attended a mostly Latino inner-city high school, and another group from a suburban, more upscale, middle school met the threshold, Austin went to the Los Angeles school district. He demanded that they either put the management of the school out to bid, or his organization would be forced to respond to the parents' demands by starting a charter school in competition with LAUSD's school.

Since each child has seven thousand dollars of potential state funding in his backpack, LAUSD agreed to Austin's demands. When 3,000 parents showed up to demonstrate their support of the concept, the school board voted 6–1 to adopt a policy mandating that competitive bids eventually be issued for the management of all 250 demonstrably failing schools, as defined by federal education law. With those successes in their pocket, the group was able to rally parents of all types, from every part of the state, to lobby for the same rights in their districts.

As part of its attempt to garner badly needed federal funds for the state's schools from President Obama's Race to the Top competitive grant process, California adopted "Parent Trigger" legislation in 2010, which embodied the bargain at the heart of the Los Angeles parent revolution (Blume 2009). Although the need for money was the impetus behind the legislature's consideration of the idea of a Parent Trigger, it was the grassroots organization, fueled by social networks and mommy blogs, that pushed the legislature into turning back pleas from their traditional union allies and enacting this earth-shattering reform.

At one point in the debate, the Democratic-controlled education committee in the California State Assembly agreed to water down the trigger provision in response to requests from its teachers unions' supporters. Under the committee's version, when a majority of parents in a school district signed a petition demanding a change in management, the district would have been obligated only to hold a hearing on the subject. The provision was so representative of the closed system that had made parents powerless in the past to influence the quality of the education their children received that it backfired when brought into the light of day. Austin posted a blog on the parent revolution Web site that was printed in California newspapers, as well. He used the vote as a prime example of why a real Parent Trigger was required. Democratic leaders in both houses quickly reversed their colleagues' decision when faced with thousands of parents asking legislators a simple question, "Why shouldn't parents get to decide what kind of school their kids go to?"

Austin believes it won't be long before the same rights are given to every parent in the country. As he points out, "the old coalitions don't apply here; it's a cause that unites parents from upper-middle-class and working-class backgrounds—white, black, and Latino alike" (interview 2010).

Bringing parents into the process of establishing successful learning environments represents the cutting edge of educational reform in this Millennial era. Our previous book, *Millennial Makeover*, predicted that stealth fighter parents would demand "models that produce superior results at lower costs and provide the aggregating mechanism for a new, decentralized, parent-controlled, educational decision-making system" (Winograd and Hais 2008, 260). When Hurricane Katrina wiped out the public school forces that might resist such reforms, the city of New Orleans took advantage of the opportunity to demonstrate how successful such a system might be.

Before Katrina, the city's schools were among the worst-performing and worst-managed in the country. So after the storm, rather than reopen these failing schools, the state created a Recovery School District

(RSD) and put all but sixteen of the city's schools under its jurisdiction. RSD schools were given the freedom to choose their educational approach, their teachers, and their principals, and to offer the resulting product to the parents of New Orleans's children in competition with other schools in the city. No student is assigned to an RSD school on the basis of geography, and any parents unhappy with their child's education can choose to send their child to a different school. The experiment attracted veteran educators and young Teach for America enthusiasts alike, with the various charter schools authorized by the district eventually enrolling over 60 percent of the city's student population (Murphy and Fausset 2010).

The results of the experiment demonstrate the potential power parents have to fix the nation's educational performance. The number of fourth graders passing the state's standardized tests has jumped from fewer than half in 2007 to two-thirds in 2010. Eighth grade test performance went up from 44 percent passing in 2007 to 58 percent in 2010. Almost half of the district's high school students meet the state's proficiency goals, a performance that is clearly not good enough, yet is still dramatically better than it was before parents were allowed to be a part of the process. The Brookings Institution found the system had demonstrated "sustained" academic growth despite the challenges of serving a student population that had an even higher proportion of low-income students, 84 percent, than before Katrina. When asked what about New Orleans was better since the hurricane, one out of four residents spontaneously answered "education" and 80 percent supported the concept of parents being able to send their child to any school in the city (Jacobs 2010).

The system New Orleans has instituted reflects the egalitarian and community orientation of a Millennial civic era and confirms a theory of how to build better learning communities that was first developed in California over a decade ago.

A UNIFIED THEORY OF LEARNING

In 1997, under the auspices of the Institute for a New California, a think tank devoted to changing California's governing institutions, educators, technologists, academics, and practitioners engaged in a year-long conversation on how to create "a society where all individuals fully participate in the development of their own and their community's learning potential" (Buffa 1997). The group's emphasis on learning, rather than education, enabled it to break through conventional thinking on the topic and establish a new framework for dealing with the problem. The framework's foundation is built on four insights gleaned from studies at the Institute for Research on Learning begun in 1986 in Silicon Valley:

- Learning takes place all the time.
- Learning is a process of friction between what we already know or believe and new experiences, people, or settings.
- Demands for learning never cease.
- The ability to know how to learn has become the most important type of learning.

On the basis of these understandings, the group developed a systemic view of how to create learning communities—usually called schools—that provide the necessary social context of interactivity, exploration, and discovery so real learning can take place. The group's theory suggested that the most successful schools would blend the four roles required for the community to function to the greatest degree possible. For example, those who contributed financial resources, or "payers" as the group defined the role, needed also to be involved as "policy makers" and help set the rules by which the community functioned. Similarly, when the role of "providers," usually thought of as teachers who delivered practices or lesson plans designed to improve learning, was sometimes played by "learners" or students, more effective learning took place as a result of the peer-to-peer interaction (Buffa 1997). A decade later, successful reforms in education, such as the increasing use of charter schools where providers ask parents to choose the unique educational policies they offer, and Parent Trigger legislation that places parents in the role of policy maker, have served to validate the unified learning theory's hypothesis.

The group also argued that "the most productive learning systems are built and sustained when the goals of the four domains [roles] are aligned through a process of consensus-building." When such an alignment around vision and values exists within a learning community, the school can reintegrate "the constituent parts of learning—subject matter expertise, pedagogy, and developmental aspects of the learner—into an effective learning environment." These ideas increased the responsibility and accountability of the learner, not just the provider or teacher, to be "an active agent in her or his learning." Finally, the system the group envisioned placed the role of technology "at the service of the new learning context, instead of the other way around" (Buffa 1997).

Although the unified theory of learning was developed in conversations overlooking the beautiful beaches, valleys, and mountains of California, entrepreneurial educators in some of the nation's toughest urban environments have been using its tenets to build learning communities that are producing the type of quantum improvements in results the report predicted. Examples of such successful learning communities include schools in the Harlem Children's Zone, charter schools in the New York area run by METSchools, Inc., and schools in cities across the country that are part of the Knowledge Is Power Program (KIPP) network. To fix the nation's educational challenges does not require inventing a new theory, but it does require leadership to implement what works in every learning community at every level of education in the country.

LEADING SUCCESSFUL
LEARNING COMMUNITIES

Doug Ross, the CEO of University Preparatory Academy in Detroit—more than 90 percent of whose urban, mostly poor, and African American students graduate high school and are accepted to college—is an example of the type of committed leader required to implement fundamental educational reforms throughout America. The former assistant secretary for education and training in President Clinton's Labor Department started his charter school in 2000 in the basement of a church, appropriately named "The Promise Land." His promise to the parents of the first 112 sixth-grade students who attended the new school that year was similar to the one Ben Austin made to Los Angeles parents: "Send your children to our school, and we will make sure that they graduate from high school and go on to post-secondary education." A decade later, his success in keeping that bargain has brought his program enough funding to support seven schools covering grades kindergarten through twelfth grade and enough interest among parents to more than fill each of them. The three key elements Ross identifies that make learning communities like his so successful—a culture of success built upon a common vision and set of values, effective teachers, and the use of data to drive performance improvements—are perfectly aligned with the principles of the unified theory of learning born in California (interview 2010).

Schools can create a culture of success by ensuring that parents, students, and teachers actively support a common vision and subscribe to the same set of values. For example, because all University Prep students are selected by lottery from a varied applicant pool, they bring a range of differing attitudes toward educational achievement into the student body. Each parent is interviewed and told about the school's vision and asked to sign a contract subscribing to its goals. But even when there is little or no parental involvement, as happens with at least one-third of University Prep's students, the school provides each student with an adult role model whose behavior reflects the school's values since, as Ross says, "our commitment is to the child." A teacher advisor stays with a group of sixteen students during every two or three years of their schooling, beginning in kindergarten and extending through high school. The mentoring continues after the student graduates from high school, with staff dedicated to providing advice and counsel to University Prep students as they experience what, for many, is the first college experience in their families. Thanks to the flexibility and commitment of its teachers, Ross's school pays for all the services within the same per-pupil resources provided by the state to regular public schools.

Creating a cultural change of the magnitude required to make a school successful becomes exponentially more difficult as the size of the learning community increases. So, although smaller size is not a magic bullet for educational reform, or even one of the key elements of success, the ability to limit the size of any given learning community clearly increases the chances of its success and the speed at which it can change its culture. At University Prep, class sizes range between sixteen and twenty-five students, and each of their communities, or school governing groups, is limited to 150 students, teachers, and administrators. In Ross's words, "This eliminates the problem of anonymity for everyone, but if you are doing the wrong thing, doing it on a smaller scale won't make things better" (interview 2010). To mold a learning community's culture, the leader needs to be able to personally reinforce behaviors that reflect the agreed-upon vision and values, and the smaller the learning community, the easier this is to do.

This need for constant personal intervention, however, creates major challenges in scaling successful models to the national level. Creating a cadre of school administrators capable of replicating proven models in more communities is an urgent, but unmet, national need. The magnitude and difficulty of the challenge suggests it won't be fully addressed until the size and unified beliefs of the Millennial Generation provide a sufficient number of new leaders dedicated to transforming the learning community in their neighborhoods.

GREAT TEACHERS ARE PRECIOUS

Developing teachers who know how to teach is the second key element required to transform America's schools. Studies have found that students learn best from teachers who have a unique type of subject-matter expertise, one enabling them to bridge the critical gap between what they know about the subject and what the student needs to understand at any given learning moment. Deborah Loewenberg Ball, dean of the University of Michigan's School of Education, and one of the nation's foremost experts on effective teaching, summarized the secret to success in this way, "Teaching depends on what other people [students] think, not what you think" (Green 2010).

Her research confirms the unified learning theory's insight that reconstituting subject-matter expertise, pedagogy, and the learner's developmental status into a new learning process can have a dramatic impact on the quality and quantity of what the student learns. Ball's approach has boosted performance in math for students from poorer socioeconomic backgrounds to the same level as students from middle-class families. Thomas Kane, a Harvard economist, has estimated that by figuring out what makes great teachers great and passing that knowledge on to the rest of the 3.7 million teachers in America today, "we could close the gap between the United States and Japan on international tests within two years, and ensure that the average classroom tomorrow was seeing the types of gains that the top quarter of our classrooms see today" (Green 2010).

The teacher who befriends and encourages the otherwise beaten and battered student in the eponymous movie *Precious* continuously demonstrates the skills needed to be a good teacher. She builds upon the slimmest glimmer of interest and ability in her student, teaching Precious what she is able to learn at the particular moment. She even exposes her student to a success-oriented culture where people "talk like folks on TV do," as Precious describes the experience. Eventually, her pupil learns enough to pass her GED exam and how to lead a productive life. Unfortunately, these critical teaching skills are just beginning to be assessed in school districts across the country.

Most of the attributes commonly associated with good teachers, such as completing graduate school, receiving a high score on the Scholastic Aptitude Test (SAT), possessing an extroverted personality, being polite or confident, exuding warmth and enthusiasm, or even passing the teacher-certification exam on the first try have not shown any ability to predict whether or not a teacher's students learn. This has led many reformers to suggest the best way to assess a teacher's skills and reward them accordingly is to base their evaluation on how much of the required curriculum at a particular level has been absorbed by the student. To eliminate any bias that might flow from the makeup of the student body in a given class, proponents of this idea suggest the rewards be based on each individual student's growth in educational proficiency as measured by standardized tests.

This so-called "value-added" approach became a hot topic of debate between the Obama administration, teachers unions, educators, and the media when the *Los Angeles Times* decided to post the value-added performance of every teacher in LAUSD online. A. J. Duffy, president of LAUSD's teachers union, voiced his objections in classic Boomer fashion, accusing the newspaper of reaching "the height of journalistic irresponsibility" by making public "these deeply flawed judgments about a teacher's effectiveness." But the 230,000 page views the information generated on the day the site went live suggested that Millennials' parents remained keenly interested in who was teaching their kids and how well those teachers were doing. Secretary Duncan suggested the real tragedy in Los Angeles "has been [that] teachers . . . desperately want this data and they've been denied it. It shouldn't take a newspaper to give it to them" (Song 2010).

As the controversy raged, Vielka McFarlane, head of the successful Celerity Charter School system in the heart of some of the city's poorest neighborhoods and a committed educational reformer, brought more of a Generation X approach to the concept. Her plan was to pay each of her teachers $25 for every step up on the state's proficiency exams each student was able to take in a year, and deduct $25 for each step backward. The bonuses were over and above the union scale wages Celerity teachers earned (McFarlane interview 2010). But even the strongest supporters of value-added assessments of teacher performance weren't arguing that improving test scores should be the only element in evaluating the teacher's skill in transmitting knowledge to students.

While its organizing rival, the National Education Association, continued to resist any linkage between student performance and teacher evaluation, the American Federation of Teachers (AFT) engaged in a Millennial-like, consensus-building effort to find solutions that worked for both teachers and schools. Pushed by the weight the Obama administration's competitive Race to the Top initiative placed on having performance evaluation agreements with unions in place as part of its evaluation of each state's grant application, school administrators began to negotiate with their AFT counterparts on systems that incorporated student performance outcomes in teacher evaluations.

Before her politically driven departure as chancellor of the District of Columbia's school district, Michelle Rhee negotiated a contract that raised the maximum pay of her AFT teachers to almost $150,000, in exchange for linking their pay to student learning performance. Even though her take-no-prisoners attitude when it came to improving student achievement, made famous in the documentary *Waiting for Superman*, often made her the national lightening rod for teacher unions' distrust of school administrators, she and her nemesis, AFT's president Randi Weingarten, were able to find common ground on the need to measure and reward outstanding performance by teachers. After two years of negotiations, the contract was approved by a four-to-one margin. To finance the pact, four private foundations agreed to supplement the district's budget with 64.5 million dollars in grants over three years. Under the path-breaking contract, those who score lowest in the evaluation process can be fired, and those who score highest can be given additional rewards (Rhee and Fenty 2010).

The AFT's willingness in this case to negotiate a process by which good teaching is rewarded—and bad teaching has consequences—made it more likely that the country will soon develop a consensus on how to ensure that good teachers, the second element of successful schools, are present in every learning community in the country.

Beyond good teachers and a culture of success, the management of each school also needs to learn how to improve their performance by using the data on student progress generated from tests. Educators could learn quite a bit about how to do that from some of their fellow public employees who deliver services that are equally valuable to the community, but who are not often thought of as role models by the educational establishment.

SCHOOLSTATS

The most successful experiment in using data to improve performance began in New York City, in 1994, when William Bratton became the city's police commissioner and was able to deliver on his promise to reduce crime by 40 percent within three years using a process he called "COMPSTATS" (Behn n.d). It captures computer-generated crime statistics to provide the data that become the focus of the shared learning experience in a police department, but the cultural change and performance improvements the process generates are far more important than the technology. COMPSTATS creates rapid and continuous information feedback loops to create a learning community among the participants, who quickly discover what works and what doesn't, to achieve a given objective.

The initial dialogue between Bratton and the New York Police Department's brass, when he first explained why the NYPD should be held accountable for the crime reductions he had promised Mayor Rudolph Giuliani, captures the essence of the cultural change that schools need to experience in order to become productive learning communities. Citing the FBI's national crime reports to push back on the concept, the Police Department's leadership team pointed out that since crime "is largely a societal problem which is beyond the control of the police," it was totally unfair to hold them accountable for reducing it (MacDonald 2010). In their opinion, since the police department was not responsible for the city's economic vitality, its housing stock, its school system, and certainly not its racial and ethnic tensions, it lacked the ability to actually reduce crime. When Bratton asked what the department was willing to be held accountable for, the leadership replied that they were prepared to accept responsibility for the "perception of crime in New York City" and that their existing tactics of high-profile drug busts, neighborhood sweeps, and the like were effective ways to manage that perception. Bratton adamantly refused to accept this definition of accountability. He created a system that not only placed accountability for crime reduction on the police department's leadership, but also drove that accountability down through the ranks of every precinct in the city and into the fabric of the department's culture.

Overall crime in New York City has dropped 77 percent since COMPSTATS was instituted, and homicide rates have fallen to the lowest level since reliable records were first kept in 1963 (MacDonald 2010). A rigorous analysis of crime data from the 1990s by criminologist Frank Zimring demonstrated that these results could not be explained by changes in imprisonment, demography, a lower birth rate due to the loosening of abortion laws under *Roe v. Wade*, or fluctuations in the economy in that timeframe (Zimring 2006). Zimring concluded that better management, particularly the introduction of the COMPSTATS process, was the key to New York's declining crime rates. "New York City had 75 percent less homicides, robberies, and thefts of autos in 2006 than it had in 1990, but essentially the same populations, schools, transportation, and economy" (Skolnick 2007).

Based on its success in reducing crime, state and local governments attempted to import the COMPSTATS concept to the delivery of other services, but without similar results, until they made the process less of a "gotcha" experience and more of a learning opportunity. For instance, departments in Los Angeles County, responsible for providing public social services, such as mental health or food stamps, spent more time in their STATS meetings educating managers and illuminating the alternative strategies for performance improvement, so that they could, in turn, explain and test the ideas with their staffs. But once this cultural adjustment was made, the results were equally dramatic. Within six to nine months, departments were achieving objectives long considered unattainable and were becoming models for similar, but much smaller, departments in government agencies across the country (Altmayer 2006).

These demonstrated examples of improved performance caused some urban school districts to import the process under the general rubric of SchoolStats. Although school officials have collected data for decades, in SchoolStats, as with COMPSTATS, the information is broken down into unusual detail and presented in elaborate charts and graphs, so those summoned to SchoolStats meetings can look for problems or trends by school, or by grade, or by classroom, that are not evident in routine reports. In Paterson, New Jersey, data is updated every three to five weeks using "relentless follow-up," according to Michael Kanarek, who plans the district's meetings. For instance, when that district's SchoolStats process looked at classroom instruction, it started keeping tabs on the number of visits by support staff, who are required to go to schools three times a week to assist in improving the instructional skills of its teachers. SchoolStats' analyses allowed the district to determine if the standard was being met; and, if not, why not; and, if so, what impact it might actually be having on student learning (Hu 2007).

Although some of the reactions from those whose performance was being tracked by SchoolStats were reminiscent of Bratton's first conversation with NYPD's precinct captains, the comments of Brenda Patterson, one of the assistant superintendants who was being held accountable under the new system, reflects the power SchoolStats has to change the culture and, therefore, the performance of schools as well. "Who wants to sit among colleagues and not know the answer? You may leave there [SchoolStats meeting] feeling uncomfortable, but you also get a direction." Just as Al Gore's taskforce on reinventing government spread the word about COMPSTATS, leading foundations are funding efforts to spread the adoption of this new way of learning to urban schools throughout the country (Hu 2007).

The results from early adopters of the process suggest that it holds great promise for improving student performance. The Montgomery County, Maryland, school district's Office of Accountability generates detailed SchoolStats data for each of its 139,000 students. Patterns that lead to failing grades trigger alarms from principals to teachers, who determine what intervention is required. Since implementing SchoolStats, 90 percent of the district's kindergarten students passed the basic reading proficiency assessment tests; in five years, fifth grade reading proficiency rose from the mid-50 percent range for minority students to 85 percent, almost completely closing the gap with white students; and the number of minority high school students passing at least one Advanced Placement Test quintupled. Secretary Duncan hopes that Montgomery County's data-driven system will become "the norm, not the exception" in districts across the country (Hechinger 2009).

In order to dramatically improve the performance of all of the nation's schools, the collection and examination of data on the performance of each teacher's students by the collective leadership of the school needs to be consistent with the vision and values of the learning community. Otherwise, school districts are likely to fall into the trap of Boomer ideological debates that fail to distinguish between responsibility and accountability. For instance, Florida's former Republican governor Charlie Crist vetoed a bill passed by the state's Republican legislature that would have linked teachers' pay to their students' learning and taken tenure and teaching certificates away from teachers whose students failed to learn. In that instance, both teachers and school administrators argued that such an approach would hold teachers "responsible for factors in students' lives beyond their control." Echoing words spoken by NYPD's brass almost two decades ago, one second-grade teacher said, "I am not a puppet master; I can't pull strings and make them perform. I can't even make them come to school" (Gabriel and Tave 2010).

The parents of Millennials are tired of these Boomer debates about who is responsible for the current state of their children's education. They want schools to take whatever action is needed to improve their child's learning performance. Bratton's COMPSTATS initiative points to a way out of the argument by clearly distinguishing what educators are not responsible for from what they should nevertheless be held accountable for. SchoolStats, deployed as part of a success-based educational model, gives school administrators another tool to use to fulfill their obligations to assess the potential of each teacher to become a great teacher, and to reward progress toward that goal. It is also very much aligned with Millennials' attitudes toward privacy and accountability.

Most of the newest teachers in the nation's schools are Millennials, a generation famous for its lack of interest in protecting personal information. While Boomers prefer to be judged by who they are on the inside, Millennials' preference for being judged by what they do on the outside is pushing schools toward a much more public discussion of performance data than many older teachers are comfortable having (N. Howe 2010b). In Celerity's schools, for example, results are posted by name by the door of each classroom, using red, yellow, or green to denote which students passed the previous week's tests. Rather than being intimidated by such an approach, the school's Millennial students rally to help any classmate whose performance was below the target. The idea is in line with Celerity leader McFarlane's belief that "No one believes you are serious [about using data] until you do something about it" (interview 2010). Furthermore, SchoolStats has the potential to draw the Gen-X parents of Millennials deeper into the learning community's decision-making process by providing the type of data and objective information about both student and teacher performance that this bottom line–oriented generation desires.

CONCLUSION

The irresistible force driving the transformation of America's educational institutions is parents, especially when they are empowered to be payers who are allowed to choose which learning community's policies they wish to support on the basis of its alignment with their vision of educational excellence and a set of values that places the future of their Millennial offspring first. As their children become learners and interact with teachers, who will have acquired new skills on how best to educate each student, parents will also become learners and providers. As a result, the national community will continue to register improvements in performance as more committed leaders continue to employ the principles of the unified theory of learning in their institutions.

Already the intense focus on education characteristic of civic eras is having an effect on student performance. In 2005, the average Millennial's SAT score was higher than in any year since 1973, when Boomers were taking the test. According to the National Assessment of Educational Progress (NAEP), math scores for ages nine and thirteen are the highest they have ever been. That's a better performance than Millennials have registered in reading, however, where scores have risen for age nine but have held steady for all other ages. More encouraging, the achievement gap for minorities has been narrowing as black and Latino students register greater improvements than their white counterparts (N. Howe 2010b).

Most Millennials, however, want to go beyond high school and acquire a degree or certificate from an institution of higher learning. Furthermore, the need to learn is no longer limited by age, location, or work status. It will become a lifelong process. In the civic era ahead, the parents of Millennials, and Millennials when they become parents, will create a demand for more and better learning communities that will transform institutions of higher education, as well as how all Americans learn throughout their lives.

CHAPTER 10

Taking Higher Education Higher

MILLENNIALS ARE CONVINCED that college is the ticket to a better life. Ninety percent of high school students say they want to get some sort of additional education when they graduate, and two-thirds enroll in a two- or four-year college within a year of completing high school. Twelve percent of eighteen-to-twenty-four-year-olds were enrolled in a two-year college in 2008, and 28 percent at four-year colleges. When trade schools, or for-profit career colleges, are included along with apprenticeships, almost 60 percent of this age group are seeking a credential of some type, a percentage never attained by any previous generation (N. Howe 2010b).

Unfortunately, the percentage of students who actually graduate from America's institutions of higher learning has been stagnant for the last thirty years. Currently, more than a quarter of the freshmen in America's four-year colleges fail to return for their second year, and the percentage is twice that number for those enrolled in two-year colleges. For every ten students who start high school, only five enroll in a post-secondary educational institution, and fewer than three complete a bachelor's degree—even after ten years (Kazis, Vargas, and Hoffman 2004, 3). Fewer than one-quarter of Hispanics who start college leave with a bachelor's degree, and almost two-thirds receive no credential at all (Boston Globe 2010).

In 2003, a conference of over 450 policy makers, practitioners, and researchers issued a call to double the numbers of Millennials from low-income and minority families who earn a postsecondary credential by 2020 (Kazis, Vargas, and Hoffman 2004). Seven years after that initial conference, the leaders of hundreds of community colleges signed a pledge to boost student completion rates to 50 percent. Achieving this goal would certainly represent a major improvement from present performance. Currently, only about 23 percent of community college students get a certificate within three years of entering college, and only 40 percent eventually complete their education. But the challenge of improving postsecondary education outcomes calls for much more transformative change than most educators may be willing to embrace (Banchero 2010).

Few college and university leaders are willing even to acknowledge the scale and scope of the changes required. Many argue that there is nothing wrong with the institutions they lead that more money wouldn't fix. For example, in 2009 the heads of three levels of California's higher education system said the state's master plan for postsecondary education, adopted in 1960, didn't "need structural changes, just a stronger commitment from the state to fund it" (Hemmilia 2009). Ignoring all of the technological and societal change that has occurred in the intervening fifty years, those college and university leaders had no vision other than to serve the institutional interests of the existing structure, and no values other than money.

The disastrously high number of students who drop out of college and fail to get a degree or certificate of completion is caused primarily by the inadequate levels of preparation for college they receive in high school, along with the financial burdens of trying to pay for a college education whose costs are escalating at rates comparable to those of health care (Jacobson and Mokher 2009). Millennials who had dropped out of college told survey researchers in 2009 that they did so because they couldn't afford it, had to work full time, and were not able to receive any help from their family to deal with the cost and time of staying in school (N. Howe 2010b) Pressure from Millennials' parents is pushing high schools to deal with the problem of inadequate preparation; but similar pressures, from parents and policy makers alike, will be needed to alter the current trajectory of price and performance in the country's system of higher education.

The best way to offer an alternative future to America's most educationally motivated generation is for everyone involved in education to give up their institutional silos and work across boundaries to reform the entire system. Organizing colleges and universities in line with the same unified theory of learning whose validity has been demonstrated in elementary and secondary education reform efforts across the country offers a framework for reform that will help ensure that students actually complete their postsecondary education. Developing a new national consensus on the value of a college education would permit educators, payers, learners, and policy makers to more fully integrate their roles and produce a system of higher education that costs less and graduates more productive citizens. Introducing Millennial-era technologies to serve these new institutional structures, as the unified theory of learning also suggests, is crucial. Taking this cross-institutional, comprehensive course of action would be the best way to "restore a balance between the costs and availability of educational services needed by our society and the resources available to support those services" (Duderstadt, Atkins, and Van Houweling 2002, 120).

In the long run, the recalcitrance of higher education bureaucrats to change their ways will be no match for the parents of Millennials, who will take the lead in demanding that their children receive the level and quality of education required for them to be successful. Those leaders who harness that parental energy to create alternative postsecondary educational futures for Millennials will reap the benefits of the changes they bring about.

Higher Education Needs to Get Its Civic Subsidy Back

As America emerged from the crises of the Great Depression and World War II, early in its third civic era, the country was confident enough of its future to embark on a major expansion of mass public education. In his 1944 State of the Union address, Franklin D. Roosevelt proposed an Economic Bill of Rights, including the right to a good education, and asked Congress to implement it. The subsequent legislation, officially named the Serviceman's Readjustment Act but almost always referred to as the GI Bill of Rights, funded an explosion in college attendance that continues to this day.

Whereas only about 25 percent of Americans had attended college by age thirty in 1930, over 60 percent had done so by 1970. Only 10 percent of Americans born in 1900 attended college; by contrast, half the Baby Boomers born in 1950 did. The resulting influx of student tuition was accompanied by a massive increase in research grants to universities, which began with the passage of the National Defense Education Act, in

1964, as America's previous civic era was coming to a close. That infusion of money from both student tuition and government grants provided the fuel that enabled America's system of higher education to become the finest in the world by the end of the century (Goldin and Katz 2008).

Unfortunately, the public's willingness to support the system declined dramatically during the idealist era from 1968 until the financial system's collapse in 2008. As incomes stagnated and state governments cut their support of higher education even further during the Great Recession, colleges and universities were forced to raise tuition even more to cover their escalating costs. As a result, since 1980 college tuition rates have grown at 3.3 times the consumer price index. Tuition rates for both public and private four-year colleges are now about 350 percent greater in real dollars than they were when the last Boomers were born (N. Howe 2010b). Not surprisingly, in 2010, Millennials ranked the cost of a college education as one of the top four issues they wanted the federal government to address (Winograd and Hais 2010a).

This increased cost is having a direct impact on which colleges students are able to attend. Forty-three percent of incoming freshmen in the first year of the Great Recession cited the ability to get financial aid as very important or essential in their choice of college, the highest level ever recorded (Pryor et al. 2010). In 2009, 70 percent of high schools reported an increase in the number of students who had abandoned the school of their dreams in favor of a college they could afford. Eighty-five percent of those who applied for aid said they wouldn't be able to pay for college without it (Block 2009). As a result, for the 2008–2009 school year, the federal government guaranteed or made $65.2 billion in student loans, an increase of 18.6 percent from the year before (Tomsho 2009). More than 62 percent of incoming college freshmen in 2010 said that the bad economy had influenced their decision on which school to attend, causing more of them to abandon their first choice and attend a school closer to home, with 17 percent deciding live at home to reduce the cost of their college education (Lipka 2011).

The unwillingness of today's older generations to subsidize the higher education of younger generations has had a particularly pernicious impact on those who see a college education as a way of improving their future economic circumstances. In 2007–2008, just about every student coming from a low-income family and attending a community college was in debt, with an average of $7,147 in unmet expenses even after taking into account any grants or scholarships they received. As a result, three-fourths of those seeking an associate degree or certificate were forced to work, leaving less time for study. Indeed, at the beginning of this civic era, only 38 percent of community college students earned a degree within six years of enrolling (Jacobson and Mokher 2009).

In order for higher education to fulfill the American dream of upward mobility in the future as it has in the past, a much greater commitment in support of its economic and social value will have to be made by elected officials at all levels of government. The Millennial Generation's civic activism and belief in the value of a college education creates a political environment that will be supportive of such initiatives. One city, made famous by the Glenn Miller orchestra toward the beginning of the last civic era, is already demonstrating the benefits such a promise can bring to communities throughout the country.

AMERICA'S PROMISE LIVES IN KALAMAZOO

Today's college graduates earn, on average, 70 percent more than high school graduates, which is twice as great a gap as that of the 1980s (Kazis, Vargas, and Hoffman 2004, 2). Those who earn an associate degree at a community college earn 27 percent more than those who fail to receive a degree of any kind. Those with a certificate, if even for only one year of post–high school education, still earn, on average, 8 percent more per year than those who failed to complete their postsecondary education (Jacobson and Mokher 2009).

To produce a better-educated, higher-earning populace as part of an overall economic development strategy, some communities are testing the impact on attendance and graduation rates of guaranteeing a free public postsecondary education to students who complete high school. In 2005, a small group of donors (who remain anonymous to this day) created the Kalamazoo Promise, which offered any graduate of the city's public schools a four-year scholarship covering all tuition and mandatory fees at any of Michigan's public colleges or universities, provided those students maintained a 2.0 grade point average in their college courses and made regular progress toward a degree. Scholarship levels varied based only upon the number of grades or years in Kalamazoo schools the student had attended, not on a determination of need or merit (Miller-Adams 2009).

The idea was born out the need to find a way to halt a decline in the city's revenues. The city manager suggested the imposition of an income tax on those who worked inside Kalamazoo's boundaries in order to balance the city's books. In an attempt to increase the tax base without raising taxes, community leaders, instead, asked residents of the area surrounding the city what would persuade them to move back into the city. Not surprisingly, the parents of Millennials expressed the greatest interest in living in a place that would provide a good public education for their children—all the way through college. Local philanthropists translated that desire into a simple program that offered full, four-year college scholarships to the city's high school graduates, with no requirement to repay the money or to reside in Kalamazoo after graduation from college. They bet the bargain would be enough to attract families back to Kalamazoo and to halt the annual 10 percent decline in the city's public school population. Five years and over $21 million later, the bet has paid off handsomely (Kitchens interview 2010).

Since the program was announced in November 2005, Kalamazoo has seen a 17.6 percent enrollment increase in its student population, and the construction of three new schools for the first time in thirty-seven years. Dropout rates have been cut in half. Ninety percent of Kalamazoo's female African American high school graduates have gone onto college. The school district's success was even noticed by President Obama, who chose to deliver the first high school commencement speech of his presidency at Kalamazoo Central High. Calling the school a model for success in the twenty-first century, Obama told the senior class he was there "because I think America has a lot to learn from Kalamazoo Central about what makes a successful school in this new century" (J. Montgomery 2010).

The community's detailed tracking of the program's progress has identified 1,600 students whose families say they are in Kalamazoo because of the Promise (Kitchens interview 2010). In direct testament to the program's strategic success, the proportion of residential construction permits issued within the district rose sharply from around 30 percent of all of those issued in the Kalamazoo area to nearly 50 percent (Miller-Adams 2009).

The Kalamazoo Promise created an expectation on the part of most residents that every public school student in the city would have an opportunity to receive a postsecondary education (Miron, Jones, and Young 2009). And the cultural shift created by the community's commitment to the vision and values of the Kalamazoo Promise has also created a mini-Race to the Top with surrounding school districts, which are passing bond issues and improving their schools to compete more effectively with Kalamazoo's schools.

It is still too early to tell, however, if the lack of any financial burden for the almost 2,000 Kalamazoo Millennials who have received scholarships so far will lead more of them to graduate from college. More than 80 percent of those who chose to enroll in a university are still attending college, but the enrollment of those who elected to go to a community college has declined from 50 percent in the first year, to the same one-out-of-four performance after three years of most other community college students (Miller-Adams 2009). Funding to pay for four years of college is available to each recipient for up to ten years after high school graduation, so it may take more time before the full effect of the Kalamazoo Promise on college graduation rates can be determined.

Nevertheless, the program's initial success has led communities across the country to search for sources of philanthropic revenue in order to make their own educational bargain with their residents (Kitchens interview 2010). Just as previous civic eras witnessed the expansion of universal educational expectations beyond elementary school to high school, this civic era will witness the emergence of a national consensus that every young American should complete a postsecondary education and graduate debt free. Eventually, Kalamazoo's promise will become America's promise.

A LEARN GRANT ACT FOR THE MILLENNIAL ERA

Federal and state governments already offer programs that support individuals wanting to go to college through tax-favored savings programs, direct grants, and tuition subsidies. Unfortunately, as the higher education commission report of President George W. Bush's secretary of education Margaret Spellings found, "a very significant fraction of public funds . . . go primarily to benefit affluent students with modest economic needs, at a time when close to a quarter of Americans are disproportionately and severely deprived of higher education opportunities" (U.S. Department of Education 2006).

During the last two decades of the idealist era, Boomer presidents George W. Bush and Bill Clinton both supported policies that attempted to deal with this problem by expanding the availability of student loans, which monetized the future income stream a college degree provided, essentially borrowing a student's future earnings to pay for current tuition costs (Winograd and Buffa 1996, 219). That policy approach proved disastrous when the economy crashed in 2008. Millennial college students were left with heavy debt loads and no immediate prospects for jobs that would provide sufficient income to pay off their loans. Ideas to create government-subsidized Individual Education Accounts, funded by capping public support for colleges and universities at current levels, failed to gain traction as the country entered a civic era, with its greater focus on economic equality and collective initiatives. In order to address this problem, in 2010 Congress, following President Obama's lead, eliminated the federal subsidy that went to banks making student loans and used most of the savings to increase the amount of grants and tuition aid available to students.

All of these ideas fall short of the sweeping public policy changes in education that the country has adopted in prior civic eras. The centrality of an educated populace to the nation's economic well-being and its democratic vitality calls for a new social contract for higher education that reflects the country's emerging civic ethos.

As a few visionary educators have suggested, it is time for a "Learn Grant Act for the Twenty-first Century," deliberately modeled after the Land Grant Acts of the Civil War fourth turning. That nineteenth-century program, which created many leading public universities, especially in the Midwest, linked federal and state government investments in new higher education institutions to a commitment by such colleges to broaden educational opportunities for the working class. Echoing the dual justifications for robust public funding of education of earlier eras, Learn Grant Act proponents argue it is time to create "a social contract aimed at providing the knowledge and the educated citizens necessary for prosperity, security and social well being in this new age" (Duderstadt, Atkins, and Van Houweling 2002, 255). But, as in the mid-nineteenth century, such government largesse would only be given to colleges and universities willing to commit to transforming the cost and quality of the education they offered. Just as the Obama administration has done with its Race to the Top initiative to spur reform in the nation's elementary and high schools, the Learn Grant Act in this civic era would provide incentives only to those institutions of higher learning that embrace both the values of Millennials and the technologies Millennials use most often, in order to deliver learning experiences that will last a lifetime.

Envisioning Higher Education in a Millennial Era

Millennial era colleges and universities will need to be redesigned to "create learning communities and to introduce students into these communities" (Duderstadt 2000, 230). Consistent with the unified theory of learning and Millennials' values, distinctions between learner and teacher will become blurred. Students will co-design and even co-instruct courses, since sharing the knowledge among peers provides the best context for learning. To prove mastery of a skill or topic, students will produce new simulations or author Web sites, and these work products will be assessed not only by faculty but also by their fellow students, to capture the value of the contribution to the larger team or learning community.

The authors of *Higher Education in the Digital Age* describe the radically different role of the faculty in such environments in this way: "Faculty members of the twenty-first-century university will find it necessary to set aside their roles as teachers and instead become designers of learning experiences, processes, and environments. . . . They may be asked to develop collective learning experiences in which students work together and learn together, with the faculty member becoming more of a consultant or a coach than a teacher" (Duderstadt, Atkins, and Van Houweling 2002, 65).

To continue to attract students in an increasingly virtual world, physical campuses will need to find new ways to serve the learning community. Apple, for instance, envisions higher education learning communities where students use high-speed, mobile devices to connect to large databases containing all the educational resources the student requires—except for the human interaction with peers and mentors that will occur on campus (Duderstadt interview 2010). In order to continue to attract students, twenty-first century universities will also find it advantageous to deploy technology on their campuses that will create augmented reality opportunities in intelligent physical spaces, thereby providing feedback to students on their smart phones as they interact with their environment, making the entire campus a learning lab (Dede 2005).

To act as a transformative catalyst of the nation's universities, civic era governments may well require universities to provide their students, and society in general, with increased access to the ideas, or intellectual property, that they generate as part of a new social contract for Learn Grant universities. Graduates, under this concept, would retain a lifelong membership in the learning community from which they received their academic credentials. As a condition of their government funding, universities would be asked to offer students whatever learning resources they require throughout their lives, and, through new information technologies, wherever they may live. Government funds for research would also come with more civic-oriented ties attached, requiring that the discoveries resulting from university-based research be placed in the public domain and that faculty who work on such projects partner with the private sector in ways that serve societal needs (Duderstadt, Atkins, and Van Houweling 2002, 256).

The main impetus for these changes in higher education, however, will come not from government but from Millennials, either as students or, later in the century, as parents and policy makers. They will want to take the responsibility for the acquisition of lifelong learning into their own hands, mashing-up or combining, as Millennials do with their favorite music, whatever resources are available to suit their individual needs. John Seely Brown and fellow futurist Paul Duguid have suggested how such a learner-centered conception of higher education might evolve. In their model, students select the type of "Degree-Granting Body" (DGB) they find most desirable and design an educational experience that draws upon a variety of faculty expertise and learning environments. Faculty, acting as independent contractors, would affiliate with various DGBs and campuses and be paid on the basis of the number of students they attract and the research grants they win. In the course of their lives, the learner's DGB would issue credentials that attest to whatever skill or knowledge level they had achieved, based on a port-folio of work and academic accomplishments (Brown and Duguid 1996). This model "is a radical departure from the traditional view of schooling with its emphasis on individual knowledge and performance and the expectation that students will acquire the same body of knowl-edge at the same time" (Beilaczyc and Collins 1999).

James Duderstadt, president emeritus of the University of Michigan, and one of the leading voices for transformative change in higher educa-tion, underlines the difficulty of introducing such deep change in exist-ing institutions of higher learning. "The challenge . . . is neither financial nor organizational; it is the degree of cultural change required. We must transform a set of rigid habits of thought and organization that are inca-pable of responding to changes rapidly or radically enough" (Duderstadt 2000, 269).

As a result, colleges willing to place this twenty-first-century under-standing of teaching and learning at the core of their business model are more likely to emerge from outside the existing postsecondary structure, just as charter schools began as experiments that did not involve tradi-tional public schools. As these new institutions grow by offering a more cost-efficient and effective learning experience for students, they will become increasingly popular among Millennials and their parents. Eventually, every campus environment will need to change in response to these competitive pressures, resulting in twenty-first-century higher education institutions as different as the land grant colleges of the nine-teenth century were from the elite Ivy League universities that were already well established when the United States became an independent nation in the eighteenth century.

Playing Serious Games

The use of digital media and online communication by Millennials has become their most distinguishing characteristic. The need to con-stantly stay in touch with each other through social networks and smart phones, whatever else they may be doing, has caused some to suggest that Millennials' ability to multitask represents a new stage in the evolution of the human brain. Although their neurons and synapses are probably not wired any differently than those of previous generations, Millennials have learned how to cope with, and even thrive upon, the vast increase in the amount of information that washes over them daily. They tag and store interesting bits of information in each data stream, so that it can be retrieved with search-engine efficiency when it needs to be processed.

Attracting Millennials and their offspring with these habits will require institutions of higher learning to embrace the technologies Millennials love to use and adapt their pedagogy accordingly. Millennials' digitally native brains will not sit still for hours at a time listening to traditional lectures that convey text-based information. As one member of the generation pointed out, "If you want to encounter distance learning, sit in the back of a 500 seat lecture" (Parry 2010). The physics department at MIT abandoned this approach in favor of a hands-on, interactive collaborative learning environment in their freshman courses and saw attendance soar and failure rates drop by more than 50 percent (Rimer 2009). To create, preserve, integrate, transmit, and apply knowledge, as they have in previous centuries, universities in the twenty-first century will have to use new, more visually intensive and immersive media and online communication.

Millennials think in images more than in words. Their increased exposure to visual media, from video games to YouTube, is considered by many to be the reason that visual IQ scores have gone up at twice the rate of verbal IQ scores over the last two decades (Greenfield 1997). Eighty-two percent of Millennial teenagers play video games and more than half of them do so online (D. Riley 2009). The University of Southern California's Institute for Creative Technologies produces virtual humans, computer training simulations, and immersive experiences, using interactive digital media technologies borrowed from the gaming and movie industry, to train members of the armed forces. As one retired admiral explained, "The video game generation learns very quickly. The typical young PackBot [robot] operator just needs about a day and a half of training to get down the basics. Much like with their gaming, they then need only a few weeks after that to figure out all the moves and reach expert level" (Singer 2009, 365).

In her path-breaking ethnographic study of the way Millennials live and learn, Mimi Ito and her colleagues identified three distinct levels of commitment and intensity in the generation's interactions with new media. The first, which she called "hanging out," is a friendship-driven genre of participation that includes social networks such as MySpace or

Facebook, as well as instant and/or text messaging. The second level she called "messing around" because of its exploratory nature. At this level, Millennials take an interest in the technology itself and produce mash-ups and other creative products. The most intense level, which she called "geeking out," is primarily found among hard core gamers and producers of original content (Ito et al. 2009).

The last two, interest-driven, levels of interaction described by Ito involve the type of trial-and-error learning that complexity economics suggests will produce the most innovative and valuable types of information. Complex ecosystems and modern economies continuously adapt and grow through a process of rewarding what works and discarding what doesn't. More trials, including more errors, produce better results. In school settings, virtual, multilevel games, which require testing a player's skills at one level before advancing to another, avoid the cost of learner errors, while providing students a chance to engage in multiple trials in simulated environments. Adopting this Millennial epistemology to the way postsecondary education is delivered is the best way to develop the creative adults America's economy will need to retain its global competitiveness.

Millennials and their parents have already demonstrated an affinity for online education at the high school level. Online delivery uses individual customization to raise the quality of education while lowering its costs, leading some to predict that half of all high school courses in the United States will be consumed over the Internet by the end of this decade (Christensen, Johnson, and Horn 2008, 88–89). The Khan Academy, a treasure trove of more than 1,400 free YouTube lectures covering individual topics in math and science, reaches one million high school and college students a month, who watch over 40,000 videos per day to help them better understand the material they are taught in school. Their system provides immediate feedback on proficiency and gives step-by-step explanations of every problem (Khan 2010). The greatest growth in online education in the future, however, will take place at the college level, which is not limited to serving a specific geographic area or physical campus, or constrained by the need to provide daytime adult supervision of its students.

Over two million college students in the United States are enrolled in online courses, with the number expected to double by 2014.

Twenty-five percent of all postsecondary students in 2008 were enrolled in at least one online course ("Online Learning" 2010). The University of Phoenix, which has four times the enrollment in virtual courses of any of its nearest competitors, has a student body of almost one-half million, greater than all of the Big Ten schools put together (N. Howe 2010b). Thanks to its highly structured courses, formatted for the student's convenience, and taught by "professionals who teach," Phoenix's enrollment is growing at 20 percent per year (Duderstadt, Atkins, and Van Houweling 2002, 127).

For all of their popularity, most online postsecondary educational offerings represent a hybrid solution to the problem of lowering cost and raising educational quality. Online college courses cost less to deliver because they use the Internet to transport video lectures and analog learning materials wherever and whenever the student may want to receive them, without heavy investments in brick-and-mortar facilities or tenured faculty. The learning that flows from such interactions, however, is not always up to the level that a more personal, but costly, educational experience can bring. But by engaging students in the type of interactive, immersive experiences that digital technologies make possible, and that movies such as *Avatar* make familiar, colleges can provide both a more effective learning experience and deliver it at a lower cost.

When postsecondary students are exposed to comprehensive, realistic experiences that produce a sense of being immersed in the action, studies have shown a very positive effect on the skill and performance of the student in subsequent, analogous real-world situations. Nothing in traditional teaching methodologies approaches the power of this type of situated learning, which combines knowing, or "learning about," with doing, or "learning to be" (Thomas and Brown 2009). "Whereas schools largely sequester students from one another and from the outside world, games bring people together, competitively and cooperatively. . . . In schools, students largely work alone with school-sanctioned materials; avid gamers seek out news sites . . . participate in discussion forums, and most importantly, become critical consumers of information" (Shaffer et al. 2004).

Beyond the acquisition of particular skills, playing serious games has been shown to have positive effects on the individual's or group's identity. "Reflecting on and refining an individual identity is often a significant issue for higher education students of all ages, and learning to evolve group and organizational identity is a crucial skill in enabling innovation and in adapting to shifting contexts" (Dede 2005). The experience of play enables what learning theorist John Seely Brown terms "learning to become" and generates the level of interest and commitment that Ito described as "geeking out."

The introduction of serious, online games into the world of higher education enables the establishment of distributed Millennial era learning communities, where everyone is involved in a collective effort, whether in person or in virtual environments. Such communities make it possible for students to continue to learn throughout their lives, "orchestrating the contributions of many knowledge sources embedded in real-world settings outside of school" (Dede 2005). Institutions of higher learning that put this technology at the service of a new model of education that integrates the roles of learners, providers, payers, and policy makers will create powerful alumni networks that span the globe and last a lifetime. These learning communities will be this civic era's contribution to the constant expansion of educational opportunities that have been a hallmark of the nation's public policy since America's founding. A fully transformed learning system of lifelong, free, public education will, once again, become the foundation for the nation's political and economic success.

CONCLUSION

The current civic era began with the collapse of the previous idealist era's economy, one built on the irrational exuberance and values of the Baby Boomer Generation. In his inaugural address, President Barack Obama suggested that, in order to build a more stable economic foundation, it was time for a new era of responsibility—one more in line with Millennials' values of collective action. Two years later, he told Congress innovation and education were two key priorities in assuring America's ability to retain its global economic leadership. Nurturing a complex economy back to health, however, will require learning what works through a series of experiments that create an environment of trust in which creativity and innovation can flourish. Apart from the need for an immediate response to the economic crisis facing the country, the long-term health of the economy requires finding new ways to work and learn that constantly enrich the country's store of knowledge.

The Millennial Generation's unique perspective has already begun to change the focus of the nation's economic activity. Corporate organizations and educational institutions are feeling the pressure to respond to this change and are searching for ways to imbue their daily routines with civic purpose and meaning in order to attract the full energy and enthusiasm of Millennials. Leaders able to envision alternative futures that align with the beliefs and behaviors of Millennials will further transform these critical sectors of our society beyond the hybrid, halting, first steps often celebrated today. Such acts of courageous leadership will produce the heroes of this civic era.

As Millennials learn and mature, the heat from the friction between the emerging generation and the experiences, people, and settings Millennials encounter along the way will throw new light on how to change and strengthen most aspects of American society. Millennials will influence not only how the nation works and learns but also every facet of daily life. From how we get our information to what music we listen to, from where we live to how we serve our community, from how we play sports to how we relate to the world, Millennials will remake American society in their image. The result will be a country more committed than ever to its founding principles, even as its institutions are reshaped to reflect the values of the Millennial Generation.

PART FOUR

Changing the Way Americans Live

Chapter 11

Millennial Family Lifestyles

The economic circumstances and educational expe-
riences of Millennials have had a profound effect on the generation's
attitudes about where they want to live and the type of families they want
to raise as they become adults. Their fundamental beliefs about religion,
marriage, and child rearing will play an important part in how Millennials
shape America's social institutions for at least the next half-century.

During the course of the next fifteen years, the youngest Millennials
will join their twenty-something siblings in young adulthood. Civic
generations, like the Millennial Generation, have historically entered this
phase of life just as the country has been faced with a major crisis; and
their heroic, team-oriented behavior has been called upon to help the
nation overcome its challenges (Strauss and Howe 1997). But coming of
age during a time of crisis has also tested the faith of civic generations and
impacted their ability to enjoy the quiet pleasures of family life, often
requiring their members to postpone marriage and child-rearing until
societal and economic circumstances make it practical for them to do so.
This same fate seems to await America's newest civic generation; but as
with many of their other circumstances, Millennials appear to be dealing
with these challenges in the distinctive and optimistic way of their own
and other civic generations.

Love and Marriage, Millennial Style

From 1920 to 1940, when members of the GI Generation, America's
previous civic generation, were about the age that Millennials are today,
the median age for a first marriage was 24.4 for males and 21.3 for
females. In 1945, the frequency of teenagers marrying and giving birth
fell to only 11 percent of all marriages and births. By contrast, in the
1950s and 1960s the median age for first marriages dropped to 22.8 for

males and 20.3 for females, when first the Silent Generation and then Boomers were in their twenties and thirties. By 1965, 18 percent of marriages and births involved a teenager.

Beginning in the late 1980s, as Gen-Xers reached their teens and twenties, the age of first marriages rose once again, and the number of teenage marriage and births began to fall, trends that accelerated in the first decade of the twenty-first century, as Millennials became teens and young adults. In the 1990s, the median age for male first marriages was 26.5 and for females, 24.5. By 2007, the median age for first marriages was 27.7 for males and 26 for females. In 2005, teens constituted only 10 percent of those getting married and giving birth, a level not seen since the 1930s and 1940s when the GI Generation was young.

These changes in the timing of family formation also influenced how each generation dealt with issues of procreation and abortion. Teen pregnancy and birth rates rose by more than 20 percent from the time the last Baby Boomers entered their teens in the early 1970s, to the early 1990s, when the greatest number of Gen-Xers were teenagers. Rates then declined by more than 35 percent from that peak until the years right after 2000, when the first wave of Millennials entered high school. Over the same period, the teenage abortion rate more than doubled, and then fell by 50 percent as Millennials reached their teen years. Abortion rates for Millennial teenagers did rise slightly in 2006 and 2007, although they never came close to where they had been when Boomers and Xers were teens, and they began to decline again in 2008 (Guttmacher Institute 2010).

Despite these positive trends, many older adults worried that the generation's "failure to launch," to quote the title of a popular movie, represented a disturbing new social phenomenon with supposedly dire consequences for the generation's ultimate ability to succeed in life. Robin Marantz Henig, writing for the *New York Times*, suggested that there was a traditional American life cycle requiring "an orderly progression . . . kids finish school, grow up, start careers, make a family and eventually retire to live on pensions supported by the next crop of kids," which seemed "to have gone off course" with many young people "forestalling the beginning of adult life" (Henig 2010). However, the elongation of youth she observed is actually a recurring characteristic of civic generations, resulting from their protected and structured upbringing as well as from the major societal crises that seem invariably to arise when civic generations emerge into adulthood.

Early in the twentieth century, psychologist G. Stanley Hall coined the term "adolescence" to describe a new life stage that seemed to delay the passage of youth into adulthood. Henig indicates that Psychologist Jeffrey Jensen Arnett is currently leading a movement to view one's twenties as a distinct life stage, which he calls "emerging adulthood" (Henig 2010). Both concepts were developed at points in U.S. history when members of a civic generation were becoming adolescents or emerging as adults.

Although civic generations may marry and start families later than the generations that precede them, it does not mean that they care less about such things. In *The Best Years of Our Lives*, an Academy Award–winning film of 1947 that portrayed the efforts of demobilized servicemen to piece together their lives after World War II, one of the returning GIs expressed the hope that peacetime would bring him "a good job, a mild future, and a little house big enough for me and my wife." Most Millennials appear to want the same thing.

Ashleigh Rainko, a blogger on *The Next Great Generation* (*TNGG*) Web site, while noticing that, like her, many of her friends in their early twenties weren't married, made it clear that fact doesn't represent a rejection of the institution by her generation. "Our evolution lies in our ability to stand out as a group of unique individuals, each progressing at his or her own pace, deciding an appropriate marriage age—if we ever decide to get married, that is. We disregard any stereotypes and marital expectations, and it's okay" (Rainko 2010). And in a finding that should give great comfort to older adults worrying about the future of American families, a Pew survey found that the two most important priorities of Millennials were being a good parent (52%) and having a successful marriage (30%), attitudes almost identical to those of older generations (Pew 2010a).

MODERN FAMILIES AND PARENTHOOD

Although most Millennials want to marry and have children, the families they will form will not look and behave like the families of previous generations because of their vastly different demographics, as well as their very different attitudes toward all things sexual. These differences are already visible enough to be captured in new family sitcoms, whose popularity reflects how the country perceives itself and what it aspires to be.

When Baby Boomers were growing up in the 1950s, TV families, such as the Andersons in *Father Knows Best*, the Cleavers in *Leave It to Beaver*, and the Nelsons in *The Adventures of Ozzie and Harriet*, were invariably white, upper middle-class, and residents of small towns or suburbs. The family unit consisted of a GI Generation father who worked in an office, a wise, warm stay-at-home mom, and sometimes mischievous, but basically good children. From the 1960s, and into the early 1980s, the years during which the often-scorned and neglected Generation X grew up, family sitcoms dropped in popularity, along with society's appreciation for the institution of marriage. Those that did air either portrayed a single mother struggling to hold her family together in a society with changing values (*One Day at a Time* and *Alice*) or completely dysfunctional and unappealing families (*Married . . . With Children*) (Winograd and Hais 2008).

In the mid-1980s and 1990s, the parents of Millennial children created a demand for a different type of family comedy show that celebrated the families they were raising and provided guidance on the best way to take on the challenges of child-rearing. As in the 1950s, these early Millennial era sitcoms portrayed intact families, consisting of a husband/father, wife/mother, and as many as four children. But there were important differences. Both partners were busy, high achievers in their work outside the home, and active, nurturing parents within it. And, although African Americans had been central characters in a number of sitcoms over the years, for the first time ever, black parents (Cliff and Clair Huxtable in *The Cosby Show*) served as a role models, demonstrating by example for their enthusiastic audiences the right way to raise kids.

Today, as members of the Millennial Generation begin to marry and raise families of their own, the style and tone of the genre is changing once again to reflect the demographics and values of the generation. Today's popular sitcoms, *Modern Family* and *Parenthood*, accurately portray the ethnically diverse, socially tolerant, attitudes of the generation. Both programs feature multigenerational and multiethnic families headed by Boomers who are resisting the inevitable aging process, even as they attempt to embrace the societal changes their children and grandchildren are driving.

In the hit show *Modern Family*, the patriarch, Jay Pritchett, is the father of two Gen Xers by a previous marriage. One, a daughter, is a conventional, homemaker mom raising three children with her husband, whose traditional attitudes are a source of constant irritation to Jay's Boomer-rebellious spirit. The other child is a gay man, who is raising an adopted Vietnamese baby with his partner. Meanwhile, Jay has remarried a much younger Colombian immigrant, whose smart and sensitive Millennial son from her own first marriage provides the wisest advice to the rest of the family in each episode. While the show's incorporation of communication technologies and self-analysis into its storyline makes each episode feel fresh and modern, perhaps its clearest reflection of the current, or indeed any other, civic era's attitudes, is its focus on emotionally satisfying endings that usually resolve all problems with a big familial hug (Wadler 2011).

The male head of the *Parenthood* family is Zeek Braverman, a liberal Boomer who has flitted between careers and causes, to the dismay of his artistically inclined and former flower child wife, Camille. Their Millennial grandchildren are the focus of their four Generation X children's lives, with the resulting portrait capturing the spectrum of intergenerational family life in the Millennial era. The oldest male portrays the dutiful son, desperately trying to build a conventional family life for himself and even for his siblings. The length to which Generation X parents will go to preserve their family is tested when the eldest's son is diagnosed with Asperger's Syndrome. One of Zeek's Gen-X daughters is a woman whose career focus and need for control cause friction with her stay-at-home-dad husband, even as they both profess undying love and devotion to their daughter. The other daughter is a single mother who returns to her parents' home to raise her Millennial son and daughter. Her children's increasing maturation only underlines the vast differences in achievement and ambition between the two of them and their Gen X mother. The youngest child, Crosby, is an unmarried male who finds new meaning in life when his African American lover turns up and informs him that he is the father of her son, Jabbar. Like children in other Millennial era movies and TV shows, Jabbar becomes the source of strength, stability, and inspiration for the interracial couple.

These family settings would have been shocking and bizarre to TV viewers during the childhoods of Boomers in the 1950s, Xers in the

1970s, or even Millennials in the 1990s. However, adult Millennials express little concern about the current trends in family life these shows portray. Most Millennials (59%) do not approve of single women deciding to have children. Even so, Millennials were less likely to condemn single parenting than the Silent Generation (72%) and Boomers (65%). Beyond this, fewer than half of all Millennials had a problem with gay couples raising children (32%), mothers of young children working outside the home (23%), couples living together without getting married (22%), and interracial marriage (5%). By contrast, a majority of the Silent Generation, and a plurality of Boomers, disapproved of gay couples raising children and unmarried couples living together. Significant percentages of both older generations also rejected the idea of mothers working outside the home. A substantial percentage of Silents (26%) also continued to resist interracial marriage (Pew 2010a). Modern families and parenthood will have an entire different look as the Millennial Generation establishes its own families and begins to raise children.

MILLENNIALS' HEARTS
ARE IN THE SUBURBS

In his autobiographical film *Avalon*, director Barry Levinson, a member of the Silent Generation, captured what he believed to be the impact of America's suburban exodus on his large and fractious family. He suggested that the weakening of the ties that bound his previously close-knit family was due to its dispersal to the suburbs, rather than to the social upheavals of the 1960s that he captured so well in the other two films in his Baltimore trilogy, *Diner* and *Liberty Heights*. From 1940 to 1960, the percentage of Americans living in suburbs doubled, from 15 to 30 percent. In the 1970s, racial tensions and the general deterioration of central cities pushed more Americans into the suburbs. By 1970, a plurality (38%) of Americans already lived in the suburbs, and by 1980, 45 percent did so. In 2000, around the time that the last members of the Millennial Generation were born, fully half of all Americans were living either in older suburbs or the new exurbs beyond them (Winograd and Hais 2008).

But the weakening of family ties, as measured by such social indicators as rising teenage crime and pregnancy rates that Levinson deplored, had more to do with the cycle of generational archetypes than did the place where Americans chose to raise a family. Now, the very same generational forces that pulled American families apart in the late 1960s and 1970s are about to return full circle to the attitudes and beliefs of a civic era very much like those that prevailed in the 1950s and early 1960s, the golden years of Barry Levinson's memories.

Millennials generally lack the animus against the suburbs that has been a major element of Baby Boomer urbanist ideology over the past few decades. Forty-three percent of Millennials describe suburbs as their ideal place to live. This dwarfs the 17 percent of Millennials that want to live in a big city and the 34 percent that favor living in either a small town or in the country. The generation's preference for suburban living is well above the preferences of older Americans. Only 36 percent of Gen-Xers, 28 percent of Boomers, and 29 percent of Silents prefer to live in the suburbs. A majority of older generations (56%) express a preference for small town or rural living, but these locations are cited by only 34 percent of Millennials as their preferred places to live (Winograd and Hais 2010a).

Millennial Generation preferences are likely to determine the outcome of the hottest debate about the future direction of U.S. urban development currently raging between Toronto-based, "cool city" advocate, Richard Florida, and Joel Kotkin, author of *The Next One Hundred Million*. Florida argues that future development in the United States will occur primarily in ultra-urban mega regions along the Atlantic and Pacific coasts where Americans will live in dense, multifamily housing within walking distance of work, shopping, and entertainment. His vision depends on the notion that young people will flock to urban environments because of a city's capacity to generate greater opportunities for social interaction and creativity.

Although Kotkin does not think that America's largest cities will completely wither and die, he believes that the greatest number of Americans will continue to reside in less densely populated suburbs, either around the coastal cities or in emerging areas in the center of the country. He sees these suburban settings as centers of economic growth, permitting their residents to work near where they live with all the amenities required to raise a family in a safe neighborhood with good schools. He maintains that the desire for homeownership is a part of the American ethos stretching back to the beginning of the country, and that it remains a goal for most Americans.

A *National Journal* article detailing the debate neatly captured the lifestyle and thinking of many young people and suggests that Kotkin's predictions are more likely to be right in the long run than Florida's. The article describes Matthew Brown, a graphic designer born on the cusp of the generational shift from Gen-X to Millennial, who rents an apartment in downtown Seattle, lives without a car, and walks to work, shops, and entertainment. His reasons for choosing this lifestyle sound as if he were channeling Florida. "I like living where there are buildings and things to do, restaurants and shops . . . I kind of like the busyness of the city." However, when Brown contemplates the future his thoughts reinforce Kotkin's predictions. "In the back of my mind, my plan when I'm ready to purchase something is to move into more of a neighborhood. I don't see myself when I'm married and living with children . . . living right here" (Hamilton 2010).

Perhaps the Millennial Generation's preference for suburban living stems from the fact that a majority (54%) of the cohort currently lives in suburban America and loves the family settings in which they have grown up. By contrast, in 1978, when Boomers were about the same age as Millennials are now, only 41 percent lived in the suburbs and many rebelled at the conformist lifestyles they experienced in that setting. Less than one-third of the Silent Generation lived in suburbs when it was young. The fact that most Millennials now reside in the suburbs may also explain why, contrary to Florida's expectations and preferred housing policies, few of them are particularly anxious to be renters any longer than is absolutely necessary. Fully 64 percent of them said it was very important to have an opportunity to own their own home. In fact, 20 percent of adult Millennials named owning a home as one of their most important priorities in life, right behind being a good parent and having a successful marriage (Pew 2010a).

The family orientation of the Millennial Generation will also reinforce the continued growth of America's suburbs. During the 1960s and 1970s, Boomers moved as far away as they could from their parents' homes in order to find themselves and express their own unique values. In the 1980s and 1990s, Gen-Xers often reacted to their relatively unloving upbringings by rejecting every aspect of their childhood, including suburban living. But Millennials actually like and respect their parents and are interested in living nearby, if not in the same household. Two-thirds of Millennials, in contrast to about half of Boomers, and one-third of Silents, believe it is a responsibility of adult children to allow an elderly parent to live with them (Pew 2010a). As a consequence, the number of senior citizens living with adult children increased by more than 50 percent in the first seven years of this decade, and there is no sign that the trend is abating. The growth of multigenerational households in the future will recreate another common feature of GI Generation childhoods (Kotkin 2010b).

Single-family dwellings with a surrounding patch of land continue to attract families of every background to the nation's suburbs, a reflection of the increasing diversity of Millennials' families. Slightly more than half of African Americans (51%) now live in large metropolitan suburbs, as do 59 percent of Hispanics, almost 62 percent of Asian Americans, and 78 percent of non-Hispanic whites. Los Angeles, for instance, which is often decried by nonresidents as simply an aggregation of suburbs with no central core, has a suburban population whose demographic profile almost exactly matches the city's population (Frey 2010). Without much fanfare, the country is getting closer than ever before to achieving a goal that many thought would never be achieved: city/suburban racial/ethnic integration, in an environment of increased tolerance inspired by Millennials' beliefs.

Barry Levinson's experience growing up with his extended family in a tight-knit urban, ethnic neighborhood will never return, but the suburban tilt of America's future lifestyle does not mean that communities sharing the joys of family and friends that Levinson longed for will become extinct. Instead, this time, most Americans will share that experience, not in central city ethnic enclaves but in suburbs or urban communities of moderate density with houses located conveniently to their work—if not actually in their Internet-wired homes. Where and how Millennials choose to live and raise their families will be the single most important force in shaping housing patterns over the next two decades. The return to Avalon will occur, in large part due to the family orientation of America's emerging civic Millennial Generation and its desire to enhance the communities that it has come to know and love.

BOYS ARE BOYS AND GIRLS ARE GIRLS . . .
OR ARE THEY?

Historically, civic generations have tended to emphasize distinctions between the sexes. In the past, it has been the role of idealist generations to advance the cause of women's rights. This includes the Transcendentalists who founded the feminist movement in the 1840s, the Missionary Generation suffragists in the early twentieth century, and the Boomers who revitalized the women's movement in the 1960s. By comparison, the eighteenth-century civic Republican Generation "began leading America toward much wider sex-role distinctions . . . having proved themselves 'men' to their beloved fathers, rising Republicans associated 'effeminacy' with corruption and disruptive passion, 'manliness' with reason and disinterested virtue" (Strauss and Howe 1991, 178).

In the twentieth century, "GI's came of age preferring crisp sex-role definitions. Raised under the influence of the strongly pro-feminist [Missionary Generation], GI's matured into a father-worshiping and heavily male-fixated generation" (Strauss and Howe 1991, 264). During World War II, as most GI Generation men went into the military, many women went to work in America's factories and on its farms, assuming jobs traditionally held by males. But at war's end, willingly or unwillingly, Rosie the Riveter and most of her sisters returned to their traditional roles as wives and mothers.

Although "no generation of American women can match the GI's for the intensity of the nurture they provided their mostly Boomer children" (Strauss and Howe 1991, 305), the parenting style of GI Generation fathers was strong, silent, and distant. In fact, many believe that the rebelliousness of Boomers in the 1960s was, in large part, a reaction against their psychologically removed fathers. The "Consciousness Revolution . . . began within families as a revolt against fathers. Older Americans who studied young radicals in the late 1960s were struck by their attachment to mothers and their 'ambivalence,' 'oedipal rebellion,' or attitude of 'patricide' toward male authority" (ibid., 302).

No such attitudes can be found among Millennial children, whose upbringing by their fully involved father and mother has helped to blur perceptions of different roles based upon a person's sex. Even as Millennial men strive to define the correct way to behave in this new environment, most of today's Millennial women are happily refusing to accept any restrictions on what they might be allowed to do, based upon their gender. The result has been vastly improved educational and income opportunities for women and a greater demand for the ability to blend work with the rest of life's responsibilities and pleasures, from both sexes.

An income gap between women and men still remains, but it has narrowed significantly. In 2010, across all occupations, women earned an average of 78 percent of what men did, compared to 60 percent in 1980. Furthermore, among urban-based Millennials, there are indications that the income gender gap has almost entirely disappeared. In some major markets, childless Millennial women in their twenties earned on average 16 percent more than men of the same age (Luscombe 2010).

Although the civic GI Generation was notable for providing equal opportunities for women and men to attend high school, the Millennial Generation is the first in American history in which women are more likely to attend and graduate from college and professional school than are men. In 2006, nearly 58 percent of college students were women. Once in college, women seem to accomplish more than men. Department of Education statistics indicate that "men, whatever their race or socio-economic group, are less likely to get bachelor's degrees. . . . Men also get worse grades than women. And, in two national studies, college men reported that they studied less and socialized more than their female classmates." In the 2005–2006 school year, women earned 63 percent of associate's degrees, 58 percent of bachelor's degrees, 60 percent of master's degrees, and 49 percent of doctorates awarded in the United States. By 2016, they are projected to earn 64 percent of associate's degrees, 60 percent of bachelor's degrees, 63 percent of master's degrees, and 56 percent of doctorates (Lewin 2006).

These achievements have produced a generation of self-confident women who, unlike many of their Boomer mothers and grandmothers, do not see themselves in conflict or competition with men. Jen Kalaidis, posting on the *TNGG* Web site, clearly expressed this new Millennial feminism: "Today's women were raised to believe we were equal to men, but we didn't have to try to *be* them to prove it. We play sports, go to college, start businesses, have babies, and travel the world *on our own terms*. We aren't constantly trying to out-man the boys, play for play" (Kalaidis 2010).

All of this female success has led some male Millennials to rethink the entire concept of masculinity. Two of them, Andrew Romano and Tony Dokoupil, issued a call for "a New Macho: a reimagining of what men should be expected to do in the two realms, home and work, that have always defined their worth" (Romano and Dokoupil 2010, 44). These two Millennials expect to see greater participation in housework and child rearing from the males of their generation than by earlier generations of men. They believe Millennial fathers will take greater advantage of paternity-leave opportunities to bond with their newborn children and support the mothers of those children, especially once such benefits are mandated by law. Remarkably, in sharp distinction to the usual partisan rancor during this period of FUD, polls show that "majorities of Republicans (62%), Democrats (92%), and independents (71%) now support the idea of paid paternity leave" (ibid., 46).The federal budget already includes money to help states start paternity-leave programs. Eventually, as part of the overall Millennial era approach of establishing national standards to empower individual action, a paid paternity and maternity leave program will become an employee-funded insurance program, similar to Social Security, which could be financed by a small payroll tax increase of about three-tenths of one percent.

The biggest changes for American men in the years ahead will come in the workplace. Economic necessity will force young men to consider, train for, and work in a range of careers that have been hitherto seen as woman's work:

> Of the 15.3 million new jobs projected to sprout up over the next decade, the vast majority will come in fields that currently attract more women than men . . . men dominate only two of the 12 job titles expected to grow the most between 2008 and 2018: construction worker and accountant . . . the social sector of the economy will gain 6.9 million jobs by 2018. But unless the complexion of the workforce changes . . . a whopping 2.5 million of them will go unfilled. The coming employment gap represents a huge opportunity for working class guys—and the families they're struggling to support. (Romano and Dokoupil 2010, 47)

Reflecting their Millennial Generation's beliefs, Romano and Dokoupil take issue with "skeptics who argue that men are 'designed' for some gigs and not for others. . . . women long ago proved that gender essentialism doesn't determine what kind of work they can do. Today women still serve as teachers, nurses, and social workers. But they're also CEOs, soldiers, and secretaries of state. The time has come for a similar expansion of what men can do for a living. . . . The percentage of nurses who are men has doubled over the past 25 years and more men are teaching elementary school than ever" (Romano and Dokoupil 2010, 48).

As the blurring of occupational gender distinctions occurs, Millennials will demand that employers provide opportunities for more work-life blending, as opposed to requests for balance so often expressed by Gen-Xers. Ryan Healy, a Millennial who blogs about his generation's experience in the workplace, argues that "I would never dream of saying I want a Family/Life balance or I want a Friend/Life balance. . . . This whole notion of needing to separate work and life implies that your career, which takes up 75 percent of your day, is something you simply try to get through so you can go home and do what you really enjoy for the other 25 percent. . . . I don't want to choose. I want a blended life" (Healy 2007). With both parents fully involved in both careers and families, employers who wish to attract top talent will have no other choice but to accommodate the generation's demand for such things as telecommuting, flexible hours, child care, and round-the-clock access to technology to create a seamless blend between working and raising a family. The result will be a new national consensus on what it means to be a man and a new respect for the full participation of both sexes in all aspects of American family life.

FAITH IN THE MILLENNIAL ERA

Millennial families will also redefine the role religion plays in their lives, increasing the rich diversity of the nation's faiths and beliefs. The vast majority of Americans believe in God in numbers that range from two-thirds to 80 percent, depending on the precise manner in which the question is posed. Millennials share this belief with other generations. Two-thirds of them (64%) are absolutely certain of God's existence, and large majorities also say they believe in life after death (75%), heaven (74%), hell (62%), miracles (78%), and angels and demons (67%). Fifty-nine percent agree with the idea that the Bible is at least a reflection of the word of God, if not the literal truth, a percentage only slightly lower than that of older Americans (Pew 2010a).

Although the large majority of the Millennials, therefore, could be described as spiritual or believers, the members of the generation are significantly less likely than older Americans to be members of a specific religious faith and to participate in traditional religious rituals. In fact, 72 percent of them describe themselves as "more spiritual than religious" (Grossman 2010). About one in five Millennials (18%) have moved away from the denominations of their childhood and are completely unaffiliated with any traditional faith; one-quarter of all Millennials are currently unaffiliated with any denomination (Pew 2010a). Some might argue that the lack of commitment to a religious faith stems simply from the skepticism of youth. In fact, however, Millennials are twice as likely to be unaffiliated as were Boomers in the 1970s, when the members of that cohort were young adults. Millennials are also one-and-one-half times more likely to be unattached to a religious denomination than Gen-Xers were in the 1990s, when they were the same age as today's Millennial Generation. Millennials are also less likely than older generations to attend religious services weekly (33%), or to read Scripture, pray, and meditate regularly (Pew 2010a).

Of particular political significance, the Millennial Generation, as with other civic generations before it, is more tolerant, and less driven by the cultural issues that have divided the United States in eras dominated by idealist generations. In the first three decades of the twentieth century, the country split along religious and geographic lines in heated arguments over women's right to vote, Prohibition, and the theory of evolution. Led by the civic GI Generation, concern with those issues receded in the 1930s and virtually disappeared for the next four decades, only to rise to prominence again during the last forty years. Millennials are likely to end these arguments in much the same way that the GI Generation did eighty years ago, by taking a live-and-let-live approach and rejecting more orthodox and doctrinal beliefs.

Nearly two-thirds (63%) of all Millennials, and 58 percent of Millennials who are affiliated with a specific religious denomination, believe that homosexuality should be accepted by society. This compares with 47 percent of all older Americans and 35 percent of members of the senior citizen Silent Generation. Similarly, a majority (55%) of all

Millennials and a plurality of the religiously affiliated members of the generation (49%), as compared with 47 percent of older Americans and one-quarter of Evangelical Protestants, believe that evolution is the best explanation for human life. Finally, only one-third of all Millennials and 36 percent of religiously affiliated Millennials agree that Hollywood and the entertainment industry are threats to American values. This is well under the percentage for older generations (44%) (Pew 2010a).

In the end, however, perhaps the biggest impact that the Millennial Generation will have on the country's religious landscape is to increase its diversity and expand the definition of what faiths are recognized as part of America's civic ethos. For most of its history, America was considered to be a Christian nation, and more specifically, Protestant. While other faiths were tolerated in the spirit of the First Amendment, the essential Americanism of Catholics and Jews was occasionally questioned. Within the past several decades, however, the description of what constituted the nation's religious mainstream was broadened and encapsulated in the phrase, Judeo-Christian. While to some this may seem like a subtle or cosmetic change, to those who listened to or still remembered the anti-Semitic screeds of Gerald L. K. Smith, Father Charles Coughlin, and Charles A. Lindbergh during America's most recent previous period of fear, uncertainty, and doubt, it was profound.

Just as the inclusive civic GI Generation spearheaded the expansion of America's religious mainstream in the twentieth century, the civic Millennial Generation will do the same in the twenty-first. Millennials are not only the most ethnically diverse generation in U.S. history; they are also the most religiously diverse. Only two-thirds of Millennials (68%) are Christian, as compared to at least 80 percent of all older generations. Fewer than half of Millennials (43%) are Protestant, in contrast to 53 percent of older Americans and almost two-thirds of the Silent Generation. At the same time, buoyed by the growth of America's Hispanic population, the percentage of Millennials who are Catholic is almost identical to that of older generations, while the number of non-Christian Millennials of all denominations is one-third larger (Pew 2010a).

The nation's religious diversity is likely to increase in coming years, as greater numbers of Americans choose spouses across denominational lines. The percentage of mixed-faith marriages rose from 15 percent in

1988 to 25 percent in 2006. The American Religious Identification Survey of 2001 indicated that 27 percent of Jews, 23 percent of Catholics, 39 percent of Buddhists, 18 percent of Baptists, 21 percent of Muslims, and 12 percent of Mormons were married to someone with a different religious identification. Millennials are particularly willing to cross denominational boundaries in selecting a life partner—fewer than one-quarter of the eighteen-to-twenty-three-year-old respondents in the National Study of Youth and Religion thought it was important to marry someone of the same faith (N. Riley 2010).

In his major work, *Protestant, Catholic, Jew*, written during the 1950s, in the heart of the nation's last civic era, Will Herberg argued that religion had a broad societal purpose that exceeded doctrine or denomination. It was the vehicle by which Americans of various ethnicities fit into and achieved acceptance within the greater society (Herberg 1955). But some in this era argue that the doctrines and actions of other denominations, especially Islam, place their followers at the edges of American society. However, the diverse nature of the Millennial Generation suggests that Buddhists, Hindus, and Muslims will inevitably join Protestants, Catholics, and Jews in the mainstream of America's religious life. Although older generations, in a time of FUD, may respond to those who spread the notion that Muslims represent a fifth column that threatens the nation's security, or worse, the history of generational cycles demonstrates that these appeals to prejudice and religious intolerance fail to resonate with civic generations and will ultimately recede from the political discourse of the country.

CONCLUSION

Millennials, like previous civic generations, are both builders and reformers of societal institutions. They believe in traditional concepts of marriage and parenthood and look forward to settling down in the comfortable suburban environments their parents have given many of them the opportunity to know and enjoy. They are also the most ethnically and religiously diverse, tolerant, and gender-neutral generation in U.S. history, and their unique attitudes about how life should be lived will cause a major transformation in the structure, composition, and behavior of the nation's families. These changes will influence how we work and worship, as well as where we live.

The Millennial Generation will also change how America entertains itself. Millennial attitudes and beliefs will change the songs the country listens to, the television programs it watches, and even the way sports are presented for the nation's enjoyment. Millennial optimism and team-oriented behavior is about to bring a breath of fresh air to a cynical, dispirited country that could use a little more-uplifting popular culture.

CHAPTER 12

Let Millennials Entertain You

WHILE CHANGES IN GENERATIONAL ATTITUDES toward such institutions as marriage and parenting effect deep and profound shifts in society, most casual observations of differences in generations tend to focus on more superficial behaviors, often beginning with the phrase, "these kids today." Millennials, for instance, are often characterized by their constant texting on mobile phones, or their need to check their Facebook profiles every few minutes, or, in the case of younger males in particular, their obsessive focus on video games. Certainly, these behavioral distinctions are real. A Kaiser Family Foundation study found that the average eight- to eighteen-year-old in 2010 spent ten hours and forty-five minutes each day exposed to a variety of media, an increase of three hours and fifteen minutes since 1999, when, for the first time, only Millennials were included in the age span of the study. One hour of that increase reflects the time the latest wave of Millennials spent on the computer, and another forty-five minutes was due to the additional time they spent playing computer games. But the same observers would be surprised to learn that, in fact, during the same ten-year time span, the percentage of Millennials reading books rose slightly (Kaiser Family Foundation 2010). Because such trends in media behavior and other popular culture activities tend to change as frequently as youthful fashions, it is easy to dismiss the entire subject as having little to do with the country's future.

Such sentiments, however, overlook the powerful pull America's popular culture has on the nation's mood and sense of confidence. Indeed, looking back at popular entertainment in prior decades often reveals as much about previous generations as studying more objective measurements of societal trends. Listening to the music of Glenn Miller, Benny Goodman, or the Andrews Sisters reminds us of the style and achievements of the youthful GI Generation as it won victory and held down the home front in World War II; hearing the Beatles, Jimi Hendrix, or Janis Joplin transports us back to the Boomer-led rebellion and societal turmoil of the late 1960s. As Millennials make their own mark on the music the country listens to, the television shows it watches, and even the way professional sports are played, their unique blend of teamwork, optimism, and individual initiative will change how America thinks about its future.

MILLENNIAL MUSIC IS A HOPEFUL MASH-UP

Music first becomes identified with a generation when its members are in their teens and twenties. However, Pete Markiewicz, an astute observer of generational trends and popular culture, maintains that the musical genre with which a generation is forever identified may not be clear until the oldest members of that cohort are in their thirties. "Typically new styles are embraced by a rising generation, and are created by the tail-end of a previous generation" (Strauss and Howe 2006, 100–101). So tween (9–14-year-old) and teenage (15–18-year-old) Millennials, during the late 1990s, absorbed the rap and hip hop music produced by their Gen-X elders, just as the GI Generation during the 1920s initially fell in love with the jazz music so intimately linked to the older Lost Generation. Boomers first found their rebellious voices in the 1950s in the early rock 'n' roll that came from the Silent Generation that preceded them. But eventually, all generations, especially a generation as large as the Millennials, puts its own unique stamp on a musical genre that retains its popularity for two decades, as the musical tastes of both the older and younger members of that generation are united. Consequently, the musical preferences of the Millennial Generation are a work in progress, and its clear choice of a genre won't be known until a few years in the future. We will know a Millennial musical genre has arrived when the songs at the top of the charts represent both a fusion of earlier styles and something completely different in both its words and music.

Recent Academy Award winners for best song demonstrate the sharp shift in lyrics that is occurring as the country moves to a more Millennial sensibility. Contrast the upbeat exhortations celebrating victory throughout the world from "Jai Ho," sung with multilingual Bollywood enthusiasm at the end of the Academy Award–winning movie *Slum Dog Millionaire*, with the rap lyrics of the 2005 winner, "It's Hard

Out Here for a Pimp." Instead of bemoaning the fact that they had "done seen people killed, done seen people deal, done seen people live in poverty with no meals," as Three 6 Mafia did in that song, the Bollywood movie looked at the very same conditions and made a hit with lyrics whose English translation focused on a dangerous and impossible love affair that proved "you are my destiny."

The creation of the next musical genre to capture the sweet spot of success won't be complete, however, until this turn toward more positive lyrics is combined with rhythms and melodies that also reflect the ethnic diversity of the Millennial Generation. Jazz, the quintessential American music from the last era dominated by a civic generation, was born from a mixture of black rhythms and melodies from European immigrants and their children who made up much of the GI Generation. The transition from the Lost Generation's small combo jazz to the GI Generation's big band swing music came with a major slowdown in tempo. Glenn Miller and Tommy Dorsey delivered a sweeter musical sound that their adoring crowds could dance to, rather than the jarring, syncopated rhythms of early jazz greats, such as Jelly Roll Morton and Louis Armstrong. The Silent Generation fell in love with the brand new up-tempo backbeat of Elvis Presley's and Fats Domino's rock 'n' roll, but Baby Boomers put their generational stamp on the genre a decade later, with the love-drenched lyrics of guitar groups like the Beatles.

Given the polyglot nature of Millennials, the country's next pop genre may combine Asian tonality with a Latin beat or, as in "Jai Ho," Asian rhythms and European lyrics. The possibilities are almost limitless. Whatever the genre's name and sound, it will represent as sharp a break from today's rap as Elvis's rock 'n' roll did from Sinatra's swing jazz crooning.

Markiewicz points out that the end of an era dominated by a musical genre is near when its proponents pronounce its eternal life the loudest. In their 1970s reprise of a 1950s Danny and the Juniors classic, Sha Na Na told "all of you hippies out there in the audience, that rock 'n' roll is here to stay. It will never die." In 1979, Neil Young repeated the claim, at about the same time that rap emerged to take rock 'n' roll's place on Top 40 radio play charts. The clearest sign of rap's imminent dethroning is the pride that its richest and most vocal devotees take in pointing to the global ubiquity of rap culture as proof of its perpetual popularity.

But, according to the Record Industry Association of America's official tally of music sales by genre, rap's popularity peaked in 2002, just as the first Millennials entered adulthood, and it has now fallen to third place behind country and rock in America's musical purchases, with sales falling faster than the industry as a whole. Even the rap that is being recorded is changing as "its audience and its performers are increasingly Millennial. The kind of hip hop we see today is very different from what it was back in the heyday of Tupac, NWA, and Biggie Smalls" (N. Howe 2010c).

The rise to fame of singer Taylor Swift personifies these Millennial-driven changes in the music industry. Unlike the late King of Pop, Michael Jackson, whose startling dance routines in music videos rocketed him to the top of the MTV charts, Taylor Swift's equally impressive rise in popularity has been driven by votes from her devoted fans on MySpace, Facebook, and Twitter. She is famous for sending text messages and instant personal responses because, like other Millennials, she believes that "it's important for the people who keep you going and support you and have your back out there in the world to know that you are thinking of them all the time" (Let'sSingIt 2008).

While Swift is most often considered to be a country singer, her appeal crosses genres. In 2009, at the age of twenty, she was named *Billboard* magazine's Performer of the Year. Her 2010 album, *Speak Now*, sold a million copies in its first week of release, the first time that had happened since 50 Cent's 2005 album *The Massacre*. No rap album has come close since, with overall album sales falling by half in the intervening years (R. Lewis 2010).

Unlike the rebellious, unconventional, and often alienated behavior of Boomer and Gen-X artists, Swift's personal life is as wholesome as the lyrics of her songs. One of her songs mashed up Romeo and Juliet, but gave it a more Millennial-like happy ending. Another, "Fifteen," which gives advice on handling the pressures of high school, was written with her best friend and younger brother in mind. When rumors arose that she was pregnant by her former boyfriend, Joe Jonas, she squashed them in characteristic Millennial fashion with an emphatic denial posted on her MySpace page. She is an active philanthropist, donating large sums to combat online sexual predators and aid flood victims in Iowa and Tennessee.

Even as Swift and other members of her generation seek to create the ultimate Millennial Generation musical genre, there is one category, mash-up, which already reflects the desire to share and the technological proficiency of Millennials. Mash-up is the combination of the music from one song with the *a cappella* version of another—with the music and vocals frequently belonging to completely different genres. Musicians are now exploring new ways to take advantage of this trend by creating interactive music videos that allow their fans to become the producers and directors of a more personalized experience. Borrowing from the popularity of video games such as "Guitar Hero," these music videos allow the viewer/listener to click a color to change the track, or to tap one of the band members to mute or un-mute the instrument they play, or create a customized remix of the song as it plays (Richey 2010). Mash-up's emergence as a distinctive musical form awaited the arrival of digital technology that made combining musical types easy to accomplish and a generation proficient in the use of that technology, with musical tastes eclectic enough to make it interested in melding one type of music with another (Winograd and Hais 2008). Its popularity attests to the generation's desire to personalize every experience.

When asked which types of music they often listen to, at least one-quarter of Millennials name four specific genres: rock (45%); rap or hip-hop (41%); rhythm and blues (30%); and country (25%). By contrast, all older generations cite no more than two genres that they especially enjoy. Similarly, when asked to indicate the appeal of specific musical performers, the top choices of Millennials spanned five decades—from the Rolling Stones, the Beatles, and Jimi Hendrix of the 1960s, to the current Coldplay, Carrie Underwood, and Kanye West, with Michael Jackson and Nirvana in between. A quarter of Millennials even named Frank Sinatra, the musical icon of the GI and Silent generations, and Elvis Presley, a Boomer favorite (Taylor and Morin 2009).

Eventually, Millennials, like other generations, will develop and adopt a music all their own. Whatever it is called and whatever it sounds like, the dominant Millennial musical genre will reflect the generation's positive, optimistic, group-oriented, constructive, and diverse character.

THIS IS NOT YOUR BOOMER PARENTS' TELEVISION

Television channels and networks, once strongly attuned to the sensibilities of older generations, will also have to change their style, tone, and programming to meet the preferences of the emerging Millennial Generation. MTV premiered in August 1981, just as the oldest Gen-Xers turned sixteen. Its edgy programs and music videos fit perfectly with the risk-taking and alienated mindset of the teens of that era. Millions of Xers heartily echoed the demand of MTV's advertising slogan, "I Want My MTV!"

By the first decade of the twenty-first century, however, a very different generation of young Americans had emerged, and the channel's ratings began to fall. To the Millennial Generation, the once cutting-edge MTV seemed out of date. At first, MTV's executives made the mistake of assuming that young people behaved the same way, held the same attitudes, and liked the same things at all times. Their initial strategy was to continue to do what had worked in the past, by providing programming that further pushed the envelope of taste, as if young Millennials were the same as young Gen-Xers.

Finally, and belatedly, MTV recognized the need for change. While introducing the channel's new programming approach, MTV's general manager Stephen Friedman acknowledged, "we held on to Generation X a little too long and our programming reflected that. It was very clear we were at one of those transformational moments, when this new generation of Millennials was demanding a new MTV" (M. James 2010). When the channel first went on the air, "the humor of young people was more cynical . . . and the idea of community seemed earnest and not cool. It's the opposite now" (Arango 2009).

As a result of these changes, MTV is enjoying a renaissance, with viewership up 16 percent over the prior year. Its biggest new hit, *Jersey Shore*, shows that the parents "come around and support each other—yes, they fight with each other, but they are a family," according to Van Toffler, the president of MTV Networks Music/Film/Logo Group. "You even see their parents come in and cook pasta for the house." Friedman underlined the change the channel was making. "Four years ago, you never would have seen that on MTV. Parents were absent!" Parenting is even the main topic of *Teen Mom*, MTV's second most popular program (Stelter 2010).

Other television programmers have had to learn the same generational lesson as MTV. In 1977, the Reverend Pat Robertson founded the Christian Broadcasting Network Satellite Service channel. In 1988, it was renamed the Family Channel and offered a blend of theologically and politically conservative informational programming and entertainment shows targeted at both the conservative half of the Baby Boomer Generation and traditionalists in older cohorts. The popularity of his television channel transformed Pat Robertson from an obscure Virginia Baptist minister to the leading televangelist (a term that did not exist when his channel was founded) of that idealist era.

By the mid-1990s, however, the reactive Generation X had entered its teen and young adult years, and the Family Channel found it difficult to attract a younger audience. Its programming was too bland for the new generation and the advertisers who targeted it, and the channel's financial position—as well as its conservative ideology—would not permit it to obtain the type of shows that would attract a Gen-X audience. In 1997, Robertson sold the channel to Rupert Murdoch, who wanted to broaden the reach of his Fox Network's brand.

In 1998, in accordance with the terms of the sales agreement, which stipulated that "family" was always to be a part of the channel's name, the network was relaunched as the Fox Family Channel. The result was a mish-mash of wholesome, family programming leavened with Fox's edgy tone that so strongly appealed to Generation X. For viewers, the blend of the sacred and profane made the channel impossible to believe and difficult to watch. TV family sitcoms, like *The Simpsons* or *Married . . . With Children*, a key part of Fox Network shows, were not nearly wholesome enough for the new channel. And, the families that were shown were not nearly edgy enough to attract a Gen-X audience. Failing to find any logical generational niche, the effort floundered and the Fox Family Channel was sold in late 2001 to the Walt Disney Company and rebranded as ABC Family.

The sale to Disney occurred just as teenage and young-adult Millennials were becoming a significant segment among television audiences. Disney decided to target Millennials with the programming of both ABC Family and the Disney Channel it already owned. According to Jack MacKenzie, president of the Millennial Strategy Program of Frank N. Magid Associates, the consulting firm that suggested this new direction, these were the "first channels ever aimed specifically at the Millennial Generation." Based on viewer research, the programming on the two channels was designed to reflect and appeal to the group-oriented, societal-concerned, upbeat, and high-achieving Millennial Generation. In particular, according to MacKenzie, the approach of the channels was to present shows depicting likeable, well-meaning, but occasionally flawed characters that, after struggling, are able to overcome the odds, do the right thing, and achieve their goals (interview 2010).

The Disney Channel carried shows aimed at tweens. Its biggest hit was *High School Musical*, whose songs contained lyrics such as "We're all in this together/Once we know/That we are/We're all stars," which summed up Millennial beliefs perfectly. Meanwhile, ABC Family aired programs like *The Secret Life of the American Teenager* and *Greek*, directed at older teen and college-age Millennials.

The focus on the Millennial Generation paid off. By the 2009 television season, ABC Family earned the best ratings in its three-decade history. As a personal reward for the job he had done, but also in recognition of the rising importance of the Millennial Generation, ABC Family's president, Paul Lee, was named president of the ABC Entertainment Group in 2010, with a special charge to import his Millennial savvy to the struggling ABC broadcast network.

Magid's research forecasts not just what type of story line is likely to appeal to Millennials but also what type of programming people will want to watch, as well. Reality TV, with its emphasis on winners and losers, is not likely to retain its current level of popularity, as a generation that thinks everyone should get a trophy becomes a larger share of the target demographic advertisers want to reach. Instead, according to Magid's research, viewers prefer comedy when the Consumer Confidence Index declines and drama when the CCI rises. In line with Magid's forecast, in fall 2010, comedies accounted for five of the eight most highly rated primetime programs. Only one drama made the list as consumer confidence continued to fall.

Sitcoms that appeal to Millennials, however, are not likely to have the same types of plot lines that were popular with rebellious Boomers in the 1960s and 1970s, or with alienated Gen-Xers in the 1980s and 1990s. New TV comedies, such as *Raising Hope*, *Community*, and *Modern Family*, reflect the generational plot line and programming lessons that Disney learned so well. Greg Garcia, the creator of *Raising Hope*, which first aired two decades ago with a more edgy Gen-X approach, expressed the new tone succinctly. "I don't want to do a show that's just outrageous and [has] funny things and shocking things. . . . It's important to me to have some heart and emotion to it." In other words, as the headline of the article in which he was quoted made clear, "You gotta have snark. But you also gotta have soul" (Kronke 2010).

PLOTTING FOR GOOD

Even comic book heroes are undergoing a generational makeover. Within a year after Disney purchased Marvel Comics, Joe Quesada, chief creative officer for the company's stable of popular superheroes, such as Iron Man, Captain America, and the Fantastic Four, announced that "Marvel Universe is going to be a more optimistic place than we've seen in quite awhile." The plan was to reflect the shifts occurring in the real world, by creating "a bold new era for the world's greatest superheroes as they emerge from darkness with a renewed sense of hope and optimism" that was much more in line with young Millennials' sensibilities (Wallace 2010).

Tim Kring had earlier demonstrated the power of this new approach in his science fiction television drama *Heroes*, which had a successful four-year run on NBC. That series told stories of ordinary people who discover they have superhuman abilities, and portrayed how the discovery impacted the characters' lives. Its popularity spawned viewer interest in magazines, action figures, interactive Web sites that included original content, graphic novels available for mobile viewing, and even cereal box promotions and giveaways. At the height of the popularity of the series, keeping up with the "voracious demand" for all of this content required the work of over 300 people on the TV show and another 50 on non-broadcast content (Kring interview 2010). But Kring drew an even larger lesson from the experience.

"It was clear that the only way to keep up with the audience was to give them the resources to craft content on their own." Rather than simply grafting Millennial attitudes onto existing formats, Kring sensed the need for a completely different entertainment experience. Instead of churning out a hybrid mix of print and video to promote virtual and real merchandise on both broadcast and mobile platforms, he decided to take a giant leap into the future and place the audience into the story as it unfolded. The result, *The Conspiracy for Good*, provided his Millennial fans with a whole new dimension in which they could exercise their penchant for mashing up content and making a positive difference in the world (Kring interview 2010).

The pilot for this experimental series recruited players to come to London to save a rap artist under attack for exposing an attempt by a fictitious corporation, Blackwell Briggs, to prevent her from building libraries for African children because it wanted the land for its oil pipeline. Nokia's app store, Ovi, generated one million downloads of the software that was the entry point for those who wanted to participate in the program's plot. A limited number then took their Nokia smart phones to London, and over four successive Saturdays engaged in a high-tech scavenger hunt using the very latest in image recognition technology, while seeking to avoid real actors playing security forces from Blackwell Briggs. Other actors assumed the roles of street musicians, shop owners, lawyers, recruiting officers, even the homeless. Each of the selected 250 players pointed their smart phone's camera at tagged images ranging from graphic graffiti-like symbols to landmarks to a painting at the Tate Modern Museum. Each of these images unlocked other clues on how to continue to the next location, so participants could find hidden information that would expose the corporation's plans. Players communicated via Twitter and staged real flash mob demonstrations to divert those playing Blackwell Briggs agents away from their target. By intermixing real actors and audience members, the simulated exercise created its own virtual reality for those playing the game, while generating online video to entertain everyone who had become attracted to the story.

The program gave positive exposure to the nonprofit Room to Read, which raised enough money from Nokia and participants to build five real libraries and provide fifty scholarships for schoolgirls in Zambia. Another nonprofit, WeGiveBooks.org, raised enough money through the show to donate 10,000 books for the libraries. *The Conspiracy for Good* demonstrated both the power and the popularity of what will become the way Millennials entertain themselves in the future.

Tim Kring calls his creation a "social benefit platform" that can be used to connect service-oriented, Internet-addicted, game-playing Millennials with corporate advertisers seeking to build brand awareness and demonstrate their good citizenship (interview 2010). By changing the very definition of audience participation, Kring's platform creates a radical new concept for both storytelling and charitable fund-raising in the Millennial era.

This Millennial sensibility, which combines purpose with the pleasure of entertainment, is also quietly infiltrating the world of sports.

HOW MILLENNIALS PLAY
THE NATIONAL PASTIME

Nielsen TV ratings and Gallup Polls since at least 1972 indicate that professional football has become America's favorite sport; but, as Ken Burns's 1994 PBS documentary *Baseball* reminds us, no other game has been as enmeshed in U.S. history and as reflective of the nation's culture as baseball. Professional baseball began with the formation of the National League in 1876, a year before the political compromise that resolved the Civil War fourth turning, and has since experienced two complete turnings of the generational cycle. As a result, America's national pastime has been shaped by these changes, with each generational archetype of players emerging onto, and then passing from the scene.

In eras in which players from values-driven idealist generations predominated, the game experienced conflicts among those seeking to advance the interests of players at the expense of team owners. In 1890, when most players were members of the idealist Missionary Generation, many joined the short-lived Player's League. Far more successful were the efforts of players from the Baby Boom Generation, who won the unprecedented right to become free agents and sell their services to the highest bidding team, after a series of strikes between 1972 and 1995.

By contrast, individual performances, often record-breaking, have characterized periods in which players from reactive generations most heavily populated major league rosters. The focus of these reactive generation athletes on proving their individual superiority, regardless of the cost to teammates or the game, has also produced crises that threatened the very existence of baseball.

Most of the ballplayers of the 1910s and 1920s were from the reactive Lost Generation and included some of the greatest names—and flawed personalities—in the history of baseball. Babe Ruth's appetites were almost as prodigious as his ability to swat home runs. More than eight decades after he retired, Ty Cobb, one of the most combative and disliked players of his era, continues to have baseball's highest lifetime batting average. Rogers Hornsby was the best right-handed batter of his era, but he was also a compulsive gambler and member of the Ku Klux Klan. And Shoeless Joe Jackson, who, along with seven of his Chicago White Sox teammates, conspired to throw the 1919 World Series, earned his greatest fame as the object of a plaintive plea from a little boy after his trial: "Say it ain't so, Joe." Baseball historian Bill James's portrayal of the players of the 1910s as "shysters, con men, drunks, and outright thieves," colorfully sums up the character of the era dominated by players from the Lost Generation (B. James 2001, 95). More recently, virtually all of those associated with steroid usage, including Mark McGwire, Sammy Sosa, Jose Canseco, Barry Bonds, Roger Clemens, Manny Ramirez, and Alex Rodriquez were born within or right on the cusp of the birth years of the reactive Generation X.

There are notable exceptions to this list of generational bad boys, such as Christy Mathewson, whose admirable style earned him the nickname, "the Christian Gentleman"; the nondrinking, nonswearing Lost Generation pitching great, Walter Johnson; and today's clean-cut Gen-Xer, Derek Jeter. However, it is the ill-behaved members of reactive generations who have most distinctly painted the picture of big league baseball in these eras.

Reactive generations are inevitably followed by civic generations, which for baseball has meant the emergence of positive, self-confident, high-achieving, and, above all, team-oriented players. Baseball historian and statistical guru Bill James describes the GI Generation ball players of the 1930s and 1940s as hard-working team players who were completely schooled in the intricacies of their craft, in sharp contrast to his characterization of players from several decades earlier. Baseball historians have described this period as the sport's golden age. Among the earliest GI Generation arrivals was the beloved Yankee first baseman Lou Gehrig, who had a quiet personal style that differed completely from that of his flamboyant Lost Generation teammate, Babe Ruth. Gehrig was followed by other iconic members of his generation, including Bob Feller, Hank Greenberg, Jackie Robinson, Stan Musial, Ted Williams, and Joe DiMaggio, all of whom were among the 400 major league players who served their country proudly and without complaint during World War II. Like all civic generations, these GI Generation baseball greats were ethnically diverse. DiMaggio, Gehrig, Greenberg, and Musial were the sons of immigrants—Italian, German, Jewish, and Polish, respectively. Feller was an Iowa farm boy. And, of course, Jackie Robinson was not only a superior athlete but also played a key role in changing the character of America by integrating major league baseball.

Members of a new civic generation, the Millennials, are just starting to fill big league rosters in large numbers. Already talented, positive, team-oriented Millennials, such as Dustin Pedroia, Evan Longoria, Joey Votto, Andre Ethier, David Wright, Kurt Suzuki, Ryan Braun, David Price, and Robinson Cano are among baseball's biggest and most promising stars. While all of the diversity of GI Generation America is represented among the current crop of Millennial ballplayers, the game has been enhanced with the addition of a large contingent of American and foreign-born Hispanics, as well as an increasing number of Asians.

It is far too early to know everything that Millennial baseball players will ultimately accomplish and exactly how they will shape the game, but the actions of one of them provides a clue. While at Arizona State University, Pedroia forfeited his scholarship to enable the recruitment of additional pitchers, thereby making it possible for his team to win the College World Series. It is difficult to imagine any member of the individualistic Lost and X generations making the same decision. As greater numbers of America's newest civic generation fill Major League rosters, baseball can look forward to its second golden era.

MILLENNIALS ARE TAKING OVER THE SPORTS WORLD

The shift from Generation X attitudes to the behavior of Millennials is having a similar impact on professional sports other than baseball. From 1999 to 2002, the Los Angeles Lakers won three straight National Basketball Association championships. They were anchored by two Generation X players—Kobe Bryant and Shaquille O'Neal. The rivalry and tension between the two individualistic Gen-Xers soon broke up this winning combination. O'Neal demanded to be traded when it became clear Laker management wanted to recreate itself around the younger Bryant; and the day after O'Neal was gone, Bryant signed a seven-year contract. But the Lakers did not win another league championship until 2009, by which time the team was restocked with a new cast of players, many of them team-oriented Millennials, who were more comfortable acting in a supporting role to Bryant than O'Neal had been.

Nearly a decade after Shaq and Kobe split, the greatest Millennial basketball player in the NBA, LeBron James, made a career move that both fascinated and upset the sports world, but which demonstrated the strong team orientation of his generation. James played for seven seasons with the Cleveland Cavaliers, just thirty miles from his hometown, but even though his individual statistics were among the best in the league, the Cavaliers never won an NBA championship. In one of the most hyped decisions in the history of sports, James announced he would play the next year on the Miami Heat alongside two of his closest friends and fellow Millennials, Dwayne Wade and Chris Bosh, who also happened to have the talent that might enable him to win the championship that had eluded him in Cleveland. James's move to Florida wasn't driven by money. He and his two new teammates all signed virtually identical contracts with Miami for less money than they would have received individually had they accepted separate offers from different teams.

Michael Jordan, the dominant basketball star of the 1980s and 1990s, and a late-wave Boomer born in 1963 on the cusp of Generation X, found their reasoning hard to fathom: "There's no way I would have called up Larry [Bird], called up Magic [Johnson] and said 'let's get together and play on one team.' . . . I was trying to beat those guys." Jordan recognized that his sport had moved to a new era shaped by the attitudes and behavior of a new generation: "But . . . things are different. I can't say that's a bad thing. It's an opportunity these kids have today" (Abbott 2010).

The willingness of Millennial athletes to leave money on the table, at least temporarily, to pursue other goals is not limited to professional athletes. For instance, Myron Rolle, a defensive back at Florida State University, could have entered the NFL draft in 2009, but instead took a year off to attend Oxford University as a Rhodes Scholar. Although he is currently a member of the Tennessee Titans practice squad, in clear Millennial fashion Rolle's long-term goal is to attend medical school, become a neurosurgeon, and build a medical clinic in the Bahamas, his ancestral country. Rolle explained his choice this way, "If the [NFL] draft works out, I think it solidifies that my dreams are realized. I want a young boy or girl in inner-city Chicago . . . to see a guy who took a year off, got smarter, got a master's degree, and came back. I want to show that you can have options" (Thamel 2009).

After winning the Most Valuable Player award at the 2010 Orange Bowl, Adrian Clayborn, a defensive end at the University of Iowa, announced he was returning for his senior year, rather than entering the NFL draft. Some questioned his decision to forgo millions of dollars, and risk injury and a fall-off in his personal statistics that could threaten his expected first-round draft selection. Clayborn simply said, "I like Iowa. I like my teammates, and I want to graduate with my class." When his statistical achievements did, indeed, drop because opposing coaches blocked him with two or three players, Clayborn embraced the opportunities for his teammates to make the tackles that he had previously made: "I enjoy seeing my friends make big plays." Clayborn was joined by his mother, who moved from St. Louis to Iowa City to experience his senior year with him. Having his mother around him at college completed the picture of an athlete who could only be a Millennial (Clayborn 2010).

CONCLUSION

The top stars of the entertainment world, including those who perform music, act on television, or play sports, inevitably become celebrities that everyone talks about. Their behavior is not just a source of gossip but also a reflection of the mores and values of the country at the time. Even though Millennials are much less inclined to think of pop culture celebrities as their heroes than were Gen-Xers, they, too, are influenced by the behaviors and beliefs of those in the news. Furthermore, the use of social media has made the daily lives and thoughts of stars vastly more accessible to their fans than in previous eras. For these reasons, the arrival of Millennial celebrities on America's pop culture scene will reinforce the considerable power the generation's attitudes wield in shaping the zeitgeist of America in the twenty-first century.

A desire to achieve, but not at the expense of others, a devotion to team success above personal gain, and a determination to make the world a better place, are all parts of the Millennial Generation's personality that have become key elements of the image today's youngest stars are trying to project. Instead of having to endure the shocking Gen-X behavior of former musical headliners such as Britney Spears or rappers Eminem and 50 Cent, or the self-above-team attitudes of Gen-X players such as Manny Ramirez, Brett Favre, or Alex Rodriguez, the country is about to enjoy decades of celebrities exhibiting the very behaviors the parents of Millennials have tried to instill in their children. The result will be a nation with greater pride in its culture and more confidence in its future.

The Millennial Generation's influence will not be confined to this country. Millennial attitudes and beliefs will also change the way in which the United States is perceived by, and interacts with, the rest of the world. America's next civic generation, community-oriented Millennials, are busily striving to change the world as decisively as their GI Generation great-grandparents did before them.

CHAPTER 13

Changing the World

MILLENNIALS HAVE BEEN TAUGHT since they were toddlers that the best way to solve a societal problem is to act upon it locally, directly, and as a part of a larger group. Tired of exalted rhetoric from Boomer leaders that rarely produced results and frustrated by their older Gen-X siblings' lack of interest in pursuing any collective action to address broad social problems, young Millennials have embraced individual initiative linked to community action. In 2009, over thirteen million American teenagers volunteered an average of three hours per week, providing over two billion hours of service to the nation (Fox 2010b). Eighty-five percent of college-age Millennials consider voluntary community service an effective way to solve the nation's problems (Winograd and Hais 2008, 262). They also think it's the right way to solve the world's problems. Applications to join the Peace Corps jumped 40 percent in 2009 after a 16 percent increase in 2008 (Kraul 2009).

This penchant for public service shapes the beliefs of Millennials about how the United States should deal with the problems it faces around the world. In the contest for the 2008 Democratic presidential nomination, Millennials believed Barack Obama was right, and Hillary Clinton was wrong, about whether to conduct direct talks with our enemies. They also thought Republican vice presidential nominee, Sarah Palin, was completely off base when she declared in her acceptance speech at the GOP convention that "the world is not a community and it doesn't need an organizer." In fact, Millennials believe that what the world needs most is thousands of community organizers, working at the local level to solve their own country's and the world's problems, linked electronically, of course, to friends around the globe.

It will take a decade or two before the impact of the Millennial Generation's belief in the need to think globally and act locally to address international challenges will be fully understood. But in the interim, the United States is certain to benefit from the generation's focus on rebuilding America, as well as the world, one community at a time.

MILLENNIALS' MULTILATERAL, CAUSE-DRIVEN WORLD

In contrast to generational stereotypes often portrayed in pop culture, Millennials are very much concerned about, and connected to, the world around them—more so, in fact, than many older Americans. Responding to questions on foreign policy in a Pew Research survey, only 9 percent of Millennials were unable to express an opinion on how well President Obama was doing in working with our allies, while almost one-quarter of senior citizens, mostly members of the Silent Generation, had no opinion on the same subject. On the knotty question of Israeli/Palestinian relations, all but 7 percent of Millennials could tell survey researchers whether or not Obama was striking the right balance between the two sides; 26 percent of senior citizens could not (Pew 2010d).

One reason for Millennials' greater degree of global sophistication is the multiethnic culture in which many were raised. It gives the generation, as one Millennial put it, "a new sense of geography. . . . Within my relatively close social circle, I can quickly think of friends whose parents come from Mexico, Israel, Iran, Brazil, Russia, Uruguay, Korea—and I'm sure there are many more. Being a first-generation American, if not an immigrant, is so commonplace that it seldom comes up in conversation" (Zwick 2009).

In addition to Millennials' frequent multicultural experiences at home, the number of college students acquiring such knowledge from studying abroad has increased fivefold since 1986, when Generation X was in college (Obst, Bhandari, and Witherell 2007). More than 260,000 students studied overseas in the 2007–2008 school year. As one Millennial observed, "through traveling, we are learning to turn off technology for a little while and get to know how to really communicate with the world and its people. We are a generation yearning to always be connected in a way that was incomprehensible to those who came before us, but we are also working harder than ever before to break down barriers" (B. Lewis 2010).

Beyond its personal exposure to many cultures, the greater degree of electronic global connectivity, which enables the generation to make virtual friends on Facebook anywhere in the world or to Twitter Iranian protesters instantaneously, provides Millennials with a unique perspective on American foreign policy. "Our computers feed us second-by-second updates on the world's diplomatic challenges" (Zwick 2009).

The results of this greater global exposure can be seen in the sharply different attitudes on specific foreign policy issues between Millennials and other generations. Americans under thirty say that more trade with China is good for the United States by a 56 percent to 37 percent margin. Those thirty to forty-nine and fifty to sixty-four years old are divided, but a majority of those sixty-five and older see increased trade with China as bad for the country rather than good (52% to 37%) (Pew 2010g). A majority of Millennials consider Al Qaeda (59%), and the nuclear programs of North Korea (51%) and Iran (55%) as major threats to the United States, but by margins 15 to 20 points lower than older generations. Other, more intractable but less direct security concerns, such as the drug trade in Mexico, China's emergence as a world power, or conflicts in the Mideast ranging from Pakistan to Palestine, are not considered a major threat by a majority of Millennials (Pew 2010d).

Rather than thinking about the world in terms of relationships between nation-states, as many foreign policy analysts have traditionally done, Millennials are more apt to view causes, such as global warming or human rights abuses, that require global solutions, as of equal, if not greater, importance. For example, the percentages of Millennials who favor or oppose military intervention to spread democracy are almost exactly the reverse of the numbers for intervening to stop genocide. Only 12 percent of Millennials are in favor of intervening to promote democracy, while 45 percent are opposed. By contrast, 42 percent of Millennials support using the U.S. military to halt genocide, while only 14 percent do not (Institute of Politics 2010). As Lee Fox, founder of the tween social network site KooDooZ, pointed out, "the Cold War, 'us versus them' mentality is obsolete for this generation. Millennials are united by global pains. They care about individuals, i.e., Nedra's death in Iran. The rigidity of national borders is softening as a result" (Fox 2010a).

This focus on causes was captured eloquently by Abigail Zwick when she was just a senior in high school. "We know there are problems that simply must be fixed. At my school, and probably at many others, the Community Service Fair is the most popular event of the school year. When we go to a concert, it's often a benefit for a cause that we may also post on the 'Causes' tab of our Facebook page" (Zwick 2009).

Given the distinctions Millennials make between the seriousness of direct military threats, such as terrorism and nuclear proliferation, and squabbles over power or territory, the focus of America's foreign policy is likely to shift toward a more multilateral, global institution-building approach as this generation takes over the country's mantle of leadership. By a three-to-one margin, Millennials agree that the United States should take the opinion of other countries into account when making foreign policy decisions, and one-fourth of them don't believe the United States currently does that frequently enough (Pew 2010d). While a plurality support intervening militarily to protect the United States from hostile countries (31% to 23%) or from terrorism (36% to 22%), only one-quarter of the generation is in favor of doing so in a preemptive manner (Institute of Politics 2010). Only 38 percent of Millennials, in contrast to a majority of all older generations, including two-thirds of those over sixty-five, agree that U.S. military strength is the best way to maintain peace (Pew 2009b).

In his speech accepting a somewhat surprising Nobel Peace Prize, President Obama quoted an earlier civic generation president, John F. Kennedy, to suggest a pragmatic way to advance Millennials' belief in a multilateral, ideals-driven approach to foreign policy. "The world should focus on a more practical, more attainable peace, based not on a sudden revolution in human nature but on a gradual evolution in human institutions." While some misread the president's remarks in this and other symbolic venues around the world as hopelessly idealistic, in the fashion of Woodrow Wilson's support for the League of Nations, his thoughts on how best to carry out America's role as a world leader were very much aligned with the pragmatic idealism of his Millennial supporters (Kagan 2009).

Two-thirds of Millennials approved of Obama's international policies halfway through his term, even after his decision to increase America's presence in Afghanistan, compared to only about half of older generations (Pew 2010d). As the president moved to change America's approach toward solving challenges as diverse as global warming and relations with the Muslim world, Millennials were right behind him, cheering his efforts every step of the way and putting their own distinctive approach to solving these problems into action.

SAVING THE PLANET ONE
INDIVIDUAL AT A TIME

Millennials have been taught to treasure nature, a theme at the heart of some of their favorite movies. In 1995, right in the middle of the generation's birth years, the heroine of Disney's animated version of the tale of Pocahontas taught Englishman John Smith to give up his culture of plunder and conquest because "we are all connected to each other, in a circle, in a hoop that never ends," as the lyrics to its hit song "Colors of the Wind" made clear. In 2009, as Millennials came of age, the story was updated with 3D technology, transported to some point in the future on another planet, Pandora, and given an even more sophisticated network of sentient beings, in the movie *Avatar*.

The movie taps deep into the belief system of Millennials by having the heroine, Neytiri, bestow her superior wisdom on the alternative identity, or avatar, of a cynical and crippled marine, Jake Sully, whose beliefs resemble those of members of a reactive generation like today's Generation X. Sully's heroic defense of the nature-loving, completely connected Na'vi people occurs after he experiences the hollowness at the center of the ruling institutions' power and abandons his previous beliefs. The wildly successful movie finished the job of imprinting in Millennials' minds the necessity of preserving nature in the face of institutional hostility.

The generation's beliefs are clearly reflected in the importance members place on addressing the challenge of global warming. In 2006, Millennials between the ages of thirteen and twenty-four years old cited the environment as the number-one problem facing their generation (CBS News/MTV 2006). In 2008, 64 percent endorsed the idea that the environment should be as high a priority for government as protecting jobs (S. Cohen 2010). And, in 2010, 80 percent of Millennials considered global climate change to be either a serious or very serious problem, ten points higher than Xers or Boomers. Twice as many Millennials as those over sixty-five thought it was a very serious problem (Pew 2010d).

Beyond these differences over the issue's importance, Millennials also disagree sharply with their elders on the best way to address the problem. As with other global causes, Millennials prefer to tackle the problem through individual initiative and grassroots action, not through the top-down approaches that many Boomers prefer. In *Avatar*, Jake Sully learned about the world of Pandora from the research of his scientific colleagues and from Neytiri's teachings about the deep connectedness of all living things. In real life, countless Millennials are using the very same combination of scientific insights and the power of community to take action to preserve the world for future generations.

In 1990, Ted Turner's TBS cable network launched the cartoon program *Captain Planet* with a message, "The Power Is Yours," designed to enlist youth in environmental causes. Twenty years later, a group of the show's original viewers created a Web site and a series of activities dedicated to creating "a global network of adult Planeteers to collaborate both locally and globally." Their manifesto captured the Millennials' approach to the challenge of global warming and suggested why the generation's attitudes would prove to be decisive in saving the planet. "We take personal responsibility for creating the world as we know it can be. As our numbers grow, so will our power" (CaptainPlanet and the Planeteers 2010).

In June 2004, thirty-one Millennials representing twenty-five organizations that had already undertaken action in their own local communities formed the Energy Action Coalition, whose purpose was to "unify a diversity of organizations that will support and strengthen the student and youth clean energy movement." Their goal was to create an umbrella organization that would work through a consensus-oriented decision-making process, in contrast to the Boomer personality-driven mentality of many of the existing environmental organizations in the United States. Melding the interests of all of its members, the coalition did its entire budgeting and fund-raising requests as one organization (Duval 2010).

As with most Millennial initiatives, its approach combined local initiative with national and international coordination and publicity. One of its efforts, the Campus Climate Challenge, has led to over 685 campuses developing plans to become climate neutral and "models of sustainability for the rest of society." The group's blog, "It's Getting Hot in Here," is now the largest issue-based youth blog in the world. During the negotiations in Copenhagen to limit carbon consumption, the coalition linked Millennials onsite to youth networks back in the United States to reinforce the need for the country to exercise its leadership responsibilities on climate change (Energy Action Coalition 2010).

The goals of Millennial environmental organizations tend to be scientifically, not politically, determined. For instance, the 350.0rg initiative was named after the 350 parts per million of carbon dioxide that scientists say is the safe upper limit for such gases in the atmosphere in order to keep the planet's climate stabilized. The locally focused, global campaign was led mostly by Millennials who made October 24, 2009, "the most widespread day of political action in the planet's history," according to CNN. Twenty-five thousand pictures from events as diverse as 15,000 students marching through the streets of Addis Ababa, Ethiopia, to an underwater cabinet meeting in the Maldives (an island nation in the Indian Ocean facing the threat of inundation) were displayed on the group's Web site, as well as on the big TV screen in Times Square. As one Millennial activist, Jared Duval, put it, "In contrast to groups for whom setting targets was a negotiable political matter, we set ours by reading countless scientific reports . . . and only after consultations with leading climate scientists . . . who made it clear the science was not negotiable" (Duval 2010, 102).

Campaigns to enhance awareness need to be connected to individual behavior, however, if they are to be more than just clever publicity stunts. Millennials believe that sharing information widely is the best way to change behavior. As a result, initiatives to help consumers connect the dots between their green impulses and their daily purchases are likely to grow in popularity. Wal-Mart, the most influential retailer in the United States, is already requiring its suppliers to disclose the environmental costs of making their products. Soon, Wal-Mart shoppers will be able to compare the Green Ratings as well as the prices of products on its shelves (Bustillo 2009). Actions to increase awareness of environmental issues might lead even Wal-Mart's highly price-sensitive consumers to choose products with a smaller carbon footprint.

The California Department of Toxic Substances Control, during Republican Governor Arnold Schwarzenegger's administration, launched a Green Chemistry initiative designed to identify the toxicity and green footprint of hundreds of thousands of products sold in the state and to create a system to share the information easily and widely. The ultimate goal is to allow consumers to be able to scan products on their smart phone as they are shopping so they can determine, for instance, if they were manufactured with coal-fired electricity in China or solar power in California. Rather than use risk assessments by experts to determine what should be offered to consumers, the system would rely upon an informed public to make those decisions at the point of each sale (Roosevelt 2009).

These initiatives respond directly to the desire of 86 percent of Millennials and 91 percent of their moms to learn about environmental issues from brands when they are shopping. The two groups carry enormous clout in the marketplace. Moms control 80 percent of household expenditures; college-aged Millennials have $40 billion of discretionary income to spend each year (Cone 2010). Before Congress ever reaches a consensus on how to reduce carbon consumption, environmental impact information will become commonplace. As a result, Millennial-influenced purchasing decisions and activism will play a key role in moving the country closer to its international environmental commitments.

One of every three adult Americans will be members of the most environmentally conscious generation in history by the end of this decade. During this period, Millennial enthusiasm for taking individual action to fulfill collective responsibilities in the marketplace, as well as in the voting booth, will tip the scales in favor of pro-green policies at both the national and international level. When the whole world learns to act locally and think globally, the Millennials' problem-solving approach will also pay off for the planet.

WILL MILLENNIALS OF THE WORLD UNITE TO SAVE THE PLANET?

While Millennial momentum is certain to alter attitudes toward climate change in the United States, without support from a new generation of leaders in other parts of the world, the global commitments necessary to deal with the problem may never become a reality. In 2010, as part of its research to create a global network that focuses on tween males, Disney XD, the Walt Disney Corporation interviewed over three thousand eight- to fourteen-year-olds in six European countries. Ninety-seven percent of those whose age, at least, would put them in the final wave of Millennials if they were Americans, believed it was important to look after the planet, and 74 percent indicated they were already recycling regularly (Disney XD 2010). Many young adults around the world share similar attitudes. Upward of 90 percent of people eighteen to twenty-nine years old in countries as diverse as Brazil, China, India, Indonesia, Japan, and Mexico believe global climate change is a serious or very serious problem, percentages actually greater than those of U.S. Millennials (Pew 2010d).

Neil Howe and other generational theorists believe that this consensus reflects an increasing global alignment of generational archetypes that has been taking place ever since World War II, especially in Europe. Indeed, many of these countries have given their generations labels that reflect the behavioral traits of their Anglo-American generational archetype counterparts. The rebellious Boomer spirit is captured in names such as Sponti, or protest generation, in Germany and Brigate Rosse (Red Brigades) in Italy for those who came of age in the late 1960s. More recently, the Null Zoff, or "no problem," tag has been applied to Germany's current cohort of young adults to describe a generation much like our own Millennials, as does Sweden's Generation Ordning (Ordered Generation) label for its present-day youth (N. Howe 2009b).

Howe looks at underlying attitudinal and behavioral social trends, such as divorce and birth rates, criminal behavior and drug use, civic participation, risk-taking, and institutional trust to compare generations across cultures (N. Howe 2009a). Survey research data that measure attitudes directly suggest, however, that in some countries at least, the generational cycle may be five or ten years behind the generational breakpoints in the United States. For instance, German and British men and women in their twenties express a level of hostility toward tradeoffs between jobs and environmental regulation that are more in line with the beliefs of thirty-something American Gen-Xers than Millennials (Pew 2010d).

Even if Howe is right that Europeans in their teens and twenties resemble American Millennials, the political power of young people in Europe is likely to be much less than in America because of Europe's declining birth rates. The United Nations projects that Western Europe will have two million fewer children under age fourteen in 2020 than it did in 2005, with the elderly making up 50 percent of its population, almost double the projected percentage of seniors in the United States

(Shapiro 2008). This lack of numbers will prevent Europe's youth, regardless of their beliefs, from being able to shape their region's destiny as powerfully as Millennials will shape America's.

Young people in many other parts of the world, however, particularly in the Middle East, do have the numbers that will make them forces to be reckoned with as events in Iran and North Africa demonstrated. Their attitudes could turn out to be a cause for concern or celebration, depending on how well the world responds to their aspirations.

Seventy percent of Iranians are under thirty, twice the proportion of that age group in the United States. They grew up during a religious awakening in the Islamic world that came later than America's Cultural Revolution in the 1960s. According to Howe, the Middle East's idealist generation, comparable to our Baby Boom generation, was not born until about 1956; their young adults' revolt against established institutions did not begin until 1979. Because of this lag, the attitude of people under thirty in Iran is more like that of our Generation X—pragmatic, individualistic, commercial, and anti-ideological. This explains some of the hostility among young Iranians to leaders, such as President Mahmoud Ahmadinejad, from the older, doctrinaire idealist generation (N. Howe 2009b).

In the immediate aftermath of Ahmadinejad's disputed reelection in 2009, text messages became the opposition's tool for organizing protests against the regime. Hundreds of thousands of tweets provided more, if not clearer, information about what was happening each day than the traditional media. It suddenly seemed as if American democratic values had erupted in the barren landscape of a theocratic society and that young people's technological capabilities might produce a regime change no one had anticipated. Clay Shirky announced, "This is it. This is the big one. This is the first revolution that has been catapulted onto a global stage and transformed by social media" (Scola 2009c).

But then the entrenched establishment fought back using the very same Internet-enabled technologies to isolate and spy on the resistance. The police posted photos of antigovernment protesters online and asked the public for tips on their identity. They also flooded the Internet with false information to heighten tensions and disrupt the opposition's plans (Morozov 2010). In the end, the government was able to turn the power of technology back on the protesters and force the resistance underground.

The same combustible mixture of a large number of young people with bleak economic prospects, coupled with technologies that provide these restless populations the ability to connect with their friends and compare their conditions to the rest of the world, sparked challenges to other authoritative regimes throughout the Middle East. In Tunisia, a video posted on Facebook of a 26-year-old college graduate who had been humiliated by the local police as they confiscated his fruit cart, setting himself on fire, created a wave of protest that abruptly ended the twenty-three-year reign of that country's autocratic president Zine el-Abidine Ben Ali. In Egypt, where half the population is under thirty, a small group of Internet-savvy political organizers who had started the April 6 Youth Movement on Facebook to protest police brutality in an earlier textile worker's strike, were able to leverage events in Tunisia to take a lead role in organizing widespread demonstrations against the three-decade long autocratic rule of President Hosni Mubarak. Unlike the government in Iran, Egypt's rulers temporarily shut down the Internet and social media services to deprive protesters of the ability to organize quickly. But by doing so, those running Egypt also lost the ability to eavesdrop on the opposition, which easily shifted its communications strategy to passing messages at daily prayers in the mosques (Kirkpatrick and El-Naggar 2011).

The contrasting outcomes of these events demonstrate that technology is neither inherently liberating nor enslaving. Instead, the values of those who use it determine whether it is a force for good or evil. In the 1930s, FDR's use of radio calmed the nation's fears, while Hitler's use of the same new technology stoked Germany's paranoia. The values of young people today in the Middle East—entrepreneurial, action-oriented, and suspicious of authority—resemble the attitudes of our own Generation X, making them hostile to dictatorial regimes throughout the region. Hard evidence for the existence of generational cycles in this part of the world is thin, however. Only time will tell if the next generation of Middle Eastern youth believes in other, more civic-oriented values, such as the power of consensus and the peaceful resolution of differences, as Millennials in America do. The desire for democracy on the part of many young people in a region that historically has been led by dictators accustomed to settling differences by force is laudable, but a major shift in values at all levels of society will be needed to build lasting democratic institutions throughout the Middle East. President Obama spoke to this challenge, ironically enough, in Cairo in 2009. His remarks were designed to initiate a "new beginning" in America's relations with the Muslim world. "All people yearn for certain things," he said. "The ability to speak your mind and have a say in how you are governed; confidence in the rule of law and the equal administration of justice; government that is transparent and doesn't steal from the people; the freedom to live as you choose. These are not just American ideas; they are human rights" (B. Obama 2009b). By turning the issue of relations between nations into a cause on behalf of civil liberties, Obama pointed the way toward a solution that young people everywhere could and, it is hoped, will embrace.

Currently, the situation is much more problematic. A majority of adults in all age groups in Pakistan and Turkey, ostensibly America's allies, express disapproval of the United States, and even more disagree with President Obama's policies regarding the region's hotspots of Israel, Iran, and Afghanistan (Pew 2010d). Pop stars with the biggest followings among Pakistani youth sing songs that condemn American interference in their country, not the Taliban (Ellick 2009).

The generational time lag in the Middle East holds out some hope, however, that this hostility to America and its leaders might not be a permanent part of the region's culture. If generational cycles apply in that part of the world, then those born in this century may represent a large civic generation, albeit one still a decade away from adulthood. While they are sure to be as patriotic and proud of their own country as Millennials are of the United States, they may also want their leaders to work with other countries to advance causes, such as human rights and the environment, creating the potential of a world more aligned with Millennial values.

China's Generational Gang of Four

China's rapid growth and the governmental policies put in place to deal with the societal strains that growth has created have had a dramatic impact on the country's generational cycles. The adoption, in 1980, of China's One Child Policy for those not living in the countryside has created a generation of urban children who are growing up in a family environment of such high expectations and minimal competition for attention that they are known as Little Emperors. Similar to our own Millennial Generation, this is a protected, pressured, conventional, civic-minded cohort of young people who revere their parents and are optimistic about their nation's future (N. Howe 2010d).

Meanwhile, China's economic growth has spurred a migration of workers from the countryside to the coast, creating a cohort of "left-behind children" who are being raised in rural poverty by aging grandparents. Nearly a quarter of China's children, and almost one-third of its rural children, are growing up without one or both of their parents present, an experience with potentially more devastating consequences than that suffered by American latchkey Generation X kids in the 1970s and 1980s (Stack 2010). No country has ever raised such diametrically different types of children simultaneously in such large numbers. It is as if the Chinese were rearing two different generational archetypes—reactive and civic—at the same time. As these two dramatically different subsets of China's youngest generation grow up, their differences in attitudes and beliefs are likely to add a major source of tension in a country already facing a series of challenges to its social stability.

Just as American Generation X managers express concern over the mental toughness of their young Millennial subordinates, Chinese leaders worry that a new generation moving from poor villages to work in factories, or unable to find work despite their education, will not tolerate the tough conditions earlier generations stoically accepted. Speaking in response to worker unrest over factory wages, Chinese Premier Wen Jiabao declared, "The government and all parts of society should treat young migrant workers as they would treat their own children" (Pomfret 2010), apparently missing the irony that many of these workers are, in fact, separated from their children. Things are not much better for roughly one-third of China's 5.6 million university students who graduated in 2008 but have been unable to find work. This concern over social instability has led to a revival of the teachings of Confucius, once called a "stinking corpse" by Mao Tse-tung. The current crop of Chinese leaders even made the sage's homilies in support of filial duty and a harmonious society a bigger part of the 2008 Olympics opening ceremonies than tributes to the nation's Maoist past (Gardner 2010).

After the sacrifices of China's civic Long March generation established the People's Republic of China in 1949, a generation of Technocrats, much like our Silent Generation after World War II, led the country through difficult times and built its modern institutions. But beginning with the Great Leap Forward and continuing through the Cultural Revolution that lasted until 1976, China was ruled by ideological zealots and their supporters in the Red Guard generation, who had little regard for the economic and cultural chaos that followed in their wake. The reaction to this upheaval was the economic reform initiative of Deng Xiaoping that began in 1978 and gave the current generation of leaders its name, Reform. Many members of the powerful Standing Committee that rules China are due to retire in 2012, however, and their replacements, including Xi Jinping, who is the heir apparent to succeed Hu Jintao as president of China, are likely to come from the generation that suffered through the Cultural Revolution when they were young. This cohort, which has experienced the worst of ideological zealotry and the best of technocratic management in their lifetimes, will be the ones who will have to respond to the challenges to the stability of China's political system that the fruits of rapid economic growth have generated.

Two of the greatest threats to the country's stability will flow from the deep differences in beliefs between rural and urban Chinese youth and the looming shortage of young people as a result of its One Child policy. The differences in generational attitudes between old and young will further exacerbate these social tensions. By 2050, 31 percent of China's population will be older than sixty, compared with barely one-quarter in the United States. There will be over 400 million elderly, with virtually no social security and relatively few children to support them. The preference for male children has also created a ticking population time bomb, with roughly 30 million more marriageable-age men than women (Kotkin 2010a). Given these challenges, China's future will ultimately be determined by how well it manages generational change and how willing its new generation of leaders will be to engage their contemporaries in other countries in peaceful competition for the world's economic and political respect.

One way to respond to domestic tensions is to unite the country behind a challenge, real or imagined, from outsiders. A senior colonel who teaches up-and-coming People's Liberation Army officers at the country's elite National Defense University, Liu Mingfu, argued forcefully in his book, *The China Dream*, that China should abandon its moderate foreign policy goals and "sprint to become world number one, the top power" (Buckley 2010). Although his writings may simply have been a part of the continuing struggle for power between the country's military and party leadership, historically "the rise of one great power at the expense of the dominant one has . . . more often than not eventually led to a war between them" (Art 2010). If the Chinese-U.S. relationship deteriorates to that point in the next decade or two, it will also confirm one of the darker scenarios of generational theory that has seen civic generations serve as cannon fodder for the global ambitions of idealist generation leaders.

An alternative path that China's leadership could follow is to try and find common ground with the United States based on mutual respect in order to build new, or remake existing, global institutions that would reflect China's increasing clout. The expanded role given to the G20 group of nations to guide international financial policies after the 2008 economic crash is a recent example of this type of accommodation. But the limits of such an approach were apparent when President Obama had to crash a gathering of developing nations convened by China at the Copenhagen conference on global warming in order to block China's attempts to dictate the outcome. A more Millennial style of consensus decision making may need to wait until a new generation of Chinese leaders is in charge.

The president's decision to engage in an online and open press conference with young Chinese leaders provided an opportunity to at least open a dialogue with that nation's future leaders on how best to achieve greater international understanding. Even as he was being criticized for not confronting the Chinese Great Firewall that limited distribution of the exchange within China, the president continued to focus on the Millennial Generation's belief in the potential of information-sharing to change the world. "I think that the more freely information flows, the stronger the society becomes, because then citizens of countries around the world can hold their own governments accountable. They can begin to think for themselves." His comments on Web censorship were carried, albeit briefly, on Xinhua, the government's official press agency. It caused one young Chinese listener to tweet, "I will not forget this morning; I heard, on my shaky internet connection, a question about our own freedom which only a foreign leader can discuss" (Branigan 2009). The incident revealed just how large a challenge China's leadership faces in managing the gap between what younger Chinese desire and the leadership's plans for the country's economic and political future.

Whether China is ultimately able to challenge the United States for global leadership and whether it chooses to do so through peaceful or military means is likely to be the key dynamic in foreign affairs during the rest of this Millennial cycle. But the Millennial Generation's desire to change the world through individual action on behalf of causes will introduce a new element into this historical mix that may give the upper hand to America's values in the contest for the hearts and minds of its generational peers around the world.

Social Networking Goes Global

Millennials are working hard to establish new institutions designed to do an end run around the post–World War II web of interlocking treaties and global policy-making bodies, by using social networks to link equally committed young people from around the world. They realize that powerful ideas can shape the world, even if there is no current guidebook on how to make such transformations occur. As one involved Millennial, Derek Gildea, commented, "To be effective, we have to both get our ideas across and make them practical" (interview 2010). The way to do that, according to Leah Garvin, a Millennial who has been producing films for nonprofits in Africa and Boston since her sophomore year in college, is to create "social spaces that foster partnership among nonprofits and their followers, a place where more followers means more resources" (interview 2010a). Many members of her generation are doing just that. Each effort has a slightly different strategy for making the world better, but all of them are committed to connecting similarly motivated individuals into networks that can tackle problems directly and locally.

Andrew Slack co-founded the Harry Potter Alliance when he was twenty-four, to "encourage our members to hone the magic of their creativity in endeavoring to make the world a better place." Leveraging the popularity of one of Millennials' favorite stories, he and his friends created a real-life Dumbledore's Army that gathered more than three-fourths of the 10,000 signatures sent to the United Nations Security Council on the issue of Darfur. Their podcast on the subject was downloaded over

120,000 times. His Army has also taken direct action to prevent geno-cide, raised funds to protect Darfur's civilian population, and donated 14,000 books around the world, including 4,000 to a youth village in Rwanda. Stack believes his "Avatar activism" is "creating the blueprint for a new kind of civic engagement that combines pop culture, social change, and new media that amplifies each voice hundreds of thousands of times" (Harry Potter Alliance [2010]).

Using a completely different strategy, Kiva.org seeks to provide dignity, accountability, and transparency for entrepreneurs around the world, by creating "a global community of people connected through lending." Over $100 million has been provided through the site's micro-financing Field Partners, who collect the entrepreneurs' stories, pictures, and loan details and publish them on Kiva.org. Ordinary citizens with as little as $25 to lend can click on the site, and Kiva handles the rest of the transaction, including providing information on the entrepreneurs' progress to those who lent them the money. Kiva was founded in 2004 by Matt Flannery, born on the cusp between Generation X and Millennials. It began as a side project he started while programming for TIVO and has since provided over $163 million to more than 400,000 entrepreneurs in over 200 countries, 82.5 percent of whom are women (Kiva [2010]).

The notion of using social networks to change the world continues to gain momentum. Jumo.com is the next project of Chris Hughes, a Millennial present at the creation of Facebook, who went on to found the Obama campaign's social network, MyBarackObama.com. *Jumo* means "together in concert" in the West African language Yoruba. It "conjures up the idea of a lot of people working on different causes simultaneously to affect social change," according to Hughes, whose reputation was enough to cause 60,000 people to sign up even before the official launch of the site. The site allows users to find interests they care about through an algorithm that consolidates everything about that cause through Facebook Connect, Twitter, e-mail, YouTube, and other platforms, as well as the ability to follow the cause and provide feedback or support to its volunteers. When asked why he chose to take on this particular project, Hughes replied in characteristically idealistic and pragmatic Millennial terms. "Why not do this? If people don't have responsibility when there is injustice, [I'm] not sure what they should be doing" (Kang 2010).

Millennial initiatives often face scorn or skepticism from older generations. Malcolm Gladwell, author of *The Tipping Point*, derided the State Department's "outsized enthusiasm for social media," by comparing the failure of Iranian protests to the success of the civil rights movement in the United States. "Fifty years after one of the most extraordinary episodes of social upheaval in American history, we seem to have forgotten what activism is" (Gladwell 2010). Like many other Boomers, such as Tom Friedman, Gladwell is not about to give up his generation's belief that its approach to social change is the only way to make it happen, despite increasing evidence that the generation's efforts are no match for the scale of the global, as opposed to domestic, challenges the Millennial Generation faces.

Garvin points out the shortcomings of Boomer-led nonprofits, which "take the issue first and social media second . . . at least they admit that they don't know how to leverage these new media tools to the advantage of their cause." But she is equally frustrated with nonprofits, often led by Gen-Xers, whose "flashy websites with animation, professional videos, and celebrity endorsements put the media before the cause." Instead, she argues, social media needs to be "used as a tool to congregate people who care about a cause," and "those connections need to support interaction" (e-mail 2010b).

Janessa Goldbeck, the field director for the Genocide Intervention Network, responding on behalf of her Millennial Generation to Gladwell's attack, made it clear what role social media can play in addressing causes. "We have to build political will, which means organizing both online and offline. Social media platforms lower the barrier to entry and provide people with mechanisms to connect and get involved—hopefully for the long haul" (Goldbeck 2010).

Millennials' dedication to working with each other on behalf of causes has spawned a host of initiatives and organizations, which will create powerful international institutions in the future. Although not all of these efforts will survive the inevitable challenges of growing to scale and expanding their reach, taken together they represent more hope for the future of the world than many initiatives led by Boomers, whose leaders' attitudes of moral superiority often limit their ability to attract others to their cause. The world is more likely to find ways to resolve differences peacefully, and build institutions capable of meeting the challenges it faces, by acting upon the Millennial Generation's values of cooperation and consensus instead.

Conclusion

America's role in the world will change as Millennials' enthusiasm for taking individual action to fulfill collective responsibilities tips the scale in favor of a more cause-oriented approach to the planet's problems. Threats to the nation's security from nonstate actors will increase at the same time that the desire of Millennials to act locally and think globally will be creating networks of new global institutions designed to relieve the worst suffering among the world's population and to provide new avenues for sustainable economic growth.

Whether the results of those initiatives will have the effect of dampening hostility toward the United States in the Mideast, China, and elsewhere, in time to avoid the global conflagrations that have engulfed earlier civic generations, remains to be seen, however. Much will depend on the nature of the political leadership in charge of managing the relationships between countries during the next few decades. Confrontational idealists, whether they are Boomers or a different manifestation of the same attitudes in other countries, are the least likely to be able to accommodate the beliefs of others for the sake of peace. Newer leaders, who may reflect a younger generation's belief in finding practical solutions to global problems, offer greater hope for a peaceful resolution of whatever disputes may emerge. Ultimately, the civic impulses of younger generations everywhere will need to be channeled into a productive, global dialogue on the best way to achieve a positive future for the planet.

For that to happen, however, the current levels of fear, uncertainty, and doubt that infects America's body politic will have to subside far enough to allow for rational dialogue about the real problems and threats the country faces. The history of fourth turnings suggests that both political parties will need to redefine themselves before the debate will end. Each strain of American political thought will have to come to grips with the realities of an American electorate and an American society fundamentally different from what it was during the last forty years. Both political parties will have to change the way they believe and act if they hope to elect leaders capable of retaining America's preeminence on a rapidly evolving global stage.

CHAPTER 14

Making Over American Politics

THE ENTHUSIASM AND UNITY of the Millennial Generation completely transformed America's political landscape in 2008, so that when Barack Obama took office his Democratic Party held the high ground. Obama's 7-percentage-point (53% to 46%) popular-vote win over John McCain was the largest victory margin of any Democratic presidential candidate since Lyndon Johnson's landslide in 1964. Over the course of two election cycles, the Democrats had gained a total of 55 seats in the House of Representatives, giving them a decisive 257 to 178 majority over the GOP in that chamber. In the Senate, the Democrats had gained a total of 13 seats. Once Pennsylvania senator Arlen Specter switched parties, the Democratic caucus, with the participation of 2 independents, swelled to 60 participants, the number needed to overcome any attempt to prevent their proposals from being considered on the Senate floor.

The Democratic Party's strength in Congress was a reflection of the positive view the public held of the party. In January 2009, Americans had an overwhelmingly favorable perception of Democrats (62% favorable to 32% unfavorable) and were even more positively disposed to newly inaugurated President Obama, 79 percent to 15 percent (Pew 2009a).

By contrast, the Republican Party was in dire straits. After winning the presidency in seven of the ten previous elections and controlling both houses of Congress between 1995 and 2007, GOP leaders came to believe that their party held a natural dominance of American politics and were shell-shocked when that advantage seemed to disappear almost overnight. Many observers considered the results of the 2008 election to be the harbinger of another realignment of American politics that would leave Republicans in a minority position for the next four decades

(Winograd and Hais 2008). Certainly, the public's opinion of the party seemed to suggest that the GOP might be facing such a plight. The same January 2009 survey that gave the Democrats an almost 2:1 favorability advantage put the public's impression of the Republican Party at only 40 percent favorable to 55 percent unfavorable (Pew 2009a).

Under these circumstances, many expected that Republicans would want to work closely with Democrats to wring whatever advantage they could obtain in their reduced capacity and that congressional Democrats would act in a unified and coordinated manner to easily pass their own and the president's program. Instead, for both parties, the opposite occurred. A unified Republican congressional membership held together in opposition to the president and congressional Democrats. Obama's efforts to reach across the aisle were consistently rebuffed, leaving the disparate factions within the Democratic congressional delegation to negotiate with one another in order to cobble together legislative majorities for each of the party's proposals.

By clarifying, rather than blurring, the clear ideological distinctions between the two parties, Republicans successfully reenergized their supporters and provided the public with a clear choice on which party's vision of the future to support. But although their dramatic gains in 2010 gave Republicans a new sense of purpose and hope in the short run, the changing demographic contours of the American electorate, particularly the growing importance of Millennials and minorities, suggested that the long-term prospects for Democratic domination of American politics in the Millennial era remained strong.

THE REPUBLICANS JUST SAY NO

Just nine days after the president took office, House Republican Whip Eric Cantor shared the results of a survey his party had conducted in order to bolster Republican resistance to the Democratic economic stimulus bill. The poll showed that President Obama was popular (71% approval) and that an overwhelming majority (64%) approved of his economic recovery plan. But it also showed that House Speaker Nancy Pelosi (34% favorable) and Senate Majority Leader, Harry Reid (20%) were far less popular. Furthermore, when asked about the specifics of the stimulus plan without Obama's name attached, the plan lost its appeal. Cantor presented the findings to wavering Republican moderates as evidence they could vote no without paying a political price. In the end, he convinced even those from districts won overwhelmingly by Obama to vote their party line (Karl and Klein 2009). The bill passed the House 244–188 with no Republican support, and by early March the GOP felt secure enough to "turn its sights on Obama" and oppose the president directly (Hulse 2009).

No one stated more clearly than Iowa senator Charles Grassley the Republican strategy of massive resistance to President Obama's and his party's legislative proposals. One of six senators (three from each party) designated to develop bipartisan health care reform legislation, Grassley said "he'd vote against any . . . bill coming out of the committee unless it has wide support from Republicans—even if the legislation contains EVERYTHING I want" (Murray and Montanaro 2009). In other words, Grassley was prepared to vote against his own bill unless a majority of his Republican colleagues were willing to join him, a virtual impossibility in the strongly partisan environment of the 111th Congress.

The unified opposition of congressional Republicans to all important aspects of the president's and the Democrat's program was, however, far more than a poll-driven strategy. It was also a clear result of the increasing level of demographic and attitudinal uniformity within the present-day Republican Party and its electoral base.

In 2010, Caucasians constituted 89 percent of those who identified as Republicans, in a nation that was only two-thirds white and in which whites will be a minority of the population by 2050. The party's demographic core was also concentrated geographically and generationally. Nearly four in ten GOP identifiers (37%) were white residents of the eleven Southern states that formed the Confederacy. Six of ten Republicans came from America's two oldest generational cohorts—Baby Boomers and Silents—and 56 percent were male (Winograd and Hais 2010a).

Republicans in the 111th Congress were even more strikingly male, white, and Southern than the GOP's electoral base. Only 10 percent of the Republicans were women, in contrast to 22 percent of the Democrats. There were no African American and only four Hispanic Republicans (all Cuban Americans from Florida) in either house. Almost half (45%) of Republican representatives and more than one-third (37%) of GOP senators were Southern.

This demographic uniformity was reflected in a growing homogeneity of attitudes among Republican Party adherents, as well. One of the eternal conflicts in U.S. politics stems from the fact that most Americans tend to be both ideological conservatives and operational liberals. On one level, Americans believe in small government, individual initiative and responsibility, and state and local authority. On another, they favor a range of specific federal government programs such as Social Security, Medicare, and grants and loans for college students. However, during the past several decades those who identify with the Republican Party have become increasingly conservative, operationally as well as ideologically. In 1987, just as the Reagan presidency was about to end, the Political Values survey conducted by the Pew Research Center classified a plurality of Republicans as middle-of-the-road on both the operational (44%) and the ideological scales (48%). Republicans who were not in the middle tilted slightly liberal on the operational spectrum (30% liberal to 26% conservative) and solidly conservative on the ideological scale (44% conservative to 8% liberal). By 2009, a plurality of Republican identifiers (48%) remained in the middle of the operational spectrum but among the rest, the balance had shifted toward the conservative side of the scale (32% conservative to 20% liberal). On the ideological spectrum, a clear majority (56%) were conservative.

TEA TIME

The emergence of the Tea Party further tightened the conservative hold on the Republican Party, which was reinforced by the demographic composition of the movement's adherents. Tea Party supporters were even less diverse than the GOP base overall. An April 2010 survey found that only 3 percent of Tea Partiers were Hispanic and 1 percent African American. Six in ten were male, and 75 percent were members of the Baby Boomer and Silent generations. Only 7 percent were Millennials. Forty-three percent were Southern (New York Times/CBS Poll 2010b).

The Tea Party movement was composed overwhelmingly of conservative Republicans. Nearly three in four (73%) called themselves conservatives (New York Times/CBS Poll 2010b) and an overwhelming majority (80%) either identified with or leaned to the Republican Party (Jones and Cox 2010). Moreover, at a time when a majority of the American electorate (53%) had an unfavorable impression of the

Republican Party, most Tea Partiers (54%) were favorable toward the GOP, while only 6 percent had a positive attitude toward the Democratic Party (New York Times/CBS Poll 2010b). Tea Party supporters also liked Republican politicians—large majorities had favorable opinions of Sarah Palin (83%) and Mike Huckabee (73%). In spite of media claims that many disdained George W. Bush for deficit spending, 73 percent of Tea Party supporters were favorable toward the former president (Jones and Cox 2010). By contrast, a plurality (37%) were unfavorable toward John McCain, the 2008 GOP presidential nominee, who had campaigned as a maverick willing to break with his party and compromise with Democrats (New York Time/CBS Poll 2010b).

Tea Party supporters were almost uniformly opposed to the economic policies advanced by the Obama administration. Large majorities rejected such key aspects of the president's health care reform legislation as requiring all Americans to have health insurance (85%) and raising taxes on those with incomes of greater than $250,000 to help pay for the health insurance of those who cannot afford it (80%) (New York Time/CBS Poll 2010b). Although the "Don't Tread on Me" signs carried by many demonstrators against "ObamaCare" suggested a strong libertarian, secular streak among Tea Partiers, majorities of its supporters see themselves as part of the Christian conservative movement (57%), believe that America has always been and is currently a Christian nation (57%), and are worried that public officials don't pay close enough attention to religion (50%). A longitudinal survey, conducted over the three months preceding the 2010 midterm elections, showed that religious conservatives became a larger component of the movement, and libertarians a smaller one, as the movement grew (Koelkebeck 2010).

There is also little evidence that the Tea Party movement is strongly composed of economic populists upset with governmental policies that benefit elites against the interests of ordinary Americans. Although three-quarters (74%) believed that the economy would have improved without providing government money to banks and other financial institutions, few Tea Party supporters (15%) blamed the Great Recession on the actions of Wall Street. Of the 53 percent of Tea Partiers who claimed to be angry with events in Washington, only 1 percent said that it was government bailouts of banks and auto companies that caused their ire (New York Times/CBS Poll 2010b). Furthermore, a large majority of Tea Partiers

(65%) were unconcerned that America may provide greater opportunities to some people than others (Jones and Cox 2010).

More than anything else, Tea Party supporters' concerns seemed to be driven by a greater degree of fear, uncertainty, and doubt about the future than those of most other Americans. Forty-one percent said they were afraid that they would drop from their current social class. A majority (58%) believed that America's best days are behind it (New York Times/CBS Poll 2010b). Colleen Owens, a stay-at-home mom, had voted Republican but was never politically active until she attended a Tea Party rally on tax day in 2009. "After Bush, I thought, 'things will get better. We'll be out of these wars.' Instead we are basically heading down a cliff" (Blackmon et al. 2010).

By the spring of 2010, it was clear that the Tea Party movement had become an important force in America and especially in the Republican Party. It brought a badly needed shot of vitality and purpose to the GOP. Candidates endorsed by the Tea Party wrested nominations in Alaska and Utah from incumbent Republican senators who were seen as Washington insiders, and defeated candidates endorsed by the Republican establishment in Colorado, Delaware, Florida, Kentucky, and Nevada. According to ABC News, eleven U.S. Senate, six gubernatorial, and nineteen House candidates received Tea Party backing in the 2010 midterm general elections. All but one, conservative Idaho Democratic Representative Walt Minnick (who rejected the Tea Party endorsement and eventually lost in November) was a Republican. Even among Republicans who did not receive the movement's endorsement, few, if any, were willing to oppose it.

A demographically and ideologically uniform base, coupled with pressure from the energetic Tea Party movement, made virtually unanimous GOP opposition to President Obama and his program all but certain. Republican unity gave the party a clear message about the direction they wanted the country to take. Whether that unity and uniformity will be as beneficial to the GOP in the long run depends on whether a majority of Americans in the Millennial era will also want to follow the direction Republicans have chosen.

THE DEMOCRATS PLAY LET'S MAKE A DEAL

During the first two years of the Obama presidency, the Democratic Party was as eclectic in its beliefs and as diverse in its composition as

Republicans were homogeneous and unified. Almost one-third (31%) of those who identified or leaned Democratic were minorities. A majority (53%) came from America's two youngest generations—Millennials and Gen-Xers—and 55 percent were women. In addition, the regional distribution of Democratic identifiers was virtually the same as that of the American population overall. White Southerners constituted only half the percentage of Democratic identifiers as they did Republican Party adherents (18% to 37%) (Winograd and Hais 2010a).

This varied demography of the Democratic electoral base was reflected in the party's sharp attitudinal diversity. In the 2009 Pew Political Values survey, Democratic identifiers, like Americans overall, skewed moderately conservative on the ideological scale and solidly liberal on the operational scale. While a majority (59%) was in the middle of the ideological scale, among the rest of the Democrats a greater number tilted slightly conservative rather than liberal (23% to 18%). Operationally, a majority of Democrats (51%) were liberal and most of the rest (40%) were in the middle. Moreover, although Republicans had become more consistently conservative both ideologically and operationally during the previous twenty years, the distribution of Democrats on the two scales has been virtually unchanged over that period of time.

The composition of the party's congressional delegation was as diverse demographically and attitudinally as its electoral base. There were three major ideological Democratic caucuses in the 111th Congress. With seventy-nine members in the House of Representatives, the Congressional Progressive Caucus (CPC) was the largest and most liberal of the three. In addition, more than half of its members were minority (thirty African Americans, nine Hispanics, and three Asians). Only 14 percent, compared with 22 percent of all Democratic members of Congress, were from the South, and most of those (eight of eleven) were African American.

Members of the CPC were the most politically secure of the three Democratic caucuses. All were elected from districts carried by Barack Obama in 2008. Democrats from such constituencies provided the Democrats' congressional governing core in the 111th Congress. In 2010, House Democrats who represented districts won by the president voted 199–8 for final approval of health care reform legislation. A year earlier, they voted 201–1 for the president's stimulus plan, 191–8 for financial reform, and 189–15 for climate-change legislation (Brownstein 2010b). However, with 218 votes required to pass legislation in the House, even these lopsided margins of support were not enough to enact the Democratic program. President Obama and his party's leadership had to look beyond this core to cobble together a majority for each of their legislative proposals.

One of the two caucuses they had to work with was the New Democrat Coalition (NDC), founded in 1997 as the congressional affiliate of the centrist Democratic Leadership Council, which positioned itself as a home for pro-business and pro-growth Democrats. In the 111th Congress the NDC consisted of sixty-eight representatives, almost rivaling the Progressive caucus in size, but with a much more ideologically conservative attitude, even as they shared many operationally liberal beliefs. The large majority of NDC members were white, but four were African American, one was Hispanic, and one Asian. Only fifteen of its members were Southern, while many represented predominantly suburban districts.

Politically, those associated with the NDC were somewhat less secure than members of the Congressional Progressive Caucus, even though most came from constituencies that usually voted Democratic. Only thirteen of its sixty-eight House members represented districts carried by John McCain. As a result, most New Democrats tended to support key administration initiatives in the 111th Congress, even as they pushed back against some of their more ideologically driven provisions. For example, only eleven representatives affiliated with the New Democrat Coalition voted against the 2010 health care reform law, and of those, nine were also members of the more conservative Blue Dog Coalition.

The smallest, and in many respects, the most atypical of the Democratic caucuses was the Blue Dog Coalition. Founded in 1995, its name is a play on words stemming from an old aphorism that Southerners would vote for a yellow dog if it ran on the Democratic ticket. Those who founded the organization to a large extent represented the ideologically conservative Southern Democratic tradition. Of the fifty-four Blue Dogs in the 111th Congress, 41 percent came from the South or a border state, and many represented rural and small town districts. Fewer than one in ten was a minority. Blue Dogs tend to be both ideologically and operationally conservative. On their Web site, they echoed former President George W. Bush's description of his philosophy as "common sense, conservative compassion" (Blue Dog Coalition [2010]). Well over half (thirty-two of fifty-four) represented districts won by John McCain. As a result, twenty-three of the fifty-four Blue Dogs voted against the Obama health care reform bill on final passage, accounting for two-thirds of all the Democrats voting nay.

Given the almost total unanimity of congressional Republicans in opposing President Obama, Democrats had no choice but to win support from at least some members of the two caucuses that were less ideologically liberal. Finding compromises involving less ideologically but still operationally liberal solutions involved elongated negotiations and deal making that many voters thought typified the very worst of politics inside the Beltway. Even President Obama called the process "ugly" and acknowledged that it hurt his party in the 2010 midterm elections.

In those elections, after two years of FUD in the country and rancor in the Capitol, a unified and unitary Republican Party squared off against a Democratic Party that was diverse in both its composition and its beliefs. In 2006 and 2008, this alignment had produced large Democratic majorities and elected Barack Obama. But in 2010, it led to a result that, at least in the House of Representatives, exceeded the Democrats' worst fears.

CHANGE COMES TO AMERICA AGAIN

On average, since World War II, the president's party has lost about 25 House and 5 Senate seats in midterm elections. The Democratic Party's loss in 2010 of 63 seats in the House of Representatives and 6 in the Senate was the greatest midterm loss suffered by any political party since Franklin Roosevelt's Democrats lost 72 House and 7 Senate seats in 1938. In both years, the country was reeling from prolonged economic pain and expressing dark forebodings about its future. Although in 1938 Democrats retained control of Congress despite their losses, in 2010 Democrats saw their filibuster-proof majority slip away in the Senate and lost their House majority completely. The Republicans also picked up a net of five governorships and a majority of the nation's state legislative seats, doing especially well in the South, where the GOP won a majority of legislators for the first time since Reconstruction.

Although the magnitude of the Republican victory was impressive, its size represented more of a continuation of the type of political volatility the country experiences during fourth turnings than a massive shift of America to the GOP and conservatism. A Pew survey taken just before the election indicated that the distribution of party identification within the electorate was little different in 2010 (49% Democratic to 39% Republican) from what it was in either 2008 (51% to 36%) or 2006 (47% to 38%), two years in which Democrats won sweeping victories at the polls (Pew 2010e). Nor did election-day exit polls show a clear endorsement of GOP positions on key issues. Only half of the voters (48%) called for repeal of the Democratic health care reform law. About the same number (47%) wanted the law left as is or even expanded. Only 39 percent of voters favored extending the Bush-era tax cuts to all Americans, including those with incomes greater than $250,000. By contrast, a majority endorsed either the Democrats' position of extending the tax cuts only for those with incomes below that level (37%), or the even more liberal position of letting the tax cuts expire for everyone (15%) (CNN 2010).

Moreover, exit polls indicated that, although the Democrats lost some ground among almost all demographics, the composition of the two parties' coalitions remained largely unchanged. The votes of Millennials (55% Democratic to 42% Republican), African Americans (89% to 9%), and Hispanics (60% to 38%) were only slightly altered from what they had been in 2006 and 2008. The Northeast (54% to 44%), the West (49% to 48%), and the nation's cities (56% to 41%) provided a firewall that helped the Democrats retain control of the Senate. The GOP did strengthen its position among its core constituencies, winning solidly among men (55% Republican to 41% Democratic) and among members of the Silent Generation, in the South, and in rural areas, all of which voted Republican by about 1.5:1 margins.

There was a demographic shift in the 2010 electorate among women, however, a group that had leaned Democratic in most elections since the 1980s. They divided their votes about evenly between the two parties. This was primarily due to the massive support of Silent Generation women for the GOP (57% Republican to 41% Democratic). Millennial women (61% Democratic to 29% Republican) and Gen-X and Boomer women (52% to 48%) continued to give majority support to the Democrats (CNN 2010).

The Democrats also lost significant ground in two other key demographic categories, the Midwest and the suburbs. In 2008, Barack Obama carried the former 54 percent to 44 percent. That margin was almost precisely reversed in 2010 (53% Republican to 44% Democratic), as Republicans won at least 25 new House seats, or about 40 percent of their pickups, in the Great Lakes watershed that stretches from upstate New York to Wisconsin. Obama narrowly won the suburbs, 50 percent to 48 percent in 2008 (CNN 2008) but, two years later, the GOP won them even more decisively, 55 percent to 42 percent (CNN 2010).

Primarily, however, the Democrats lost ground because those who turned out to vote in 2010, in contrast to the electorate or the population as a whole, were substantially more likely to identify with the Republican Party than two years earlier. As polls showed throughout the campaign, Republicans were more concerned with the outcome of the election and therefore more likely to vote, creating an enthusiasm gap between them and Democrats. In 2008, Democrats constituted 39 percent of those who voted, a number that fell to 35 percent in 2010. By contrast, the contribution of Republicans rose by 3 percentage points (from 32% to 35%). The contribution of conservatives rose by 8 points (34% to 42%), while that of liberals fell from 22 percent to 20 percent, and that of moderates, a group that is composed primarily of Democrats, dropped from 41 percent to 38 percent (CNN 2010 and 2008).

One of the reasons for this shift in the makeup of the 2010 electorate, compared to 2008, was a drop in the contribution from Millennials. Although turnout among those eighteen to twenty-nine years of age was comparable to previous midterm elections, the percentage of Millennials within the electorate dropped dramatically from the presidential election of 2008, falling from 18 to 12 percent (CNN 2010 and 2008). Twenty-three percent of all Millennials eligible to vote did so, slightly more than in 2002, but a point less than the 24 percent turnout in the 2006 midterm elections. It was the first time young voter participation failed to increase since the first Millennials became eligible to vote. Those Millennials who did vote preferred Democratic candidates in almost all contested elections and approved of Barack Obama's handling of his job as president by a 60 percent to 40 percent margin. Reflecting the generation's demographics, Millennial voters were more racially and ethnically diverse than the electorate as a whole. Two-thirds were white, 16 percent black, 14 percent Hispanic, and 5 percent Asian or some other racial category (CIRCLE 2010). The degree to which the drop in Millennial participation reflected their frustration with the slow pace of the country's economic recovery, or with the president's failure to quickly change how Washington worked, or with a lack of resources devoted by the various campaigns to ensure they voted, is difficult to determine. But one thing was clear, in contrast to all other generations, Millennials remained overwhelmingly Democratic and both ideologically and operationally liberal in their political orientation.

If the 2008 election was a victory for young Millennials, the 2010 midterms were a triumph for senior citizens. A big part of the increase in votes for Republican candidates came from the Tea Party movement's older supporters who turned out in droves. A solid plurality (40%) of 2010 voters claimed to be Tea Party supporters and nearly nine in ten (87%) of them voted for Republican candidates for the U.S. House of Representatives (CNN 2010). Still, the Tea Party was a mixed blessing for the GOP. Tea Party–endorsed candidates lost Senate races in Colorado, Delaware, Nevada, and Washington, elections some Republicans said more traditionally conservative candidates would have won, thereby costing the GOP an opportunity to gain a majority in the Senate (Elliott 2010). Even so, after the 2010 elections, the Republicans claimed a mandate from the American people to once again change the direction in which the country was headed, and the Democrats were left wondering what had happened to the mandate they believed they had won in 2008.

PARTY ON

The demographic and partisan composition of those who vote in any particular election are a reflection of events and the appeals of each party that are especially effective in bringing voters who agree with those appeals to the polls. In 2010, a stagnant economy and a less-than-persuasive narrative from President Obama and the Democrats about the usefulness of the operational programs they had enacted to improve the economy muted the enthusiasm of the party's base. Meanwhile, the GOP's clear emphasis on ideological themes, built around civic era concerns about the nature and scope of government, inspired their frightened and frustrated base to turn out in record numbers to prevent what they perceived to be a dangerous drift toward liberal hegemony.

It is clear that the programs that the Democrats had put in place to alleviate the nation's economic pain had not worked fast enough or with enough credibility to convince the electorate that hope was on the horizon. A clear majority (62%) of those who voted in 2010 named the economy as the most important issue facing the country; 87 percent said that they were worried about it. Almost half (41%) claimed that their own financial situation was worse than a year earlier (CNN 2010). With the unemployment rate stuck at about 9.5 percent, President Obama's claim, supported by the nonpartisan Congressional Budget Office, that the American Recovery and Reinvestment Act, or stimulus, had added 1.4 to 3 million jobs to the U.S. economy and that 1.1 million private sector jobs had been created during the first ten months of 2010, seemed less than inspiring.

While the president and Democrats argued that the bank and auto industry bailout programs, begun during the Bush administration and implemented during the Obama presidency, saved the nation from a financial and economic catastrophe that would have rivaled the Great Depression, many believed that these programs benefited economic elites, not ordinary Americans. Investors, who benefited from a 22 percent gain in stock prices after Obama was elected, and corporations, which saw profits rise by 60 percent between the fourth quarter of 2008 and the third quarter of 2010, were clearly better off. But economic statistics showed homeowners and working and middle-class Americans, particularly those who were undereducated or looking for work, were worse off than when the Great Recession began (Newman 2010).

Even the historic health care reform act was not a net positive in the minds of those who voted in the 2010 midterm elections. Popular programmatic elements of the law, including the expansion of health insurance coverage to more than 30 million Americans and the ban on insurance companies denying coverage to those with preexisting conditions or dropping coverage for people who need costly medical care, did not take effect until 2014. Those delays satisfied the budget scorekeepers in the Congressional Budget Office and the more fiscally cautious Democrats in Congress, so that the administration could claim that the legislation would eventually lower the nation's health care costs; but they cost Democrats in 2010 most of the political benefits that might have flowed from passing health care reform after almost an entire year of congressional deliberations.

In the end, however, most of those who voted in 2010 had little good to say about either party. Almost identical majorities among those who voted had an unfavorable opinion of the Democratic and Republican parties. Reflecting the opinions of some of their Tea Party supporters, even one-fourth of Republican voters expressed a negative perception of the GOP (CNN 2010). After three successive change elections, each party was left in the position of persuading voters that its approach was the best option for the country to choose. Going forward, each party still needs to convince its core constituencies to stick with their growing partisan preferences and express them consistently and enthusiastically on Election Day if it hopes to establish a more permanent majority. Since realignment theory suggests that it takes two presidential elections before the country's new political dynamic clearly takes hold, the 2012 elections should be decisive in determining whether the operational programs of Democrats or the ideological crusades of Republicans will be the dominant motif in American government and politics in the decades ahead.

FINDING THE WINNING SWEET SPOT IN THE AMERICAN ELECTORATE

Neither party can afford to ignore either the ideological conservatism of a majority of Americans or the public's support for many of the operationally liberal programs that have become a part of the country's civic ethos. Suggestions to reduce the deficit by cutting back, or even phasing out, Social Security or Medicare benefits inevitably run into opposition because of this inherent conflict in voter attitudes. The toughest challenge for leaders in each party in U.S. politics in the coming years will be to find a balance that reflects both strands of America's political DNA.

Because their office holders and electoral base are more diverse attitudinally and demographically, the Democratic Party and Barack Obama face a particularly difficult challenge in this regard. The actions of two post–World War II Democratic presidents—Harry Truman and Bill Clinton—who were forced to deal with circumstances similar to those now facing President Obama, offer alternative lessons on how to deal with the problem.

When Truman came to the White House from the vice presidency in 1945 after the death of Franklin Roosevelt, and Clinton was elected to the office in 1992, both witnessed large Democratic losses in the first midterm election of their presidencies. In 1946, after the tension of thirteen years of economic depression and world war, voters answered affirmatively to the Republican campaign question, "had enough?" The GOP gained 55 House and 13 Senate seats, winning Republican majorities in both houses of Congress for the first time since 1930. In 1994, the GOP gained 54 House and 9 Senate seats, achieving Republican majorities in both houses for the first time since 1954.

Truman and Clinton reacted to the midterm election defeats of their party in very different ways. Truman fought back vigorously, strongly leaning toward the operationally liberal base of his Democratic Party. He sent an array of progressive economic proposals to Congress, vetoed conservative legislation, such as the Taft-Hartley labor bill, that the Republican congressional majority sent to him and enthusiastically "gave Hell" to the "good-for-nothing" 80th Congress. By contrast, Clinton took a more centrist position, called at the time triangulation, between the conservative Republicans in Congress and the liberal base of his own party. He utilized ideologically conservative themes, even announcing that "the era of big government is over" in his 1996 State of the Union Address. He tacked toward operational liberalism, however, when he vetoed reductions in Medicare spending, leading to a temporary shutdown of the federal government. But he also sought common ground for programmatic reforms, on crime and welfare, for instance, leaving his Democratic base restless and dissatisfied. To the surprise of contemporary observers, both Truman and Clinton won reelection two years later, although Truman's coattails enabled him to restore the Democrats' congressional majority, whereas Clinton faced a Republican majority throughout the rest of his presidency.

In the aftermath of the 2010 elections, depending on their ideological preferences, observers were quick to point to either Truman or Clinton as the model Obama should follow. Liberals, such as Katrina Vanden Heuvel, editor of *The Nation*, called on the president to "channel Harry Truman" (Vanden Heuvel 2010), as did *New York Times* columnist Frank Rich, who, at the same time, expressed concern that Obama "lacks the will to fight" as had Truman six decades earlier (Rich 2010).

Conservative analyst Jay Cost, on the other hand, who believes Obama operates in a political environment more akin to that of 1994, argued that Clinton would be a better role model for the current Democratic president (Cost 2010). The successful political maneuvers of President Obama during the lame duck Congressional session that followed the midterms, as well as the background and beliefs of his new senior White House staff, suggested he was more inclined to follow the Clinton model, while searching for his own unique political synthesis.

Although the choice did not seem as urgent for the victorious Republicans, the GOP will face a similar need to balance operational and ideological concerns. Immediately after winning control of the House, Republican leaders pledged to repeal "ObamaCare," cut the federal budget back to 2008 levels, and permanently extend the Bush-era tax cuts for upper-income Americans. These ideas spoke directly to the ideologically conservative core of the party from establishment Republicans to newly elected Tea Partiers. However, the GOP's insistence on not raising the federal debt ceiling without major cuts in discretionary programs failed to address the operational liberalism of the American electorate and gave President Obama an opportunity to regain his political momentum as the budget battles unfolded.

Only a few Republican voices seemed willing to suggest that their party needed to consider operational as well as ideological concerns. One, former Republican governor, William Milliken of Michigan, a member of the GI Generation, spoke in the language of his civic generation, in seeing government as a useful, problem-solving, force in American life. "I believe government serves an important and necessary purpose, and can be a positive influence . . . unlike the kind of approach that's being used by the Tea Party people . . . who feel that we have too much government" (Wheeler 2010). And another civic generation Republican, Millennial Megan McCain, in her book *Dirty Sexy Politics*, suggested the "ideological narrowness" of her father's party was costing Republicans important support among members of her generation. "Rather than leading us into the exhilarating fresh air of liberty, a chorus of voices on the radical right is taking us to a place of intolerance and anger" (McCain 2010, 7). George W. Bush's former speechwriter, Michael Gerson, a consistent spokesman for moderate Republicanism, succinctly described the choice between ideological conservatism and operational liberalism confronting his party: "In the current case, there is a genuine uprising in favor of fiscal responsibility and job-creating growth—but there is no mandate for the destruction of the modern state" (Gerson 2010).

In the short run, the ideological orientation of each party's congressional representation will push both parties toward their ideological poles. Flush with victory, top House Republicans and strategists said they saw "little distinction between incumbent members and those who would be joining them as freshman . . . both benefited from the Tea Party activism that helped them trounce Democrats" and said that "the support deserved to be rewarded" (Hulse and Herszenhorn 2010).

Congressional Democrats are now more ideologically uniform, as well. Virtually all of the members of the Congressional Progressive Caucus (95%) were reelected in 2010, as were a clear majority (59%) of New Democrats. By contrast, a majority of the conservative Blue Dog Coalition (54%) were either defeated or saw their open seats won by Republicans. In all, the Progressive Caucus accounted for only 5 percent of all Democratic losses and the Blue Dogs 45 percent. Together, these changes meant that, for the first time since these organizations were formed in the 1990s, the Congressional Progressive Caucus was larger than the Blue Dogs and New Democrats combined.

In spite of the internal structural forces impelling each toward ideological uniformity, the party that will guide the nation in the Millennial era will be the one that most effectively synthesizes operational liberalism and ideological conservatism. The external, demographic changes reshaping the United States will give both parties no other choice, if they hope to establish a stable majority during the next few decades.

Conclusion

The three key demographic components that will cause this shift are Millennials, minorities, and women. America's largest and most diverse generation is joining the electorate in ever larger numbers. Millennials will account for 24 percent of voting-age Americans in 2012 and 36 percent in 2020. Minorities collectively now comprise about one-third of all Americans. By 2050, the United States will be majority-minority nation. More than one in four Americans will be Hispanic by 2050. Nonwhites are close to a majority of Americans who are of high school age or younger. Ever-increasing numbers of women are attending and graduating from college, and women are becoming a larger component of the country's workforce and are holding high-status jobs more often than ever before.

So far, in spite of its 2010 losses, the Democratic Party has been more effective than the GOP in appealing to this emerging America. Liberal columnist Harold Meyerson pointed out that the number of newly elected Republican senators in "genuinely contested" races who carried eighteen- to twenty-nine-year-old voters was "zero" in 2010, and describes the Republican victory as looking "more like the wave of the past than the wave of the future" (Meyerson 2010).

Some Republicans also recognize the problems these demographic changes present to their party in the future. David Frum, another George W. Bush speechwriter, spoke of an "electoral generation gap," that could overtake the Republicans in 2012 as Millennials rejoin the electorate in larger numbers (Frum 2010). Kristin Soltis, a young Republican pollster, warned of the longer-term danger for her party: "The Millennials can point to the election of Barack Obama as a critical formative event in their political lives that will echo in their voting behavior for decades to come. The risk [for Republicans] is that another generation remains voting heavily Democratic for the rest of their political lives" (Soltis 2010). The lopsided support of Hispanics for Democratic senatorial candidates in California, Colorado, and Nevada and for Democratic House candidates across the country caused Gary Segura, a Hispanic pollster, to sum up the Republican's future quandary this way: "They lost in every racial and ethnic group except whites. They haven't . . . broadened their coalition. And, the question is—with whites declining as a share of the population, what's the future for them to build a vote base?" (Jaffe 2010).

The GOP made a few initial steps to take on this challenge in 2010, electing two Hispanic governors, a female Indian American governor, and a Cuban American senator, along with two African American congressmen, although most of these victorious Republicans received only a small percentage of minority votes. The Republicans also made major gains in America's suburbs, where the greatest number of Americans of all ethnicities and generations, including Democratic-leaning Millennials, African Americans, and Hispanics, now live. The party that is able to win over suburban voters with a message that is both ideologically and operationally appealing will gain the strategic high ground in the battle over the nation's political direction in 2012 and beyond.

Shaped by some of the most profound demographic changes in American history, the key to future success for both the Democrats and Republicans will be to develop a civic ethos that synthesizes the two strands of America's political DNA. The party that most effectively accomplishes that goal will be the dominant political force in the emerging Millennial era.

CHAPTER 15

Building a New Civic Ethos

THE CONSTITUTIONAL CONVENTION of 1787 is often thought of as the decisive moment when the country finally resolved the paradox of popular rule and the need for a strong, stable, national government. In fact, however, the adoption of the document was just the beginning of vigorous, and often riotous, debate over the new nation's civic ethos. As the process of ratification wound its way through the thirteen states, the same fundamental questions of individual freedom and collective action that have been intertwined in the country's political DNA ever since were at the center of each state's deliberations. "The vast majority on both sides of the issue wanted a decentralized federal system of limited government, responsive to the people and protective of their rights. The difference was over how to achieve this" (McConnell 2010).

As in other periods of FUD, the debate turned ugly. On July 4, 1788, supporters of the Constitution in Albany, New York, staged such a noisy celebration that their opponents assaulted them and burned a copy of the document. Later that month, Thomas Greenleaf, publisher of the *New York Journal*, had to run out the back door in order to escape an angry mob that had thrown his printing equipment into the street to prevent him from publishing essays critical of the Constitution (McConnell 2010).

The conflict was ultimately resolved by an agreement on the part of the pro-ratification side to have the Congress consider amendments, some of which were adopted and that later came to be known as the Bill of Rights. This addressed the concerns of the Constitution's opponents, who feared an overreach by the federal government that would threaten individual liberties. The ten amendments that were ultimately adopted outlined a set of values to govern relationships between the federal government and either the people or state governments; the

Constitution itself laid out a vision of how democracy could function more effectively, while restraining the natural instincts for power of those elected to serve. The country threw off the ineffective, hybrid governing structure established by the Articles of Confederation, and created a completely new type of government, unlike anything anyone had ever experienced before. By coming to a consensus on both vision and values, the Constitution, coupled with the Bill of Rights, established the basic civic ethos by which the country has been governed ever since.

During every fourth turning, however, the same questions raised in the ratification debate are reopened, and the same concerns about the values that should govern the relationship between the government and the nation's citizens are expressed by those fearful of where the nation is headed. The question of whether or not the liberties guaranteed in the Bill of Rights should be applied to slaves could only resolved by a civil war. Afterward, the country's new understanding of its civic ethos was enshrined in the Thirteenth, Fourteenth, and Fifteenth amendments to the Constitution. During the 1930s, the expansion of the federal government's power had to be validated by changes in the thinking and composition of the Supreme Court before Franklin Roosevelt's sweeping vision of a New Deal for the common man could be realized. That Tea Party supporters have a propensity to put on eighteenth-century dress to underline their desire to see the country return to its fundamental values, as they understand them, is just the latest example of this type of civic era debate. The equally vigorous counterargument by President Obama and his supporters that the country needs a new vision to succeed in a new century and that America's values need to be reinvigorated in the context of contemporary life is also a part of the country's search for a redefined civic ethos suitable for the Millennial era.

The volatility and vociferousness of American politics in the current period of FUD will only end when the country finds a way to resolve its disagreements over vision and values, abandons some of the patchwork, hybrid solutions it has adopted, and comes to an agreement on a new way to organize its public and private sectors. The heart of this consensus will be found in the beliefs and attitudes of the Millennial Generation, whose numbers and unity will provide the foundation for the nation's new civic ethos.

MILLENNIALS LOVE TO SERVE THEIR COUNTRY AND THEIR COMMUNITY

In 2009, during the worst of the Great Recession, the number of people volunteering to serve their communities in the United States rose to an all-time high of 63.4 million, representing 26.8 percent of all Americans over the age of sixteen. It was the largest single-year increase for both these statistics since 2003 (Corporation for National and Community Service 2010). Approximately 1.3 million more Millennials offered their time without compensation to nonprofit organizations in 2008 than in 2007, providing over a billion hours of volunteer service. This increase among Millennials represented all of that year's gain in volunteerism. The increase among young people was most pronounced among those attending college, who registered a 10 percent gain in participation in voluntary service. But even those in high school increased their volunteer rates by 5 percent. Reflecting the difficult economic times, the single largest increase of volunteer activity came from those working with neighbors in their communities. Almost two-thirds of youthful service work was done through religious or educational nonprofit institutions. All of this Millennial volunteer activity contributed over $22 billion worth of economic value to the nation's nonprofit sector (Corporation for National and Community Service 2009).

The instinct to perform public service in order to improve the local community can be found even among Millennials in grade school. Lee Fox, founder of KooDooZ, a cause-based social networking site for "kids who want to make money while making a difference," sees a real hunger on the part of her site's users to close the gap between the challenges society faces and the ability of individuals to make an impact (Fox 2010b). Another Web site, DoSomething.org, has inspired two million teenagers who have recognized the need to do something, believed in their ability to get it done, and then taken action to serve a cause of their choosing, often by starting their own nonprofits (DoSomething.org 2010).

Zach Bonner has been working to help raise awareness of, and money for, homeless youth since 2004, when he was just six years old. One year later, he established the Little Red Wagon Foundation and solicited donations for backpacks filled with food and supplies for homeless children. In 2010, after many successful fund-raising activities and presidential recognition of his volunteer work, Zach decided to create even greater public awareness of his cause by walking 2,478 miles across America. His journey was sponsored by McDonald's, K12 Education, the Office Depot Foundation, and the Philanthropy Project, and garnered truckloads of donations for homeless youth. The next step for the precocious, yet not completely atypical, middle-school Millennial is the production of a mini-documentary that will tell the world about his philanthropy and his work to end youth homelessness (Fox 2010b).

The spirit of service permeates the entire generation. In 2009, the percentage of college freshmen who believed it is "essential or very important to help people in need" rose to its highest level (70%) since 1970, when the last of the idealistic Baby Boomers entered college. Virtually all of the entering class of 2009 (93%) had performed some sort of volunteer work in high school. Almost half (48%) expected to participate in community service while in college, and almost as many (44%) considered it essential or very important that they become a leader in their community (Higher Education Research Institute 2009). More than one-third (35%) of all adult Millennials have participated in some form of voluntary community service (Institute of Politics 2010).

Ben Wofford, a University of Pennsylvania undergraduate, says the "service bug is part of his generation's DNA." During his senior year, he used the organizing lessons he had learned as a volunteer in the Obama campaign to turn the relatively inactive National Honor Society chapter at his high school into a source of volunteers who performed service in the community as frequently as two weekends per month. Upon entering Penn, he joined that college's Civic Scholars program, which required a commitment to service throughout his four years of college. "What they require are things I would probably have done anyway," he explained. "What it really does is take the idea of the 'best and the brightest' and apply it to service. It creates the opportunity for our generation's most powerful philanthropists and innovators to one day look back and say, 'Remember when this all began?'" (interview 2010).

Ninety-four percent of Millennials agree with Ben that community service is an effective way to solve problems at the local level, and 85 percent believe that is true for national problems as well. Almost 60 percent of Millennials are "personally interested in engaging in some form of public service to help the country." This spirit of service is strongly supported regardless of gender or party affiliation (Institute of Politics 2008).

Addressing the participants at the National Conference on Volunteering and Service in San Francisco on June 22, 2009, First Lady Michelle Obama made clear the level of importance she and her husband placed on the role of service in the country's evolving civic ethos. "This new Administration doesn't view service as separate from our national priorities, or in addition to our national priorities—we see it as the key to achieving our national priorities." Her explicit invocation of the role of community-based, nonprofit service organizations and the public's participation in activities to support them perfectly captured the Millennial Generation's belief in the ability of individual action, supported by collective commitment to a cause, to solve the nation's problems.

> Our government can rebuild our schools, but we need people to serve as mentors and tutors in those schools, to serve on the PTA and chaperone those field trips. Our government can modernize our health care system, but we need people to volunteer to help care for the sick and help people lead healthier lives. Our government can invest in clean energy, but we need people to use energy-efficient products, keep our public spaces clean, and train for the green jobs of the future. (M. Obama 2009)

The enactment of the Kennedy Serve America Act in the first year of the Obama administration increased from 75,000 to 250,000 the number of opportunities for Millennials to serve communities at home or abroad through programs of the Corporation for National and Community Service, such as AmeriCorps and Learn and Serve America, while providing Pell Grant–level support for the future education of those who served. Demand for CNCS positions quickly overwhelmed the supply.

This spirit of service also helped fill the ranks of the nation's volunteer military. Of the approximately two million men and women who have served in Iraq and Afghanistan, more than 60 percent, or almost 1.26 million, are members of the Millennial Generation. But more than one in five veterans between the ages of eighteen and twenty-four has had difficulty finding work when they return home. To address this problem, Mobilize.org, led by a fellow Millennial, Maya Enista, brought more than five dozen Millennial veterans of the two wars, representing all branches of the armed services, together for three days to develop service solutions for the major problems facing returning veterans. Joined by civilian Millennials and interested nonprofits, the summit, "Beyond the Welcome Home," prioritized the issues that needed to be addressed using the latest in interactive technologies. Although the most important issues the group identified did not sound very different from those facing veterans returning from earlier wars, the solutions that received the most support from the participants had a distinctly Millennial flavor. Many emphasized the group solidarity that Millennials feel so intensely. As one participant put it, "The way to deal with these issues is with veterans taking care of each other, just as we did in Iraq." Or as another participant said, "We need to do things ourselves, not have DOD [Department of Defense] do it" (Winograd 2010).

The Millennial Generation's determination to overhaul the institutions its elders built or, failing that, to start new ones was also evident in the suggestions offered at the conference. "We should use the established Veteran Service Organizations, but if they don't work, we should create new ones." Nor were the participants daunted by the challenge of taking on two of the federal government's biggest bureaucracies—the Department of Defense and the Veterans Administration. The generation's penchant for political action was evident in two of the more popular suggestions: "We need to become active and aware of political issues that involve veterans and encourage our fellow Millennials to vote for legislators who support veterans' issues." "By sharing information and becoming advocates we can get DOD and VA to respond."

Millennials also demonstrate an interest in serving their communities after they graduate from college, serve in the armed forces, or choose an occupation. Catherine Aranda, who graduated from Stanford in 2010, was heavily involved with public service throughout her undergraduate career, including co-directing a mentoring program for middle school students and working to coordinate family workshops for early childhood literacy. "I've always known that regardless of what I end up doing as a profession, public service is going to be a part of my life no matter what" (Jacobsen 2010).

Thanks to such attitudes, Teach for America, which places college graduates in low-income schools, saw a 42 percent increase in applications over 2008, with 35,000 students seeking to fill about 4,000 slots (Pope 2009). In 2009, TFA received 35,178 applications but was only able to find positions for 15 percent of those who applied (Jacobsen

2010). In addition to these governmental service programs, private sector employers have found it necessary to include the opportunity to serve the community as part of their recruitment messages to Millennials.

Despite this enthusiasm for community service among Millennials, not everyone believes that government involvement is the right way to encourage volunteerism. Although legislation to expand national service opportunities enjoyed bipartisan sponsorship in both the Senate and the House, a majority of Republicans voted against it. Senator Jim DeMint (R-SC) explained his opposition on his Web site: "We need to recognize that this bill does represent a lot of what's wrong with our federal government today. . . . Civil society works, because it is everything that government is not. It's small, it's personal, it's responsible, and it's accountable" (DeMint 2009). And Louisiana Senator David Vitter suggested, "This new federal bureaucracy would, in effect, politicize charitable activity around the country" (Broder 2009). Their arguments illustrated the wide gulf in political philosophies concerning what role, if any, government should play in rewarding those who serve their country in some capacity.

During America's last civic era, this debate was settled decisively on the side of government support, at least where returning veterans were concerned. The GI Bill of Rights sent millions of World War II servicemen, the Millennials' great-grandparents, to college. By exponentially increasing the number of college-educated workers, the program helped pave the way for a long period of postwar growth and vastly expanded the size of the country's middle class. If history is any guide, the civic Millennial Generation will follow in the footsteps of the civic GI Generation and, through its dedication to public service, leave America an even stronger country than the one it inherited.

ENVISIONING AMERICA IN 2040

In 2004, after a frustrating experience that found them knocking on doors but not being asked to contribute ideas to the presidential campaign, a few college students decided to form the first think tank run by and for Millennials. Their efforts generated a connection across civic generations through Anne Roosevelt, a granddaughter of Franklin Roosevelt, who told them, "We [the Franklin and Eleanor Roosevelt Institute] have been waiting for fifty years for this to happen" (Dunlop

2010). By 2010, more than 8,000 Millennials had become involved in one of the eighty-six chapters of the Roosevelt Institute Campus Network across the country.

In March 2010, the group launched its Think 2040 project, "a program designed by and for Millennials," in the words of its national director, Hilary Doe, "to empower the generation to reframe the challenges and opportunities facing America and design the future that we want to inherit." The project's ultimate goal is to "leverage our unique generational characteristics, transform our communities nationwide, and redefine the American dream" (Doe e-mail 2010). Within a year, the project involved over 2,000 young people, representing the full diversity of the Millennial Generation, in group discussions to design a "Blueprint for the Milllennial America" (Doe and Kolodin 2010).

Their vision of America in 2040 is a country "that continues to be a model for the world in terms of innovation, productivity, and strength . . . [and] a moral leader as well." The participants wanted America to live by three core values: "a deeply held concern for equity, respect for the individual and society, and a belief in community empowerment and self-determination." Together, these values and the group's vision paint a picture that "uniquely represents the world Millennials aspire to create: more accessible, more equitable, more community-driven, more entrepreneurial, more inclusive, and better prepared to tackle the long-term challenges our country faces." Participants were appalled at the inequities of the country's current educational system, "the foundation of our economy and democracy," and placed its reform at the top of their list of priorities. They committed to changing the system's unequal outcomes, but didn't want American schools to "lose their essential creativity and civic function in an effort to meet federally mandated standards." Rather, as part of their generation's focus on acting locally, they favored "an eclectic mix of federal incentives and local power and creativity to revitalize American education."

Millennials in Think 2040 approached America's environmental problems with the same values that informed their broader vision. Because they believed that "environmental challenges fundamentally alter the texture of communities," they proposed solutions that respected "the needs of America's communities," so that no one would be asked to "make sacrifices without fully considering the cost to communities across the United States." To accomplish this goal, which clearly reflects the special sensibilities of Millennials, the report prioritized the development and usage of renewable sources of energy above all other environmental solutions. The participants argued that "creating a thriving domestic market for renewable sources of energy, fostering a strong green-jobs sector, and achieving energy independence . . . was essential for the long-term health of the country's environment and its economy," as well as for "maintaining national and global security and preserving biodiversity."

Just as, after World War II, the previous civic generation created "a system of global cooperation to promote human rights, poverty reduction, and conflict resolution," these globally minded Millennials shared "an overwhelming belief that it is the moral duty of the United States to reduce global conflict by reinvigorating international institutions." "The rise of genocide in the 20th century has led to a fundamentally different conception of America's international responsibility" to guide the country's foreign policy. In their Millennial America, the United States would work "with its allies across the globe to promote sustainable development, capacity building, and community ownership, instead of invading and occupying enemy territory," and use "defense, diplomacy, and development as equal pillars of U.S. foreign policy."

At home, Think 2040 participants wanted "to build an American economy that supports and rewards creativity, ingenuity, and personal determination to succeed," leading them to endorse banking reform, infrastructure investment, and strengthening of the social safety net. Their safety net would "lower barriers to entrepreneurship, enable workers to rebound in times of need, and combat intergenerational poverty by allowing children the opportunity to succeed regardless of their family challenges." As Aaron Cohen, a student at American University told his peers, "We need more than a social safety net, we need a social safety trampoline."

Millennials in Think 2040 also support "a culture of wellness in America [to] keep health costs down for both citizens and the government, and ensure that no one lacks care because he or she cannot afford insurance." Their more holistic vision of a healthy America in 2040 focused on equitable access to health care based upon "a diet built on local food; a citizenry more fully equipped with knowledge of how to stay healthy; and a culture of medicine more oriented toward promoting wellness than treating sickness" (Doe and Kolodin 2010).

Exemplifying their generation's penchant for combining high ideals with pragmatic solutions, the Blueprint's action plan suggested Millennials "demand change, but act locally. Work to combat challenges, but do so from within the system. Create change, but not just through protest. . . . What allows us, as communities, to overcome obstacles . . . is collaborative action." The report emphasized the need not only for high levels of civic engagement by the generation, but the need for reforms in the political system to reduce the role of money in elections, thereby creating "a more open, accountable, and democratic electoral system." Doe is confident of her generation's ability to effect the changes the Blueprint advocates because "our shared experiences have made us socially empathetic, tolerant, informed, collaborative, engaged, innovative, entrepreneurial, effective problem solvers both capable and willing to work together to overcome the challenges that we face" (Doe e-mail 2010).

WHICH CIVIC ETHOS
WILL AMERICA ADOPT?

One insightful commentator, Gregory Rodriguez, wrote that if the United States "was a cartoon character, it would be a cheerful fellow with his head in the clouds and his feet planted squarely on the ground" (Rodriguez 2010). This combination of idealism and pragmatism, which Millennial Generation beliefs and attitudes epitomize, was also visible at the beginning of America's first fourth turning. As Harvard historian Bernard Bailyn wrote, "The blending of realism and idealism permeates the entire history of the Revolutionary era." He suggests that "if Thomas Jefferson's intellectual idealism had not been tempered by the 'hard-headed pragmatism' he learned as a 'man of business,' he wouldn't have played such a powerful role" in the nation's history (Bailyn 2003, 47). Or, as Robert Penn Warren expressed the dynamic, "realism is the burr under the metaphysical saddle of American idealism" (Walter and Ellison 1957).

America's next civic ethos, therefore, must encompass the nation's highest ideals, while presenting realistic solutions to today's challenges, in order to become the consensus by which the country manages its affairs. This new synthesis of ideology and pragmatism can only be found by embracing the beliefs of Millennials in both bottom–up, peer-to-peer problem solving and the use of government to generate a collective commitment to deal with the nation's most pressing problems. Just as Millennials who participated in the Think 2040 project sought to define a new vision to direct the nation's progress and a set of values to live by, the nation's political leaders will have to enunciate their own vision of the type of country they want America to become and a clear statement of the values that should guide it on that journey. As in previous fourth turnings, the current volatility of American politics will subside when one side or the other convinces a majority of the country that its proposed civic ethos is best suited to advance the ideals and welfare of the United States in this century.

As the Millennial era dawned, the leadership of both political parties misread the task before them and focused on the partisan battles of the present, instead of gaining the upper hand in the debate over what vision and set of values should guide the country's future development.

Initially, Republicans took a defiant, just-say-no attitude toward any suggestion that the country needed to hear an alternative vision from its leaders. But spurred by the energy and enthusiasm of what was at the beginning a bottom-up movement, the Tea Party, Republicans eventually found new power and possibilities from a vision built on individual liberty and smaller government. With a pledge to never again abandon their values of fiscal discipline and free market capitalism, the party's leadership was able to win over enough skeptical Tea Party adherents to at least be given what newly elected House Speaker Republican John Boehner called a "second chance" to prove they could govern according to this new civic ethos.

Republicans quickly and effectively adopted the tools of social media in their candidates' campaigns immediately after 2008 and married them with vast new sums of corporate spending from undisclosed sources in 2010 to communicate a disciplined message that reflected their vision and values. By focusing on deficit reduction, lower taxes, economic entrepreneurialism, and cutbacks in government programs as a way to grow the economy, Republicans were able to recruit and elect messengers who believed in the same civic ethos. There was a certain irony that the party of Lincoln, responsible in the mid-nineteenth century for the first major expansion of the role of the federal government since the Constitution's adoption, gained power in the current civic era by swearing allegiance to the document as originally written. The Republican campaign did, however, provide a clear choice between its values and those of the Democratic Party's new leadership.

Harder to understand was the failure of Barack Obama to carry forward the vision and values that elected him president into the governing style of his administration. On the campaign trail in 2008, the values of inclusivity and bottom-up participation were built into the campaign's stunningly successful strategy. But once in office, his vision of an America with expanded opportunities, guaranteed through a caring government's intervention in nonfunctioning markets and protection of civil liberties, was obscured by the burden of bureaucratic processes and the obfuscation inherent in legislative compromise. Only when the electorate sent him a sharp rebuke in the midterm elections did the president acknowledge that, in the rush to deal with what was clearly an economic crisis, he had too quickly diluted his commitments to also change how government worked: "We were in such a hurry to get things done that we didn't change how things got done. And I think that frustrated people" (Nicholas and Oliphant 2010).

The cognitive dissonance between the empowering promise of the campaign and the top-down nature of many of Obama's policies grew so loud that supporters did indeed turn away in frustration, or as one put it, "exhaustion." The failure to connect his campaign's vision and values with his governing approach even enabled the president's opponents to suggest that the former community organizer was out of touch with the American people.

After the midterm elections, the president's supporters, such as Marshall Ganz, who helped devise the grassroots organizing model for the Obama campaign, accused the president of abandoning his transformational leadership approach in favor of a more transactional leadership style that operates "within the routine, and is practiced to maintain, rather than change, the status quo." He urged the president to return to his campaign approach and engage his "followers in the risky and often exhilarating work of changing the world," based on "shared values that become the wellsprings of the courage, creativity and hope needed to open new pathways for success" (Ganz 2010). Doing so would require confronting, rather than compromising with, the alternative civic ethos put forward by a resurgent Republican Party ready to contest him on every vote in the Congress.

Even in an otherwise disastrous election for the Democrats in 2010, the Republican Party's vision and values failed to attract much interest or support from Millennials. They felt that its focus on individual liberty at the cost of national community, and its unwillingness to embrace the full spectrum of American life in order to preserve traditional beliefs, did not reflect their values. The Republican vision of smaller government also flew directly in the face of Millennials' belief in the importance of using collective action to improve the welfare of each member of the group. By focusing so much on only the ideologically conservative strand of America's political DNA, the leadership of the Republican Party left the door open for Democrats to propose an alternative conception of an American civic ethos that would be more in line with the demographic destiny of the country. As a result, there is still of time for President Obama, as the leader of the Democratic Party, to win support for a civic ethos much more aligned with Millennials' values and beliefs than the one offered by the opposition. The presence of a competing picture of the future, which will now need to be expressed in real legislative alternatives by House Republicans, provides both the president and his party a valuable opportunity to debate which civic ethos the country should adopt.

To win that debate, however, the president will have to govern in accord with the vision and values that animated his successful 2008 campaign, whether Democrats in Congress follow his lead or not. He will need to make clear to the American public, as he did to the 2010 graduating class at the University of Michigan, his instinctive and distinctive understanding of both strands of America's political DNA. The programs and policies of the rest of his administration will need to reflect that vision and those values if he hopes to be successful in using to use the bully pulpit of the presidency to pull America toward the adoption of his proposed civic ethos.

Just as previous syntheses of America's belief in both individual freedom and collective action found a way to appeal to both the ideological and operational attitudes, or the idealism and pragmatism, of Americans in earlier eras, the new Millennial era consensus will need to integrate national purpose with individual choice.

A MILLENNIAL ERA CIVIC ETHOS

The new Millennialist view of how to resolve the central paradox of American democracy will not be a rehash of, or a return to, New Deal progressivism, which so many ideological liberals continue to advocate. A generation raised on technologies that enable it to customize each choice it makes, so that it is uniquely "my space," is not about to embrace programs that offer only one-size-fits-all solutions or centralize decision making in an unresponsive bureaucracy. But conservative policies that deny the value of social equity and community effort are equally unappealing to Millennials. The Millennial civic ethos will instead allow for both consensus and customization. It will use democratic processes to determine national priorities and rules for permissible behavior by both individual and groups, including corporations and nonprofits, even as it provides incentives for greater individual and local initiative and creates the environment for greater equality of opportunity. Examples of these new approaches already exist in both the public and private sector, but neither party has been able or willing to fully embrace them and articulate a compelling civic ethos to guide the country in the twenty-first century.

For instance, this brand new way for American democracy to work requires a more central role for Millennial era technologies in changing government than the Obama administration was initially willing to adopt. Rather than create hybrid processes that patch social network technologies on top of a very opaque and aloof government bureaucracy, the new governing approach would use the principles of open systems and group involvement to build alternative ways to administer and initiate government programs. It would require devolving responsibility for designing the details of program administration to the local level, where Millennials believe action can have the most impact. The federal government's role would be to make clear to localities and communities the national rules they would need to follow and use information technologies to collect the data to ensure that they do. This can be done using the same incentives-based approach of the administration's Race to the Top school performance-improvement grants or, less effectively, by establishing the type of mandates imposed by the new health care legislation on individual and institutional behavior. Gaining acceptance for this new approach would require abandoning the one-to-many broadcast model of communicating the administration's message through existing media filters, in favor of involving the president's supporters directly in the process of both developing and selling the administration's programs, just as companies are doing every day with their customers on social networks.

With Democrats in control of the Senate and Republicans running the House, the country has a unique opportunity to discover which party is most willing to throw off the habits and perquisites of congressional deliberations in order to embrace a different approach to law making. The Republican House Transition Office's call for participatory reform of congressional processes, by having "smaller, more focused legislation" written only "in committee in plain public view" and then posted online for three days before any vote is taken, was the opening volley in a debate over which party is more willing to involve the public in the legislative process (Boehner 2010). President Obama quickly found common ground with Republican congressional leaders after the election on eliminating earmarks, or individual expenditures mandated by a senator or representative for their home districts, but this was more of a symbolic, hybrid reform, than a new way to decide how to spend taxpayer's money.

Instituting a new appropriations process altogether would mean using objective data on what programs are working at what cost to achieve an agreed-upon set of priorities as the basis for spending taxpayer money, rather than upon the personal preferences of elected officials. Authorization legislation, which establishes the policy parameters within which agencies must administer the law, would also need to be developed using a more interactive approach. Similar to the e-Democracia experiment in Brazil, policy would be developed in a Millennial-like, continuous, and comprehensive conversation with lawmakers' constituents. Until these new ways to legislate are put in place, Congress will continue to be the most scorned branch of the federal government, regardless of which party controls it.

Nowhere is the need for a Millennial era approach to the nation's problems greater than in our economic and educational institutions. Unfortunately, economic policy has a long tradition of being determined more by outdated ideologies than by creative new ideas. The ideological roots of the current debate over whether to use Keynesian demand stimulation or to have the government withdraw from the economic arena in order to restore the nation's economy go back at least eight decades. As a result, finding new ways to stimulate innovation and creativity at the local level with the full support of national government institutions, an approach which ultimately is the key to economic growth in this era, will not be easy. As Dan Carol, a fellow at the NDN think tank in Washington, explained, "overcoming 20th Century government and creating new bottom-up innovation won't succeed by re-arranging the hardware of government on a white board. We need new thinking and collaborative software to effectively re-wire our economic circuitry" (Carol 2010a). Policies that harness local efforts in both the public and private sector to national resources and priorities break the mold of current economic thinking. Their implementation would create innovative economic programs that would be both more effective and better aligned with Millennial Generation beliefs and behaviors.

Although bipartisan agreement on any aspect of economic policy, let alone proposals based on a new economic theory, is unlikely in the near future, there is greater potential for reaching a consensus on a new way to properly educate the Millennial Generation and its younger siblings for the inherently global economic competition of this century. Already, the demonstrable failure of the current system of public education has led both parties to inch toward agreement on a new approach. Fortunately, an alternative design built upon a common vision and set of values has demonstrated success. What is now required for this change to take hold is for both parties to take off their ideological blinders and see what can be done when both collective will and individual initiative are joined in common purpose. The nation's universities will also need to join in the transformation of America's most important intellectual infrastructure and embrace the benefits of a more student-centered approach to higher learning. As more and more Millennials become parents, support for a complete overhaul of the nation's educational institutions will become a key part of the country's new civic ethos.

While governmental institutions experiment with new ways to make democracy work, the private sector will also have to give up old habits and find new ways to incorporate Millennials' need for meaning and purpose into the daily routine of commerce. A July 2009 Young & Rubicam national survey showed that "a majority of Americans already say they have changed their lifestyles and the way they behave in the marketplace. . . . People are returning to old-fashioned values . . . and they are applying these ideals in their relationships and their careers and in their consumption habits as well." On the basis of personal interviews across the country, it was clear that consumer behavior had moved "from mindless consumption to mindful consumption," with Millennials leading the way (Gerzema and D'Antonio 2010). From media to music and from sports to organized religion, private-sector institutions will find they need to give up trying to tweak existing approaches and, instead, respond to these new values in order to bond with their supporters in the emerging Millennial era.

As tumultuous as these changes will be, the bedrock beliefs of Millennials will cause America to adhere firmly to its traditional values of family and community, individual initiative and collective effort, personal freedom and social justice. The generation's willingness to perform extraordinary acts of service and sacrifice to strengthen the country and its institutions will provide the stability the country will need to successfully make the transition to a new era. Although it remains the responsibility of the country's political leadership to guide the nation and accelerate its progress, it will ultimately be up to each individual citizen to ensure that the vision and values the country endorses are commensurate with the challenges the country faces. To maximize its chances for success, the United States would be well advised to let its next great generation provide the country the wisdom and guidance to shape America's civic ethos in the Millennial era.

Note on Data Sources and Analyses

The Ideological and Operational scales referenced in chapter 3 were originally developed by Lloyd A. Free and Hadley Cantril using data collected in specially commissioned national surveys conducted in 1964 by Gallup. To develop the Ideological Spectrum, respondents were asked to agree or disagree with five statements dealing with the relative roles of the federal and state government, regulation of business, and the proper balance between individual initiative and governmental social welfare efforts. The more answers a respondent gave that reflected a belief in a limited role for government, especially the federal government, the more strongly conservative he or she was considered to be.

To calculate the Operational Spectrum, respondents were asked to indicate their support of or opposition to five government programs, all of which related to specific initiatives proposed by President Lyndon Johnson as part of his Great Society program: federal aid to education, Medicare, low-rent public housing, urban renewal, and anti-poverty efforts. An answer indicating support for any of the programs described in the questions was considered to represent a liberal attitude. The more liberal answers a respondent gave, the more strongly liberal he or she was considered to be.

Data drawn from the Pew Survey Research Center's Political Values and Core Attitudes Survey conducted periodically since 1987 offered a reasonable facsimile of the 1964 Gallup surveys. Three questions included in Pew's 1987, 1994, 2002, and 2009 surveys were used to recalculate the Ideological Spectrum:

1. Government regulation of business usually does more harm than good.
2. The federal government should run ONLY (Pew's emphasis) those things that cannot be run at the local level.
3. The federal government controls too much of our daily lives.

Agreement with each of these statements was considered a conservative belief. The more conservative answers a respondent gave, the more strongly conservative the respondent was considered to be on the scale.

The questions used to calculate the Operational Scale all related to the responsibility of government to provide economic assistance to those in need:

1. It is the responsibility of government to take care of people who can't take care of themselves.
2. The government should help more needy people even if it means going deeper in debt.
3. The government should guarantee every citizen enough to eat and a place to sleep.

Agreement with any statement was considered a liberal belief. The more such answers that were given, the more liberal a respondent was scored.

The generational analysis of U.S. survey data cited extensively in chapter 2 was drawn primarily from the May 2009 Pew Political Values and Core Attitudes Survey. The generational analysis of international survey data cited in chapter 13 was drawn from the June 2010 Pew Global Attitudes Survey. In both instances, Pew generously made that data available and provided special generational cross-tabulations broken out for our use in this book.

References

Abbott, H. 2010. "The Michael Jordan View of LeBron James." ESPN, July 19. http://espn.go.com/blog/truehoop/post/_/id/18416/the-michael-jordan-view-of-lebron-james.

Allee, V. 2010. Telephone interview with Morley Winograd, January 7.

Allstate/NationalJournal. 2010. "Allstate/NationalJournal Heartland Monitor Poll Topline: Generation Y." *National Journal,* April 22–26. http://www3.nationaljournal.com/img/news/topline_adults_100506.pdf.

Altmayer, C. 2006. "Moving to Performance Based Management." *Government Finance Review,* June 8–14.

Anderson, D. 2010. Millennials Will Save the World—You'll See." *The Next Great Generation (TNGG),* June 21. http://www.thenextgreatgeneration.com/2010/06/21/millennials-save-world/.

Arango, T. 2009. "Make Room Cynics; MTV Wants to Do Some Good." *New York Times,* April 18. http://www.nytimes.com/2009/04/19/business/media/19mtv.html?scp=1&sq=arango%20make%20room%20%20mtv%20wants%20to%20do%20some%20good&st=cse.

Art, R. J. 2010. "The United States and the Rise of China." *Political Science Quarterly* (Fall), 359–391.

Austin, B. 2010. Telephone interview with Morley Winograd, January 11.

Bailyn, B. 2003. *To Begin the World Anew: The Genius and Ambiguities of the American Founders.* New York: Knopf.

Baker, P. 2010. "Education of a President." *New York Times Magazine,* October 12. http://www.nytimes.com/2010/10/17/magazine/17obama-t.html.

Banchero, S. 2010. "Two-Year Colleges Seek More Graduates." *Wall Street Journal,* April 21.

Bannon, S. K. 2010. *Generation Zero: A Cultural History of the Great Depression.* Motion picture trailer. N.p.: Citizens United Productions. http://www.generationzeromovie.com.

Beaudry, M. 2010. Telephone interview with Morley Winograd, January 7.

Beck, Glenn. 2008. "Trophy Kids." Glenn Beck program, October 22. http://www.glennbeck.com/content/articles/article/198/17145/.

Behn, R. D. n.d. "The PerformanceStat Potential." Unpublished manuscript. Cambridge: Kennedy School, Harvard University.

Beilaczyc, K., and A. Collins. 1999. "Learning Communities in Classrooms: A Reconceptualization of Educational Practice." In *Instructional Design Theories and Models: A New Paradigm of Instructional Theory,* volume 2, ed. C. M. Reigeluth 269–291. Mahwah, N.J.: Lawrence Erlbaum Associates.

Beinhocker, E. D. 2006. *The Origin of Wealth: Evolution, Complexity, and the Radical Remaking of Economics.* Boston: Harvard Business School Press.

Beinhocker, E., N. Hanauer, and E. Liu. 2008. "The Progressive Economy: A Primer on Complexity Economics, and a New Paradigm for Policy." Unpublished memo to the Democracy Alliance.

Bendixen and Amandi Associates. 2010. "National Study of Young Hispanics." June 10. http://democracia-ahora.org/national_study_of_young_hispanics_signup/.

Blackmon, D. A., J. Levitz, A. Berzon, and L. Etter. 2010. "Birth of a Movement: Tea Party Arose from Conservatives Steeped in Crisis." *Wall Street Journal,* October 29.

Block, S. 2009. "In a Recession, Is College Worth It?: Fear of Debt Changes Plans." *USA Today,* August 31.

Bloomberg BusinessWeek. 2010. "Obama's Corporate Messaging." February 22.

Blue Dog Coalition. [2010]. "The Blue Dog Coalition: 15 Years of Leadership." U.S. Congress, House of Representatives. http://www.house.gov/melancon/BlueDogs/10%20Years%200f%20Leadership.html. (accessed November 2010).

Blume, H. 2009. "Legislation Would Give Parents New Powers to Trigger Change at a School." *Los Angeles Times,* December 7. http://latimesblogs.latimes.com/lanow/2009/12/legislation-would-give-parents-new-powers-to-trigger-change-at-a-school.html.

Boehner, J. 2010. "What the Next Speaker Must Do." *Wall Street Journal,* November 5. http://online.wsj.com/article/SB10001424052748703805704575594280015549088.html.

Boston Globe. 2010. "Enrollment Is Just the First Step." *Boston Globe,* July 5. http://www.boston.com/bostonglobe/editorial_opinion/editorials/articles/2010/07/05/enrollment_is_just_the_first_step/.

Branigan, T. 2009. "Barack Obama Criticises Internet Censorship at Meeting in China." *Guardian,* November 16. http://www.guardian.co.uk/world/2009/nov/16/barack-obama-criticises-internet-censorship-china.

Broder, D. S. 2009. "A Bipartisan Bill Worth Celebrating." *Washington Post,* April 5.

Brokaw, T. 1999. *The Greatest Generation Speaks: Letters and Reflections.* New York: Random House.

Brown, John S., and P. Duguid. 1996. "The University in the Digital Age." *Change* (July), 10–19. http://www.johnseelybrown.com/The%20University%20in%20the%20Digital%20Age.pdf.

Brownstein, R. 2009. "The Left's Fatal Abstraction." *National Journal,* December 24.

————. 2010a. "Obama Stays the Course." *Los Angeles Times,* March 19.

————. 2010b. "Dems' Governing Core Stays Intact." *National Journal,* April 3. http://www.nationaljournal.com/njmagazine/nj_20100403_2313.php.

————. 2010c. "Children of the Great Recession." *National Journal,* May 8.

————. 2010d. "Obama's Two Front Challenge." *Los Angeles Times,* September 10.

Buckley, C. 2010. "China PLA Officer Urges Challenging US Dominance." *Reuters,* February 28. http://www.reuters.com/article/idUSTRE6200P620100301.

Buffa, D. W. 1997. "Learning in the Information Age: A Conversation for California's Future." Unpublished report. Lafayette: Institute for the New California.

Burke, E. [1774] 2010. "Speech to the Electors of Bristol." Library of Economics and Liberty. *http://www.econlib.org/library/LFBooks/Burke/brkSWv4c1.html*.

Burns, C. 2009. "Bizarro World," Bob Cesca blog, December 23. http://www.bobcesca.com/blog- archives/2009/12/bizarro_world.html.

Burstein, D. D. 2010. "What the New York Times Missed about Twenty-Somethings." *Huffington Post*, August 25. http://www.huffingtonpost.com/david-d-burstein/what-the-new-york-times-m_b_694728.html.

Bustillo, M. 2009. "Wal-Mart to Assign New 'Green' Ratings." *Wall Street Journal*, July 16.

Campbell, A., P. E. Converse, W. E. Miller, and D. E. Stokes. 1960. *The American Voter*. New York: Wiley.

Caplow, T., L. Hicks, and B. J. Wattenberg. 2001. *The First Measured Century: An Illustrated Guide to Trends in America*. Washington, D.C.: American Enterprise Institute.

Captain Planet and the Planeteers. 2010. "Who We Are." Web site description. http://captainplanet.me/about/about-this-website.

Carberry, M. 2009. "Is Obama's Health Care Maelstorm [*sic*] the Birth of American Politics?" *Huffington Post*, August 6. http://www.huffingtonpost.com/maegan-carberry/is-obamas-health-care-mae_b_252218.html.

Carol, D. 2010a. "Rebooting 20th Century Government: New Software Needed." NDN blog, May 27. http://ndn.org/blog/2010/05/rebooting-20th-century-government-new-software-needed.

———. 2010b. "The Acceleration Agenda: Job Creation, Innovation, and Economic Development in the 21st Century." Online working paper. New Policy Institute, September. http://www.newpolicyinstitute.org/wp-content/uploads/2010/09/AccelerationAgenda.pdf.

Carr, A. 2010. "The 100 Most Influential Congressional Tweeters: Nancy Pelosi, Republicans Dominate." *Fast Company*, November 18. http://www.fastcompany.com/1703747/the-100-most-influential-house-reps-on-twitter-nancy-pelosi-michele-bachmann-republicans-dom.

Cave, Damien. 2010. "A Generation Gap over Immigration." *New York Times*, May 17. http://www.nytimes.com/2010/05/18/us/18divide.html?pagewanted=2&hp.

CBS News. 2009. "Economic Burdens Mount for New Grads." *CBS News*, May 19. http://www.cbsnews.com/stories/2009/05/19/national/main5024909.shtml.

CBS News/MTV. 2006. "Environment and Diversity." Monthly Poll #3. Interuniversity Consortium for Political and Social Research (*ICPSR*), May 30–June 9. http://icpsr.umich.edu/icpsrweb/ICPSR/studies/04618.

Chait, J. 2009. "And the Rest Is Just Noise." *New Republic*, December 24. http://www.tnr.com/article/politics/just-noise?utm_source=TNR+Daily&utm_campaign=edb8bf56c3—TNR_Daily_122409&utm_medium=email.

Charnwood, L. 1996. *Abraham Lincoln: A Biography*. Lanham, Md.: Madison Books.

Chernow, R. 2010. "The Feuding Fathers." *Wall Street Journal*, June 26–27.

Christensen, C., C. W. Johnson, and M. B. Horn. 2008. *Disrupting Class: How Disruptive Education Will Change the Way the World Works*. New York: McGraw-Hill.

CIRCLE. 2010. "Youth Voters in the 2010 Election." Center for Information and Research on Civic Learning and Engagement, November. http://www .civicyouth.org/youth-voters-in-the-2010-elections/.

Clayborn, A. 2010. Interview on ESPN during the Iowa-Penn State football game, October 2.

Clift, E. 2010. "A Modern Day LBJ?" *Newsweek*, January 15. http://www.newsweek .com/2010/01/14/a-modern-day-lbj.html.

CNN. 2008. "Election Center 2008: Exit Polls." CNN, November. http://www .cnn.com/ELECTION/2008/results/polls.main/.

———. 2010. "Election Center: Exit Polls." CNN, November. http://www .cnn.com/ELECTION/2010/results/polls/#USH00p1.

CNN Wire Staff. 2010. "Obama Says He Should Have Advertised Policies Better." CNN, October 22. http://edition.cnn.com/2010/POLITICS/ 10/21/obama.back.yard/index.html.

Cohen, N. 2008. "A Political Agitator Finds a Double-Edged Weapon." *New York Times*, July 6. http://www.nytimes.com/2008/07/06/us/ politics/06website .html?_r=2.

Cohen, S. 2010. "Growing Public Support for Sustainability." *Huffington Post*, April 19. http://www.huffingtonpost.com/steven-cohen/growing-public-support-fo_b_542600.h.

Cohn, J. 2010. "Wanted: More Fraud, Abuse in Government Spending." *New Republic*, October 4. http://www.tnr.com/blog/jonathan-cohn/78149/ stimulus-recovery-spending-waste-fraud?utm_source=ESP+Integrated+ List&utm_campaign=1a9badd030-TNR_Daily_100510&utm_medium=email.

Collins, J. 2001. *Good to Great: Why Some Companies Make the Leap . . . and Others Don't*. New York: HarperCollins.

Cone. 2010. "2010 Cone Cause Evolution Study." Cone Web site, September 17. http://www.coneinc.com/cause-marketing-remains-strong.

Connery, M. 2008. "The Pundits Are on Board." Future Majority blog, November 13. http://www.futuremajority.com/node/4003.

Continetti, M. 2004. "The Real Grover Norquist." *Weekly Standard*, September 28. http://www.weeklystandard.com/Content/Public/Articles/000/000/004/ 695jwmmb.asp.

Coppered. 2007. "The Millennials." Durban Bud blog, November 13. http://www.durbanbud.com/blog/archives/2007/11/the_millennials_1.html.

Corporation for National and Community Service. Office of Research and Policy Development. 2009. "Volunteering in America: Research Highlights." Washington, D.C.: Corporation for National and Community Service, July. http://www.volunteeringinamerica.gov/assets/resources/VolunteeringInAme ricaResearchHighlights.pdf.

———. 2010. "Volunteering in America: National, State and City Information." Washington, D.C.: Corporation for National and Community Service. June. http://www.volunteeringinamerica.gov/assets/resources/IssueBriefFINALJune 15.pdf.

Cost, J. 2010. "Would He Rather Fight Than Switch?" *Weekly Standard*, November 1. http://www.weeklystandard.com/articles/would-he-rather-fight-switch_511749.html.

Davidson, V. M. 2009. "Ronald Reagan's Clarity . . . 'The Gipper' Speaks out Against Socialized Medicine." Frugal Café blog, June 22. http://www.frugal-cafe

.com/public_html/frugal-blog/frugal-cafe-blogzone/2009/06/22/ronald-reagans-clarity-the-gipper-speaks-out-against-socialized-medicine/.

Dede, C. 2005. "Planning for Neomillennial Learning Styles: Implications for Investments in Technology and Faculty." In *Educating the Net Generation*, ed. D. G. Oblinger and J. L. Oblinger, 15.1–15.22. Boulder, Colo.: Educause.

DeMint, J. 2009. "National Service Act Represents Flawed Government." GOP12 blog, March 25. http://www.gop12.com/2009/03/demint-national-service-act-represents.html.

Dempsey, C. 2010. "Smart Transportation: Changing Urban Mobility." Presentation to 20th annual Regional Plan Association assembly, Waldorf Astoria Hotel, New York, April 20.

DeWolfe, C. 2009. Interview with Morley Winograd. Los Angeles, February 4.

Dickstein, M. 2009. *Dancing in the Dark: A Cultural History of the Great Depression*. New York: Norton.

Dionne, E. J. 2010a. "The Right Court Fight." *Washington Post*, April 26. http://www.washingtonpost.com/wp-dyn/content/article/2010/04/25/AR2010042502987.html.

———. 2010b. "Obama Needs to Relearn the Art of Politicking." *Washington Post*, August 30. http://www.washingtonpost.com/wp-dyn/content/article/2010/08/29/AR2010082902899.html.

Disney XD. 2010. "Generation XD-Disney Releases Biggest Ever Study of Tweens in Europe." Marketwire press release, January 11. http://www.marketwire.com/press-release/Generation-XD-Disney-Releases-Biggest-Ever-Study-of-Tweens-in-Europe-1099550.htm.

Doe, H. 2010. E-mail exchange with Morley Winograd, November 5.

Doe, H., and Z. Kolodin, eds. 2010. "Blueprint for the Millennial America—A Report on the Results of Think 2040 Phase I." *Roosevelt Institute Campus Network*, December 1. http://www.think2040.0rg/.

Dolan, M., and S. Terlap. 2009. "GM/Ford Gird for Small Car Showdown as Consumers Shun SUVs." *Wall Street Journal*, December 7. http://online.wsj.com/article/SB10001424052748703939404574568463753957326.html.

DoSomething.org. 2010. "Who We Are." Web site description. http://www.dosomething.org/about.

Douthat, R. 2009. "A Generation in the Balance." *New York Times*, November 29. http://www.nytimes.com/2009/11/30/opinion/30douthat.html?_r=2&hp.

Duderstadt, J. J. 2000. *A University for the 21st Century*. Ann Arbor: University of Michigan Press.

———. 2010. Interview with Morley Winograd. Ann Arbor, August 22.

Duderstadt, J. J., D. E. Atkins, and D. Van Houweling. 2002. *Higher Education in the Digital Age: Technology Issues and Strategies for American Colleges and Universities*. Westport, Conn.: Praeger.

Duncan, A. 2010. "Crisis in the Classroom." Interview by Christiana Amanpour, *This Week*. ABC News, August 29. http://abcnews.go.com/watch/this-week/SH559082/VD5582230/crisis-in-the-classroom.

Dunlop, T. 2010. "How the Journey Began." Roosevelt Institute Campus Network blog, April 8. http://www.rooseveltcampusnetwork.org/blog/how-journey-began.

Duval, J. 2010. *Next Generation Democracy: What the Open Source Revolution Means for Power, Politics and Change*. New York: Bloomsbury USA.

Edelman, R. 2010. "2010 Edelman Trust Barometer: An Annual Global Opinion Leaders Study. Executive Summary." www.edelman.com/trust/2010/docs/2010_Trust_Barometer_Executive_Summary.pdf.

Ellick, A. B. 2009. "Pakistan Rock Rails against the US, Not the Taliban." *New York Times*, November 11. http://atwar.blogs.nytimes.com/2009/11/11/tuning-out-the-taliban-in-pakistan-pop/?partner.

Elliott, P. 2010. "Upset Republicans Believe Tea Party Cost GOP Senate Control." *Huffington Post*, November 6. http://www.huffingtonpost.com/2010/11/06/upset-republicans-believe_n_779924.html.

Energy Action Coalition. 2010. Web site description. http://energyactioncoalition.org/content/about.

Faria, C. F. 2010a. "Can People Help Legislators Make Better Laws? Brazil Shows How." Personal Democracy Forum blog, April 29. http://techpresident.com/user-blog/can-people-help-legislators-make-better-laws-brazil-shows-how.

———. 2010b. Telephone interview with Morley Winograd, June 16.

———. 2010c. E-mail communication with Morley Winograd, November 11.

Fernandez, J. 2010. "Remarks Prepared for Delivery: by John Fernandez, Assistant Secretary of Commerce for Economic Development, NADO Annual Conference." San Diego, Cal., U.S. Economic Development Administration (EDA), August 31. http://www.eda.gov/NewsEvents/Speeches/NADOSpeech.xml.

Fox, L. 2010a. Interview with Morley Winograd. Los Angeles, April 24.

———. 2010b. "Generation Z—the New Philanthropists." Koodooz blog. September 29. http://koodooz.wordpress.com/2010/09/09/generation-z-the-new-philanthropists.

Free, L. A., and H. Cantril. 1968. *The Political Beliefs of Americans: A Study of Public Opinion*. New York: Simon and Schuster.

Frey, W. H. 2010. "The State of Metropolitan America: Demographics, Cities, Regions and States." Brookings Institute, May 9. http://www.brookings.edu/reports/2010/0509_metro_america.aspx.

Friedman, B., and J. Rosen. 2010. "The Battle over the Court." *New Republic*, April 14. http://www.tnr.com/article/politics/the-battle-over-the-court.

Friedman, M. 1970. "The Social Responsibility of Business to Increase Its Profits." *New York Times Magazine*, September 13. http://www.colorado.edu/studentgroups/libertarians/issues/friedman-soc-resp-business.html.

Frum, D. 2010. "The GOP's Electoral Generation Gap." *FrumForum*, October 23. http://www.frumforum.com/the-gops-electoral-generation-gap.

Gabriel, T., and D. Tave. 2010. "Florida Governor Splits with GOP on Teacher Pay." *New York Times*, April 15.

Ganz, M. 2010. "How Obama Lost His Voice . . ." *Los Angeles Times*, November 3.

Gardner, D. K. 2010. "The Useful Sage." *Los Angeles Times*, October 1.

Garrett, E. 2003. "The Impact of Bush v. Gore on Future Democratic Politics." In *The Future of American Democratic Politics*, ed. G. Pomper and M. Weiner, 141–160. New Brunswick: Rutgers University Press.

Garvin, L. 2010a. Telephone interview with Morley Winograd, October 6.

———. 2010b. E-mail exchange with Morley Winograd, October 15.

Gerson, M. 2010. "Political Blips, Disguised as 'Eras.'" *Washington Post*, November 2. http://www.washingtonpost.com/wp-dyn/content/article/2010/11/01/AR2010110105103.html.

Gerzema, J., and M. D'Antonio. 2011. *Spend Shift: How the Post-Crisis Values Revolution Is Changing the Way We Buy, Sell, and Live*. San Francisco: Jossey-Bass.

Gildea, D. 2010. Telephone interview with Morley Winograd, October 6.

Giuliano, P., and A. Spilimbergo. 2009. "Growing up in a Recession: Beliefs and the Macroeconomy." Washington, D.C., National Bureau of Economic ResearchSeptember. http://www.nber.org/papers/w15321.

Gladwell, M. 2010. "Small Change: Why The Revolution Will Not be Tweeted." *New Yorker*, October 4. http://www.newyorker.com/reporting/2010/10/04/101004fa_fact_gladwell?currentPage=all#ixzz124jp7Dvl.

Goldbeck, J. 2010. "Does Social Media Matter in the Fight to End Genocide?" Movements.org. blog, October 15. http://www.movements.org/blog/entry/genocide/.

Goldberg, J. 2008. "Idle Youth Vote." *National Review*, September 1.

Golden, C. 2010. Interview with Morley Winograd. Washington, D.C. March 3.

Goldin, C., and L. F. Katz. 2008. *The Race between Education and Technology*. Cambridge: Belknap Press of Harvard University Press.

Green, E. 2010. "Building a Better Teacher." *New York Times Magazine*, March 2. http://www.nytimes.com/2010/03/07/magazine/07Teachers-t.html.

Greenfield, P. 1997. "Rising IQ." *All Things Considered*. NPR, September 17. http://www.npr.org/templates/story/story.php?storyId=1037879.

Grossman, C. L. 2010. "Survey: 72% of Millennials More Spiritual than Religious." *USA Today*, October 14. http://www.usatoday.com/news/religion/2010–04–27–1Amillfaith27_ST_N.htm?loc=interstitialskip.

Guffey, B. 2010. "Answers! Visions of Your Ideal Career!" McAmerica.org. blog. January 17. http://www.mcamerica.org/blog/2010/2/17/answers-visions-of-your-ideal-career.html.

Guttmacher Institute. 2010. "U.S. Teenage Pregnancies, Births, and Abortions: National and State Trends and Trends by Race and Ethnicity." January. http://www.guttmacher.org/pubs/USTPtrends.pdf.

Hamilton, J. A. 2010. "America's Future: The Heartland vs. the Coasts." *Atlantic*, October 26. http://www.theatlantic.com/business/archive/2010/10/americas-future-the-heartland-versus-the-coasts/65162/.

Hamsher, J. 2009. Firedoglake blog. http://action.firedoglake.com/page/s/killthisbill?source=email&subsource=122109.

_____. 2010. "Blogs, Populism and Power." Remarks delivered at the Personal Democracy Forum Conference, New York City, June 3.

Hannity, S. 2010. "Exclusive Look at 'Generation Zero.'" *Fox News*, February 24. http://www.foxnews.com/story/0,2933,587349,00.html.

Harper, M. 2009. "Uploading Hope: An Inside View of Obama's HQ New Media Video Team." Lecture. Amherst: University of Massachusetts, April 17. http://youtubeandthe2008election.jitp2.net/keygues/mharper.

Harry Potter Alliance. [2010]. HPA. http://thehpalliance.org/press/success-stories/.

Hart Research Associates. 2010. "Better, Not Smaller: What Americans Want from Federal Government." Center for American Progress, May. http://www.americanprogress.org/events/2010/07/av/dwwpresentation-hart.pdf.

Healy, A. R. 2007. "Twentysomething: Why I Don't Want Work/Life Balance." Penelope Trunk's Brazen Careerist blog, April 2. http://blog.penelopetrunk.com/2007/04/02/twentysomething-why-i-dont-want-worklife-balance/.

Hechinger, J. 2009. "Data-Driven Schools See Rising Scores." *Wall Street Journal*, June 12.

Hemmilia, D. 2009. "Higher Ed Master Plan Needs Funding Not Fixing." University of California newsroom, December 12. http://www.universityofcalifornia.edu/news/article/22505.

Henig, R. M. 2010. "What Is It about 20-Somethings?" *New York Times*, August 18.

Herberg, W. 1955. *Protestant, Catholic, Jew: An Essay in American Religious Sociology*. Chicago: University of Chicago Press.

Hewlett, S. A., L. Sherbin, and K. Sumberg. 2009. "How Gen Y and Boomers Will Reshape Your Agenda." *Harvard Business Review* (July–August): 71–76.

Higher Education Research Institute. 2010. "The American Freshman National Norms Fall 2009." CIRP Freshman Survey 2009 Cooperative Institutional Research Program. Higher Education Research Institute, January. http://gseis.ucla.edu/heri/PDFs/HERI-CIRP_Portfolio.pdf.

Hoffer, P. C., W. H. Hoffer, and N.E.H. Hull. 2007. *The Supreme Court: An Essential History*. Lawrence: University Press of Kansas.

Howe, J. 2006. "The Rise of Crowdsourcing." *Wired*, June. http://www.wired.com/wired/archive/14.06/crowds.html.

Howe, N. 2009a. E-mail exchanges with Morley Winograd, June 20–26.

———. 2009b. "The Winter of History: An Interview with Neil Howe on the Fourth Turning." DVD. Great Falls, Va., LifeCourse Associates.

———. 2010a. "Meet Mr. and Mrs. Gen X: A New Parent Generation." *School Administrator* 67, no. 1 (January): 18–23.

———. 2010b. *Millennials in the Workplace: Human Resource Strategies for a New Generation*. With R. Nadler. Great Falls, Va.: LifeCourse Associates.

———. 2010c. E-mail exchange with Morley Winograd, October 22.

———. 2010d. "Millennials in China." LifeCourse Associates blog, November 8. http://blog.lifecourse.com/

Hsu, T. 2010. "Satisfied at Work? It's a Rare Benefit." *Los Angeles Times*, January 6.

Hu, W. 2007. "Statistics Pinpoint Problems in Paterson Schools." *New York Times*, December 2. http://www.nytimes.com/2007/12/02/nyregion/02stat.html?pagewanted=1&ei=5124&en=ae71a3b95bff5e8b&ex=1354338000&partner=permalink&exprod=permalink.

Hulse, C. 2009. "G.O.P. Turns Sights on Obama." The Caucus (*New York Times* blog), March 4. http://thecaucus.blogs.nytimes.com/2009/03/04/gop-turns-sights-on-obama/.

Hulse, C., and D. M. Herszenhorn. 2010. "Tea Party Moves Quickly to Flex Muscle." *New York Times*, November 4. http://www.nytimes.com/2010/11/05/us/politics/05repubs.html.

Institute of Politics. Harvard University. 2008. "Fall 2008 Survey: Obama Retains Strong Lead in Presidential Race among Energized Youth Vote, Harvard Poll

Finds." October 22. http://www.iop.harvard.edu/Research-Publications/Survey/ Fall-2008-Survey.

———. 2010. "Survey of Young Americans' Attitudes toward Public Service and Politics 17." January 29–February 22. http://www.iop.harvard.edu/var/ezp_site/ storage/fckeditor/file/100307_IOP_Spring _2010_Topline.pdf.

Ito, M., H. Horst, M. Bittanti, D. Boyd, B. Herr-Stephenson, P. G. Lange, C. J. Pascoe, and L. Robinson. 2009. *Living and Learning with New Media: Summary of Findings from the Digital Youth Project.* Cambridge: MIT Press.

Jacobs, L. 2010. "After the Deluge, a New Education System." *Wall Street Journal,* August 30.

Jacobsen, S. 2010. "Postgraduate Service Rising in Popularity." *Stanford Daily,* October 21. http://www.stanforddaily.com/2010/10/21/postgraduate-service-rising-in-popularity-at-stanford/.

Jacobson, B. 2009. "Obama's Online Army Creaks into Action on Health Care Reform (Or, What a Difference a Year Makes)." Comment on a post by Colin Delany. Personal Democracy Forum blog, September 2. http://techpresident. com/blog-entry/obamas-online-army-creaks-action-health-care-reform-or-what-difference-year-makes.

Jacobson, L., and C. Mokher. 2009. "Pathways to Boosting the Earnings of Low Income Students by Increasing Their Educational Attainment." Hudson Institute. http://www.hudson.org/files/publications/Pathways%20to%20Boosting.pdf.

Jaffa, H. V. 1982. *Crisis of the House Divided: An Interpretation of the Issues in the Lincoln-Douglas Debates.* Chicago: University of Chicago Press.

Jaffe, I. 2010. "Latinos May Have Saved Senate for Democrats." NPR, November 5. http://www.npr.org/templates/story/story.php?storyId=131100975.

James, B. 2001. *The New Bill James Historical Baseball Abstract: The Classic Completely Revised.* New York: Free Press.

James, M. 2010. "MTV to Shake Up Content." *Los Angeles Times,* November 10.

Jamieson, K. H. 2009. *Electing the President, 2008: An Insider's View.* Philadelphia: University of Pennsylvania Press.

Jefferson, T. 1789. "Thomas Jefferson to Richard Price." Washington, D.C.: Library of Congress. http://www.loc.gov/exhibits/jefferson/60.html.

Johnson, H., and D. Broder. 1997. *The System.* Boston: Little, Brown.

Johnson, L. B. 1964. "President Lyndon B. Johnson's Remarks at the University of Michigan, May 22, 1964." Lyndon Baines Johnson Presidential Library and Museum Archives. http://www.lbjlib.utexas.edu/johnson/archives.hom/ speeches.hom/640522.asp.

Jones, R. P., and D. Cox. 2010. "Religion and the Tea Party in the 2010 Election: An Analysis of the Third Biennial American Values Survey." Public Religion Research Institute, October. http://www.publicreligion.org/objects/uploads/ fck/file/AVS%202010%20Report%20FINAL.pdf.

Jordan, S. 2008. Interview with Morley Winograd. Los Angeles, November 18.

Judd, N. 2010. "Transparency Is Not Enough." Personal Democracy Tech Forum blog, May 26. http://techpresident.com/blog-entry/transparency-not-enough.

Judis, J. J. 2010 "Tea Minus Zero." *New Republic,* May 27.

Kagan, R. 2009. "Woodrow Wilson's Heir." *Washington Post,* June 7. http://www.washingtonpost.com/wp-dyn/content/article/2009/06/05/AR 2009060502615.html.

Kaiser, D. 2010. "American Anger." History Unfolding blog, May 29, http://historyunfolding.Blogspot.com/search?q=fourth+turning+explosion+anger.

Kaiser Family Foundation. 2010. "Generation M2: Media in the Lives of 8- to 18-Year-Olds, 2010." January 20. http://www.kff.org/entmedia/mh012010pkg.cfm.

Kalaidis, J. 2010. "The GOP Feminista." *The Next Great Generation (TNGG)*, October 18. http://www.thenextgreatgeneration.com/2010/10/18/the-gop-feminista/.

Karl, J., and R. Klein. 2009. "GOP Strategy: Oppose Pelosi, Not Obama." *ABC News*, January 29. http://blogs.abcnews.com/thenote/2009/01/gop-strategy-op.html.

Kang, C. 2010. "Facebook Co-founder Hughes Builds New Social Network for Causes." *Washington Post*, November 8. http://voices.washingtonpost.com/posttech/2010/11/facebook_co-founder_hughes_bui.html.

Katie Mae. 2009. "Millennials and Opinions of Congressional Performance." Millennials Changing America. McAmerica.org, think tank blog, December 1. http://www.mcamerica.org/thinktank/post/947043.

Kazis, R., J. Vargas, and N. Hoffman, eds. 2004. *Double the Numbers: Increasing Credentials for Underrepresented Youth*. Cambridge: Harvard Education Press.

Keen, A. 2008. "The Foolishness of Crowds." *Democracy: A Journal of Ideas* n0.8 Spring: 78–83.

Kelly, C. 2009. Interview with Morley Winograd. Santa Monica, Cal., December 12.

Kennedy, D. M. 1999. *Freedom from Fear: The American People in Depression and War, 1929–1945*. New York: Oxford University Press.

Khan, S. 2010. "YouTube U. Beats YouSnooze U." *Chronicle of Higher Education,* November 5, B36.

Kinzie, S. 2010. "D.C. Teams Boosting Focus on Charitable Giving." *Washington Post*, August 15.

Kirkpatrick, D.D., and M. El-Naggar. 2011. "Protest's Old Guard Falls in Behind the Young." *New York Times* January 30. http://www.nytimes.com/2011/01/31/world/middleeast/31opposition.html?pagewanted=1&_r=2&hp.

Kitchens, R. 2010. Telephone interview with Morley Winograd, April 27.

Kitfield, J. 2005. "Coast Guard Official Fills Leadership Void in Katrina Relief Effort." *Government Executive*, September 23. http://www.govexec.com/dailyfed/0905/092305nj1.htm.

Kiva. [2010]. "Facts and History." *Kiva, Web site description*. http://www.kiva.org/about/facts.

Koelkebeck, T. 2010. "Is the Religious Right Taking over the Tea Party?" *Huffington Post*, October 27. http://www.huffingtonpost.com/tim-koelkebeck/post_1153_b_774964.html.

Kolodin, Z. 2009. "Millennials and Opinions of Congressional Performance." Millennials Changing America, McAmerica think tank blog, December 8. http://www.mcamerica.org/thinktank/post/947043.

Kotkin, J. 2010a. "The China Syndrome." *New Geography*, August 24. http://www.newgeography.com/search/node/china+syndrome.

———. 2010b. *The Next One Hundred Million: America in 2050*. New York: Penguin.

Kraft, M. 2010. "Frontline: Digital Nation: The Crowd." PBS, March 4. http://webcache.googleusercontent.com/search?q=cache:urGfLzWpUpQJ: www.pbs.org/wgbh/pages/frontline/digitalnation/forum/thecrowd/+mark+ kraft+pbs&cd=1&hl=en&ct=clnk&gl=us&client=firefox-a.

Kraul, C. 2009. "More Americans Turning to the Peace Corps." *Los Angeles Times*, June 2. http://articles.latimes.com/2009/jun/02/world/fg-peacecorps2.

Kring, L. 2010. Telephone interview with Morley Winograd. November 15.

Kroft, S. 2010. "Transcript: President Barack Obama, Part 2." *60 Minutes. CBS News*, November 7. http://www.cbsnews.com/stories/2010/11/07/60 minutes/main7032277_page3.shtml?tag=contentMain;contentBody.

Kronke, D. 2010. "You Gotta Have Snark." *Los Angeles Times*, October 12.

Kundra, V. 2009. Notes made by Morley Winograd on remarks delivered at Personal Democracy Forum conference, New York, June 29.

Kwok, J. 2010. "Phaeton: Learning by Doing." *ASK 37,* Winter. http:// askmagazine.nasa.gov/issues/37/37d_in_this_issue.html.

Lazer, D., M. Neblo, K. Esterling, and K. Goldschmidt. 2009. "Online Town Hall Meetings: Exploring Democracy in the 21st Century." Congressional Management Foundation. http://www.cmfweb.org/index.php?option=com_ content&task=view&id=296.

Lehrer, J. *How We Decide*. 2009. Boston: Houghton Mifflin Harcourt.

Let'sSingIt. 2008. "Taylor Swift Releases Her 'Fearless' New Album." Let'sSingIt, August 11. http://artists.letssingit.com/taylor-swift-taylor-swift-releases-her-fearless-new-album-vp6xw/news/287104/1.

Levey, N. 2010. "State's Health Lawsuit Moves Ahead." *Los Angeles Times*, August 3.

Levy, N. N., and J. Hook. 2009. "How Harry Reid Shepherded Healthcare Reform through the Senate." *Los Angeles Times*, December 24.

Lewin, T. 2006. "The New Gender Divide: At Colleges Women Are Leaving Men in the Dust." *New York Times*, July 9.

Lewis, B. 2010. "Communication Best Learned through Wine, Friends and Food." The Next Great Generation (TNGG), August 27. http://www .thenextgreatgeneration.com/2010/08/27/communication-best-learned-through-wine-and-friends.

Lewis, P. 1976. "Nixon's Economic Policies Come Back to Haunt the GOP." *New York Times*, August 15. http://select.nytimes.com/gst/abstract.html? res=FB0717FE345E1A738DDDAC0994D0405B868BF1D3.

Lewis, R. 2010. "Sales at a Swift Pace." *Los Angeles Times*, November 4.

Lewis-Beck, M. S., W. G. Jacoby, H. Norpoth, and H. F. Weisberg. 2008. *The American Voter Revisited*. Ann Arbor: University of Michigan Press.

Liff, S., and P. A. Posey. 2004. "Seeing Is Believing: How the New Art of Visual Management Can Boost Performance throughout Your Organization." New York: AMACOM Books.

Lipka, S. 2011. "Economy Changed Freshmen's Plans but Didn't Shake Their Confidence." *Chronicle of Higher Education*, January 27. http://chronicle.com/ article/Economy-Changed-Freshmens/126069/?sid=cc&utm_source= cc&utm_medium=en.

Liptak, A. 2010. "A Sign of the Court's Polarization: Choice of Clerks." *New York Times*, September 6. http:// www.nytimes.com/2010/09/07/us/politics/07 clerks.html.

Luscombe, B. 2010. "Workplace Salaries—At Last, Women on Top." *Time*, September 1. http://www.time.com/time/business/article/0,8599,2015274,00.html.

Lustig, N. 2009 "Millennials and Opinions of Congressional Performance." Millennials Changing America, McAmerica think tank blog, November 30 http://www.mcamerica.org/thinktank/post/947043.

MacDonald, H. 2010. "A Crime Theory Demolished." *Wall Street Journal*, January 5.

MacKenzie, J. 2010. Interview with Michael D. Hais. La Canada, Cal. August 19.

Malone, T. W. 2004. *The Future of Work: How the New Order of Business Will Shape Your Organization, Your Management Style and Your Life*. Boston: Harvard Business School Press.

Marcus, R. 2009. "An Illegal Mandate? No." *Washington Post*, November 26. http://www.washingtonpost.com/wp-dyn/content/article/2009/11/24/AR2009112402815.html.

Marston, A. 2010. "Remarks on Behalf of Graduating Class of 2010." University of Michigan News Service. http://ns.umich.edu/index_nr.html?commencement_2010.

Matthew. 2009. "Millennials and Opinions of Congressional Performance." Millennials Changing America Think Tank blog *McAmerica.org.*, November 24. http://www.mcamerica.org/thinktank/post/947043.

McCain, M. 2010. *Dirty, Sexy Politics*. New York: Hyperion.

McConnell, M. W. 2010. Review of *Ratification: The People Debate the Constitution* by Pauline Maier. *Wall Street Journal*, October 23–24.

McFarlane, V. 2010. Telephone interview with Morley Winograd, August 12.

Meister, J. C., and K. Willyerd. 2010. *The 2020 Workplace: How Innovative Companies Attract, Develop, and Keep Tomorrows Employees Today*. New York: HarperCollins.

Merrill Lynch. N.d. "Merrill Lynch Overview." Web site description. http://www.ml.com/index.asp?id=7695_8134_8296.

Meyerson, H. 2010. "A Post-election Numbers Game." *Washington Post*, November 5. http://www.washingtonpost.com/wp-dyn/content/article/2010/11/04/AR2010110406639_pf.html.

Middlekauff, R. 1982. *The Glorious Cause: The American Revolution, 1763–1789*. New York: Oxford University Press.

Miller-Adams, M. 2009. *The Power of a Promise: Education and Economic Renewal in Kalamazoo*. Kalamazoo, Mich.: W. E. Upjohn Institute for Employment Research.

Mintizberg, H., R. Simons, and K. Basu. 2002. "Beyond Selfishness." *MIT Sloan Management Review* 44, no. 1: 67–74.

Miron, G., J. N. Jones, and A. J. Kelaher Young. 2009. "The Impact of the Kalamazoo Promise on Student Attitudes, Goals and Aspirations." Working Paper #6. May. Kalamazoo, Mich.: Western Michigan University.

Montgomery, J. 2010. "President Obama Delivers Commencement Speech at Kalamazoo Central High School." June 7. MTV. http://www.mtv.com/news/articles/1641004/20100607/story.jhtml.

Montgomery, L. 2010. "Report Gives Stimulus Package High Marks." *Washington Post*, October 1. http://www.washingtonpost.com/wp-dyn/content/article/2010/09/30/AR2010093007382.html.

Moore, J. 2009. "US Grads Job Expectations on Hold." *Christian Science Monitor*, May 28. http://features.csmonitor.com/economyrebuild/2009/05/28/us-grads-job-expectations-on-hold/.

Morozov, E. 2010. "The Digital Dictatorship." *Wall Street Journal*, February 20. http://online.wsj.com/article/SB10001424052748703983004575073911147404540.html?mod=WSJ_article_MoreIn.

Motor Trend. 2006. "Interview with Rick Wagoner." June, 94.

Murphy, K., and R. Fausset. 2010. "Five Years after Katrina, New Orleans Still Caught between Storms." *Los Angeles Times*, August 29.

Murray, A. 2010. "The End of Management." *Wall Street Journal*, August 21–22.

Murray, M., and D. Montanaro. 2009. "GOP Support Most Important for Grassley." MSNBC, August 17. http://firstread.msnbc.msn.com/_news/2009/08/17/4436230-gop-support-most-important-to-grassley.

Nagourney, A., and M. Thee-Brenan. 2010. "Poll Finds Edge for Obama over GOP among the Public." *New York Times*, February 11.

Neuman, J. 2010. "A Familiar Tune on Healthcare." *Los Angeles Times*, March 28.

New York Times/CBS News Poll. 2010a. "Mood of the Country as Midterms Approach." September 10–14. http://documents.nytimes.com/new-york-timescbs-news-poll-new-york-timescbs-news-poll-mood-of-the-country-as-midterms-approach?ref=politics.

———. 2010b. "National Survey of Tea Party Supporters." *New York Times*. http://documents.nytimes.com/new-york-timescbs-news-poll-national-survey-of-tea-party-supporters?ref=politics.

Newman, R. 2010. "Who's Gained and Lost under Obama So Far." *US News and World Report*, October 26. http://money.usnews.com/money/blogs/flowchart/2010/10/26/whos-gained-and-lost-under-obama-so-far.

Nicholas, P., and J. Oliphant. 2010. "Obama vs. GOP House." *Los Angeles Times*, November 4.

Noonan, P. 2010. "Look Ahead with Stoicism—and Optimism." *Wall Street Journal*, January 2.

Noveck, B. S. 2009. "Wiki Government: How Technology Can Make Government Better, Democracy Stronger, and Citizens More Powerful." Washington, D.C.: Brookings Institutional Press.

Noyes, A. 2009. "Behind the Curtain." *Government Executive*, April 1. http://www.govexec.com/story_page.cfm?filepath=/features/0409–01/0409–01s1.htm&oref=search%20Government%20Executive.com.

Obama, B. 2007. *Dreams from My Father: A Story of Race and Inheritance*. New York: Crown.

———. 2008. "Obama Says Special Interests Are Blocking Energy Reform, Proposes Short-term Steps to Relieve the Pressure of Rising Prices." Barack Obama Web site, April 25. http://www.barackobama.com/2008/04/25/Obama_says_special_interests_a.php (site now discontinued).

———. 2009a. "Remarks of President Barack Obama—As Prepared for Delivery. Address to Joint Session of Congress, Tuesday, February 24, 2009." White House Press Office, February 24. http://www.whitehouse.gov/the_press_office/Remarks-of-President-Barack-Obama-Address-to-Joint-Session-of-Congress.

_____. 2009b. "President Obama's Speech in Cairo: A New Beginning." White House blog, June 4. http://www.whitehouse.gov/blog/newbeginning/transcripts/.

_____. 2009c. "Remarks to Joint Session of Congress on Health Care, U.S. Capitol, Washington, D.C." White House Press Office, September 9. http://www.whitehouse.gov/the_press_office/Remarks-by-the-President-to-a-Joint-Session-of-Congress-on-Health-Care/.

_____. 2009d. "Full Text of Obama's Nobel Peace Prize Speech: Remarks of the U.S. President in Oslo." MSNBC, December 10. http://www.msnbc.msn.com/id/34360743/.

_____. 2010. "Remarks by the President at University of Michigan Spring Commencement, Big House, University of Michigan, Ann Arbor, Michigan May 1, 2010." *White House Press Office.* http://www.whitehouse.gov/the-press-office/remarks-president-university-michigan-spring-commencement.

_____. 2011. "State of the Union 2011: Winning the Future" White House Press Office. January 26. http://www.whitehouse.gov/state-of-the-union-2011.

Obama, M. 2009. "Remarks of First Lady, Michelle Obama." United We Serve, June 22. http://www.serve.gov/remarks_flotus.asp.

Oberlander, J. 2010. "Beyond Repeal—The Future of Health Care Reform." *New England Journal of Medicine,* November 17. http://healthpolicyandreform.nejm.org/?p=13113.

Obst, D., R. Bhandari, and S.Witherell. 2007. "Meeting America's Global Education Challenge: Current Trends in U.S. Study Abroad and the Impact of Strategic Diversity Initiatives." *Institute of International Education,* no. 1 (May). http://www.iie.org/en/Research-and-Publications/Research-Projects/~/media/Files/Corporate/Membership/StudyAbroad_WhitePaper1.ashx.

Oliphant, J., and K. Hennessey. 2010. "Obama's Voter Coalition Frays." *Los Angeles Times,* September 12.

"Online Learning." 2010. *Chronicle of Higher Education,* November 5, B28.

Parry, M. 2010. "Tomorrow's College." *Chronicle of Higher Education.* Online Learning Edition, November 5, B3.

PBS Newshour. 2010. "The Khan Academy." PBS, September 21. http://www.khanacademy.org/video/pbs-newshour-on-the-khan-academy?playlist=Khan%20Academy-Related%20Talks%20and%20Interviews.

Pew. 2007. "Trends in Political Values and Core Attitudes 1987–2007: Political Landscape More Favorable to Democrats." Report, *Pew Research Center for the People and the Press,* March 22. http://people-press.org/reports/pdf/312.pdf.

_____. 2009a. "January 2009 Political Survey. Final Topline." Report, Pew Research Center for the People and the Press, January 15. http://people-press.org/reports/questionnaires/483.pdf.

_____. 2009b. "Independents Take Center Stage in Obama Era." Report, *Pew Research Center for the People and the Press,* May 21. http://people-press.org/report/?pageid=1521.

_____. 2009c. "Gen Next Squeezed by Recession, But Most See Better Times Ahead." Report, *Pew Research Center for the People and the Press,* June 5. http://pewresearch.org/pubs/1245/gen-next-squeezed-recession-most-see-better-times-ahead.20.

————. 2009d. "Mixed Views of Economic Policies and Health Care Reform Persist." Report, Pew Research Center for the People and the Press, October 8. http://people-press.org/report/551/.

————. 2010a. "Millennials: A Portrait of Generation Next." Report, *Pew Research Center for the People and the Press*, February. http://pewsocialtrends .org/files/2010/10/millennials-confident-connected-open-to-change.pdf.

————. 2010b. "The Millennials: Confident. Connected. Open to Change." Report, *Pew Research Center for the People and the Press,* February 24. http://pewresearch.org/pubs/1501/millennials-new-survey-generational-personality-upbeat-open-new-ideas-technology-bound.

————. 2010c. "Trust in Government Survey." Report, *Pew Research Center for the People and the Press, April 18.* http://people-press.org/report/?pageid=1698.

————. 2010d. "Pew Global Attitudes Reasearch." Unpublished data. April-May.

————. 2010e. "Independents Oppose Party in Power . . . Again." Report, Pew Research Center for the People and the Press, September 23. http://people-press.org/report/658/.

————. 2010f. "GOP Likely to Capture Control of House." *Pew Research Center for the People and the Press,* October 31. http://pewresearch.org/pubs/1787 /2010-pre-election-survey-gop-win-house-wide-turnout-advantage-engagement-gap.

————. 2010g. "Public Support for increased Trade, Except with South Korea and China: Fewer See Benefits from Free Trade Agreements." Report, Pew Research Center for the People and the Press, November 9. http://people-press.org/report/673/.

————. 2010h. "How a Different America Responded to the Great Depression." Report, *Pew Research Center for the People and the Press*, December 14. http://pewresearch.org/pubs/1810/public-opinion-great-depression-compared -with-now.

Phillips, C. 2010. "Earth to Gen Y: NASA's Millennial Makeover." Millennial Marketing blog, October 9. http://millennialmarketing.com/2010/10/earth-to-gen-y-nasas-millennial-makeover.

Phillips, D. T., and J. M. Loy. 2003. *Character in Action: The U.S. Coast Guard on Leadership.* Annapolis, Md.: Naval Institute Press.

Platts, A. 2010. "Answers! Visions of Your Ideal Career." Millennials Changing America, McAmerica blog, February 17. http://www.mcamerica.org/blog/2010/2/17/answers-visions-of-your-ideal-career.html.

Plouffe, D. 2009. *The Audacity to Win: The Inside Story of Barack Obama's Historic Victory.* New York: Viking Penguin.

Pomfret, J. 2010. "China Urges Improvements at Work as Honda Strike Ends." *Reuters,* June 15.

Pope, J. 2009. "College Grads Face Worst Job Market in Years." *USA Today,* April 3.

Portfolio.com. 2009. "Portfolio's Worst American CEO's of All Time." CNBC, April 30. http://www.cnbc.com/id/30502091?slide=4.

Powe, L. A. 2009. *The Supreme Court and the American Elite, 1778–2008.* Cambridge: Harvard University Press.

Pryor, J. H., S. Hurtado, L. DeAngelo, L. Blake, L. Palucki, and S. Tran. 2010. "The American Freshman: National Norms for Fall 2009." Los Angeles: Higher Education Research Institute, January. http://www.heri.ucla.edu.

Rainko, A. 2010. "'I do' . . . But in a Few." *The Next Great Generation (TNGG)*, September 12. http://www.thenextgreatgeneration.com/2010/09/12/i-do-but-in-a-few/.

Rhee, M., and A. Fenty. 2010. "The Education Manifesto." *Wall Street Journal*, October 30/31.

Rich, F. 2010. "Barack Obama, Phone Home." *New York Times*, November 6. http://www.nytimes.com/2010/11/07/opinion/07rich.html.

Richey, J. 2010. "Engage My Eyes, My Ears, My Computer." The Next Great Generation (TNGG), October 22. http://www.thenextgreatgeneration.com/2010/10/22/engage-my-eyes-my-ears-my-computer/.

Riley, B. 2010. Interview with Morley Winograd. Jet Propulsion Laboratory, Pasadena, Cal., January 12.

Riley, D. 2009. "Among American Kids Ages 2–17, 82 Percent Report They Are Gamers." NPD Group *press release,* December 2. http://www.npd.com/press/releases/press_091202.html.

Riley, N. S. 2010. "Interfaith Marriages Are Rising Fast, But They're Failing Fast Too." *Washington Post*, June 6. http://www.washingtonpost.com/wp-dyn/content/article/2010/06/04/AR2010060402011.html.

Rimer, S. 2009. "At M.I.T. Large Lectures Are Going the Way of the Blackboard." *New York Times*, September 13.

Roberts, S. 2009. "Economy Is Forcing Young Adults Back Home in Big Numbers, Survey Finds." *New York Times*, November 24. http://www.nytimes.com/2009/11/24/us/24boomerang.html.

Rodriguez, G. 2010. "Realistic, Idealistic Americans." *Los Angeles Times*, January 25.

Romano, A., and T. Dokoupil. 2010. "Men's Lib." *Newsweek*, September 20.

Roosevelt, M. 2009. "State Officials Launch 'Green' Initiative." *Los Angeles Times*, September 17.

Rosenberg, S. 2009. Telephone interview with Morley Winograd, December 11.

Rosenthal, S. A., S. Moore, R. M. Montoya, and L. A. Maruskin. 2009. "National Leadership Index 2009: A National Study of Confidence in Leadership." Report. Cambridge: Kennedy School Center for Public Leadership, Harvard University. http://www.merrimanriver.com/files/NLI2009.pdf.

Rospars, J. 2008. "Response from Barack on FISA and Discussions with Policy Staff." Organizing for America, July 3. http://my.barackobama.com/page/community/post/rospars/gGxsZF/).

Ross, D. 2010. Telephone interview with Morley Winograd, February 23.

Rubin, B. M. 2010. "Stalled on the Road to Security: For Millennials, Traditional Markers of Adulthood Prove Elusive." *Chicago Tribune*, May 27.

Santmyer, H. H. 1982. . . . *And Ladies of the Club*. Columbus: Ohio State University Press.

Sasso, B. 2010. "Class of 2010 New Members of Congress." *National Journal*, November 11. http://www2.nationaljournal.com/member/magazine/class-of-2010-new-members-of-congress-20101111.

Savage, D. G. 2010. "States Fighting Health Care Don't Have Precedent on Their Side." *Los Angeles Times*, March 27. http://articles.latimes.com/2010/mar/27/nation/la-na-constitutionality27–2010mar27.

Schwartz, B. 1993. *A History of the Supreme Court*. 1993. New York: Oxford University Press.

Scola, N. 2008. "Worldchanging Interview: David Moore of Open Congress." *Worldchanging*, November 4. http://www.worldchanging.com/archives/008959.html.

———. 2009a. "Getting Our 'Open for Questions' Legs" Personal Democracy Forum blog, March 26. http://techpresident.com/blog-entry/getting-our-open-questions-legs-making-sense-whitehousegov-experiment.

———. 2009b. "Obama's Internet Q&A." Personal Democracy Forum blog, March 27. http://techpresident.com/blog-entry/obamas-internet-qa-pretty-exciting-canned-experiment-amazing-okness.

———. 2009c. "Iran Roundup: Facts and Framing." Personal Democracy Forum blog, June 17. http://techpresident.com/blog-entry/iran-roundup-facts-and-framing.

———. 2009d. "Can Obama's Army Convert to a Peacetime Force? Plouffe Responds." Personal Democracy Forum blog, November 25. http://techpresident.com/blog-entry/.

———. 2010a. "Sunlight's Miller Takes a Dim View of Obama's Transparency." Personal Democracy Forum blog, September 7. http://techpresident.com/blog-entry/sunlights-miller-takes-dim-view-obamas-transparency.

———. 2010b. "Connecting the Dots on Stimulus Fraud." Personal Democracy Forum blog, September 8. http://techpresident.com/blog-entry/connecting-dots-stimulus-fraud.

Seib, G. 2010. "Get Ready for an Anti-Incumbent Wave." *Wall Street Journal*. September 7.

Shaffer, D. W., K. R. Squire, R. Halverson, and J. P. Gee. 2004. "Video Games and the Future of Learning." University of Wisconsin–Madison and Academic Advanced Distributed Learning Co-Laboratory, December. www.academiccolab.org/resources/gappspaper1.pdf.

Shapiro, R. J. 2008. *Futurecast: How Superpowers, Populations, and Globalization Will Change Your World by the Year 2020*. New York: St. Martin's Press.

Shirky, C. 2008. *Here Comes Everybody: The Power of Organizing without Organizations*. New York: Penguin.

Sifry, M. L. 2009. "Inside the 'Hope Factory': Max Harper on the Obama Media Machine." Personal Democracy Forum blog, May 4. http://techpresident.com/blog-entry/inside-hope-factory-max-harper-obama-media-machine.

———. 2010a. "Can the Internet Counter the Coming Gusher of Money in Politics?" Personal Democracy Forum blog, January 21. http://techpresident.com/blog-entry/can-internet-counter-coming-gusher-money-politics.

———. 2010b. "Strong Ties, Weak Ties and Obama's 'New Realities.'" Personal Democracy Forum blog, October 1. http://techpresident.com/blog-entry/strong-ties-weak-ties-and-obamas-new-reality.

———. 2010c. "Point-and-Click Politics." *Wall Street Journal*. October 30/31.

Silverman, B. E-mail exchange with Morley Winograd, October 25.

Simon, Julian. 2003. *A Life against the Grain: The Autobiography of an Unconventional Economist*. New Brunswick, N.J.: Transaction.

Singer, P. W. 2009. *Wired for War: The Robotic Revolution and Conflict in the 21st Century*. New York: Penguin Press.

Skidelsky, R. 2010. *Keynes: The Return of the Master*. New York: Public Affairs.

Skolnick, J. 2007. "Good Cop." *Democracy: A Journal of Ideas*, no. 4 (Spring): 92–98.

Skowronek, S. 2008. *Presidential Leadership in Political Time: Reprise and Reappraisal*. Lawrence: University of Kansas Press.

Smith, W. H. 2008. "A Proper Eulogy." *RateLab*. Speech at Merrill Lynch shareholders' meeting. http://dealbreaker.com/_old/images/thumbs/RateLab%20A%20Proper%20Eulogy.pdf.

Soltis, K. 2009. "Young Voters One Year Later" *Pollster.com* blog, December 1. http://www.pollster.com/blogs/young_voters_one_year_later.php.

———. 2010. "Generation O and the Switch to Generation GOP." Daily Caller, February 25. http://dailycaller.com/2010/02/25/generation-o-and-the-switch-to-generation-gop/.

Song, J. 2010. "Teachers Blast Times for Rankings." *Los Angeles Times*, August 30.

Stack, M. 2010. "Mom and Dad Don't Live Here Anymore." *Los Angeles Times*, September 30.

Steed, A. 2010. "On the Millennial Work Ethic." Millennials Changing America, McAmerica blog, April 5. http://www.mcamerica.org/blog/2010/4/5/on-the-millennial-work-ethic.html.

Stelter, B. 2010. "MTV Is Looking Beyond 'Jersey Shore' to Build a Wider Audience." *New York Times*, October 24. http://www.nytimes.com/2010/10/25/business/media/25mtv.html?pagewanted=1&_r=1.

Sternberg, A. 2008. "Obama Thanks Campaign Staff at Chicago HQ." Andy Sternberg's Blog, June 8. http://netzoo.net/video-obama-thanks-campaign-staff-at chicago-hq/.

Sternstein, A. 2009. "The Public Eye." Nextgov, June 12. http://www.nextgov.com/nextgov/ng_20090612_9850.php.

Stewart, M., and J. Bird. 2009. "Transcript: OFA's Mitch Stewart and Jeremy Bird Speak to TPMDC." TPMLivewire blog, November 11. http://tpmlivewire.talkingpointsmemo.com/2009/11/transcript-ofas-mitch-stewart-and-jeremy-bird-speak-to-tpmdc.php.

Strauss, W., and N. Howe. 1991. *Generations: The History of America's Future 1584 to 2069*. New York: Morrow.

———. 1997. *The Fourth Turning: An American Prophecy*. New York: Broadway Books.

Strauss, W., and N. Howe, with P. Markiewicz. 2006. *Millennials and the Pop Culture: Strategies for a New Generation of Consumers in Music, Television, the Internet, and Video Games*. N.p.: LifeCourse Associates.

Tapscott, D., and A. D. Williams. 2006. *Wikinomics: How Mass Collaboration Changes Everything*. New York: Penguin Group.

Taylor, P., and R. Morin. 2009. "Forty Years after Woodstock, a Gentler Generation Gap." Pew Research Center, August 12. http://pewsocialtrends.org/2009/08/12/forty-years-after-woodstockbra-gentler-generation-gap/.

Thamel, P. 2009. "On the Way to the NFL Draft, a Year of Fulfillment in England." *New York Times*, October 24.

Thomas, D., and J. S. Brown. 2009. "Learning in/for a World of Constant Flux: *Homo Sapiens, Homo Farber*, and *Homo Ludens* Revisited." Paper presented at the 7th Glion Colloquium. Geneva, Switzerland. by J. S. Brown. June. http://www.johnseelybrown.com/Learning%20for%20a%20World%2000f%20 Constant%20Change.pdf.

Tomsho, R. 2009. "Tuition Ammunition: A Happy Lesson on Lending." *Wall Street Journal*, January 6.

Tulgan, B. 2009. *Not Everyone Gets a Trophy: How to Manage Generation Y*. San Francisco: Jossey–Bass.

Twenge, J. M. 2006. *Generation Me: Why Today's Young Americans Are More Confident, Assertive, Entitled, and More Motivated Than Ever Before*. New York: Free Press.

U.S. Department of Education. Commission on the Future of Higher Education. 2006. *A Test of Leadership: Charting the Future of U.S. Higher Education*. Washington, D.C.: Department of Education, September 19.

Vance, M., and D. Deacon. 1996. *Break out of the Box*. Pompton Plains, N.J.: Career Press.

Vanden Heuvel, K. 2010. "An Undeserved Win for the GOP." *Wall Street Journal*, November 5. http://online.wsj.com/article/SB100014240527487035069045 75592900976030696.html.

Vargas, J. 2008. Obama Responds to Online FISA." *Washington Post*, July 3. http://blog.washingtonpost.com/44/2008/07/03/obama_responds_to_online_ fisa.html.

Ventsias, T. 2009. "U.S. Study Shows Congressional Use of Twitter Falls Short." University of Maryland, press release, September 15. http://www.newsdesk .umd.edu/culture/release.cfm?ArticleID=1964.

Viger, D. 2009. "Millennials and Opinions of Congressional Performance." Millennials Changing America McAmerica think tank blog, November 24. http://www.mcamerica.org/thinktank/post/947043.

Wadler, J. 2011. "What 'Modern Family' Says about Modern Families." *New York Times*. January 23.

Wallace, L. 2010. "First Look at Marvel's Hopeful New 'Heroic Age'" *Wired*, January 27. http://www.wired.com/underwire/2010/01/marvel-heroic-age/.

Walter, E., and R. Ellison. 1957. "Robert Penn Warren, the Art of Fiction No. 18." *Paris Review* (Spring–Summer). www.theparisreview.org/interviews/ 4868/the-art-of-fiction-no-18-robert-penn-warren.

Warrior, P. 2010. Interview with Morley Winograd. Los Angeles, March 10.

Wasow, O. 2008. "The First Internet President: How Obama Tapped Internet Netizens to Transform American Politics." The Root blog, November 5. http://www.theroot.com/views/first-internet-president.

Weiner, E. 2007. "Stan O'Neal: The Rise and Fall of a Numbers Guy." NPR, October 29. http://www.npr.org/templates/story/story.php?storyId=15738661.

Weisman, J. 2008. "Et Tu You Tube?" *Washington Post*, April 11. http://www .washingtonpost.com/wp-dyn/content/article/2008/04/10/AR200804 1003584.html?nav=hcmodule.

Wertman, A. 2008. "Society and Business Lab Establishes New Models for Social Entrepreneurship." Marshall School of Business, University of Southern California, n.d. http://marshall.usc.edu/news/all-articles/society-and-business 84417.htm.

Wessel, D. 2008. "In Turmoil, Capitalism in U.S. Sets New Course." *Wall Street Journal*, September 20.

Wheeler, J. 2010. "Bill Milliken, Michigan's Moderate." *Glen Arbor Sun* 15, no. 8.

Will, George F. 2010. "That Rock in the Health Care Road? It's Called the Constitution." *Washington Post*, January 14. http://www.washingtonpost .com/wp-dyn/content/article/2010/01/13/AR2010011303460.html.

Winograd, M. 2010. Notes recorded by Morley Winograd at "Beyond the Welcome Home." Mobilize.org conference, Los Angeles, April 1–3.

Winograd, M., and D. W. Buffa. 1996. *Taking Control: Politics in the Information Age*. New York: Henry Holt.

Winograd, M., and M. D. Hais. 2008. *Millennial Makeover: MySpace, YouTube and the Future of American Politics*. New Brunswick: Rutgers University Press.

———. 2010a. "Twenty-first-Century Political Coalitions: Two Parties Headed in Opposite Directions. A Twenty-first-Century America Report." NDN, March 4. http://ndn.org/sites/default/files/paper/21st%20Century%20America %20Project%20March%202010%20PPT%20Presentation.pdf.

_____. 2010b. "A Twenty-first-Century America Report." NDN, June. http://ndn.org/sites/default/files/paper/JunePollPresentation.pdf.

Wofford, B. 2010. Telephone interview with Morley Winograd, November 1.

Yahoo! News. 2010. "Bush Women Run Afoul of GOP Orthodoxy." June 14. http://news.yahoo.com/s/ynews/ynews_p12570.

Zimring, F. E. 2006. *The Great American Crime Decline*. New York: Oxford University Press.

Zuckerman, A. 2010. "Congressional Twitter Usage Results Are In!" Finding Zuckerman, June 16. http://www.findingzuckerman.com/2010/06/ congressional-twitter-usage-results-are.html.

Zwick, A. 2009. "Millennial Perspective: The Global View." New Geography, March 15. http://www.newgeography.com/content/00662-millennial- perspective-the-global-view.

Index

ABC Family (cable channel), 216–217
abortion, 10, 30, 32–34, 52; and
  family lifestyles, 194; and legislative
  branch, 55, 58; and Supreme Court,
  75, 170
accountability, 61, 88, 113, 125, 242;
  and civic ethos, 270, 273; and
  education, 164, 171–172; and
  NYPD, 169–170, 172
Adams, John, 19, 67
adaptive generations, 14. *See also*
  Silent Generation
Adventures of Ozzie and Harriet, The
  (television sitcom), 196
Affordable Care Act. *See* health care
  reform
Afghanistan War, 28, 229, 237, 268
African Americans, 27; and education,
  161, 164, 173, 180; and
  entertainment, 212, 222; and family
  lifestyles, 197, 201; and politics,
  105, 247–248, 251–252, 254–256,
  262. *See also names of individual*
  African Americans
agriculture, 46, 73–75, 135, 157, 202
Ahmadinejad, Mahmoud, 235
AIG, 123
Alice (television sitcom), 196
Alito, Samuel, 79
Allee, Verna, 144–145
Allen, Thad, 108
All in the Family (television sitcom),
  29
Al Qaeda, 228

American Federation of Teachers
  (AFT), 168–169
American Revolution, 15–20, 22, 24,
  98–99, 103–104, 273
American Voter, The (Campbell et al.),
  40–41
American Voter Revisited, The
  (Lewis-Beck et al.), 41
AmeriCorps, 122, 268
Anderson, Derek, 4
. . . *And Ladies of the Club* (Santmyer),
  22–24, 42
Andrews Sisters, 210
anger, 83, 85, 105, 114, 249
anti-Semitism, 74, 207
Apple, 111–112, 183
Aranda, Catherine, 269
Armstrong, Louis, 212
Arnett, Jeffrey Jensen, 195
Asian Americans, 27, 142, 201, 212,
  222, 251–252, 256
Audacity to Win, The (Plouffe), 2–3
Austin, Ben, 160–161, 164
auto industry, 36, 115–116, 123,
  127–129, 249, 257
Avalon (movie), 198–199, 201
Avatar (movie), 188, 230–231, 242
Awakening Generation, 19. *See also*
  idealist generations

Baby Boom Generation (1946–1964):
  childhood of, 28–29; and civic
  ethos, 267; and corporate
  leadership, 124, 126–127;

Baby Boom Generation (1946–1964)
(*continued*)
and corporate life, 138–139,
147–149, 151; and the economy,
116, 121, 124, 126–128, 135; and
education, 159, 167, 172–173; and
entertainment, 211–214, 216–217,
220, 223; and family lifestyles, 194,
196–203, 206; and GI Generation,
10, 23; and global change, 226,
230–231, 234–235, 243–244; and
health care reform, 45, 56, 58–59;
and higher education, 177, 182,
189; and Millennials, 10, 13, 27,
30–31, 33–34, 148–149, 151, 159,
203; and Obama, 5, 59; and
operational/ideological attitudes,
50–53, 56, 58–59; and politics, 85,
247–248, 254; and Social Security,
24; and Supreme Court, 65, 74, 79.
See also idealist generations
Ball, Deborah Loewenberg, 166
Bank of America, 123, 127
banks/banking, 46, 73, 87, 145; and
bailouts, 87, 116, 123, 249, 257;
and corporate leadership, 124–125;
and student loans, 182
Bannon, Stephen, 23–24
Baptists, 208, 216
Barney (television character), 31
baseball, 220–222
Baseball (PBS documentary), 220
basketball, 222–223
Beatles, 211–212, 214
Beaudry, Michelle, 147–148
Beck, Glenn, 29
Beinhocker, Eric, 131, 140
Ben Ali, Zine el-Abidine, 236
Berkley, Busby, 26
Best Years of Our Lives, The (movie),
195
"Beyond the Welcome Home"
(conference), 268–269

Biden, Joe, 14
Biggie Smalls, 213
Bill Cosby Show, The (television
sitcom), 29, 196
Bird, Larry, 223
birth rates, 14, 194, 234–235
blogs, 93, 99, 102, 111, 142, 161,
205. *See also titles of individual blogs*
"Blowin' in the Wind" (song), 59
"Blueprint for the Millennial
America," 271–273
Boehner, John, 274
Boeing, 145
Bollywood, 211–212
Bonds, Barry, 221
Bonner, Zach, 266–267
Boomers. *See* Baby Boom Generation
Booth, John Wilkes, 20
Bosh, Chris, 223
Bossie, Dave, 23–24
Boston bus system, 111–112
Boyd, Dana, 112–113
Brandeis, Louis, 73–75
brand loyalty, 128–129, 152, 219
Bratton, William, 169–172
Braun, Ryan, 222
Brazilian House of Representatives,
96–97, 100, 278
Breakfast Club, The (movie), 29
Breyer, Stephen, 81
Briand, Aristide, 38
Brigate Rosse (Italy), 234
British Petroleum (BP), 107–108
Brokaw, Tom, 14
Brown, John Seely, 184–185, 189
Brown, Matthew, 200
Brown, Michael, 108
Brown, Scott, 57
Brownstein, Ron, 60
Bryant, Kobe, 222–223
Buchanan, James, 67, 69
Buddhists, 208
Burke, Edmund, 98–99

Burke, James, 150
Burns, Ken, 220
Burstein, David, 30–31
Bush, Barbara, 50–51
Bush, George H. W., 50
Bush, George W., 13, 47, 56, 249–250, 253; campaign model of, 150; children of, 50–51; and economy, 17, 116, 123, 128, 249, 254, 257, 260; and higher education, 181–182; and presidential leadership, 102, 116; and Supreme Court, 77, 81–82; and telecom immunity, 98–99
business. *See* corporations
Business.com, 147–148
Butler, Pierce, 73–74

campaign contributions, 86–89, 91–92, 95, 97, 100
Campus Climate Challenge, 231
Cano, Robinson, 222
Canseco, Jose, 221
Cantor, Eric, 13, 246
Cantril, Hadley, 45–48, 50, 281
capitalism, 21, 23, 44, 274
Capitalism, Socialism, and Democracy (Schumpeter), 131
Captain Planet (television cartoon program), 231
Capuano, Michael, 89
Carberry, Maegan, 53
Card, Andrew, 128
Cardozo, Benjamin, 73–74
Carol, Dan, 279
Carville, James, 2–3, 4
Catholics, 27, 207–208
Catron, John, 70
cell phones, 52. *See also* smart phones
Center for Progressive Leadership, 153
Cermak, Anton, 21
Chait, Jonathan, 57

Chambers, John, 144
charitable fund-raising, 153–155, 220
child-rearing practices, 28–30, 193, 195–198, 200, 204–205, 208, 215
China, 24, 228, 237–241, 244; One Child Policy, 237–239
China Dream, The (Liu), 239–240
Christians, 207–208, 249
Chrysler, 115–116, 123
Churchill, Winston, 38
Cisco, 143–144
Citigroup, 125
Citizens United Productions, 23
civic ethos, 55–60, 264–280; and community service, 266–270, 280; and education, 158, 182, 266–267; and executive branch, 103–105, 109–111, 114, 117–118; and family lifestyles, 207; and health care reform, 16–17, 55–60; and Millennials, 265–280; and Obama, 11, 16–17, 42, 54–55, 60, 105, 109, 114, 117–118; and politics, 258, 263, 269, 273–280; and regeneracy, 16–17, 55–57; and Supreme Court, 67, 80; and Think 2040 project, 270–274
civic generations, 5, 13–15; childhoods of, 27–31, 109, 146, 155; and civic ethos, 270, 272; and corporate life, 139, 190; and economy, 27–28, 30, 34–37, 123–124, 127–129, 133, 135, 256; and education, 157–159, 162, 173–174; and entertainment, 212, 221–222; ethnic diversity of, 221–222; and executive branch, 103–104, 107, 109, 111, 115; and family lifestyles, 28, 193–195, 197, 199, 202–203, 206–208; and fourth turning, 18, 22–23, 25; and global change, 237–238, 240, 242, 244;

civic generations (*continued*)
and health care reform, 45, 54, 58,
60, 79–80; and higher education,
178–179, 181–184, 189–190; and
legislative branch, 83–84, 88, 98;
and operational/ideological
attitudes, 44–46, 50–54, 58, 60–61,
260; parents of, 28, 159; and
Supreme Court, 65, 71, 76, 79–80,
88. *See also* GI Generation;
Millennial Generation
Civic Scholars program (Univ. of
Pennsylvania), 267
Civil War, 12; and baseball, 220; and
education, 157–158; fourth turning,
15–18, 20, 22, 24, 42, 61, 265;
Land Grant Acts, 182–183; and
presidential leadership, 103–105,
146; and Supreme Court, 69–71,
73, 77, 82
Clayborn, Adrian, 224
Clemens, Roger, 221
Clift, Eleanor, 105–106
Clinton, Bill, 2, 13, 47, 77, 122, 128,
164, 182; and legislative branch, 52,
91–92, 258–260
Clinton, Hillary, 52, 146, 226
Coast Guard, 107–109
Cobb, Ty, 220–221
Cohen, Aaron, 272
Coldplay, 214
Cold War, 28, 228
collaboration, 53, 97, 136, 186, 231;
and civic ethos, 273, 279; and Coast
Guard, 108; and corporate life, 140,
144–145, 148–149; and executive
branch, 106, 108, 136; and
legislative branch, 95, 97; "mass
collaboration," 140
collective action, 16, 26–27, 36, 42;
and civic ethos, 264, 268, 276,
279–280; and education, 172, 182,
189; and global change, 226, 233,

244; and presidential leadership,
114, 117–118, 137
college. *See* higher education
Collins, Jim, 146
"Colors of the Wind" (song), 230
communication technology, 1, 14
52; in Brazil, 96–97; and civic
ethos, 266–267, 269, 274, 277–279;
and corporate life, 140–144; and
education, 164; and entertainment,
210, 213–214, 219; and executive
branch, 106, 111–114; and family
lifestyles, 197, 201, 205; and global
change, 226–229, 231, 235–236,
240–244; and higher education,
177, 183–189; and legislative
branch, 83, 89–100; and politics,
89–93, 97, 141; and Supreme
Court, 87–88; and 2008 campaign,
4–5, 91–94, 98–99, 141–144, 146,
242; video communication,
141–144, 146, 155, 219, 236, 243.
See also social media/networks
Community (television sitcom), 217
community organizers, 53, 226, 275
community service, 11–12, 27, 30,
122, 152; and civic ethos, 266–270,
280; and global change, 226,
228–229, 231
complexity economics, 130–132,
134–135, 137, 140, 187
COMPSTATS, 169–172
Cone Cause Evolution Study (2010),
152
Confederacy, 16–17, 20, 22, 69–70,
158, 247
Congress. *See* House of
Representatives; legislative branch;
Senate
Connections (Burke), 150
consensus, 17, 66, 103, 108, 117, 123,
135, 144; and civic ethos, 265, 273,
276–277, 279; and Coast Guard,

108; and education, 163, 168–169, 177, 181; and global change, 231, 233–234, 236, 240, 244; and health care reform, 57–59, 61; and operational/ideological attitudes, 57–59, 61

conservatives, 13, 23–24, 102, 109, 123, 247–250, 252–255; and age-influenced attitudes toward government, 38–40; Conservative PAC (CPAC), 23–24; and *Generation Zero* (Bannon), 23–24; and *Ground Zero* (documentary), 32–33; and health care reform, 77–78, 92, 249; and legislative branch, 85, 90, 92, 250, 252–256, 259, 261; and Supreme Court, 73–74, 77–79. *See also* ideological conservatism; *names of individual conservatives*

Conspiracy for Good, The (video series), 218–220

Constitution: amendments, 68, 104, 207, 264–265; and health care reform, 61, 77, 82; interstate commerce clause, 77–78; ratification of, 18, 19–20, 66, 264–265; and Supreme Court, 66, 68, 70, 74, 77, 82

Constitutional Convention (1787), 44, 264

consumers, 14, 116, 128, 136, 152–154; and civic ethos, 279–280; Consumer Confidence Index (CCI), 217; and global change, 232–233

Corporate Average Fuel Efficiency (CAFE) standards, 128

Corporation for National and Community Service (CNCS), 268

corporations: in auto industry, 36, 115–116, 123, 127–129; and Business Roundtable, 124; CEOs of, 124–129, 144–145, 147–148, 155; and civic ethos, 277; and communication technology, 140–144; and corporate life, 138–155; and corporate welfare, 128; and creativity, 139–141, 143–147, 150–151; and the economy, 124–128, 135–137, 257; in financial services industry, 36, 87, 116, 123–127; generational divide in, 147–149; as hybrid organizations, 153–155, 190; and innovation, 140–141, 143–147, 150–151, 155; leadership of, 124–129, 132, 137, 145–147, 155; and legislative branch, 87–88; and meaningful work, 151–155; and organizational proprioception, 143, 149–151, 155; and social responsibility, 124–125; as workplace, 138–144. *See also names of individual corporations*

Cost, Jay, 260

Coughlin, Charles, 207

creativity: and civic ethos, 271–272, 275, 278; and corporate life, 139–141, 143–147, 150–151; creative destruction, 131, 139–140; and the economy, 1, 129, 131, 136–137; and global change, 241–242; and higher education, 189; and Obama campaign, 145–147

crime, 10, 30, 169–170, 198, 234, 259

Crist, Charlie, 172

crowdsourcing, 93–94, 96

Cuban Americans, 247, 262

Culberson, John, 89

Cureton, Linda, 149

Danny and the Juniors, 212

Darfur (Sudan), 241–242

Dean, Howard, 47, 56, 150
Defense Department, 269
Deloitte, 152
DeMint, Jim, 53, 270
democracy: and civic ethos, 265, 271, 276–277, 279; and corporate life, 140, 144, 150, 155; and the economy, 129; and education, 157–158, 182; and executive branch, 10–11, 55, 104–105, 111; and FUD (Fear, Uncertainty, and Doubt), 44; and global change, 228, 235–237, 240; and legislative branch, 97–99; and open participation, 97–99, 111; and Supreme Court, 65–67
Democracy Alliance memo, 130–132, 134
Democrats, 245–246, 249, 250–263; and age-influenced attitudes toward government, 37–42; Blue Dog Coalition, 252–253, 261; and civic ethos, 275–276, 278; and Civil War, 69–70, 82; and communication technology, 89, 91–94; Congressional Progressive Caucus (CPC), 251–252, 261; Democratic Leadership Council, 252; Democratic National Committee (DNC), 91–92, 94; and the economy, 130–133, 257; and education, 161; and executive branch, 102–103, 105–106, 110, 116; and family lifestyles, 204; and fourth turnings, 20–24; and GI Generation, 37–39, 42; and health care reform, 43, 53, 55–59, 77, 79–80, 84, 92–93, 254, 257; and legislative branch, 83–85, 89, 91–94, 245–247, 251–262; and Millennials, 37–38, 40, 42, 83–84, 245–246, 256; and New Deal, 71, 73–74; New Democrats, 47, 252,

261; and operational liberalism, 47, 50–53, 55–59, 251–253, 256, 258–261; Southern Democratic tradition, 252; and Supreme Court, 69–71, 73–74, 76–77, 79–80; and 2010 midterm elections, 53, 59, 102–103, 106, 110, 116–117, 251, 253–262, 276. *See also names of individual Democrats*
Deng Xiaoping, 239
Devaney, Earl, 113
DeWolfe, Chris, 147
Dilbert (comic strip), 138
DiMaggio, Joe, 221–222
Diner (movie), 198
Dingell, John, 58–59
Dionne, E. J., 78–79, 103
Dirty Sexy Politics (M. McCain), 260
Disney Channel, 216–217
Disney University, 143
Disney World, 143
Disney XD, 233–234
Doe, Hilary, 271
Dokoupil, Tony, 204
Domino, Fats, 212
Donahue, Josh, 122–123
Dorsey, Tommy, 212
DoSomething.org, 266
doubt. *See* FUD (Fear, Uncertainty, and Doubt)
Douglas, Stephen A., 20, 44, 67
Douthat, Ross, 41–42
Drucker, Peter, 124
drug trade/use, 28, 30, 170, 228, 234
Duderstadt, James, 184–185
Duffy, A. J., 167
Duguid, Paul, 184–185
Duncan, Arne, 157, 167, 172
Dunne, Peter Finley, 66
Durban Bud (blog), 147

Economic Bill of Rights (1944), 179

economic equality/inequality, 15, 28, 59, 182; and complexity economics, 131–132; and governmental activism, 34, 36–37, 41–42, 249–250

economy, the, 1, 10, 121–137; and auto industry, 36, 115–116, 123, 127–129, 249, 257; and bailouts, 17, 36, 87, 115–116, 123, 129, 249, 257; in childhood of civic generations, 27–28, 30, 41; and civic ethos, 266, 271–272, 274–275, 278–279; and complexity economics, 130–132, 134–135, 137, 140, 187; and Congressional Budget Office, 257; and corporate leadership, 123–129, 132, 139, 257; and deficit spending, 46, 50, 116, 121, 130, 249, 258, 260, 274; and education, 131–132, 134, 157–159; and elites, 249, 257; and executive bonuses, 116; and executive branch, 104, 106, 110–111, 113–118; and family lifestyles, 193, 203–204; and free markets, 35, 42, 49, 123–125, 130–131; and global change, 228, 237–241, 244; and governmental activism, 34–37, 41–42, 115–116, 121, 123, 130–136, 249–250; and health care reform, 131–134, 249, 257–258; and higher education, 122, 135, 158, 178–179, 182, 187, 189–190; and infrastructure spending, 35, 73; and Keynesian economics, 123–124, 130–131, 278; and legislative branch, 17, 87, 123, 128, 133–136, 251–252, 260; and neoclassical economics, 81, 124–125, 130; and New Deal, 17, 21, 71–74, 104, 115, 123, 129–134; and operational/ideological attitudes, 50, 133, 135, 256; and politics, 129, 135, 246–247,

249–250, 256–257; and stimulus bill, 17, 35–36, 111, 113–114, 246–247, 251, 257; and Supreme Court, 71–78, 81; and unemployment, 21, 34–35, 113, 115, 121–123, 130, 136. *See also* Great Depression; recessions

e-Democracia Project, 96–97, 100, 278

education, 1, 45, 109, 153, 156–174, 203; and Celerity Charter Schools, 168, 173; and charter schools, 160, 162–164, 168, 173, 185; and civic ethos, 266–268, 271, 277–279; and class size, 165–166; and "common schools," 157–158; and compulsory attendance laws, 157–158; and District of Columbia schools, 168; and the economy, 131–132, 134, 157–159; and entertainment, 213; and GED exams, 167; and global change, 228–229, 238; and Harlem Children's Zone, 164; and "helicopter parents," 159; K12 Education, 267; and Kalamazoo Promise, 180–181; and Knowledge Is Power Program (KIPP), 164; and learning communities, 162–166, 169, 172–173; and Los Angeles Unified School District (LAUSD), 160–161, 164, 167–168; and METSchools (New York), 164; and Montgomery County, Md., school district, 171–172; online, 187; and "Parent Trigger" legislation (Calif.), 160–161, 163; and Paterson, N.J., school system, 171; and Race to the Top, 109, 160, 168, 181, 183, 277; and Recovery School District (RSD; New Orleans), 161–162; and role models, 165, 169; and SAT scores, 167, 173;

education (*continued*)
and SchoolStats, 171–173; and standardized tests, 30, 162, 167–169, 171–173; and "stealth fighter parents," 159–162; and teachers' unions, 161, 167–169; and Teach for America, 122, 151, 162, 269; and teaching effectiveness, 166–169, 171–173; and unified theory of learning (Calif.), 162–166; and University Preparatory Academy (Detroit), 164–166; and value-added performance, 167–169; and women, 33, 158, 203, 261–262. *See also* higher education
Egyptian protesters, 236
Elachi, Charles, 148
elections: 1828 election, 69; 1856 election, 68–69; 1860 election, 20, 70; 1862 midterm elections, 20; 1864 election, 17, 20; 1868 election, 22; 1876 election, 18, 82; 1896 election, 71; 1932 election, 21–23, 38, 71, 73; 1934 midterm elections, 73; 1936 election, 17, 21–22, 46, 61, 75–76, 133; 1938 midterm elections, 253; 1946 midterm elections, 259; 1948 election, 259; 1964 election, 47, 52; 1992 election, 91–92, 259; 1994 midterm elections, 49, 52, 259–260; 1996 election, 259; 2000 election, 81–82; 2002 midterm elections, 255; 2004 election, 40, 150; 2006 midterm elections, 253–255; 2008 election, 1–5, 10, 15, 43–44, 52, 83, 86–87, 89, 91–93, 95, 98–99, 101, 105–106, 115, 141–143, 145–147, 150, 226, 242, 245, 254, 256, 275–276; 2010 midterm elections, 42, 49, 53, 59, 80, 83–84, 88, 93, 102–103, 106, 110, 115–117, 246, 249–251, 253–258, 262, 275–276; 2012 election, 1, 17, 80, 258, 261, 263; 2016 election, 17; 2020 election, 261
Ellis, Steve, 113
Emanuel, Rahm, 91–92
Eminem, 224
energy, 1, 128–129, 132, 135; and civic ethos, 268, 272; and global change, 231–233; and Partnership for a New Generation of Vehicles (PNGV), 128–129
Energy Action Coalition, 231
Enista, Maya, 268–269
entertainment, 26, 209, 210–225; and audience participation, 218–220; and family lifestyles, 199–200, 207, 215–216; music, 184, 190, 209, 210–214, 224, 280; sports, 211, 220–225, 280; superheroes, 4, 218–220; television, 29, 196–197, 209, 211, 214–220, 224. *See also* movies
entrepreneurs, 135–136, 154–155, 164, 236, 242, 271–274
environment, 1, 45, 151, 228–234, 237, 252; and auto industry, 128–129; and civic ethos, 271–272; and global climate change, 228–234, 240; and Gulf oil spill, 106–108
Ethier, Andre, 222
ethnic diversity: and entertainment, 212, 221–222; and family lifestyles, 31–32, 196–197, 201, 207–208; and politics, 247–248, 251–252, 255–256, 261–262. *See also* race; *names of individual ethnic and racial groups*
evolutionary theory, 34, 206–207
executive branch, 61, 101, 102–118; and the economy, 104, 106, 110–111, 113–118; and executive orders, 87, 106, 113; four priorities

of, 102–110, 113–118, 135, 137; Jobs and Innovation Partnership, 135–136; Office of Management and Budget, 113; Office of New Media, 114; and open participation/transparency, 106–114, 117; and presidential leadership, 102–110; Race to the Top, 109, 160, 168, 181, 183, 277; State of the Union addresses, 47, 110, 117, 179, 259; and Supreme Court, 66–67, 69–70, 73–77, 80. *See also names of individual presidents*

Facebook, 91, 96, 141, 149, 153, 187, 210, 213; Facebook Connect, 242; and global change, 228–229, 236, 242
faith. *See* religion
family lifestyles, 193–209; and child-rearing practices, 28–30, 193, 195–198, 200, 204–205, 208; in China, 237–238; and the economy, 193, 203–204; and entertainment, 215–216; ethnically diverse, 31–32, 196–197, 201, 207–208; and gender neutrality, 32–33, 202–205, 208; and marriage, 193–196, 200, 207–208, 234; and maternity/ paternity leave programs, 204; multigenerational, 196–197, 201; and religion, 193, 205–208, 280; and role models, 29, 196; and suburbs, 198–201, 208
Faria, Cristiano Ferri, 96–97
fascism, 9, 28, 34
Father Knows Best (television sitcom), 196
Favre, Brett, 225
Fay, Scotty, 122
FBI, 151, 169
fear. *See* FUD (Fear, Uncertainty, and Doubt)

Federal Deposit Insurance Corporation (FDIC), 134
Federal Emergency Management Agency (FEMA), 108
Federal Housing Administration (FHA), 134
Federal Reserve, 87, 123
Feller, Bob, 221–222
feminism, 33–34, 129, 202–203
Fernandez, John, 136
Field, Stephen, 70
"Fifteen" (song), 213
50 Cent, 213, 224
financial crises. *See* Great Depression; recessions
financial services industry, 36, 87, 116, 123–127, 135, 249
Firedoglake (blog), 56–57, 87
Flannery, Matt, 242
Florida, Richard, 199–200
football, 153, 220, 223–224
Ford Motor Company, 128
Foreign Intelligence Surveillance Act (FISA), 98–99
foreign policy, 2, 18, 28, 39, 226–230, 240–241, 244, 272. *See also names of specific wars*
42nd Street (movie), 26
fourth turnings, 15–25, 264–265; American Revolution, 15–20, 24, 103–104, 273; catalyst, 16, 18, 23, 25, 50, 55–56; and civic ethos, 273–274; Civil War, 15–18, 20, 22, 24, 42, 61; climax, 16, 17–18, 66, 70; and executive branch, 103–105, 109; and FUD (Fear, Uncertainty, and Doubt), 18–25, 44, 61; New Deal, 15, 17–18, 21–24, 61, 71–77, 104, 115; and Obama, 16–17, 19, 21, 25, 34, 76–77, 79; regeneracy, 16–17, 55–57, 74; resolution, 16, 18, 25; and Supreme Court, 65–66, 69–77, 79–80, 82

Fox, Lee, 228, 266
Fox Family Channel, 216
Fox Network, 51, 216
Frank, Barney, 123
Frankfurter, Felix, 65, 76
Frank N. Magid Associates, 216.
    See also Magid surveys
Free, Lloyd A., 45–48, 50, 281
Freedom from Fear (D. M. Kennedy),
    133–134
French Revolution, 19
Friedman, Milton, 81, 124–125, 130
Friedman, Stephen, 215
Friedman, Tom, 243
Frum, David, 262
FUD (Fear, Uncertainty, and Doubt):
    and the economy, 116, 123; and
    education, 157; and executive
    branch, 103–105, 116; and family
    lifestyles, 204, 207–208; and fourth
    turnings, 18–25, 44, 61, 103–105,
    264–265; and global change, 244;
    and Great Depression, 26, 71, 73;
    and health care reform, 43, 45, 59,
    80; and immigration, 31; and
    politics, 250, 253, 256–257, 265;
    and Supreme Court, 65, 67, 71,
    73, 80
Futurecast (Shapiro), 139–140
Future of Work, The (Malone),
    140–141, 144

Gallup polls, 46–48, 75, 220, 281.
    See also survey research data
gaming: and entertainment, 210,
    214, 219; and higher education,
    186–189; and military service, 186
Ganz, Marshall, 275
Garcia, Greg, 217–218
Garrow, David J., 79
Garvin, Leah, 241, 243
gays/gay rights, 32–33, 52, 197–198,
    206

Gehrig, Lou, 221–222
Geithner, Timothy, 125
gender neutrality, 32–33, 202–205,
    208
General Electric, 145
General Motors (GM), 115–116, 123,
    127–129
generational archetypes, 12–15, 42,
    51, 65, 79, 220; and family
    lifestyles, 198–199; and global
    change, 234, 238
generational cycles, 5, 12–25, 50,
    208; and global change, 234,
    236–237. *See also* fourth turnings
Generational Dynamics (Xenakis),
    32–33
generational stereotypes, 195, 226
Generation Ordning (Sweden), 234
*Generations: The History of America's
    Future 1584 to 2069* (Strauss and
    Howe), 12
Generation X (1965–1982), 13, 27,
    29–30, 32–34; and age-influenced
    attitudes toward government, 38;
    and corporate life, 138, 147, 149,
    151; and the economy, 34,
    135–137; and education, 159–162,
    168, 173; and entertainment, 211,
    213, 215–217, 221–225; and
    family lifestyles, 194, 196–201,
    205–206; and global change,
    226–227, 230, 234–236, 238,
    242–243; and Millennials, 27, 30,
    32–33, 147, 149, 159–162; and
    Obama, 5, 59–60, 98–99; and
    operational/ideological attitudes,
    53; and politics, 251, 254. *See also*
    reactive generations
Generation Zero (Bannon), 23–24
genocide, 228, 241–243, 272
Genocide Intervention Network, 243
Gerson, Michael, 260–261
Giffords, Gabrielle, 110

GI Generation (1901–1924): and
age-influenced attitudes toward
government, 38–40, 42; and
Boomers, 10, 23; childhood of,
27–31, 201–202; command-and-
control approach of, 1, 139; and
the economy, 27–28, 30, 34,
36–37, 121, 133; and education,
158–159; and entertainment,
210–212, 214, 221–222; and
family lifestyles, 28, 193–196,
201–203, 206–207; and Millennials,
1, 9, 11, 14, 26–31, 33–36, 270;
and operational/ideological
attitudes, 50, 260; parents of, 28,
158–159; and Supreme Court, 71.
See also civic generations
Gildea, Derek, 241
Gingrich, Newt, 24, 49–50, 52
Giuliani, Rudolph, 169
Giuliano, Paola, 41
Gladwell, Malcolm, 243
Glee! (television sitcom), 26
global change, 145, 226–244, 272;
and China, 24, 228, 237–241, 244;
and education, 156, 187, 189; and
environment, 228–234, 237, 240;
and foreign policy, 2, 18, 28, 39,
226–230, 240–241, 244, 272; and
Middle East conflicts, 227–228,
235–237, 244
Global Health Corps, 50–51
Godwin, Bev, 114
Goldbeck, Janessa, 243
Goldberg, Jonah, 2–3, 4
Goldman Sachs, 126
Goldwater, Barry, 52
Goodman, Benny, 210
Gore, Al, 81–82, 114, 128–129, 171
governmental activism, 15, 17–18, 21,
34–42; and age-influenced attitudes
toward government, 37–42; and
civic ethos, 270, 274; and the

economy, 34–37, 41–42, 115–116,
121, 123, 130–136, 249–250; and
executive branch, 115–116; and
operational/ideological attitudes,
51, 55, 60; and Supreme Court, 73,
76. *See also* New Deal; operational
liberalism; regulation, governmental
Graham-Felsen, Sam, 93
Grant, Ulysses S., 22
Grassley, Charles, 247
Great Depression, 9, 21, 24, 26, 34,
36, 40, 42, 46, 56, 104, 129,
132–134, 137, 179, 257; and
Supreme Court, 71–75, 77. *See also*
recessions
Greatest Generation, The (Brokaw), 14
Greek (television sitcom), 217
Greenberg, Hank, 221–222
Green Chemistry initiative (Calif.),
232–233
Greenleaf, Thomas, 264
Grier, Robert, 67
Ground Zero (documentary), 32–33
Guffey, Bryan, 152
Guffey Coal Act, 74
"Guitar Hero" (video game), 214
Gulf oil spill, 106–108

Hall, G. Stanley, 195
Hamel, Gary, 140
Hamilton, Alexander, 66
Hamsher, Jane, 56–57, 87
Hannity, Sean, 23–24
Harper, Max, 141–143
Harry Potter Alliance, 241–242
Hayes, Rutherford B., 82
health care reform, 1, 17, 34, 43, 45,
51–61; and civic ethos, 272–273,
277; and "death panels," 52; and
the economy, 131–134, 249,
257–258; and employer mandates,
54; and health insurance, 54–56,
60, 77–78, 109, 249, 257, 272;

health care reform (*continued*)
and legislative branch, 45,
51–59, 61, 77–78, 80, 84, 92–95,
247, 251–254, 257, 260; and
operational/ideological attitudes,
51–61, 251–253; and preexisting
conditions, 54, 257; and public
option, 56, 60; and single payer
system, 60; and Supreme Court, 61,
77–82; and universal coverage, 43,
58, 60
Healy, Ryan, 205
Hendrix, Jimi, 211, 214
Henig, Robin Marantz, 194–195
Herberg, Will, 208
Here Comes Everybody (Shirky), 93–94
Heroes (television drama), 218
Hewlett Packard, 143
hierarchical organizational structures:
"clusters of experts," 144;
command-and-control, 1, 108–109,
139–140, 142, 144, 231; and
corporate life, 138–140, 142–144,
150–151; flatter hierarchies, 94;
loose hierarchies, 143, 144, 155
higher education, 159, 174, 175–191;
and civic ethos, 177–179, 266–272,
279; and communication
technology, 177, 183–189; and
community colleges, 175–176, 179,
181; cost of, 176–184, 188; and
"Degree-Granting Body" (DGB),
184–185; and dropouts, 175–176,
178–181; and the economy, 122,
135, 158, 178–179, 182, 187,
189–190; and family lifestyles, 203;
and gaming, 186–189; and GI Bill
of Rights, 177, 270; and global
change, 227, 231, 238; and
Individual Education Accounts,
182; and intellectual property, 184;
and Kalamazoo Promise, 179–181;
and Land Grant Acts, 182–183,

185; and "Learn Grant Act,"
181–185; and learning
communities, 183–184, 189; and
lifelong learning, 174, 184, 189;
and mentoring, 183–184; online,
187–188; and peer interaction,
183–184; and research grants,
177–178, 184, 248; and
scholarships, 179–183; and student
loans, 109, 177–179, 181–183, 248;
and teaching effectiveness, 167; and
unified theory of learning, 176–177,
183; and University Preparatory
Academy (Detroit), 164–165; and
videos, 186–188. *See also* education
Higher Education in the Digital Age
(Duderstadt et al.), 183–184
High School Musical (television show),
26, 217
Hindus, 208
Hispanics, 35, 175, 201, 207, 222;
and politics, 247–248, 251–252,
254, 256, 261–262
Hitler, Adolf, 236
Holmes, Oliver Wendell Jr., 72
homeless youth, 266–267
homeownership, 116, 126–127, 134,
199–201, 257
homosexuality, 33, 206. *See also*
gays/gay rights
Hoover, Herbert, 73
Hornsby, Rogers, 221
House of Representatives, 47,
246–247, 251–253; and civic ethos,
274, 276, 278; and communication
technology, 89–90, 94; and the
economy, 87, 136, 246–247;
Financial Services Committee,
123; Franking Commission, 89;
and health care reform, 55, 58–59;
and Millennials, 83, 245; and
2010 midterm elections,
251–253, 255–256, 259–262.

See also legislative branch; *names of individual representatives*
Howe, Jeff, 93–94
Howe, Neil, 5, 12, 15–18, 23, 25, 159–160, 234–235
Huckabee, Mike, 249
Hudson, Henry E., 77
Hughes, Charles Evans, 74–75
Hughes, Chris, 242
Hu Jintao, 239
human rights abuses, 228, 237
Hunt, Al, 57
hybrid organizations, 153–155, 190

idealist generations, 13–15, 44; and age-influenced attitudes toward government, 37–38, 41; and the economy, 28, 124–125; efforts to eliminate addictive substances in, 28, 34; and entertainment, 216, 220; and executive branch, 104, 115; and family lifestyles, 202, 206; and fourth turning, 18–19, 22, 25; and global change, 235, 240, 244; and higher education, 178, 182, 189; and New Deal, 71–74; and operational/ideological attitudes, 46–47, 49–53; parents of, 13, 28–29; and slavery, 67–70; and Supreme Court, 65, 67–74, 76, 79. *See also* Awakening Generation; Baby Boom Generation; Missionary Generation; Transcendental Generation
ideological conservatism, 45–60, 48*tab.*, 248, 251–253, 256, 258, 260–263, 281–282; in America's DNA, 10–11, 55, 248, 258, 263–264, 276; and civic ethos, 273–274, 276–277; and the economy, 50, 133, 135, 256; and entertainment, 216; and Supreme Court, 65, 69, 73–74, 76–77, 79, 82

immigrants/immigration, 14, 27–28, 31–32, 227; and entertainment, 197, 212, 222
Indian Americans, 262
individual freedom/responsibility, 47, 49; and civic ethos, 264, 268, 274, 276–277, 279–280; and corporate life, 140, 146, 150–151; and education, 164, 172, 189; and executive branch, 109, 114, 117–118, 146; and global change, 226, 231–233, 235, 241–242, 244
Industrial Revolution, 104
innovation, 1; and civic ethos, 267, 271, 273, 278–279; and corporate life, 140–141, 143–147, 150–151, 155; and the economy, 129–132, 135–137; and higher education, 189
Institute for a New California, 162–163
Institute for Research on Learning, 163
Institute for Social Research (Univ. of Michigan), 40–41
international affairs. *See* foreign policy
Internet, 87–89, 96–97, 102, 187–188, 201, 235–236, 240. *See also titles of specific Web sites, blogs, etc.*
Iranian protesters, 228, 235–236, 243
Iraq War, 28, 268–269
iScale, 145
Islam, 208, 229, 235, 237
Ito, Mimi, 186–187, 189
"It's Getting Hot in Here" (blog), 231
"It's Hard Out Here for a Pimp" (song), 211–212

Jackson, Andrew, 69
Jackson, Michael, 213–214
Jackson, Shoeless Joe, 221
"Jai Ho" (song), 211–212
James, Bill, 221

James, LeBron, 223
Jefferson, Thomas, 67, 157, 273
Jersey Shore (television reality show), 215
Jeter, Derek, 221
Jet Propulsion Laboratory (JPL), 148–149
Jews, 27, 74, 207–208, 222
job creation, 1, 113, 135–136, 204–205, 257, 261. *See also* unemployment
John Birch Society, 87
Johnson, Lyndon B., 9–10, 105–106, 245, 281
Johnson, Magic, 223
Johnson, Walter, 221
Jones, Courtney, 115
Joplin, Janis, 211
Jordan, Michael, 223
judicial branch. *See* Supreme Court
Jumo.com, 242

Kagan, Elena, 79
Kaiser Family Foundation, 210
Kalaidis, Jen, 203
Kanarek, Michael, 171
Kane, Thomas, 166
Katrina (hurricane), 102, 108, 161–162
Kelly, Chris, 96
Kennedy, Anthony, 75, 78
Kennedy, David M., 133–134
Kennedy, John F., 11, 229
Kennedy, Ted, 54, 57
Kerry, John, 40
Keynes, John Maynard, 123–124, 130–131, 278
Khan Academy, 187
Kiva.org, 242
KooDooZ (social network site), 228, 266
Kotkin, Joel, 199–200
Kring, Tim, 218–220
Ku Klux Klan, 221

Landon, Alf, 21–22, 61, 75, 133
Latinos, 27, 115, 160–161, 173, 212
League of Nations, 28, 229
Learn and Serve America, 268
Leave It to Beaver (television sitcom), 196
Lee, Paul, 217
legislative branch, 15, 44–45, 61, 83–101, 246–263; Agricultural Adjustment Act, 74; backroom deals/concessions in, 57, 84, 88, 99; in Brazil, 96–97; and campaign contributions, 86–89, 95, 97, 100, 274; and civic ethos, 270, 274–279; and communication technology, 83, 87–100; and Congressional Budget Office, 257; and Congressional Management Foundation, 97; and Congressional Progressive Caucus (CPC), 251–252, 261; and corporate power, 87–88; Economic Recovery Act (2009), 17, 35–36, 111, 113–114, 246–247, 251, 257; and the economy, 17, 87, 123, 128, 134–136, 251–252, 260; Electoral Count Act (1886), 82; and environment, 252; and fourth turning, 20–21; GI Bill of Rights, 177; and global change, 233; and health care reform, 45, 51–59, 61, 77–78, 80, 84, 92–95, 247, 251–254, 257, 260; and higher education, 179, 182, 189; Kansas-Nebraska bill (1854), 67–68; and Millennials, 81–86, 88–89, 94–100; Missouri Compromise (1820), 67–68, 80; and New Deal, 71, 73–75; and 1946 midterm elections, 259; and 1994 midterm elections, 49, 52, 259–260; and operational/ideological attitudes, 49, 51–59, 251–253, 258–261; and partisanship, 84–86, 246–248; and

slavery, 67–70; and special interests, 84, 86–87, 95, 100; and Supreme Court, 66–71, 73–78, 80–82, 87–88; Taft-Hartley labor bill, 259; and 2010 midterm elections, 53, 59, 83–84, 88, 102–103, 106, 246, 249–251, 253–261. *See also names of individual legislators*
Lehman Brothers, 123
Levinson, Barry, 198–199, 201
liberals, 23, 29, 33, 38, 41–42, 121; and health care reform, 54, 56–57, 59–60, 78, 87; and legislative branch, 251–256, 259; and Supreme Court, 73–74, 76, 78–79. *See also* operational liberalism; *names of individual liberals*
libertarians, 51–52, 80, 87, 139, 249. *See also names of individual libertarians*
Liberty Heights (movie), 198
Life against the Grain, A (Simon), 139
limited government, 24–25, 35, 47, 49, 115; and civic ethos, 274–276; and the economy, 121, 133, 136, 260–261. *See also* ideological conservatism
Lincoln, Abraham, 10, 16–18, 20, 22, 44, 274; and presidential leadership, 103–105, 146; and Supreme Court, 67, 69–70, 76
Lindbergh, Charles A., 207
Little Red Wagon Foundation, 266–267
Liu Mingfu, 239–240
lobbyists, 86–88, 128
Long, Huey, 21
Long March generation (China), 238
Longoria, Evan, 222
Los Angeles Lakers, 222–223
Los Angeles Unified School District (LAUSD), 160–161, 164, 167–168

Lost Generation (1883–1900), 58, 76, 126, 211–212, 220–221
Loy, James, 107–108

MacKenzie, Jack, 216–217
Magid surveys, 40, 81, 216–217
Malone, Tom, 140–141, 144, 150–151
Mann, Horace, 158
Mao Tse-tung, 238
marijuana, 78, 111
Markiewicz, Pete, 211–212
Married . . . With Children (television sitcom), 196, 216
Marshall, John, 66
Marston, Alex, 12
Marvel Comics, 218
Massacre, The (album), 213
Mathewson, Christy, 221
MCAmerica.org, 151–152
McCain, John, 3, 14, 89–90, 142, 245, 249, 252–253
McCain, Megan, 260
McCarthy, Kevin, 13
McConnell, Mitch, 56
McDonald's, 267
McFarlane, Vielka, 168, 173
McGwire, Mark, 221
McKinley, William, 71
McReynolds, James, 73–74
Medicare, 45, 78, 136, 248, 258–259, 281
Memorandum on Transparency and Open Government, 111
men: and education, 158; and entertainment, 210; and family lifestyles, 33, 193–194, 197, 202–205; and politics, 247–248, 254. *See also* gender neutrality
mentoring, 148–149, 165, 183–184, 269
Merrill Lynch, 123, 126–127
Metropolitan Bay Transportation Authority (MBTA), 111–112

Meyerson, Harold, 262
Middle East conflicts, 227–228, 235–237, 243–244
Middlekauff, Robert, 19
military service, 28, 122, 202, 268–269; and draft, 20, 39; and gaming, 186
Millennial Generation (1982–2003): and age-influenced attitudes toward government, 37–38, 40–41; and Boomers, 10, 13, 27, 30–31, 33–34, 148–149, 151, 159, 203; childhood of, 27–31, 109, 146, 155; and civic ethos, 265–280; as civic generation, 5, 9–12, 14–15, 25–31, 33–37; and Coast Guard, 107–109; and corporate life, 138, 140–144, 146–155; and the economy, 1, 10, 34–37, 114–116, 121–123, 125, 128–129, 131–133, 136–137; and education, 45, 122, 156–162, 166–168, 172–174; and entertainment, 210–215, 217–220, 222–225; ethnic diversity of, 27, 31–32, 196, 201, 207–208, 212, 222, 227, 255–256, 261–262; and executive branch, 101, 106–109, 111–118; and family lifestyles, 28, 193–209; and Gen-Xers, 27, 30, 32–33, 147, 149, 159–162; and GI Generation, 1, 9, 11, 14, 26–31, 33–36, 121; and global change, 226–238, 240–244; and governmental activism, 34–38, 40–42; and health care reform, 45, 51–54, 58–61, 80, 117; and higher education, 159, 175–179, 181–190; and legislative branch, 81–86, 88–89, 94–100; moving back home, 122, 178; and operational/ideological attitudes, 50–54, 56, 58–61, 260–261; parents of, 27–31, 45, 109, 122, 146, 149,

155–156, 158–162, 167, 172–174, 176–177, 196, 201, 208, 224–225, 233, 238; and politics, 245–246, 248, 250–251, 254–256, 261–263; pragmatic idealism of, 30–31, 42, 45, 53, 60, 109, 229, 242, 273, 276; and Supreme Court, 80–82; and Think 2040 project, 270–274; and 2008 campaign, 1–5, 10, 15, 40, 49, 91, 98–99, 101, 141–143, 150, 226, 242, 255–256, 262, 267, 275. *See also* civic generations
Millennial Makeover (Winograd and Hais), 4–5, 14, 161
Millennials Changing America (Web site), 84–85, 152–153
Millennial Strategy Program, 216
Miller, Ellen, 112
Miller, Glenn, 179, 210, 212
Milliken, William, 260
Minnick, Walt, 250
Missionary Generation (1860–1882), 71–72, 74, 76, 202, 220. *See also* idealist generations
Mobilize.org, 268–269
moderates, 47, 133, 246–248, 251, 255
Modern Family (television sitcom), 196–197, 217
Moore, David, 95–96
Mormons, 208
Morton, Jelly Roll, 212
movies, 26, 29, 57, 136, 197, 230–231. *See also titles of specific movies*
Mr. Smith Goes to Washington (movie), 57
MTV, 213, 215
Mubarak, Hosni, 236
Murdoch, Rupert, 216
Musial, Stan, 221–222
music, 184, 190, 209, 210–214, 224, 280; big band swing, 179, 210, 212;

country, 213–214; hip hop, 211, 213–214; jazz, 211–212; mash-up, 213–214; Pakistani, 237; rap, 211–214, 224; rhythm and blues, 214; rock, 211–214

Muslims, 208, 229, 235, 237

MyBarackObama.com, 91, 98–99, 142, 242

Mycoskie, Blake, 154–155

myImpact.org, 153–154

MySpace, 141, 147, 186, 213

NASA, 148–149, 151

National Assessment of Educational Progress (NAEP), 173

National Basketball Association, 222–223

National Conference on Volunteering and Service (San Francisco, 2009), 268

National Defense Education Act (1964), 177–178

National Education Association, 168

National Football League, 223–224

National Honor Society, 267

National Industrial Recovery Act, 74

National Study of Youth and Religion, 208

New Deal: and civic ethos, 265, 276; and the economy, 17, 21, 71–74, 104, 115, 123, 129–134; and executive branch, 104–105, 115; fourth turning, 15, 17–18, 21–24, 61, 71–77, 104, 115; and operational/ideological attitudes, 44–46, 59; and Supreme Court, 66, 71–77, 80

New Foundation, 133

New York Police Department (NYPD), 169–172

Next Great Generation, The (*TNGG*; online publication), 4, 195, 203

Next One Hundred Million, The (Kotkin), 199

9/11 terrorist attacks, 28, 49

Nirvana, 214

Nixon, Richard M., 130

Nokia, 219

nonprofit organizations: and civic ethos, 266–268, 277; and corporate life, 139, 144–145, 152–155; and global change, 241, 243. *See also* names of individual nonprofit organizations

Noonan, Peggy, 125

Norquist, Grover, 38–40

Not Everyone Gets a Trophy (Tulgan), 151

Noveck, Beth, 111

nuclear threat, 228–229

Null Zoff (Germany), 234

Obama, Barack: and America's DNA, 10–11, 55, 58, 276; birth of, 59; and campaign contributions, 86–87, 142; and civic ethos, 265, 268, 275–278; and communication technology, 4–5, 91–94, 106, 111–114, 141–143; and the economy, 10, 17, 35, 42, 110, 114–118, 121, 125, 131–137, 251, 257; and education, 109, 157, 160, 167–168, 180–181, 183, 189; and fourth turning, 16–17, 19, 21; and global change, 227, 229–230, 237, 240; and Gulf oil spill, 106–108; and health care reform, 43, 45, 51–55, 57–61, 77, 80–82, 92–93, 249; inauguration of, 3, 40, 189; and legislative branch, 84, 86–87, 91–94, 246, 250–252; and Nobel Peace Prize, 229; and operational/ideological attitudes, 51–55, 57–60;

Obama, Barack (*continued*)
and presidential leadership,
102–103, 105–110, 113–118, 135,
137, 146–147, 150, 256, 275–276;
sister of, 142; speech on race
(March 2008), 142; State of the
Union addresses, 110, 117,
135–136; and Supreme Court,
76–77, 80–82; and 2008 campaign,
1–5, 10, 40, 42, 49, 83, 86–87,
91–93, 98–99, 101, 105–106, 115,
141–143, 145–147, 150, 226, 242,
245–247, 251, 255, 262, 267,
275–276; and 2010 midterm
elections, 102–103, 106, 110,
115–117, 250, 253, 255–257,
275–276; and 2012 election, 1, 17,
80, 258–260; University of
Michigan speech of, 9–12, 276
Obama, Michelle, 268
Oberlander, Jonathan, 80
Obey, David, 59
O'Conner, Sandra Day, 75
Office, The (television sitcom), 138,
148
Office Depot Foundation, 267
O'Neal, Shaquille, 222–223
O'Neal, Stan, 126–127
One Day at a Time (television sitcom),
196
OpenCongress.org, 95–96
Open Government Initiative,
109–114
open participation, 11, 34; in Brazil,
96–97, 100; and Coast Guard,
108–109; and corporate life,
141–142; and executive branch,
106–114, 117; and legislative
branch, 94–100; and Obama
campaign, 141–142; and online
town hall meetings, 97, 110–111.
See also transparency
open-source software movement, 94

operational liberalism, 45–60, 48*tab*.,
248, 251–253, 256, 258–263,
281–282; in America's DNA,
10–11, 55, 258, 263–264; and civic
ethos, 273–274, 276–277; and the
economy, 50, 133, 135, 256; and
Supreme Court, 82
Organizing for America (OFA),
92–94
Origin of Wealth, The (Beinhocker),
131
Orkut (Brazil), 96–97
Orszag, Peter, 113
Ovi, 219
Owens, Colleen, 250

Pacific Islanders, 142
Palin, Sarah, 13, 226, 249
Parenthood (television sitcom),
196–197
parentrevolution.org, 160–161
Participatory Politics Foundation,
95–96
partisanship, 10–11, 45; and civic
ethos, 274; and executive branch,
102, 104; and FUD (Fear,
Uncertainty, and Doubt), 18–19;
and legislative branch, 84–86,
246–248, 258; and Supreme Court,
70, 74, 76, 78–79
Patterson, Brenda, 171
Paul family, 80
Peace Corps, 11, 122, 151, 226
Peckham, Rufus, 72
Pedroia, Dustin, 222
Pelosi, Nancy, 55, 246
Pepsi Refresh Everything contest,
153–154
performance (presidential priority),
102, 104–106
Pew Research Center: Political
Values and Core Attitudes Survey,
48, 248, 251, 281–282; survey on

economy, 34, 121–122; survey on ethnic diversity, 31; survey on family lifestyles, 195; survey on foreign policy, 227; survey on government activism, 35, 36–38; survey on legislative branch, 84; survey on operational/ideological attitudes, 48–49, 48*tab.*, 51, 53–54, 248; survey on politics, 248, 251, 254; survey on women's rights, 32. *See also* survey research data

Phaeton program (JPL), 148–149

philanthropy, 179–181, 213, 266–267

Philanthropy Project, 267

Platts, Asher, 151–152

Plouffe, David, 2–3, 93, 150

policy (presidential priority), 102–103, 105–106, 109, 114–115, 117

Political Beliefs of Americans, The (Free and Cantril), 45–48, 50

politics, 14–15, 245–263; and age-influenced attitudes toward government, 37–42; and campaign contributions, 86–89, 91, 273; and civic ethos, 269, 273–280; and communication technology, 89–93, 97, 141; and the economy, 129, 135, 246–247, 249–250, 256–257; and education, 161, 168, 179; and global change, 232, 234–236, 239–241, 243–244; and health care reform, 1, 17, 43, 45; and legislative branch, 86–93, 97, 245–247; and party identification, 40–41, 254; and political efficacy, 38, 42; as presidential priority, 102–106, 109–110, 114, 117–118; and Supreme Court, 65–71, 73–76, 79–82. *See also* elections; ideological conservatism; operational liberalism; *names of specific political parties*

Polk, James, 70

polling. *See* survey research data

popular culture. *See* entertainment

Posner, Richard, 81

poverty, 36, 41, 46, 130, 271–272; in China, 238; and education, 164–166, 168, 178–179

Powe, Lucas, 76

pragmatic idealism, 30–31, 42, 45, 53, 60, 109, 229, 242, 273, 276

pragmatism, 30, 53, 55–57, 60, 229, 235, 273, 276

Precious (movie), 167

Presidential Partners, 91–92

presidents. *See* executive branch; *names of individual presidents*

Presley, Elvis, 212, 214

Price, David, 222

Prince, Charles, 125

Procter and Gamble, 145

progressives, 47; and corporate life, 153; and the economy, 87, 130; and executive branch, 107, 111–112; and expertise, 95, 107, 111–112; and legislative branch, 87, 95, 252, 259; and Supreme Court, 73–74, 78. *See also names of individual progressives*

Prohibition, 28, 34, 206

proprioception, organizational, 143, 149–151, 155

Protestant, Catholic, Jew (Herberg), 208

Protestants, 207–208

Prudential Insurance Company, 139

public opinion. *See* survey research data

public relations (presidential priority), 102–110, 113–118, 135, 137

Quesada, Joe, 218

race: and education, 161, 170, 173; and family lifestyles, 31, 197–198, 201. *See also* ethnic diversity; *names of individual ethnic and racial groups*

Rainko, Ashleigh, 195
Raising Hope (television sitcom),
    217–218
Ramirez, Manny, 221, 225
reactive generations, 13, 126,
    220–221, 230. *See also* Generation
    X; Lost Generation
Reagan, Ronald, 18, 38, 47, 49, 59,
    77, 115, 125, 136, 248
recessions, 27–28, 41; Great
    Recession (2008), 16, 34–36, 49,
    106, 116, 121, 123, 130, 132–134,
    137, 178, 249, 257, 266
Reconstruction, 18, 82, 158, 253
Recovery Accountability and
    Transparency Board, 113
recovery.gov (Web site), 113
Red Guard generation (China), 239
Reform generation (China), 239
regulation, governmental: and the
    economy, 124–125, 130, 134–136;
    and education, 109; financial
    regulation, 34–35, 73, 115,
    124–125, 135; and health care
    reform, 56, 60; and New Deal,
    73–74; and Supreme Court,
    73–75, 81
Reid, Harry, 56, 246
religion, 193, 205–208, 249, 266, 280
Republican Generation, 202
Republicans, 245–251, 253–256,
    258–263; and age-influenced
    attitudes toward government,
    38–40, 42; and civic ethos, 270,
    274–276, 278; and Civil War, 68,
    70, 82; and communication
    technology, 89, 92, 94; and the
    economy, 113, 116, 121, 133–134,
    136–137, 260–261; and education,
    172; and executive branch, 113,
    116; and family lifestyles, 204; and
    fourth turnings, 20, 22, 24; and
    global change, 226, 232; GOP

Convention (1964), 52; and health
    care reform, 53, 55–59, 61, 80, 84,
    92; and ideological conservatism,
    47, 49–53, 55–56, 59, 248, 251,
    253, 256, 258–261, 276; and
    legislative branch, 84–85, 88–89,
    92, 94, 245–250, 253–256,
    258–261; and New Deal, 71,
    73–74, 134; and Supreme Court,
    68, 70–71, 73–75, 77, 79–80; and
    2010 midterm elections, 59, 88,
    246, 249–250, 253–256, 258–262;
    and 2012 election, 262. *See also*
    names of individual Republicans
Revolutionary War, 15–19, 24
Rhee, Michelle, 168
Rich, Frank, 259
Roberts, John, 79–80
Robertson, Pat, 215–216
Roberts, Owen, 74–75
Robinson, Jackie, 221–222
Rockefeller, Nelson, 52
Rodriguez, Alex, 221, 225
Rodriguez, Gregory, 273
Rolle, Myron, 223–224
Rolling Stones, 214
Romano, Andrew, 204
Room to Read (nonprofit
    organization), 219
Roosevelt, Anne, 270
Roosevelt, Franklin Delano, 17,
    21–23, 26–27, 38, 44, 46, 270;
    death of, 259; and the economy,
    133–134, 137, 253; fireside chats of,
    104, 236; and higher education,
    179; and presidential leadership,
    103–105, 107; and Supreme Court,
    66, 71, 73–76, 265. *See also* New
    Deal
Roosevelt, Theodore, 10, 107
Roosevelt Institute Campus
    Network, 270–271
Rosenberg, Simon, 91–92

Rospars, Joe, 150
Ross, Doug, 164–165
Rove, Karl, 102
Rush, Benjamin, 157
Ruth, Babe, 220–221
Ryan, Paul, 13

Sanders, Bernie, 56–57
Santelli, Rick, 116
Santmyer, Helen Hooven, 22–24, 42
Scalia, Antonin, 65, 78, 88
schools. *See* education; higher
   education
Schumpeter, Joseph, 131
Schwarzenegger, Arnold, 232
science, 136, 187, 232
Secret Life of the American Teenager, The
   (television drama), 217
Securities and Exchange Commission
   (SEC), 134
Segura, Gary, 262
Senate, 245–247; and civic ethos,
   278; and communication
   technology, 89–90, 93–94; and the
   economy, 87, 135; and health care
   reform, 56–58, 93, 247; and
   Millennials, 85, 245; and Supreme
   Court, 69, 75; and 2010 midterm
   elections, 250, 253–254, 256, 259,
   262. *See also* legislative branch;
   names of individual senators
"Senator Obama Please Vote NO on
   Telecom Immunity—Get FISA
   Right" (group), 99
Sha Na Na, 212
Shapiro, Rob, 139–140
Sharepoint, 149
Shaw, George Bernard, 38
Shirky, Clay, 93–94, 160, 235
Silent Generation (1925–1945), 14,
   27; and entertainment, 211–212,
   214; and family lifestyles, 30,
   32–33, 194, 198–201, 206–207; and

global change, 227, 239; and
   legislative branch, 55, 58–59; and
   politics, 85, 247–248, 254; and
   presidential leadership, 116–117.
   See also adaptive generations
Simon, Julian, 139
Simpsons, The (television cartoon
   program), 216
Sinatra, Frank, 212, 214
Six Sigma, 145
60 Minutes (television news show),
   117
Skidelsky, Robert, 123–124
Skowronek, Stephen, 44, 61, 117
Slack, Andrew, 241–242
slavery, 20, 22, 44, 104, 126, 265; and
   Supreme Court, 67–70, 80, 82
Slum Dog Millionaire (movie),
   211–212
smart phones, 1, 88, 111–112, 148,
   184–185, 219
Smith, Adam, 81, 132
Smith, Gerald L. K., 207
Smith, Winthrop Jr., 127
socialism, 59, 92, 133–134
social justice, 54, 280
social media/networks, 1, 4, 26, 241;
   in Brazil, 96–97; and civic ethos,
   266–267, 274, 277–278; and
   corporate life, 140–144, 147–148,
   150, 153–154; and education, 161;
   e-mail/text messages, 91, 142,
   153, 210, 213, 235, 242; and
   entertainment, 210, 213, 219, 224;
   Facebook, 91, 96, 141, 149, 153,
   187, 210, 213, 228–229, 236, 242;
   and global change, 227–229, 231,
   235–236, 240–244; and hashtags
   (#), 90; and higher education,
   185–187; and legislative branch,
   88–96, 98–99; MySpace, 141, 147,
   186, 213; and Obama campaign,
   91–93, 98–99, 142, 150, 153;

social media/networks (*continued*)
Orkut, 96–97; Twitter, 89–91, 94, 96, 213, 219, 228, 235, 240, 242; videos, 141–144, 146, 155, 219, 236, 243; "virtual water coolers," 144; YouTube, 52, 143, 146, 186–187, 242. *See also* communication technology

Social Security, 21, 24, 39, 46, 61, 104, 204; and the economy, 133, 136; and politics, 248, 258; and Supreme Court, 74–75

Soltis, Kristen, 38, 262

Sosa, Sammy, 221

Sotomayor, Sonia, 79

Souter, David, 75

Southern states, 247–248, 251–254. *See also* Confederacy

Spacebook (intranet), 149

Speak Now (album), 213

Spears, Britney, 224

Specter, Arlen, 245

Spellings, Margaret, 181–182

Spilimbergo, Antonio, 41

Sponti (Germany), 234

sports, 209, 211, 218, 220–225, 280

Stage Door (movie), 26

Star Is Born, A (movie), 26

Stark, Mike, 98–99

State Department, 151, 243

Steed, Alex, 152–153

Stevens, John Paul, 81, 88

Stewart, Jimmy, 57

Stewart, Mitch, 93

stock market crash (1929), 16, 71, 73, 129

Stone, Harlan Fiske, 73–74

Strauss, William, 5, 12, 15–18, 23, 25

Stupak, Bart, 55, 58–59

suburban lifestyles, 198–201, 208; and politics, 252, 255, 262

Sunlight Foundation, 112

superheroes, 4, 218–220

Supreme Court, 61, 65–82, 265; appointments to, 65, 69–71, 73–76, 79; *Bush v. Gore*, 81–82; *Butler v. U.S.*, 74; *Carter v. Carter Coal*, 74; *Citizens United*, 87–88; and Civil War, 69–71, 73, 82; and contractual freedom, 72–75, 77; *Darby, United States v.*, 75; dissenting opinions, 72, 81, 88; *Dred Scott v. Sandford*, 68–70, 81; "Four Horsemen of Reaction," 73–75; *Gonzalez v. Raich*, 78; and health care reform, 61, 77–82; *Helvering v. Davis*, 74; and interstate commerce, 77–78; *Jones & Laughlin Steel Corp. v. NLRB*, 74–75; and judicial activism, 78–82, 87–88; and judicial review, 66–67; laissez-faire approach, 71–73, 76; and law clerks, 79; and legislative branch, 66–71, 73–78, 80–82, 87–88; *Lochner v. New York*, 72–75, 81; *Marbury v. Madison*, 66–67; and marijuana, 78; and minimum wage laws, 74–75, 78; *Morehead v. Tipaldo*, 74; and national labor standards, 75; and New Deal, 66, 71–77, 80; and Obama, 76–77, 80–82; *Planned Parenthood of Southeastern PA v. Casey*, 75; and precedent, 77–79; Prize Cases (1863), 70; "Revolution of 1937," 75–76; *Roe v. Wade*, 170; *Schechter Poultry Corp. v. U.S.*, 74; and slavery, 67–70, 80; and Social Security, 74; "Three Musketeers," 73–75; *West Coast Hotel Co. v. Parrish*, 75; *White v. Texas*, 70; *Wickard v. Filburn*, 75. *See also names of individual justices*

survey research data: and age-influenced attitudes toward government, 40–41; on civil ethos,

266–267, 279–280; and
COMPSTATS, 169–172; on
corporate life, 138, 148, 151–152;
on the economy, 34, 114–116,
121–122, 124–125; on education,
156, 162, 169–173; on
entertainment, 210, 216–217, 220;
on executive branch, 112–114,
125; on family lifestyles, 31–32,
193–195, 198–201, 203, 205–208;
on FUD (Fear, Uncertainty, and
Doubt), 19; on global change,
227–230, 233–234, 239; on
governmental activism, 35, 36–38;
on higher education, 175–180, 186;
on legislative branch, 83–85, 90,
100, 125, 246–247; on 1936
election, 21–22, 75; on open
government, 112–114; on
operational/ideological attitudes,
46–49, 48*tab.*, 51, 53–54, 248,
281–282; on politics, 245–257, 259;
and SchoolStats, 171–173; on
Supreme Court, 75, 79, 81; on
Twitter, 90; on 2008 election,
3, 5, 40
Sutherland, George, 73–74
Suzuki, Kurt, 222
Swift, Taylor, 213
Symantec, 145

Taft, William Howard, 73
Taney, Roger Brooke, 68–69
taxation, 37, 180, 204, 249–250, 274;
Bush-era tax cuts, 254, 260; and
operational/ideological attitudes,
50, 54, 136
Taxpayers for Common Sense, 113
Teach for America, 122, 151,
162, 269
Tea Party movement, 23, 51–52, 59,
246–250, 261, 265, 274; and
executive branch, 116; and

legislative branch, 87, 92, 94–95,
256, 258, 260–261; and Supreme
Court, 80. *See also names of specific
persons in movement*
Technocrats (China), 238–239
Teen Mom (television drama), 215
teen pregnancy, 30, 194, 198
telecom immunity, 98–99
Telepresence (virtual conference
room technology), 144
television, 209, 211, 214–220, 224;
coverage of health care reform, 58,
61; and family lifestyles, 29,
196–197; and global change, 231;
reality TV, 217–220. *See also titles of
individual television shows*
terrorism, 28, 49, 229
Tetlock, Philip, 2–3
Think 2040 project, 270–274
Thomas, Clarence, 79
Three 6 Mafia, 212
350.org, 232
Tilden, Samuel J., 82
Tipping Point, The (Gladwell), 243
TNGG Web site. *See Next Great
Generation, The*
Tocqueville, Alexis de, 65
Toffler, Van, 215
tolerance, 33–34, 42, 196, 201, 206,
208
TOMS shoes, 154–155
town hall meetings, 51–52, 54;
online, 97, 110–111
Transcendental Generation
(1792–1821), 69–70, 72, 202.
See also idealist generations
transparency: in Brazilian House of
Representatives, 96–97; and Coast
Guard, 107–109; and corporate life,
151; and executive branch, 106–114,
117, 129; and global change, 237,
242; and legislative branch, 58,
61, 84, 88, 92, 94–96, 100;

transparency (*continued*)
  and Obama campaign, 92, 110,
  142–143; and open-source software
  movement, 94. *See also* open
  participation
Treasury Department, 123
Trippi, Joe, 150
Truman, Harry, 258–259
trust, 26; and corporate life, 140–141,
  145–146, 149, 151, 155; and the
  economy, 116, 124–125, 129,
  132, 136; and global change, 234;
  and higher education, 189; and
  legislative branch, 37, 85; and
  Obama campaign, 143
Tulgan, Bruce, 151
Tunisian protesters, 236
Tupac, 213
Turner, Ted, 231
tweens, 211, 217, 228, 233–234
Twitter, 88–91, 94, 96, 213, 219; and
  global change, 228, 235, 240, 242

uncertainty. *See* FUD (Fear,
  Uncertainty, and Doubt)
Underwood, Carrie, 214
unemployment: and the economy,
  21, 34–35, 113, 115, 121–123, 130,
  133–137, 257; and executive
  branch, 113, 115, 135; and family
  lifestyles, 204–205; and veterans,
  268–269
unions, 37; baseball, 220; teachers',
  161, 167–169; UAW, 128
United Nations, 234–235; Security
  Council, 241–242
University of Michigan, 9–12,
  40–41, 276
USA.gov, 114

Value Network Analysis (VNA),
  144–145
Van Buren, Martin, 70

Vance, Mike, 143
Vanden Heuvel, Katrina, 259
Van Devanter, Willis, 73–74, 76
Veterans Administration, 143, 269
videos: and corporate life, 141–144,
  146, 155; and entertainment,
  213–215, 219; and global change,
  236, 243; and higher education,
  186–188
Vietnam War, 10, 28
VINNOVA, 145
Vinson, Roger, 77
Vitter, David, 270
volunteerism. *See* community service
Votto, Joey, 222

Wade, Dwayne, 223
Wagner Act, 74
Wagoner, Rick, 129
Waiting for Superman (documentary),
  168
Wal-Mart, 232
Walt Disney Company, 216, 233.
  See also entries beginning with Disney
Warren, Robert Penn, 273
Washington, George, 22, 103–104
Wealth of Nations, The (A. Smith), 132
Weber, Max, 107
WeGiveBooks.org, 219
Weingarten, Randi, 168
Welch, Jack, 145
Wen Jiabao, 238
Wertman, Adlai, 153
Wessel, David, 123
West, Kanye, 214
Wiki Government (Noveck), 111
Wikinomics (Tapscott and
  Williams), 140
Wilhelm, David, 91
Will, George, 78–79
Williams, Ted, 221
Wilson, Woodrow, 74, 229
Wofford, Ben, 267

women: and education, 33, 158, 203, 261–262; and executive branch, 115; and family lifestyles, 32–34, 193–194, 198, 202–204, 206; and microfinancing, 242; and politics, 85, 247, 251, 254, 261–262. *See also* gender neutrality

World War I, 28, 38

World War II, 1, 24, 28–30, 40, 42, 272; and entertainment, 211, 221; and executive branch, 104–105; and family lifestyles, 195, 202; and global change, 234, 236, 239; and higher education, 179, 270; Pearl Harbor attack, 18

Wright, David, 222

Xenakis, John J., 32–33

Xi Jinping, 239

Young, Neil, 212

Young Americans for Freedom, 52

Young Guns (Cantor, McCarthy, and Ryan), 13, 136

Youth Movement (Egypt), 236

YouTube, 52, 143, 146, 186–187, 242

Zambian libraries, 219

Zangara, Giuseppe, 21

Zimring, Frank, 170

Zwick, Abigail, 228–229

About the Authors

MORLEY WINOGRAD AND MICHAEL D. HAIS are co-authors of *Millennial Makeover: My Space, YouTube, and the Future of American Politics*, published by Rutgers University Press in 2008 and named one of the *New York Times*'s ten favorite books that year. They are fellows with NDN, a Washington, D.C.–based think tank, and the New Policy Institute.

MORLEY WINOGRAD is a senior fellow at the University of Southern California's Annenberg School's Center on Communication Leadership & Policy. He served as senior policy advisor to Vice President Al Gore and director of the National Partnership for Reinventing Government (NPR), from December 1, 1997, until January 20, 2001. He is also president and CEO of Morwin, Inc., a strategic planning consulting company for government and nonprofit organizations. He is the co-author, with Dudley Buffa, of *Taking Control: Politics in the Information Age* (Holt, 1996). Mr. Winograd earned a Bachelor of Business Administration from the University of Michigan in 1963 and attended Law School there, as well. He resides in Arcadia, California.

MICHAEL D. HAIS served for a decade as vice president, entertainment research and for more than twenty-two years overall at Frank N. Magid Associates, where he conducted audience research for hundreds of television stations, cable channels, and program producers in nearly all fifty states and more than a dozen foreign countries. Prior to joining Magid in 1983, he was a political pollster for Democrats in Michigan and an assistant professor of Political Science at the University of Detroit. He received a B.A. from the University of Iowa, an M.A. from the University of Wisconsin–Madison, and a Ph.D. from the University of Maryland, all in political science. He currently resides in Arcadia, California, and Puerto Vallarta, Mexico.